MADDER RED

CAUCASUS WORLD
SERIES EDITOR NICHOLAS AWDE
www.caucasusworld.co.uk

Other books in the series include:

PEOPLES OF THE CAUCASUS & THE BLACK SEA

CAUCASUS LANGUAGES

Previous page: Detail of a woollen tapestry-woven rug from Daghestan, pre 1865. The bristling medallion glows with an unusual shade of madder red that inspired this book. (Author's photo)

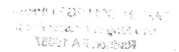

MADDER RED

A history of luxury and trade

*Plant dyes and pigments in
world commerce and art*

Robert Chenciner

CURZON

CAUCASUS WORLD

CAUCASUS WORLD

First published in 2000
by CURZON PRESS
51a George Street, Richmond
Surrey TW9 1HJ
England
www.curzonpress.co.uk

Reprinted 2001

© Robert Chenciner 2000

Typeset and designed by Nicholas Awde/Desert♥Hearts
Scans by Fred Hill
Covers & world map by Nick Awde

Printed and bound in Great Britain by
Bookcraft, Midsomer Norton, Avon

British Library Cataloguing in Publication Data
A catalogue record for this book is available from the British Library

ISBN 0 7007 1259 3

Contents

For
Robert Williams, Harold Bailey & Clive Wainwright
great teachers and beloved friends
Peter Fuller, Anthony North & Robert Irwin
'timor mortis conturbat me'

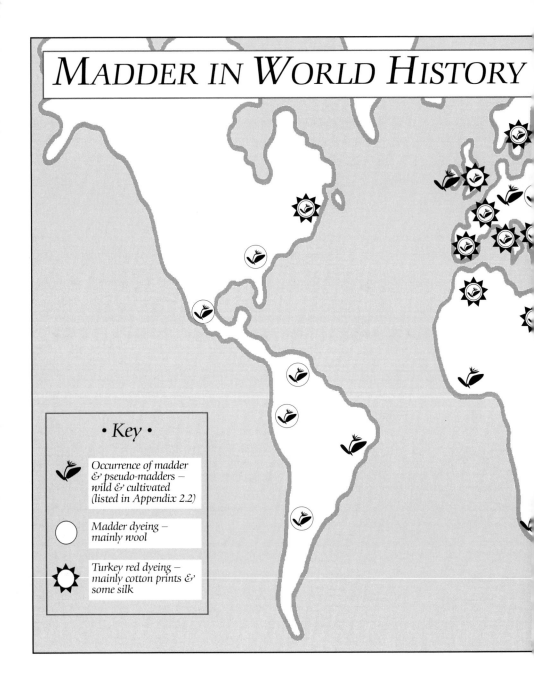

MADDER IN WORLD HISTORY

· Key ·

Occurrence of madder
& pseudo-madders –
wild & cultivated
(listed in Appendix 2.2)

Madder dyeing –
mainly wool

Turkey red dyeing –
mainly cotton prints &
some silk

A qualitative sketch-map
(developed from Gustav Schaefer's CIBA map)

Acknowledgements

In addition to those already mentioned:

Nicholas Awde
for enlightened design & editing
and
Alan Alston
June Anderson
Kate Anetts
Dr Jenny Balfour-Paul
David Beech
Dr Harald Böhmer &
Renate Böhmer
Prof Edmund Bosworth
Paul Bygrave
David Caldwell
Gill Cannell
Lisa Chaney
Dr Rosemary Crill
Harry Dagnall
Lord Ralf Dahrendorf
Dr Andrew Dalby
Dr Stephanie Dalley
Dr R A Donkin
John Edmonds
Andrew Edmunds
Prof Ronald Emmerich
Dr John Gage
Dr Renate Germer
Godfrey Goodwin
Hero Granger-Taylor
Su Grierson
Paul Grinke
Dan & Madeleine Harman
John Hutchings
Robert Irwin
Dr Esra Kahn
Dr Jo Kirby

Dr Hermann Kuhn
Christopher Mendes
Andrew Middleton
Anthony North
Nuala O'Sullivan
Caroline Oates
Dr Richard Parkinson
Emma Pearce
& Joan Joyce
& Winsor & Newton
Mark Poacher
Su Pratt
Dr Peter Priester
Anthony Ray
Paul Rix FCA
John Roberts
Barnaby Rogerson
Prof Hilary Rose
Prof Stephen Rose
Dr Helmut Schweppe
Dr Orit Shamir
Dr Harry Shukman
Prof Nicholas Simms-Williams
Dr Robert Skelton
Tim Stanley
Dr Joan Thirsk
Dr Roger Tomalin
Dr Gillian Vogelsang Eastwood
Prof Clive Wainwright
Harlan Walker
Dr Penelope Walton Rogers
Dr John-Peter Wild
Ghislaine Williams
Prof Ad van der Woude
Dr Theodore Zeldin

Note that some transliterations will vary on account of the differing periods and languages covered.
Every effort has been made to trace copyright holders of material that appears in this book.

Foreword:
The gifted eye

SINCE THE 1960s more books have been written about art objects than ever before. All this worthy study has explored their manufacture, materials, iconography, design development, technical analysis, historical, economic, religious and social context, and provenance, all of which confirms their dating. The progress of technology means that it is now conceivable that handy computer discs will one day conveniently illustrate every single object. The official authorities who merely had the keys to the libraries will not be needed in future.

However the suspension of judgement which resulted from a generation of egalitarian objectivity has transformed the aesthetic perception of material art into a lottery of 'treasures' in the attic — the British fin-d'empire philosophical message behind the all-conquering televised antiques shows. Modern museums do not single out the most beautiful — rather the loftiest provenance or the highest price paid.

In the face of such popular and official conceptions, it is more difficult and accordingly rare to propose that an object is beautiful or to discuss the eye or taste of the patrons, artists and their heritors, the collectors. Response is confined to a few learned journals[1] and society's token wildmen critics such as the late Peter Fuller who, for example, attacked the overvalued work of the celebrated New York painter Julian Schnabel.[2] Perhaps the most accessible way to understand the gifted eye is through the reawakening appreciation of colour. The most popular colour is red (see chapter 17) and the best natural reds at present available are produced from the madder root. Madder's historic rival, cochineal (made from insects), is largely used up as a food colorant today.

I was amazed to find evident an unending fascination with the colours of madder — reds, purples, browns, oranges and blacks — throughout history and over all the world. Colour is of course essential to display all art and is an art in itself. Indeed the rightness of a bright pure colour was recognised through that gifted eye which was shared by generations of connoisseurs. While there would appear to have been little choice of pre-synthetic natural reds, in fact alongside a small number of right reds there were a host of miscoloured dyes and pigments — the products of poor quality raw materials or inadequate techniques. The master dyers, pigments makers, painters and weavers and their patrons knew what was required and the second-rate was rejected. The quest for eternal quality proved irresistible . . .

A more mundane thread of events led through the labyrinthine story of madder red. In 1983 thanks to my interest in carpets, I had penetrated the virtually closed Soviet Caucasus. As a result, in 1987 I shared a paper at the International Conference on Oriental Carpets in Vienna to introduce an unknown group of woollen flat-woven rugs from Daghestan in the Caucasus. As with other textiles, these *dums* and *davaghins* woven before about 1865 used natural dyes, while later examples used garish chemical dyes — noticeable in the puces, beiges, oranges and reds. In the earlier rugs, while the most common background colour was indigo blue, which was imported from India, the next most frequent colour was a local madder red. This red was of an unusual deep rose hue which set it apart from other madder dyes found in the rugs of Turkey, Central Asia, Persia and even the Caucasus.

While I was certainly working around textile art, in retrospect there seems to have been a defining moment when I focused on madder. I had become a friend of Dr Ilya Gershevitch of Cambridge University through our common interest in the Ossetes of the northern Caucasus. He was one of the select group of philologists of Iranian languages, who had studied this northernmost Iranian people. During the same year he generously invited me to dine at High Table at Jesus College. His purpose was for me to meet Dr R. A. Donkin, the unconventional geographer who had written of mannah, pearls, Muscovy ducks and — of especial interest — cochineal, the red insect dye. He was bemused that within the same week his monographs on cochineal had been noticed by both myself and an American academic. This was because the work had been published some ten years previously and had elicited no previous interest. Some don remarked that Mahler had fared far worse with his music.

Years later I remained puzzled by the *davaghin's* special shade of red. My research in Daghestan had evolved into ethnographic study on local subversion of the socialist system. During a break from fieldwork, I was working in the library in Makhachkala where I stumbled on the monumental botanical works of the late Alexander Alfonsin Grossgeim of the Azerbaijani Academy of Sciences.[3] Back in London, I discovered that one of his bibliographies contained a reference to the earliest book about Caucasian madder, as far as I knew then. However *About the Dyeing Properties of Derbent Madder*, by I. O. Arkhipov, published in 1869[4] was not in the British Library.

On my next trip to Russia, I arranged to pass through the freshly renamed St Petersburg. As an honorary member of the Daghestan Filial of the Academy of Sciences of the USSR, I had been provided with a red identity card or *udostoverenie*, which on August 13th, 1993 allowed me to enter the

Russian National Library Saltikov-Shchedrin. Fortunately I was accompanied by my long-standing friend and ethnographic collaborator from Daghestan, Dr Magomedkhan Magomedkhanov and his old friend Dr Michael Shumilov who was then engaged in research in the library. We scanned the general book catalogue in vain and I suggested that we searched the author and subject card indexes. They politely insisted that they would do the work for me. That, in retrospect, was the critical moment when I insisted that I could not return to Britain — in particular to my sponsors at St Antony's College Oxford — without physically looking through the cards. We nervously went to a side room where a stern matronly figure confirmed that the Stalin-era regulations stated that: 'The pre-1931 author index was proscribed to all . . .' 'The only exception was for holders of a special permit which was extremely rarely granted . . .' 'It would take several months for the necessary procedures to be observed.' I begged to see the subject index. 'It had to be quick as this was most irregular . . .' *Marena* is the Russian word for madder. There were several other subjects within the relevant box. I counted 47 cards of which 17 were books or articles about madder.

I chose the three earliest, which had been commissioned to encourage the expansion of madder cultivation, ironically just before cheap chemical red dyes were to flood the market. Two were published in 1859[5] and the third in 1863.[6] There were two more later works in Russian, one by a dissident young chemist whom I had met at a conference in Baku in 1983 when he nervously promoted natural dyes against the Party line[7] and the other by V. A. Petrov, from Azerbaijan, who had written several earlier books quoted by Grossgeim.[8] Here were some 500 pages of virtually unknown material in Russian. There was no time to examine the texts at leisure, so after my departure Michael Shumilov used his arcane knowledge of the library to generously have all the texts photocopied. In due course the package arrived in London. The Russian accounts proved complementary to Philip Miller of the Chelsea Physick Garden's 38-page treatise of 1758, which similarly failed to fire the English to cultivate madder industrially.

There was little other regional material available. In one of the observant traveller P. S. Pallas' articles in German in the 1777 *St Petersburgisches Journal* there was alas only reference to an unspecified ten-page account of the Oriental method of dyeing cotton with powdered madder in Astrakhan; O V Marggraf the late 19th-century anthropologist too had a brief but rewarding chapter on dyeing techniques in his account of North Caucasian manufactures;[9] and Prof Kh-M Khashaev, a leading academic who stuck to the truth during the dark days of Soviet repression in Daghestan, wrote quantitatively about the central role of madder, carpets and other textiles in the 19th-century local economy.[10] My attempts to confirm and enlarge the Russians' assertions led to my discovery of additional mountains of non-Russian works.

The book proper starts with a botanical account of 'dyers' madder' with its medicinal use and a list of all the other varieties of wild and cultivated madder prized for their dyestuffs. Their ancient and worldwide presence is confirmed by the existence of words for madder in a wide array of ancient and modern languages, from Babylonian and Pharonic Egyptian to Khotanese, Chinese, Turkish and all the European tongues.

It is just as well that this book has taken some time in gestation as its three pillars, the interwoven historical chapters on the cultivation of madder, dyeing and pigment have been extensively rewritten by archaeologists, scientists and historians during the last decades. The histories have been written in broad chronological bands moving from region to region following trade, for example the Levant company, or technical interchange, for example Flachat's bringing the Turkey red process to France. In a similar way, the ancient dyeing tradition of the Micmacs or Berbers are seen through their contact with colonial France. Sometimes it has been necessary to cover broad time periods, such as describing the ancient Micmac techniques which mainly survived much later about 1600. From time to time it seemed worthwhile to bring together material from different countries on a particular topic such as the banning of exports of madder shoots to protect local farmers. I have tried to avoid duplication of some events which are relevant to more than one history, by mentioning them in outline with a reference to where they are described in detail. An example is the 17th and 18th century European craze for printed cotton indiennes and their substitution caused by the rise of the European industries after the 1760s. I have used the well-documented 19th-century surge in cultivation of Derbent madder and the growth of the Russian textile industry as detailed examples of the worldwide textile-led boom in specialised chapters.

If the Russian material was sometimes conflicting, it covered a logical and multidisciplinary progression. The first commercial large-scale plantations resulted from the stability of the *pax Russica* imposed on Imam Shamil's north-eastern Caucasus. The Russians subjugated the Caspian plains from 1805 to 1828 and the mountains by 1869. Clearly there were both resultant economic and political reasons for the Russian studies. Their writings included techniques of cultivation compared with the best methods known in Avignon and Schouwen in Zeeland. The complex care began with clearing and preparing the land and fertilisation. Special methods of planting seeds or shoots, were followed by precise irrigation, ridging and care for varying periods of growth from eighteen months to six years. Finally the laborious extraction to harvest the roots which then had to be dried. Any slip-up in this expensive long-term agricultural project resulted in poor quality dyestuff or dead plants, which explains the constant if surprisingly sophisticated financial analysis.

Detailed costings flesh out the meticulous records of the complicated care required for successful cultivation. A variety of idiosyncratic profit and loss calculations of the many different crop combinations according to age and size of the roots, stalks for cattle fodder and seeds for resale have been discovered and appeared by chance at regular intervals from 1620 until 1850. I have embellished these with risk analysis, modified by my accountants Deloitte Touche's current agricultural practice, in order to try to define and calculate optimal yields. There were even contemporaneous assessments of the impact of madder on the local economy.

All the efforts of cultivation were in vain if the product could not be sold well and on time. On the marketing side, there were tables of annual weights and prices, imports from Europe and Asia, and the gradual increase of 'home' production, which spanned the period 1800 to 1860. The Dutch who were for centuries world leaders in cultivation kept price records from 1580 until 1900 which Dr Peter Priester has magisterially assembled and related to the mysterious fluctuations in wheat prices. The use of the dye went hand in hand with the rise of the cotton cloth manufacturing industry, and with its crashes caused by the American Civil War and the Crimean War. While the accounts were written from Russian, Dutch, French or English points of view, an early form of globalisation became increasingly evident, where the very international market frequently intruded.

There was continuous financial incentive to develop the product from dried root to the more convenient ground krap, and the more concentrated super products like garancine, which was produced by washing krap in water and then sulphuric acid and finally fermentation. In addition, the advantages and practice of 'modern' quality control were recorded since the Middle Ages and must have existed hand in hand with the far earlier criminal practice of adulteration, the commercial equivalent of bearing false witness.

Intensive chemical research started before 1830, with the aim of increasing the yield of dyestuff from the root. The large profits to be gained from the textile-led madder boom attracted the sharpest financial brains including chemists.[11] The logical consequence was for a progressive analysis of the chemical dye compounds. The result was that alizarin, the principal red agent was isolated in 1869. At the same time other chemists achieved the initially empirical synthesis of red dye stuffs from gas street-lighting coal tar by-products. Soon after by 1873 root madder was substituted by a chemical compound at a tenth of the price. There is an inevitable progression as this particular snake of chemical activity devoured its own tail to destroy the industry that it was trying to exploit. Yet from the new chemistry grew the famous names of the German and Swiss chemical industries which changed the world (see chapter 15).

Madder never quite disappeared. William Morris attempted to revive natural dyes for a time. But the recent renaissance in natural dyeing was started by Harald Böhmer whose DOBAG project in Turkey now includes two co-operatives and has been imitated many times over, and created employment for about 8000 weavers. In other parts of the world there are also other ever-varying old and new traditional dyeing methods. The Dobag project is both cause and evidence of increased aesthetic awareness of the beauty of the vibrant colours obtained from madder red compared to the flatness of synthetic reds. My underlying purpose must be to pass on enthusiasm for the natural colour.

Finally there was the puzzle of how dyers with no scientific knowledge were able to rediscover 30-step processes for dyeing madder red. It seemed worthwhile to explore the place of colour in their minds. They would have been aware of different versions of classical colour theory, the folklore of red and some alchemical and later Romantic mystical interpretations of 'analogues' and 'harmonics'. The resulting effect on the dyers' practical attitude was described by three unique accounts of the discovery of different dye methods. The tribal method was typified by a folk-tale of the Micmac Amero-Indians, brilliant dyers of porcupine quills. In urban contrast, as a son of the Industrial Revolution, George Field the colourman's notebooks told the mystical story of how he created the finest madder lakes of the 1800s. Then there is the contemporary testament of John Edmonds, who turned himself into a medieval woad dyer and as a result in 1998 rediscovered the method of dyeing Tyrian purple lost with the fall of Constantinople in 1453.

My research has always been subject-led rather than editor-requested, so I needed a publisher. By coincidence, my publisher Malcolm Campbell had recently released Dr Jenny Balfour-Paul's book about indigo blue. So a new series was born.

Among the many proper distractions from writing this book, there was my marriage to Marian and the births and energetic early years of our jewels, Louisa and Isabel and the consequent search, purchase and restoration of our meandering London house. Two other books were written in line with earlier commitments. Further study was required to answer questions which arose from the ghoulish popularity of the (now two) Chechen-Russian wars, the awakened interest in oil and criminality and asylum advice. There was more to discover about madder than I ever imagined, so the size of the book has grown substantially since it was first conceived.

LONDON
APRIL 2000

MADDER RED

Flourishing 'dyer's madder' plant
(photo E. Tivey; Goodwin)

1

Russian dreams
of the bearded root

Profitable study

WE BELIEVE that there are excellent prospects for Derbent madder production, depending on the ability of madder production to satisfy demand while keeping prices sufficiently high . . . It is therefore of interest to study madder production in Europe.[1] The French figures are of importance to Russia because the climates in Alsace and Avignon are similar to the climates in the Caucasus.

This version of the story of madder is based on the three Russian sources written about 1860. Naturally they do not entirely agree with each other, drawing from different informants and covering an encouragingly wide range of disciplines. Where possible, later sources are used to fill in the gaps and to update various discoveries in areas such as dye analysis, archaeology and history. For convenience the three sources are referred to as Shtorkh, Karpov and The Ministry. These were written against a background of a 40-year boom in the world and Russian textile industries and consequent demand for madder red dyestuff.

The longest account, some 270 octavo-sized pages in Russian, was written by P. A. Shtorkh, who was an active member of the Imperial Economists' Society, the Imperial Russian Geographical Society and so on. He assembled an impressive amount of quantitative information about the 19th century, concentrated on the second 30-year period. His manual on the cultivation and economics of madder was written with a view to persuading the Russian reader — whether farmer, landowner, investor or banker — that it was a profitable enterprise.

In his foreword to the second account, Lt Karpov of the Ural Cossack Corps outlined his mission in terms of trade warfare against Central Asian madder:

The quantity of dried madder roots from the Derbent region and the rest of the Caucasus is not sufficient to supply the growing demand of the Russian textile industry. Proof of this is the amount of madder imported to Russia via Orenburg from the Bukhara region. Even though the quality of the Bukharan madder roots leave much to be desired, their price is relatively high. According to Orenburg statistics for 1857, 20,499 poods 10 pounds from Bukhara were sold for 57,420 roubles 25 kopeks in silver. To save payment of 20,000 silver roubles a year to Bukhara, the Governor-General of the Orenburg and Samara region decided to start cultivating madder on vast tracts of the Urals and Syr. Accordingly, Governor A. A. Katenin has sent me to Derbent to research accurately about madder seeds and madder cultivation. The Governor-General has requested the Governor of the Caucasus to assist me in my research and indeed he has been most helpful. The following 37-page article about madder is the result of my journey to the Caucasus . . .

The third 63-page account made up of several anonymous extracts from the *Kavkaz' Gazet* was published by the Ministry of Agriculture and Industry for the Caucasus and Zakavkaz, based in Tblisi. The self-evident purpose was to encourage economic development in the region. In 1850, as Prof Kh.-M. Khashaev pointed out, the governor of Derbent stated that madder had even overtaken the traditionally most important local manufacture of arms.[2]

The Caucasus was subdued by the Russians over a lengthy and hard-fought war against the Daghestanis and Chechens, who were led by Imam Shamil from 1831. The war lasted from 1800 to his final surrender in 1859. The madder rich regions of Daghestan near Derbent were under Russian control from the early 1800s and organised madder cultivation was the prize of stability from Russia's new colony.

2

The word & the plant

A worldwide word

ONE WAY of finding out where something existed is to see which languages have a word for it. A refinement is to date the earliest occurrences of the word by its appearance in ancient languages. Words for madder appear in the Ancient Oriental languages, in Biblical period languages, in Classical and Old European languages, and in modern Oriental and European languages. There are also words for artist's madder lake in several languages (see appendix 2.1, page 313).

The English word 'madder' is derived from Old English *mædere*, which corresponds to Old High German *matara* and Old Norse *ma'dra*.[1] 'Madderise' appears to be the only related English word, used to describe white wine which is brown or turning brown with the effect of oxygen with age.[2] Gustav Schaefer, who wrote thoughtfully about madder, recognised "how closely the madder plant is linked with the idea of red is revealed by the names given to it in various languages." The Greeks called it *erythrodanon*, *ereuthedanon* and *teuthrion*[3] (*erythros* = red), and *phenix*, *phoinix*;[4] the Romans *rubia*, *rubidus*, *rubeo* or *rubia passiva*;[5] and the Germans *rote*, with Germanic Old English *reeod*, *reead*, *rauudas*. Names in other languages include: Arabic فوة *fuwwa*, Hebrew פוּאָה *pu'ah*, Coptic Ⲁⲡⲉⲓ *apei*, Ancient Egyptian 𓏏𓆓𓃀𓏤 *jp3*, Chinese 茜 *qian*. All these names are the commonest terms for red in their respective languages.[6]

A recent study of how ordinary English people, meaning 'non-colour-specialists', attach names to colours, received 10,000 responses: 200 different colours were classified in six main categories from 'basic' to 'elaborate' and 'idiosyncratic'. It was found that the colour names of past centuries that would fall into their "elaborate" category, "such as madder," "have not survived."[7] Perhaps this book will show that such popular judgement was premature.

"His hands are red with jp3, as one who is smeared with his own blood" — *Ancient Egytian hieroglyphs (Germer)*

Dyer's madder

There is a difference between the botanist's and the dyer's meanings of the word 'madder'. The botanical term refers to members of the Rubiaceae natural family, most of which grow wild. Dyers generally use cultivated madder and by far the most commonly used madder is *Rubia tinctorum* known as 'dyer's madder'. Diderot and Le Pileur referred to '*Rubia tinctorum sativa*'.[8]

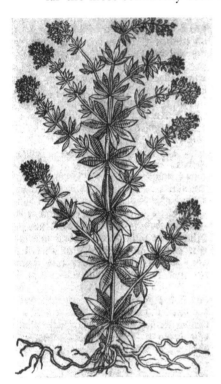

*Rubia sylvestris, wild madder,
by Theodore Zwinger, Basle, 1744
(Schaefer, CIBA Review)*

Other madder dyes were also used to supply the world-conquering Indian printed cotton industry which flourished until the 1750s. For completeness I have listed all the other dye-containing members of the Rubaiceae family and all other plants which contain red dye in their roots, which are strictly speaking pseudo-madders (see appendix 2.2, page 314).

With the exception of the Indian dyes, the other dyes appear in a far smaller number of textiles or other dyed objects in countries where *Rubia tinctorum* was not indigenous and was not planted. Small quantities of wild madder such as *Rubia peregrina* and *Rubia sylvestris* were used for dyeing, but the roots of the cultivated *Rubia tinctorum* traditionally contained the richest dyestuffs and the plant was an excellent propagator. These plants may be distinguished by analysis because cultivated *Rubia tinctorum* contains mainly alizarin and the wild varieties do not. They contain purpurin and other colourants (see Glossary).

Botanical description of Rubia tinctorum

The New Royal Horticultural Society Dictionary of Gardening states that the Rubiaceae or Madder family contains 630 genera and 10,400 species. Only a small proportion were used as dye plants. Madder is a native Rubiaceae evergreen of the eastern Mediterranean and Central Asia, where the Climatic Zone 6 of hardiness prevails — that is minimum temperatures of 0° to 10°F.[9] It does not grow north of 52° longitude, though seeds have been reputedly found in Aberdeen. Madder belongs to the variety *stellatae* — star-leafed.[10] It belongs to a class of plants which have an annual stalk but a perennial taproot.[11] It is a hardy growth, reaching a height of between two and four feet.

Rubia tinctorum is the most common cultivated variety of madder. The long, weak, jointed stems are square and hairy. It has spear-shaped, elliptic leaves, 3in long and 1in at their widest, disposed in verticils in groups of four to six, hispid underneath the leaf, but smooth on the upper surface. The small yellowish flowers which appear in its second and third year of growth spring from loose branchy spikes, growing from opposing pairs of branches which proceed from the joints of the stem. The corollas of the flowers are divided into four parts and resemble stars. The flowers are succeeded by black shiny berries.[12] The dried seeds have the appearance of peppercorns (see page 92).

Dyer's madder (Rubia tinctorum) — six botanical impressions (clockwise from top left): Reynault, La Botanique, 1774 (Harley; ack. Royal Horticultural Society); Culpeper's Complete Herbal (ed. Kelly 1821 [1653]; ack. Anthony Ray); Gerard's Herball, 1597, recut by Pomet (Adrosko); attr. to Mattioli, . . . Dioscorides de materia medica, 1562 (ack. Christopher Mendes & Paul Grinke, CIBA Review); Elisabeth Blackwell, Sammlung der Gewäschse, 1754 (Schweppe); Theodore Zwinger, Herborium, 1596 (Sandberg)

Karpov's more personal botanical comments breathed life into the plant: "When the spring weather was favourably wet and warm, the seeds produced their first shoots in two to three weeks. At first, two oblong

fluffy leaves appeared with the empty seed husk and soon after the fragile stem with three leaves followed, which was why some people thought that the seed produced five leaves at the same time. During the first year, there was only one stem, but during the second and third years several stems appeared from a single root. The stem and leaves were covered with microscopic thorns which gave the plant a sticky feel and caused it to grow along the ground. During the second year a few seeds could already be seen among the flowers."

Rhind was a more professional observer: "The root is perennial, having an annual stalk, and is composed of many long thick succulent fibres, about a quarter of an inch in thickness. It is joined at the top in a head like asparagus and runs deep into the ground. Many side roots issue from the upper part or head of the parent root, and they extend just beneath the surface of the ground to a considerable distance. In consequence the plant propagates itself very rapidly, for these numerous side roots send forth many shoots, which, if carefully separated in the spring soon after they are above ground, become so many plants."[13]

The large quantity of long, reddish roots grow up to 3cm in diameter and 80cm in length, and a single plant can produce at least 250gms of fresh roots.[14] Decaisne's 1837 drawings of the structure of the madder roots show it at different stages of development.[15] From its roots a dyeing agent containing alizarin is extracted by fermentation (see chapters 5, 7 & 8) The juice from its root produced the famous Turkey red when treated with greasy mordants and alum, a secret jealously preserved by Eastern peoples until the mid-18th century, when it became known throughout Europe (see chapters 4, 11 & 12).

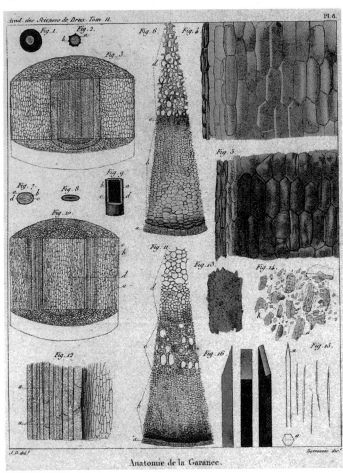

The structure of madder roots at different stages of development according to J. Decaisne, 1837, Mémoires couronnes par l'Academie . . . Bruxelles, 12, 'Recherches anatomiques et physiologiques sur la garance' (ack. British Library; Kirby & White)

The other 'madders'

From at least the early 17th until the second half of the 18th century India was the largest supplier of patterned printed cottons and linens to Europe. They used different varieties of madder for red. Most widely used was *Rubia cordiofolia L.* (*munjeet* = *Rubia munjista* Roxb.). The main colourants of *munjeet* are munjistin, pururin, pseudopurpurin and purpuroxanthin. *Rubia sikkimensis* Kurz produced the 'reds of Naga' which made famous the north-eastern provinces of India. The main colourants of here are munjistin, purpuroxanthin and purpurin. These two wild madders — though they were sometimes cultivated, as was munjeet in Darjeeling — together with *Rubia tinctorum* L., which was also cultivated in Kashmir and Sind, made up the red dyes used in Indian cotton prints in northern and eastern India, Sikkim, Butan, Nepal and Tibet. *Munjeet* was used in the chintzes, indiennes and painted cloths which dominated the European markets. In the south of India the Jesuit Father Coeurdoux in 1742 and later Roxburgh, the British botanist confirmed that the rind of the roots of *Oldenlandia umbellata* L. (*chay*) were used to dye cotton red, notably the bandanas and paisleys of Madras.[16] The rind of the roots of *Morinda citrifolia* L. and *Morinda tinctoria* Roxb. (*suranji*) were used to produce 'Indian red' on the printed cottons of Bombay. When Britain took over the printed cotton industry in the late 18th century, the Indian red dyestuffs were imported instead of the printed textiles.

Also listed are wild *Galiums* (from the Greek *gala* meaning 'milk') and *Asperulas* which were used for coral and rose dyes in the far north, in Scotland, the Scandinavian countries and French Canada. Surprisingly, the same families of plants were used at the other end of the world in South-East Asia.[17] Notwithstanding their apparent popularity, the dyestuff is relatively weak and the roots are small which make the dye difficult to extract.

The lists and duplicate names

In *Prodromous*, c. 1800, by the French botanist Augustin Pyramus de Candolle (1778-1841), 43 varieties of madder were listed, but only the varieties containing dyestuffs are described below (see appendix 2.2, page 314). His book was an early recognised scientific work published not long after, and augmenting Linnaeus' *Species Plantarum*, 1753.[18] In turn, his list is broadened by other authors. The more comprehensive list is complicated by the unavoidably empirical nature of botanical nomenclature. It is worth including all the names which could be found and also giving their duplicated names as they appeared in Hooker and Jackson's *Index*[19] (see appendix 2.2).

The medicinal root

Although there is far earlier evidence of madder dyes and pigments, in classical and medieval herbals madder is usually described for its medicinal properties. Pharmaceutical use of madder was mentioned by Hippocrates,[20] Pliny,[21] Dioscorides[22] and Theophrastus.[23] John Gerard who was a late-16th-century *chirugien* enumerated its "vertues" biblically: "The decoction . . . is every where commended for those that are bursten, brused, wounded, and that are fallen from high places . . . they be mixed with potions, which the later physicians call wound drinks."[24]

Nicholas Culpeper gave a full list of medicinal and cosmetic uses with methods of preparation:

> It hath an opening quality, and afterwards to bind and strengthen. It is a sure remedy for the yellow jaundice, by opening the obstructions of the liver and gall, and cleansing those parts; it opens also obstructions of the spleen, and diminishes the melancholy humour. It is available for the palsy and sciatica, and effectual for bruises inward and outward and is therefore much used in vulnerary drinks . . . It stops looseness, the hemorrhoids, and the menses.
>
> The root for all those aforesaid purposes, is to be boiled in wine or water, as the cause requires, and some honey and sugar put thereunto afterwards. The seed hereof taken in vinegar and honey, helps the swelling and hardness of the spleen. The decoction of the leaves and branches is a good fomentation for women that have not their courses. The leaves and roots beaten and applied to any part that is discoloured with freckles, morphew, the white scurf, or any such deformity of the skin, cleanses thoroughly, and takes them away.[25]

Hilton added dropsy to the list of treatable ailments.[26]

Flachat noted that three-year-old madder for medicinal purposes was gathered when in flower, not in autumn when the plants were exhausted after growth.[27] The travelled diplomat Paul Bergne remembered that madder flowers were made into a tea in Ancient Egypt and modern Germany. Cardon mentioned that the tisanes from the *sommites* of the flowers of *Asperula odorata* were long appreciated in eastern France and Germany for their tranquilising properties. In Germany they used it in the traditional *Maitrank* or 'May-wine'. The active ingredient contains a heteroside of coumarine.[28]

Alternative agriculture historian Joan Thirsk confirmed that the root was also used for colouring medicines, perhaps to make them more palatable or to provide reassurance in their efficacy. In addition, the ability of ingested madder to stain bones had been used by Scottish physicians to study bone growth (see chapter 8).[29]

Food colouring

Alan Davidson confirmed that food was traditionally coloured red with kermes and cochineal with some use of sandalwood, cudbear, alkanna, paprika, beetroot and elderberry.[30] However, Charles Perry has found two linked isolated uses of madder (*fuwwa*) in the 14th century Arabic *Book of Familiar Foods* (*Kitab Wasf al-At'ima al-Mu'tada*).[31]

In the recipe for *sir mathun* (milled dried fish), madder was used to colour a curry-garlic pickled rissole mix, in proportion 15 to 1 by weight of fish and madder. In *al-sahna al-jayyida*, where milled dried fish was spiced, ground and salted to form a mincemeat which was stirred for seven days, the madder content was weaker at 20 to 1. Perry thought that the intention was to make the fish look like meat, similar to modern nut rissoles.

Geographical occurrence of madder

The long list of madder plants which contain a dyeing agent for the colour red are cultivated in most parts of the world. Schaefer wrote that the genus *Rubia* occurred in many countries of the tropical and temperate zones. It is native to Mexico, but is most widespread in Europe and Asia. The best madder is grown in the East Indies, Asia Minor, the Caucasus and the north coast of Africa. Schaefer added that most varieties are indigenous to India, Persia, Asia Minor and Europe.

The best madder in Europe was produced in Turkey, Greece, Spain, France, Holland, Lombardy in northern Italy, Sicily,[32] Germany and certain areas of Russia. In Holland, the largest producer, madder was grown in Zeeland on the islands of South Beveland, Schouwen, Walcheren, Georre, Flakkee, Tolen and in Geldern on the mainland.[33] Madder grown in Europe originated from the east and was firstly brought to France, then spread to the other countries, reaching Russia last. In France, which equalled Holland as largest producer in the 1840s, 18th century plantations flourished near Montpellier, Avignon, Orange, Carpentras, Isle-en-Provence and elsewhere.

Wild madder can be found in southern and central Europe, in Russia and along the rivers Irtysh and Ob in southern Siberia, though its quality is poor. Much wild madder is found in the Balashov and Atkarsk (river Ters) areas of the Saratov region, the latter being of better quality.[34] Grossgeim's list of all Caucasian plants which produce red, with Harald Böhmer's comments, can be found in appendix 2.4 (page 317, and see chapter 16 for Böhmer's work).

3

The 5,000-year-old root: history in the Old World

The first colours

THERE ARE SEVERAL THEORIES on the origin of religion. The following layman's narrative links one theory with the use of red. In the beginning, to use animal imagery, there were ruminant humans who were quite happy and hunters who were not. This was put eloquently by the author(s) of Genesis in the description of Adam before and after the Fall. The unhappy ones focused on the insoluble and admittedly more interesting problems of survival. Different aspects of survival attained their own pre-eminence: the weather, the harvest, fertility, disease, enemies who had better living conditions and of course inevitable death. However widely the hunters roamed and conquered, these quandaries never seemed to retreat.

So their leaders, who were both the most unhappy and articulate, constructed a parallel universe and in common belief became variously witch-doctors, sorcerers, hierophants or shamans. Such roles could only exist because the leaders were genuinely convinced that they could act as bridges between the real and the spiritual worlds. The parallel universe, being imaginary, resided in their minds, but in order to communicate their revelation more convincingly to their people who were less unhappy or even happily ruminant, they had to give their story a physical form. This also meant that these hierophants (used as a general term) could invent or reveal ritual which when brought to bear on this parallel universe would change it as required and subsequently by a process of spiritual osmosis change the real world.

Nowadays, this is known as sympathetic magic. Roughly, if they chose convenient problems, half the time they were right and if not, often everyone either went away or even died, which silenced dissent. Otherwise, the disillusioned people rose up and the hierophant or king was expelled or *in extremis* put to death. If the religious idea had caught on with the people, and it certainly did fill both a spiritual and a political void, then a successor appeared or was chosen. The simplest physical manifestation was for the witch-doctor to decorate himself and his acolytes with both colour and pattern. The consequence was to adorn the sacred place of worship with pictures of the hierophant or king, who, partly could speak with the god(s) and partly was god. In addition to exaggerated physical attributes and animal appendages worn whenever the hierophant appeared, a simple way of making this representation more permanent and repeatable was by applying colour to the body or the wall. The witch-doctor was thereby changed into the god or portrayed as the god.

Red ochre pigment (see Glossary) was used in the earliest surviving primal-religious art apparently in preference to other colours, either because it was more easily obtained or because it possessed significant meaning. The frequent occurrence of animated red earth figurines in Creation stories as well as the variety of dualistic meanings peculiar to red in folklore are discussed later. One common meaning is 'red as blood'. That is a convenient symbol as it substitutes for real blood, which does not need to be shed and the pigment colour also lasts better than blood. If several of the above ideas can be considered as aspects of human-divine inversion, then having blood symbolically move from inside to outside the body would be a personal example of inversion and a manifestation of defying death.

Red in pre-history

The history of colour follows the history of civilisation. Koren considered that the art of dyeing most probably started independently in different geographical locations.[1] While the above ideas are by their nature conjectural, what follows is based on firmer evidence. Red ochre, a mineral colour pigment, appeared about 30,000 BC in Europe, Southern Russia, Japan, and the Great Lakes in America, colouring the cranium and breast of human corpses. With the ability to store seed and fruit for nourishment, it is known that colours extracted from plants were used during the Neolithic Period from 7000 BC to 2000 BC. During this period, man changed from being a hunter to a farmer, a result of the development of stone and wood implements to cultivate the earth. Where the climate was cold, man needed to provide covering for his body. However the herds of wild beasts which had provided Palaeolithic man with skins had largely disappeared. Man was accordingly obliged to find a substitute and felting and weaving evolved, using plant fibre such as flax and cotton and animal fibre such as wool and silk.[2]

Needles made of mammoth ivory tusks survive from Upper Palaeolithic cultures, for sewing skins together, while finer needles made of bone have been discovered in southern Europe where the climate was warmer. Spinning, necessary for the preparation of threads for weaving, was known in Neolithic times, with the survival of spindles to make continuous, consistent thread. A weaving loom was found in the prehistoric lake village at Robenhausen in

Switzerland. It consisted of a large square frame standing vertically on the earth. Threads were held in tension by weights hung from the frame on which a simple canvas was woven, similar to Classical Greek looms.[3]

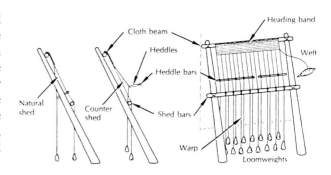

Classical Greek warp-weighted loom
(Barber, 1991)

Neolithic man had a highly developed aesthetic sense and dyes were developed to decorate ceramics and clothing. Decoration using colour and shape was used to make the object graceful or beautiful or to invest it with a primal religious meaning. Forbes thought that reds in prehistoric Europe were probably obtained from *Chenopodium album*, *Gallium palustre* and perhaps *Rubia tinctorum*.[4] In order to dye wool brightly, it is generally necessary to start with white wool. Penelope Walton Rogers (who founded Textile Research in Archaeology in York and publishes the authoritative journal *Dyes in History and Archaeology*) observed that the first wild sheep were brown with occasional white bellies. So it was only after sheep were domesticated that it was possible to breed to a whiter sheep. Also other grey stock with black and white fibres was available for cross breeding.[5] Rogers also found a possibly unique example of grey wool overdyed with madder in a single Anglo-Scandinavian textile from 6-8 Pavement, York.[6]

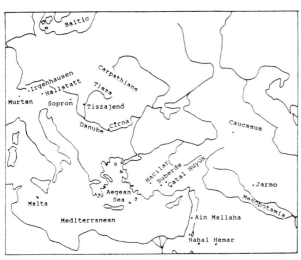

Map of Neolithic sites important to the early history of textiles
(Barber, 1994)

The earliest signs of impressed cotton textiles with a few surviving threads have been found in Dhuweila in eastern Jordan, and radiocarbon dating places them between 4450 and 3000 BC. The threads were 'Z' spun which is typical of other Asian and Indian textiles and so could have been imported.[7] Historical evidence seems to indicate that in antiquity there were places where particular materials were dyed. Silk was dyed in China, cotton in India, wool in Mesopotamia (though Brunello said that he had not come across madder in ancient Mesopotamia), and cotton and wool in Persia.

The earliest indication of coloured thread may be from Catal Huyuk in Turkey and the beginning of the sixth millennium BC. At this Early Neolithic Anatolian site a group of beads was found with traces of red inside the string holes, which suggested that the now-missing thread was originally coloured red.[8]

What may be one of the most ancient coloured or dyed textiles ever found consists of woollen fragments from the fourth millennium BC during the Chalcolithic period, from the Cave of the Treasure at Nahal Mishmar in the Judean desert in Israel. The colours are reported to include red.[9]

To cope with the volume of history, the cultivation of madder, dyeing with madder and madder pigment have been treated separately.

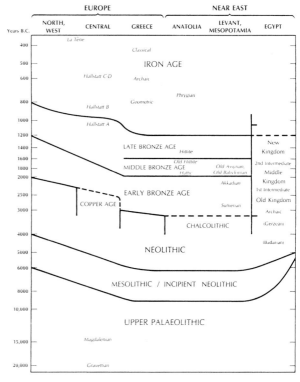

Chronology of main eras from 20,000-400BC
(Barber, 1991)

	Greece	Crete	Anatolia	Mesopotamia
400				
		Classical		
600		Archaic		Neo-Babylonian, Neo-Assyrian
800			Phrygian	
		Geometric		
1000			Neo-Hittite	
	Sub-Mycenaean			
1200	—	M Y C	—	
1400	Late Helladic	E N	Late Minoan	Hittite
1600	—	A E N	—	
1800	Middle Helladic		Middle Minoan	Old Hittite
				Old Babylonian, Old Assyrian
2000	—		—	Hattic
2500	Early Helladic	Early Minoan	Early Bronze	Neo-Sumerian, Akkadian
3000				Sumerian

Chronology of later cultures from 3000-400BC
(Barber, 1991)

Madder red dyes in archaeology and ancient writings

Traders and merchants, especially the Phoenicians, undoubtedly helped spread dyestuffs and textiles from one area to another. Ancient wars and conquests forced craftsmen to move from one country to another which also helped disseminate dyeing techniques.

Sir John Marshall noted that few textiles had survived in Mohenjo-daro. He described two small silver vessels, similar in form to a perfume jar and a salt cellar which were once wrapped in coarse purple cotton, found in Room 8 of House VIII in the VS Area, Section A. Only small scraps adhered to the outside of the lid of No 3 (the 'salt cellar'). Though very brittle, the fragments had survived thanks to impregnation with silver salts. The scraps had been examined by A. N. Gulati and A. J. Turner of the Indian Central Cotton Committee, Technology Laboratory, Dehli. They identified the cotton as an almost extinct Indian variety *Gossypium arboreum* and thought that it was one of the earliest examples of cotton

Front of House VIII, Mohenjo-daro (Marshall)

cloth. Brunello speculated that it was this plant which can grow to a height of six or seven metres which astonished the Greek invaders under Alexander the Great (c. 320 BC) who called it the wool tree.[10] The technologists also thought that the purple dye was "probably of the madder class," but omitted to add that the c. 3000 BC date would make it the earliest use of madder. The widespread Indo-iranian words for madder may be found in appendix 2.1 (page 313).

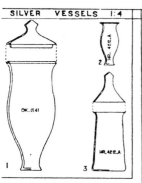

SILVER VESSELS 1:4

Silver vessels once wrapped in madder pirple cotton (Marshall)

Frustratingly, the fragments are now lost — presumably crumbled away. To extract from Marshall's full reasoning for the dating, several of the large number of artefacts from Mohenjo-daro resemble others from Elam and Mesopotamian cultures and the proto-historic culture of Sumer. Excavations at Mohenjo-Daro identified at least seven flooded levels of settlement which yielded antiquities of uniform character. This indicated what Marshall described as "a generous 500 year period" from 3250 to 2750 BC.[11]

Renata Germer cited later evidence for the use of madder in Ancient Egypt.[12] Firstly, the earliest occurrence of the hieroglyph for madder is in the 20th

Left: The girdle of Rameses III (Germer)
Right & below: Elaborate sashes from Tutankhamen's tomb (ack. Griffith Institute, Oxford; Vogelsang-Eastwood)

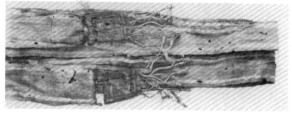

Dynasty (1189-1069 BC) sentence from papyrus Lansing. In agreement with the earlier philologist Victor Loret, Germer identified *'jp3'* as madder as well as its much later Coptic derivative (see p21).[13]

Madder did not grow wild in Egypt but was imported from Palestine either as a root or as a plant. The oldest dyed linen is yellow-brown-red from Pepi's I and Merenres's pyramids dating from the Sixth Dynasty (2323-2150 BC) but the red is not madder or henna, safflower or *alkanna*. During the Old Kingdom Fifth Dynasty, despite modern rumours of madder-dyed pink linen, the red pigment has consistently been analysed as ochrous earth — iron oxide.[14]

Another canard was recently shot down. Near Fayium in Illahum the pyramid of Sesostris II was built after 1888BC during the Middle Kingdom period, with its construction workers' dwellings in nearby Kahun. Flinders Petrie found red wool at Kahun which McDowell in 1986 analysed as madder with alum.[15] The next earliest madder dyeing which occurred during the 18th Dynasty at Tel el-Amarna c. 1370 BC, see below, was without metal salts which appeared much later during the 21st Dynasty, c. 1000 BC. Moreover, all the known red linen from the Middle Kingdom period was dyed with iron oxide. Of the 4000 New Kingdom fragments known, only one per cent are wool — sheep's wool in 38 items with two of goat's wool. The rest are linen. So Germer concluded that either the wool came from Palestine or that the dating was wrong.[16]

The Egyptian painted tomb of Khnumhotep in Beni Hassan in Palestine of the 12th Dynasty, Early Middle Kingdom, is the sole example in Palestine contemporary with Kahun, but the reds there are iron oxide and no wool was found. Avigail Sheffer wrote of two fragments of the earliest, rarely found wool, dyed red, from the Hathor temple site in Timna in eastern Sinai dating from the later 19th-20th Dynasties — after 1304 BC. There was insufficient dyestuff in the sample for analysis, but Sheffer was able to identify the wool as locally produced (ie non-Egyptian) from its twist and weave.[17] So it appears that Flinders Petrie's red wool was from later New Kingdom or Roman remains which have also been found at Kahun. Germer decided on the Roman dating as alum mordanted wool was not known in the Middle Kingdom period.

Gillian Eastwood examined the 4000 pieces of cloth found in the rubbish dump of the workmen's village at Tel el-Amarna, which can be dated to c. 1370 BC when they built the pyramid. Only 35 were dyed and with Dr G. W. Taylor she analysed the earliest known madder on red linen flax and violet linen, dyed with a mixture of indigo and madder.[18]

King Tutankhamen's 'belt' as well as some other textiles found in his tomb are said to be coloured with madder red — 1350 BC;[19] a steel dagger was also found there indicating the technical level needed to produce metal salts for mordanting.[20] Madder was also found in red linen from the Royal Cachette from the 21st dynasty, 1085-945 BC.[21]

In Mesopotamia traces of a woven fabric dating from c. 2500 BC were found in the Great Death Pit at the Royal Tombs of Ur and they seemed to be coloured from a brilliant red ochre.[22] Several tools names were derived from Mesopotamian words for kermes and cochineal, but not madder.[23] Dr Stephanie Dalley of the University of Oxford wrote that while hundreds of new cuneiform texts come to light every year, at present the earliest occurrence of the Akkadian

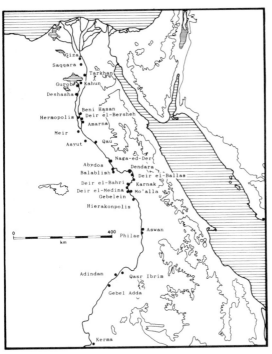

Sites and Tombs of Ancient Egypt
(Vogelsang-Eastwood)

word for madder, *hūrratu*, is from c. 1900 BC (this date and the next are plus or minus 180 years) in a text from the Larsa region in lower Mesopotamia and from texts c. 1400 BC from Ugarit on the coast of Syria.[24]

Further, Dalley knows of no texts which mention where madder was grown, so when textiles are mentioned they may have been made with local or imported dyes. From dictionaries, the Middle Akkadian c. 1300 BC word *hūrratu* is cited as a root of sweet wood and dye for red wool when used with alum *'gabu'* and tanning.[25] The red wool which the town of Arvad had to pay as tribute to the Assyrians in neo-Assyrian times (c. eighth century BC) was a shell dye. In other towns, tribute was probably also paid in madder dyed wool.[26]

In the Caucasus, the oldest coloured textiles were found in Tsarskaia (renamed Novosvobodnaia) in the Kuban region, dating from 2500-2000 BC. This was an undergarment, probably of linen, belonging to a buried tribal chieftain, which was brightly decorated with purple colour and covered with tassel-like red threads.[27] Unfortunately, there is no analysis available.

Various historians state that the Babylonians, Assyrians and Chaldeans wore rich multicoloured clothing. The Akkadian Old Babylonian c. 1800BC word for colour *bir-mu* also means coloured textiles or goods, which is analogous to the Hebrew *b'romin* in Ezekiel.[28] In the Bible three plants are mentioned from which dye was obtained: henna, saffron and *pu'ah*, meaning madder. *Tola* (crimson) and *puvah* or *pu'ah* are mentioned in Genesis, Chronicles and Judges[29] as proper names borne by the sons of Issachar, and suggest that this tribe was skilled in the production of these dyes or as dyers.[30] Spelled differently with an *'ain* it is also the name of one of Pharaoh's midwives who was ordered to kill the Hebrew first-born in Exodus.[31] *Pu'ah* is also mentioned later in the Mishna, compiled c. 200 AD from traditional oral sources.[32] Dr Esra Kahn of Jews' College, London, remarked that *pu'ah* is also known as a sound which pacifies a crying baby. Madder is indigenous to Edom, Esau's home, in present-day Trans-Jordan, and many species grow wild in Israel.

Detail of the dancing lady's skirts with red bands, inner crosses and squares. Blue, brown and white also bring out the designs —
15th century BC, Hagia Triada sarcophagus, Candia museum, Crete
(Barber, 1991)

The earliest of the sparse archaeological finds of textiles in present-day Israel was at Kuntillat Arjud on the Negev-Sinai border in the remains of a Jewish religious centre dated eighth-ninth centuries BC, known as the First Temple Period.[33] The religious nature of the site was partly indicated by one of the linen fragments which was unusually decorated with a stripe of madder red woollen thread between two stripes of blue linen thread among the warps. The mixture of linen and wool — *sha'atnez* — was forbidden to be worn by Jews.[34] However the High Priest's vestments and the hangings of the tabernacle were made of *sha'atnez*.[35] More generally, Canaanites are depicted in Egyptian art as dressed in colourful garments. In the Bible there were several references to coloured garments and to coloured threads. What the colours actually were remains a mystery in 'Joseph's coat of many colours'[36] or the divers colours of 'needlework' which Sisera's mother waited so eagerly to receive.[37]

Brunello argued that the 15th-century BC Late Minoan I period painting of the dancing lady's many-coloured skirts on the Hagia Triada sarcophagus at Candia museum coupled with evidence of Egyptian and Eastern Mediterranean alum trade,[38] showed that madder and kermes reds were used by the Cretans. They gave these dyes to the Greeks. To expand on this, Andrew Dalby noted that the number of references definitely to madder, *erythrodanon* or *ereuthedanon*, in other Greek texts is actually very small, and none of them goes into details of the use for dyeing as opposed to medicinal uses. It was mentioned by Herodotus,[39] who said that the Libyan nomads used it to dye shaved goatskins. But he did not mention that the Lydians did (see below), which was unfortunate because he knew Lydia pretty well. In Theophrastus[40] both the wild and cultivated plants were described briefly, with their pharmaceutical effects.

In general Greek references were actually to *phoinix*. This term is sometimes understood as 'the Phoenician dye', murex: but that may well be a misunderstanding since the word seemed to belong to Lydian dyes, which had nothing to do with Phoenicia. It really seemed to mean 'blood-red', and Dalby accepts the argument that madder is what was really meant. *Phoinix* was mentioned in the Homeric poems (Iliad and Odyssey) which are now generally dated shortly after 700 BC. The Iliad had one very interesting simile: blood from a wound spreading over skin "like a Maeonian (Lydian) or Carian woman making a cheek-piece for a horse, dyeing the ivory with *phoinix*."[41] The Odyssey said that Odysseus gave his marriage bed ox-hide straps (as springs? — not clear) which were coloured *phoinix*.[42]

The women of Lydia and Caria in Asia Minor were credited by Brunello as purple dyers in Homer and as specialists in colouring red leather thongs for sandals in Sappho. Actually, Sappho said that "a multicoloured *poikilos* sandal *masthles* (the word is totally unknown: it could as well be a rug) of fine Lydian workmanship covered her feet." That is all we have of the poem: we do not know the context, there is nothing to say how the colouring was achieved, nor the material it was on.[43] The Sappho fragment survived because it was quoted incidentally in an ancient commentary on the play *Peace* by Aristophanes. The commentator said: "Lydian dyes were noteworthy, see Homer (the Iliad quotation above) and Sappho (the quotation just given)." The passage in Aristophanes which is being commented on talked about "a cloak of bright *phoinikis* colour, which they call a Lydian dye."[44]

Again Brunello misinterpreted that Aeschylus described Agamemnon being welcomed back from Troy by Clytemnestra who got her slaves to spread some *porphyra* — not red — carpets from Hermione (in Argolis) on the ground. Aeschylus did not actually mention Hermione so it did not interest him.[45] Hermione is said in a handy Classical encyclopaedia[46] to have had important purple fisheries in antiquity. They have two sources for this statement: one is the passage about Alexander from Plutarch below, the other is from a late historical fiction writer, Alciphron, who talked of the loss of a slipper of Egyptian linen dyed with *porphyra halourgos* from Hermione. Alciphron usually had some reason in early texts for the things he mentioned, so his "sea-purple from Hermione" has to be taken seriously.[47]

Plutarch related that Alexander's booty at Susa included 5000 talents (25kg) of *porphyra Hermionike*, "purple from Hermione," which had been stored for 190 years and was still fresh in colour. He continued: "The reason was said to be that honey was used in the purple dyes, *halourgon*, and white oil in the whites, *leukon*: and the latter were equally clean and bright in appearance, though they were of the same age." *Porphyra halourgos*, 'sea-worked purple' was an odd phrase usually understood as meaning genuine murex purple. Brunello's[48] description of the materials as "white with sides dyed red and purple" comes from a misreading of Plutarch. There are only two colours mentioned, purple and white.[49]

The Spartans dyed their battle dress scarlet to hide bloodstains and make their warriors appear invulnerable. The famous Spartan red footwear came from the workshops at Amiclea, again possibly dyed with madder.[50] Forbes quoted the contrary story that the Spartans chased the dyers from their country as they robbed the wool of its beautiful natural colour and that was why the word *delun* in their dialect meant both 'dye' and 'cheat'.[51]

Another example of the difficulties of colour naming in ancient languages recently appeared. Lloyd Lewellyn-Jones has put forward that '*krokus*', the colour of Ancient Greek wedding veils, was not saffron crocus yellow but red. He added that red veils were widely used in other veil rituals and usually were metaphors for the broken hymen of the wedding night.[52]

According to an ancient legend, come down from the Greek alchemists, the first person to collate information about dyes was the famous philosopher, Democritus (c. 350 BC) or perhaps a pseudo-Democritus called Bolos who lived in Lower Egypt during the Ptolemaic era. During the former's visit to Memphis, the priests of the temple revealed to him secrets concerning both alchemy and the art of dyeing. There could be some truth in this, as certain Greek papyri dating from the third century AD, found in the necropolis of Thebes last century, consisted entirely of transcriptions of formulae from the temples at Memphis.

Grave robbers found two of these miraculously preserved papyri in 1828. They were placed on either side of the mummy of a priest who judging from the surrounding vases and ornaments, was an alchemist. One, now known as Papyrus Leydensis, eventually reached the museum of Leiden, the other Papyrus Holmiensis passed from Stockholm to Upsala. These stimulated much study, analysis and experimentation. The latter gave very detailed recipes for dyeing and dyestuffs including one using madder for purple, but kermes and archil for red. While these papyri were probably collections of earlier works, they represent the earliest sources available (see chapter 12).[53]

R. A. Donkin, in his magisterial account of cochineal, mentions *De Coloribus*, which perhaps was written c. 300 BC by a member of the school of Aristotle. It said that "many things are coloured by the flowers of plants, many by the roots, many again by bark or wood or leaves or fruit . . ."[54] As well as Ancient Greek and Latin references to madder, such as *erythrodanon* in Greek from Hippocrates and Theophrastus, where both wild and cultivated plants were described briefly[55] and *rubia* and *voerantia* in Latin,[56] it was also well known to the Jews from Old Testament times.

Later textiles from the cave of Wadi ed-Daliyeh in Eastern Samaria dated fourth century BC during the Persian period were dyed with madder.[57] An assortment of Roman-period textiles have been found in the caves of Muraba'at, Qumran, from the first century AD (but there were no reds)[58] and the Cave of Letters in the Judean Desert, second century AD. Decorated fabrics were used for wrapping scrolls.[59] The wrappings found in the Cave of Letters had colourful bands dyed with madder, indigo and saffron. The wrapper found in Masada, decorated on the upper side with a pattern of seven triangles, was woven with blue threads and embroidered with madder-dyed threads around the edges.[60]

The Mishna (c. 200 AD)[61] — the collection of ancient Hebrew laws and precepts which formed the basis of the Talmud (c. 425 AD) — permitted the growing of madder though only for domestic, and not commercial use. There was a discussion of the methods of uprooting it in a sabbatical year.[62] Only wooden implements were allowed to be used at the harvest. This reminded Jill Goodwin, a contemporary British dyer, of the Ancient Druids' rule to use a golden sickle for harvesting mistletoe.

Drawing of a madder plant in the Vienna Codex Aniciae Julianae with a label added in Arabic (Faber; CIBA Review & Brunello)

Strabo wrote in AD 25 that 'Colossian' wool was a common term for wool dyed with madder,[63] while Pliny the Elder (AD 23-79) mentioned[64] that best quality *rubia* was grown in the market garden area near Rome c. AD 50 and that the Italian plant was better than foreign ones, including those from Sardis, near Salihli inland from Izmir,[65] where he thought, without giving a reason[66] that dyeing with madder was invented.[67] Poor people who started to cultivate madder, which was at that time used for dyeing wool and leather, soon became rich[68] and Pliny also stated that in the vat there dissolved a single colour but after brief immersion, the textile showed several colours according to the nature of the absorbing product used. Brunello reasonably thinks that this is describing madder as the various mordants — alum, iron salts or copper salts — were well known at the time.[69]

Pliny's contemporary, the physician to Emporer Claudius, Dioscorides of Cilicia was the best authority on botany and pharmacology in ancient times,[70] and he was the author of the *Materia Medica*. He noted that the dyers distinguished between the inferior wild madder and the richer cultivated variety. Difficulties in identifying plants described by him brought about the preparations of his illustrated Herbal which is the oldest example of a Greek herbarium that has survived. He also identified a particularly excellent quality of madder grown near Ravenna, planted among the olive trees. There is a drawing of a madder plant in the Vienna manuscript, *Codex Aniciae Julianae*, dated AD 515 with later comments written in Arabic. This was roughly contemporary with silk worms being smuggled from Turkestan to Persia and Byzantium.[71]

The bright red military dress of the Romans was probably dyed with madder, which according to St Matthew was the colour of the vestment or *sagum*, known as the robe of Jesus.[72] The reason that Brunello doubted that this was kermes was because Vospicus wrote that Homisdas King of Persia sent as homage to Aurelius a precious mantle of red wool which was brighter that the imperial purple.[73] From that time the Roman dyers were ordered to search the East for this new and splendid dye which was kermes. But they were unsuccessful and could only refer vaguely to a kind of madder of unique quality.[74] W. M. Flinders Petrie discovered a fully equipped dye workshop among the Hellenistic Egyptian ruins of Anthribis near present day Sohag. Of the 16 well-cemented tubs fixed on a large stone bench that ran along three of its metal-lined walls, one contained a residue of a red colour that was perhaps madder (see chapter 12).[75] In the destruction of Pompeii on August 24th, AD 79, the largest *officina tintoria* belonging to one Ubonius, contained a number of well-preserved flasks, with the remains of various dyestuffs one of which was thought to be madder.[76] Madder may also have been grown in Gaul as early as the Roman period.[77]

During the Roman period coloured leather was a luxury good. Mommsen wrote that a skin of red Babylonian leather cost an exorbitant 500 *denarii*. Babylon was probably only the market as such skins were also made in India. Gansser suggested that a madder dye was used for red leather, which graced the Roman emperor's red laced top-boots.[78]

Strabo in AD 25 noted that 120 ships plied between Egypt and India each year,[79] which is taken as evidence of the textile and dye trades. Pfister discovered madder on Chinese silk textiles found in two graves in Palmyra in Syria. One tomb was inscribed with the name of Jambelicus and dated AD 83; the other was inscribed with the name of Elahbel son of Mannay and dated AD 103. The Byzantine period Egyptian papyrus Anastasi (probably post fourth-century AD) bemoaned "the finger of a dyer has the smell of rotten fish" (perhaps referring to *garum*, the Byzantine condiment made from rotting fish guts). "His eyes are red from fatigue" — noxious fumes from fermentation or stale urine. The tanner breathed no better air: "All covered with tannin and stinking with a special odour. His hands are red from madder like those of a man covered with blood."[80] This may be taken from the more ancient Egyptian hieroglyph in chapter 2. Petrov wrote that some late first century BC or earlier textiles found in Khakassia and Noin-Ula in Mongolia were dyed with madder.[81]

A Relbunium plant and roots, Atacocha, Peru (photo Kay & Erik Antunez de Mayolo, c. 1986; Saltzman)

There was an early equivalent to madder in America too. G. A. Fester, the pioneering researcher of South American textiles, has shown that red dyes found in the necropolis of Paracas (1000-200 BC) were not the usual cochineal, but based on colouring principles similar to madder, which was then non-existent in America. Dyestuff was obtained from the roots of local plants of the genus *Relbunium*.[82] The species is spread from Patagonia as far as Salta and Correntes.[83] Prof M. Saltzman of UCLA analysed 141 Paracas textiles which were nearly all dyed with *Relbunium* with only three testing for the wrongly-expected cochineal.[84] Sandberg quoted confirmation from analysis by M. Ekroth-Edebo at the Goteborg Ethnographic Museum, where ten Pre-Columbian textiles also showed the same dye continuing from the Paracas period through the Nasca period — 200 BC to AD 600 — and the Pachacamac around AD 1000.[85] After the colonisation of America *Rubia tinctorum* was imported and can now be found on the banks of the Rio Mayo in Chile and alongside the Godoy Cruz.

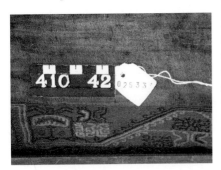

Fragment of a Paracas mantle with a band decorated with a double-headed puma, c. 100BC dyed with Relbunium (Saltzman)

This contrasted with Whitehead's studies of porcupine-quill decoration in North America.[86] The earliest "textile fragments in which porcupine quill was used as the bonding element in a wrapped twine process" were recovered from the deepest level of Lovelock Cave, Nevada. Other material from the same level has been carbon-dated to c. 500 BC. This evidence suggests the existence of a developed tradition. Other examples only survived in much later finds or were still being made when the first Europeans collected them. An example of another technique, quill stitchery, appeared on a pair of moccasins from the Promontory Point cave site in Utah, c. AD 1200-1300.

The French explorer Champlain was the first European to describe porcupine-quill ornament which he saw being worn at an Algonquin victory dance in 1603: "*qu'ils teigneant de diverses coullers*" — dyed various colours, the quills were worked into armbands, necklaces and other jewellery.

Micmac porcupine quillwork box lid, made c. 1780-90 (Whitehead)

The Micmac Indians who speak an Algonquin language and are culturally nearer to the Wabanaki cluster, were specialists in all aspects of quill decoration. The admiring 17th-century French writers recorded five types of technique which the Micmac had mastered, of which sadly only one, bark insertion, continued in use. In one traveller's account, Marc Lescarbot in 1606 was met at sea off Cape Breton Island by two shallops manned by Frenchmen and local Indians. One of the native men had left "his fair beaver gown" at home "because the weather had been foul" and "had but one red piece of frieze upon his back and *matachias* about his neck, at his wrists, above the elbow and at his girdle." *Matachias* were woven quillwork panels, "which they dye black, (natural) white and red, as lively as possibly may be." The Micmacs moved from the Gaspe and Maritime Provinces to parts of New England and Newfoundland, and their dyes were not specified in the earlier writings although Peter Kalm, a Swedish botanist travelling in Canada in 1750, identified *Galium tinctorum* for the reds.

After the Roman Empire

In the Orient, the Byzantines' successors in the Eastern Roman Empire continued to practise the same dye technology. Textiles found in En-Boqeq (Western Dead Sea) in Israel, from the seventh century have madder red dyes.[87]

Petrov wrote that early information about madder cultivation in present day Azerbaijan occurred in Armenian and Arabic texts of the ninth-tenth centuries. Minorsky apparently quoting Istakhri's report, c. 951 on Arran, Sharvan (Shirvan) and al-Bab (Derbent) from his passage on the commercial activity of Derbent, mentioned trade in local products, namely madder, saffron and linen.[88] The Arab writer mentioned that valley areas of north-east

Azerbaijan, such as the left bank of the Samur river, had been exporting madder for centuries through Derbent. The madder was sold beyond the borders of the Caliphate, even to India. The Arab geographer Makadassi writing in the tenth century noted that madder formerly grown in Egypt had been superseded by lac from India.[89] Al-Biruni (973-1048), the Arab scholar and scientist, described dyer's madder, which was imported from Balkh and Armenia to Persia and India.[90] Ibn Hawqal (c. 943-88) remarked on marshy isles in the Caspian (perhaps including the Terek delta in northern Daghestan) which produced madder of a superior quality which was exported by sea to Gurgan and thence by land to India.[91]

The three Classical philosophical theories of colour by Aristotle and others were translated into Arabic during this period (see chapter 17). The eleventh-century manuscript by the Persian Abu Mansur bin Ali Harawi is famous for having explained the properties of a great number of plants to the Europeans. He examined several plant dyes including madder but only from a pharmacological standpoint.[92]

In Europe, surviving records are also sporadic though there seemed to be continual interest in the root. We next hear of madder growing in the vicinity of Paris. In France madder was cultivated even before Dagobert I's reign (622-638). A ninth-century forged charter of King Dagobert purported to allow the inhabitants of Quentovic to sell madder at the Landit fair of St Denis.[93] In this document foreign merchants from England and Friesland were said to have purchased it there. Dagobert was supposed to have founded the fair at the abbey of St Denis and entrusted the Counts of Paris with the collection of dues. The forgery is not without historical value as it implied a need 200 years later to assert the earlier trade. Madder was also cited in the founder's charter of the Abbey of Treport and in the tithe rights of the Abbeys of Trun and Saint-Wandrille, but the dates were not given.[94] Isidore the seventh-century Bishop of Seville quoted in the 13th century 'Eraclius' (no. LIII), mentions *garancia* identified with *sandis(x)* (see chapter 10).[95] A century later madder was one of the plants which Charlemagne (768-814) ordered to be cultivated on his estates. In his *Capitulare de Villis vel Curtis Imperialibus*[96] the word used for madder is *warentia*.

De Coloribus et Artibus Romanorum was written in Latin hexameters in the tenth century and attributed to Heraclius. Though it was based on Pliny's *Heraclius*, the author's name may have been a mythological one meaning 'touchstone', anthropomorphised by medieval writers. Although the book deals mainly with painting, there are some recipes for dyeing leather red with madder and alum.[97] It may be that the custom of the medieval peasant to plant his rotational fallow field with madder dates from this time[98] (see chapter 5).

Recent active archaeology in Britain has resulted in many madder finds especially in Coppergate in York and late Anglo-Saxon London. The madder-dyes on raw wool from the ninth to eleventh centuries were applied before spinning. Penelope Walton Rogers thinks that as the summers of the period were a little warmer than today, the madder could have been grown locally near York.[99] She also translated Winric of Treves' (fl. 1068-97) verses, where the sheep are given tongues to describe the woollen cloths of Europe. Of Britain, the sheep observed, "Not blood, not sun, not fire, glows as red as you, Britain, glow ruby in my coat." The madder reds of Coppergate, London, Thetford and Winchester belong to the Anglo-Saxon rather than the Scandinavian tradition.

At the Coppergate excavation site in York, ninth to eleventh-century 'Viking' layers of red-brown earthy material were discovered[100] which were analysed by Su Grierson as madder roots thrown out by the local dyer after he had extracted the red colours. It was astonishing that after almost a thousand years in a waterlogged site, all the other unused dye principles, that is the peach and yellow shades, had survived and were identical to those from a modern sample. Madder was mentioned in two leechdoms and a Herbal of the 11th century, but these could well be based on classical texts. The same problem may call into question a late-11th century document in which the planting of madder is referred to as one of the duties of a reeve.[101] However in the 13th-14th centuries when madder seems to have been the most commonly used red dye,[102] there is no record of the importation of the dyestuff. Carus-Wilson suggested that that sufficient madder was being grown locally to meet demand and there was the ecclesiastical reference in 1270 in East Anglia mentioned elsewhere. Yet in the early 14th-century *Book of Brother Stephen* of St Augustine's Canterbury the list of prices of colours includes 'red-lead' (*plumbum rubrum*), 'vermilon' and 'ocre' but not madder, unless that was the source of 'brun'.[103]

There was another Viking madder find from further north. In 1904 at Oseberg on the western bank of Oslo Fjord, a tumulus was found to cover a wooden sarcophagus. It contained the disinterred corpse of Queen Asa, second wife of King Gudrod, who lived about 800 AD. Around the royal remains were weaving implements and receptacles with residues of plants used in dyeing. One was identified as madder which would have been imported that far north.[104] The Vikings are also known to have travelled down the Volga to Itil near later Astrakhan and southwards across the length of the Caspian to Gurgan and thence overland to Baghdad.[105] A further example of the breadth of the textile trade at this time is that the Arabs introduced cotton to China during the eighth century.[106]

City-state trade in the later Middle Ages

Divers trade records indicate the growth of international textile and madder trade during the Middle Ages. The important Oriental trade was gradually challenged by European production which grew as a result of technological

European Trade Routes of the Ottoman Empire, 1300-1600
(Inalcik, 1994; for eastern half of map, see p239)

advances. There was comple-mentary increase in European distribution, both internally through the development of annual fairs and externally through advances in maritime technology.[107] The few Oriental records which follow imply a substantial and long established trade in madder. In the 12th century ships loaded madder at Aden bound for India, according to a report by Choa-Jou-Coua, a Chinese inspector of trade.[108] He would appear to have had more

Indian 12th century printed cotton of armed combat (Wescher, CIBA Review)

than a passing interest in madder, for J. Wouters has recently analysed Chinese silks from Tibet dated from the 12th to the 14th century and found madder present in the reds and violets of 32 of the 33 samples.[109]

In about 1100, a shipment of madder brought a price of 5½ dinars in Old Cairo, with customs duties of ¼ dinar, about five per cent, paid in Alexandria.[110] R. Pfister analysed a red-brown dye on wool imported to Egypt before the ninth century as *Morinda umbellata* L. from the Indies or China.[111]

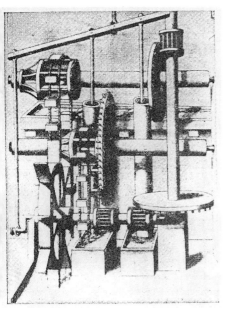

Jacopo da Strada's 1580 design of a water pump: if the function of the pistons is reversed, the machine changes into a tilt-hammer — see page 127 (Forbes, 1958)

In Fustat, the old Islamic capital of Egypt, Pfister also found post-1200 Indian coarse cotton cloths decorated with woodblock prints, where the design was transferred to the fabric by wax or (curiously) starch coloured with madder red.[112] Archbishop Eurare in his letter from Turkey in 1185 mentioned that Turkey was the largest European producer, while the 14th century traveller L. Varthema confirmed the continuing trade through Aden where he noted that every year some 15 or 20 ships sailed for India, loaded with 'rubricke' or madder.[113] About 1340 Pegolotti mentioned Turkmen exports including gall nuts, alum, Turkish silk and madder.[114] The traveller Bertrandon de la Brocquiere joined a 3000 camel caravan on the 50-day journey by land from Damascus to Bursa in 1432, where they were met by Florentine and Genoese merchants. Inalcik mentioned that the caravan was carrying dyestuffs.[115]

The opinion that madder was not cultivated in Europe until the 16th century can only be justified as far as that period marked the beginning of larger scale cultivation. Madder had already become part of the trading culture of the various European city-states and played an important role in their economic growth. Forbes understood that increase in industrial output depended on mechanisation where the textile industry was a leader. He mentioned that tilt- or lift-hammer machines were introduced in the early Middle Ages for fulling.

T' Bouck van Wondre, frontispiece, 1513 (Brunello)

Plictho, frontispiece, 1540 (Brunello)

Fulling involved beating or compressing woven cloth in water to make it stronger. Later, though still before 1300, the spinning wheel was first introduced in Europe.[116] Diffusion of dyeing techniques was accelerated by the invention of printing. The first printed book on dyeing appeared in Brussels in 1513, called *T' Bouck van Wondre*, 'The Book of Marvels'. The greatly popular *Plictho* (or 'Binder') by Gioanventura Rosetti first appeared in Venice in 1548 and was frequently reprinted during the following 200 years. About a third of the 107 formulae dealt with red and several others with blacks.[117] Several Jewish dyers realised that the future lay in technological change and became printers. One of the earliest was Abraham ben Hayyim dei Tintori of Pesaro, whose name appeared in a printed commentary on Job published in Ferrara in 1477.[118]

The Italians developed a constructive relationship with the Islamic world and became leaders of European commerce. From the tenth to thirteenth centuries Florence, Pisa and Genoa were thriving dye-trade cities and for many years Genoa had a monopoly on the alum trade.[119] Pigments were exported across the Alps from Italy. From 1400, madder was mentioned in the tariffs of Basle and later during the century in the tariffs of Como and Strasburg. A market existed in Prato near Florence evidenced in the accounts of Nicolo di Piero's Dyers' Company — both wool-weaving centres — dated March 8, 1394, where the inventory of madder roots was estimated at eight gold florins. In Venice in 1413, a decree forbade the use of cattle and goat's blood to be mixed with madder[120] (see illustrations, page 181).

The industrious Low Countries had to compete with the Italians by specialisation. Duke Guido in his letter from Flanders in 1282, mentioned that Flanders was the largest European producer.[121] Thirsk noted that during the first experience of alternative agriculture after the Black Death, madder was grown in Zeeland in 1326 and about then also in Flanders and mentioned earlier in East

Anglia which had close contact with Flanders, in 1274 (see below).[122] Detailed instructions governing the planting and tending of madder were issued by the town of Goes in Holland in 1494. They reveal a high standard of cultivation, which continued for the following three centuries ensuring Holland's top position in the business. The moist climate and the alluvial soil of the delta islands of Zeeland were ideal conditions for growing madder.

Around 1300, *The Book of Master Peter of St Omer on Making Colours* appeared, with borrowings from his contemporary Theophilus, which mentioned madder. Regulations have survived from the 1330s to 1490s for several districts in Flanders and Artois where madder was cultivated. Within a day's drive from Calais, madder was cultivated and/or processed in St Omer, Hainaut, Cambrai, Malines, Tournai, Douai, Lille, Arras, Aire, Bethune, Hesdin, Berst near Dixmude, Bruges, and nearby Micheem, now called Dudzele and Oostkerke. Quality standards were enforced at the markets at Valenciennes, Ypres, Riemerswaal, Amsterdam and de Courtrai.[123]

In 1510 there was an action in Antwerp brought by a local merchant against two Frankfurt dealers who had supplied him with three bags of inferior red dye (possibly forbidden *'mul'* from Flanders, Artois or distant Breslau, see chapter 9). It was sufficiently serious that the opinion of the witnesses — two brothers from Gouda and a merchant from Diest in Brabant, all of them dealers in red cloths — was sealed by the mayor, the sheriffs and the town council. Emperor Charles V (1519-56) was at pains to encourage

A view of Genoa 1482, retouched in 1597: the port of Genoa was only limited in size by the mountains behind. Genovese e dunque mercato' — 'Genoese and therefore a merchant' (popular saying). (Mazzino, 1974)

this profitable form of agriculture and granted far-reaching privileges to the people living in the region of Zuider Zee. To ensure that quality standards were maintained, he issued a decree in 1537, according to which madder-growers in Schouwen had to be sworn. Additional regulations which he imposed ensured the excellent reputation and success of the Dutch industry and were observed right through to the 19th century. In 1758 Miller estimated that the Dutch regularly exported £180,000 a year.[124]

Philip III
(Wescher, CIBA Review)

Further south, the fairs of Champagne became important trade centres for textiles and dyestuffs. In January there was the Fair of Lagny, in April the Fair of Lille, in autumn the Great Fair of Provins and in winter the 'Cold' Fair of Troyes. In 1121, Count William V in his testament refers to the scarlet cloth of Montpellier (Languedoc) which was chiefly made for export. By 1204 a regulation decreed that only kermes should be used for scarlet dyeing, and not madder, to compete with the products of Genoa, Lucca and Marseilles. The Italian competition was ever vigilant. The Statutes of the Dyers of Lucca drawn up in 1255 and signed by 86 dyers, forbade the purchase of *radicem tingendi*, 'roots for dyeing', which Brunello reasonably affirmed was madder, by contemporary definition. The substitution of madder for kermes had become a common practice in Lucca and even Venice. The penalty for dyeing with madder was severe — a 1000 lire fine or cutting off the dyer's hand.[125] Until the end of the 13th century the finest woven cloth was sent from Flanders, England, Brabant and Normandy to the Calimala in Florence for dyeing and finishing. At the beginning of the 14th century dyeing-workshops developed in Flanders which amongst other colours dyed madder and mignonette reds.

Count Jacob II ordered that the quantity of dyestuffs used for scarlet be increased and re-authorised the use of madder. However the superior cloths dyed with kermes were guaranteed with the town seal. Madder and alum, its mordant, were mentioned in the Fair tariffs of the mid-13th century. In 1248 a large consignment of alum, 32 loads left the south of France for the May Fair of Provins. Trade warfare was complicated: Philip III the Bold, king of France (r. 1270-1285) in 1277 forbade all export of wool to protect the French trades. But this was neutralised by his successor Philip the Fair (r. 1285-1314), who gave monopolies to two naturalised Milanese merchants Biccio and Moschietto, who had assisted with his credit requirements.[126] By 1346 Montpellier had 37 master dyers. Just over the present-day French border, records from 1361 told that alum was for sale, but apparently not madder during the well-attended fair at Geneva. This was remedied at the Basle Fair where tariff lists in 1400 included madder from Baghdad.[127]

While France looked to the Mediterranean, German trade had traditional links with Central Europe. When wool weaving developed into one of the principle trades in 13th-century Frankfurt, commerce in dyestuffs expanded rapidly. In Germany from the early 14th century, dyers of the lower category could handle black (*Schwarzfarber*) and dyers of the higher category (*Schonfarber*) had mastered madder, kermes and woad.[128] In Frankfurt, dyeing with woad from neighbouring Thuringia became a large scale industry. Co-operative purchasing by the weavers guild was recorded only from the close of the 15th century, a development of the tired woad trade established by a former Frankfurt wool weaver turned wholesale merchant, Claus Scheid (c. 1440-1501). He bartered wine for woad, securing customers in all the weaving towns in Hesse and on the Rhine. Before long the business reached Breslau and Cracow where his agents bought large quantities of madder, wax and pelts. Eastward traffic was shortly swelled by Butzbach (Hesse) cloth, Swabian fustian, Lübeck herrings, saltpetre, spices, Salzburger onion seed and Dutch cheese. Thus the pattern was set for Frankfurt's wholesale merchants who always expanded the dyestuffs trade in conjunction with other commodities.

Thanks to immigrant artisans from the Low Countries, from the 1550s the dyers' trade at Frankfurt blossomed into one of the main branches of the economy. Silk dyeing establishments multiplied and by 1600 an official count listed 153 dyeing vats with 45 dye masters, the majority of whom were immigrants. The Thirty Years War (1618-1648) ruined the trade. At the close of the century Frankfurt wholesale traders in groceries — known as 'materialists' — had their own agents in Amsterdam, Antwerp and London which reflected the new trade order. Wide areas of Germany and beyond were supplied with spices, southern fruit, foodstuffs and stimulants, fats and oils, no less than with dyes and tanning agents such as madder, woad, indigo, dye-woods, gall-nuts, alum, blue vitriol, sulphur and tartare.[129]

Another outlet for madder was in flock pseudo-velvet cloth. Its first mention was in the *Kunstbuch*, written at St Catherine's Convent in Nuremberg about 1460, which contained 100 recipes, the majority of which were about engraving and preparing wood blocks for printing and painting textiles. The nuns collected wool waste from cloth clippings, which had been dyed with madder (or woad or saffron). They boiled it in lye ash to reduce the keratin content of the wool and dried the residue for conversion. The friable fibres were pulverised into minute particles and spread over a cloth where the pattern had been drawn in a gluey paste of resin or linseed oil.[130] During the same period madder lake pigments were also made from textile cuttings which are described later in chapter 10. According to Entwisle,[131] the earliest flock wallpaper in England was mentioned as a monopoly of the Painters-Stainers Company in 1626, about the same time as the Frenchman M. le François began production in Rouen.

Central Europe looked towards Germany and Russia for trade. During the 16th century madder cultivation also flourished in Bohemia, but it also ceased during the Thirty Years War. Regulations concerning madder issued in Breslau in 1504 show that it was grown in Silesia at that time. Though

Silesian madder was of inferior quality to Dutch, it was cheap and adequate for certain purposes. While Silesian madder continued to be on the market until the 19th century, it made little impression on the European market but had more success at the Nizhegorodsky Fair on the Volga (see chapter 13). By 1737 Silesia's neighbours in Saxony posed serious competition and forced Breslau to ban the export of shoots.[132]

Maddermarket Theatre postcard

Whilst the English climate and soil may have provided better conditions for the cultivation of madder than their rivals in the Low Countries, it was broadcloth-dyeing and mercantile trade which were the preferred sources of English profit from the root. In Norwich, under the shadow of the church of St John once stood the ancient market square where countrymen used to sell their crops of madder. The site is now marked by the eponymous Maddermarket Theatre. The place name 'Maddermarket Alley' has been recorded since 1232.[133] Thirsk thought that the vigorous trading links between the Netherlands and King's Lynn probably explained why madder was also recorded growing in Norfolk on monastic lands at Catton in 1274 and Monk's Grange in 1305, almost certainly for medicinal purposes.[134]

During the difficult years for English shipping on routes to the Ottoman empire, from 1552 to 1570, Italian merchants continued importing various commodities to London including dyes.[135] Local madder-growing was nevertheless confirmed in 1524 by Sir Edward Guildford. The influential Kentish gentleman from Romney Marsh was given a license to export madder and hops against imports of wine, woad and canvas. Import substitution was an aim of Henry VIII's ministers and in 1559 the need to grow madder and woad in the realm was affirmed. Publicity was given to a patent in 1568 that allowed a Dutchman from Brabant to collect wild madder in Ireland. The same year the botanist William Turner, who had visited the Low Countries, recorded in his *New Herball* that he had seen his "fairest and greatest" specimens of madder on the road from Winchester to Southampton.[136]

The grant of 'capitulations' or trade concessions to national group(s) by the

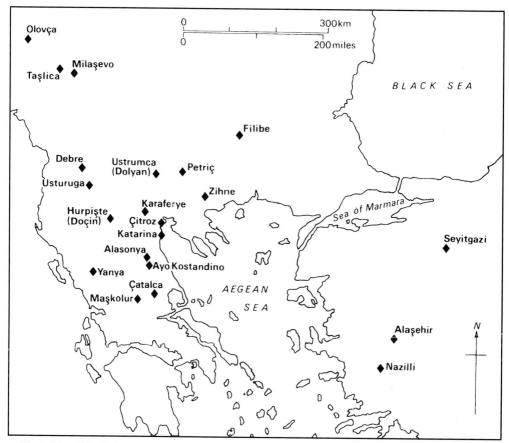

Trade fairs of the Balkans and Anatolia, 16th-17th centuries: the Ottoman economy was greater than the whole of Europe combined (Faroqhi, 1978; Inalcik, 1994)

Ottoman Sultan in 1580 led to the import of Eastern dyestuffs — mainly indigo — for English dyed woollen broadcloth. The English woollen industry was effectively released from its dependence on Flemish and Italian middlemen for the dyeing and finishing of their white cloth. As a result England replaced Venice in the wool trade in the Levantine markets of Istanbul, Izmir and Aleppo.[137] On 11 September 1581, the Levant Company was founded by Royal Charter and by 1630 English consuls had settled in Istanbul, Izmir, Aleppo and Alexandretta. The island of Chios, off the coast of Asia Minor was an important trade entrepot for English shipping and also grew madder.[138] Written in 1599, Gerard's *Herball* had accepted madder's wider role, when he confirmed that English madder was gathered and "sold to the use of Diers and Medicine."[139]

In independent Scotland, the reformer King David I (1084-1153) took customs rights from the monks and gave them to the towns of Perth, Stirling,

St Andrews and Aberdeen. The earliest local trade records, the *Assisa de Tolloneis*,[140] are attributed to his reign. Taxable imports were listed and included madder, woad and brazilwood. During the 12th and 13th centuries permanent trading links were set up between Scotland and the Low Countries.

At the end of the 15th century, a Scottish merchant Andrew Hallyburton became 'agent' in the Netherlands. His ledgers for 1492-1503 included dyes of which

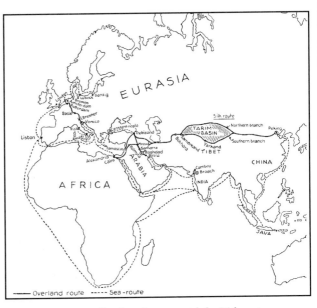

Important medieval trade routes and the 16th-century Cape sea route (Schaefer, CIBA Review)

only madder, woad and alum were being sent to Scotland. There are records of York merchants importing madder from there to Hull during the 16th century.[141] In fact, the dyers' guilds were in typical conflict with Parliament and in 1564 strong action was taken to protect standards of dyeing in a variety of colours that included "thay now nane of thame in ony time cuming sall lit ony manner of Cullor . . . nor lit ony Blakis with . . . Gallis . . . or sicklike fals Cullors." But it was more likely the result of poor workmanship than bad dyes.

4

The venturers' legacy

Trade routes, banking and technology

THE 1600s marked the beginnings of European colonisation and the gradual appropriation by Europeans of the lucrative Oriental trade. Basra continued to be one of the great entrepots of the Orient and international traffic included huge caravans from Baghdad, Damascus and Aleppo, which also carried red dye for Persia and India.[1] Venetian ships still returned from Egypt and Syria plying the old trade routes, loaded with spices, drugs, dyestuffs, silk and cotton.[2] But the European navigators' new sea routes around the Cape were faster, safer and cheaper than traditional land transport, which duly diminished. The control of trade changed from the relatively small city-state economies to the newly organised national economies represented by the trading companies of Britain, Holland and France.

Godfrey Goodwin recalled that about 1700 a quarter of Britain's trade was with the Ottoman empire. The Ottoman empire became the greatest market

Camel caravan (Leix, 'Trade routes of the Middle Ages', CIBA Review, 314)

in the world, yet allowed its export trading advantage to pass into European hands. At the same time, the focus of trade was skewed away from the Orient by the industrialisation of Europe. The rapid progress in dyeing techniques during the second half of the 18th century was in contrast to the equipment which remained virtually unchanged from the Middle Ages. In marked contrast machines gained a forceful entry into the spinning and weaving industries. Marketing followed as Bonaparte's Minister of the Interior Chaptal *inter alia* conceived the idea for the first industrial exhibitions which took place in 1798 and 1801, rather earlier than Britain's Great Exhibition in 1851.

Dominant Holland

The brilliance of Dutch horticulture which led to the amazing tulip craze was also continually evident in the cultivation of madder (see chapters 5, 6 & 7). The Dutch set the standards and made the profits that every other producer desired to emulate. Dutch methods provided the benchmarks of cultivation, processing and quality that are described in detail later. A mark of Dutch mercantile professionalism is that they were the only country to keep continual records of madder prices from 1600 to 1900 (see page 234).

Cardon considered that both civil and foreign wars were the cause of the disappearance of madder cultivation in France during the 16th century. This left a virtual monopoly in Dutch hands.[3] The Edict of Nantes which was enforced from 1598 to 1685 was also to Catholic France's loss and Holland's gain, with the great success of the Hugenot growers who settled and prospered in Zeeland.[4] It was only during the 18th century that France recovered. After centuries of effort, France only overtook Holland in the 1850s with newer processing methods to deal with the increased quantity of madder grown in Provence and North Africa.

France's challenge

Since the Middle Ages the government of France had appreciated the profitability of madder cultivation and subsidised the spread of the industry throughout the land especially in the south of France. By the 1550s Charles V had decreed the establishment of madder cultivation in Alsace. Flachat mentioned tax advantages for growers granted in 1607 and 1641 as precedents for his successful request in 1756 for another moratorium.[5] Yet there was a general decline until the reorganisations of all industries under Louis XIV. Jean Baptiste Colbert (1619-83), from 1661 Comptroller General of Finances, came from a family of cloth makers and merchants in Rheims, and naturally devoted

First Industrial Exposition, Champ-de-Mars, Paris, 1798 (Giedion)

his energies to this industry. He was also reacting to the craze for indiennes (see page 186). The import of Indian printed textiles would reach its dizzy peak in 1685, and seriously undermined the French and the other European industries.[6]

There was competition from Europe too. In 1666 Colbert had begun subsidising madder in Avignon — but it was not a lasting success. This was to prevent imports of madder or *lizari* from Holland and Asia Minor which consumed French finances. In 1671 D'Albo, under instructions from Colbert, published a set of detailed regulations for the dyeing of textiles which signalled a serious attempt to compete with Flanders. Seven good red dyes were recommended. One was a process where madder was reinforced with the addition of arsenic and salt to allegedly equal to the Flemish dyestuff. An exploratory (and ineffectual) test for fastness by boiling in slightly acidic water was also proposed. It was all an attempt to put dyeing on a more scientific basis.[7] This needed to be complemented by scientific cultivation. Roughly a century later a certain M. Dambourney of the Société d'Agriculture de Rouen still was attempting to cultivate a variety of madder which was native to Normandy, but his experiments proved unsuccessful.[8]

During the 18th century the art of textile printing developed in parallel to the art of dyeing. In the first half of the century prohibitions in several major European countries were made against the popular indiennes printed cottons — both imported and home-made — to protect local woollen industries. Jean Hellot (1685-1765) in 1737 was sent on a scientific research trip to Persia to study the Oriental procedure for dyeing silk red with kermes. His chief work, on wool, *L'Art de la Teinture des Laines et des Étoffes de Laines, au Grand Teint et au Petit Teint*, was published in 1750 in Paris. *Grand teint*, dyeing for tapestries and other luxury textiles, included the reds and although Hellot was more

& *fur les Arts.* 353

ARRÊT DU CONSEIL D'ÉTAT DU ROI,

*Qui ordonne que ceux qui entrepren-
dront de cultiver des plantations de
garance dans des marais & autres
lieux non cultivés , ne pourront
pendant vingt années être impofés
à la taille , eux ni leurs employés
à ladite exploitation , pour raifon
de la propriété ou du profit à faire
fur l'exploitation defdits marais &
terres cultivées en garance.*

Du 24 Février 1756.

Extrait des Régiftres du Confeil d'Etat.

Le Roi étant informé que plu-
fieurs terreins en marais & inon-
dés feroient propres à produire de
la garance , que l'on eft obligé de
tirer des pays étrangers , & que
quelques perfonnes s'offriroient à faire les frais néceffaires pour cultiver
cette plante & deffécher lefdits marais , s'il lui plaifoit les faire jouir
de quelques exemptions & privileges , & nommément de ceux qui

1756 Decree (Flachat; ack. LSE Library)

interested in methods of mordanting cochineal and the manufacture of Venetian scarlet with kermes, but he also wrote about gum lacquers and madder. *Petit teint* covered the less durable colours for low cost materials, for ordinary short-term use.

More tantalising, in 1760 during an experiment on indigo, Hellot distilled indigo in the presence of quicklime and accidentally discovered aniline, which was destined to revolutionise the dyeing industry a century later. He named it after the Portuguese name for indigo, *anil*, but he and his scientific peers were unaware of its significance. Hellot also wrote about the Polish custom of dyeing their horses' tails red — but the dyestuff used was cochineal, not madder. Polish cochineal insects were raised on the Ukrainian estates of Marschal Konitzpolski and other noblemen.[9]

About 1750 Henri Bertin (1720-92), Louis XV's Minister of State invited M. J. Altken, a Persian who was also known as Althen (in fact, he was an Armenian from Julfa near Isfahan called Johannis Althonian, who was colourfully described by Diderot, through Cardon, as a "former slave and bigamist") to the county of Venaissin near Avignon to experiment with wild madder. His name survives in the marshy village of Althen-des-Paluds.[10] Altken discovered that the dyestuff obtained from the native wild madder was inadequate, so he imported seeds from Asia Minor, which were successful, but still failed to arouse the interest of the local people.[11]

The attitude to cultivating madder changed on February 24th, 1756 when the State Council exempted all madder farmers from taxes for 20 years. To encourage local cultivation of the dyestuff, in 1762, four years after Miller's book was published in England, Duhamel du Monceau wrote a similar 54-page instruction on growing and drying madder in his 'Elements of Agriculture'.[12] He was more successful than his English counterpart in gaining envied government concessions to growers.[13] Unfortunately because of the local climate, the yield gradually decreased. So the government gave madder farmers seeds from Cyprus and Smyrna (Izmir).

Hellot who studied wool, formed one of a trinity of French experts. The second was Pierre Joseph Macquer (1718-84) son of an emigrant Scottish painter, who specialised in silk, and introduced the frisson of *craquant* silk.

The third was the pseudonymous Le Pileur d'Apligny (see later) who specialised in the lowly cotton, which would grow larger than all the other textile industries, as well as flax and hemp. In the 1770s he wrote his *Disertation sur la Culture de l'Indigo, du Pastel et de la Garance.*

The spread of Turkey red dye-works in France from 1747 (see chapter 11), meant that ten years later France was

The tradition of pollution: rinsing dyed goods from a secured barge in mid-river, Macquer, 1759 (Sandberg)

still obliged to import madder to the value of 50,000 livres, but 25 years on, production had increased so much that it was predominant in Europe. From 1789, ominously the new seeds from Smyrna started producing good crops and cultivation spread in the south of France, Normandy and Poitou. Dyers followed close behind the cultivators. After some Greek dyers had settled in Marseilles, Turkey red dye-houses mushroomed there and in Rouen, Nimes and Normandy. The Greeks at Rouen were duly sacked when their knowledge had been utilised. They quickly found their way to Mulhouse in Alsace where they founded another Turkey red industry. Later, excellent quality madder was grown in Algeria from the 1850s under French rule, although Schaefer wrote that the quantity was low.[14]

Emperor Charles V had been less successful when he attempted to establish madder-growing in Alsace, which was only revived more than 200 years later in the 1760s. Two men — a landowner named Frantzen[15] and an entrepreneur named Hoffman had plantations near Hagenau, Bischwiller and Strasbourg. The industry became well run. Three kinds of Alsatian madder were recognised. 'Black' madder rarely bloomed and never bore seeds. 'Turkish' madder frequently bloomed but did not bear fruit, whereas the 'new' madder of Avignon, grown from fresh French seeds always bloomed and bore fruit.[16]

Cotton printing flourished in France: the most successful

Portrait of Philipp Oberkampf (1738-1815) (Brunello)

Portrait of C. L. Berthollet (1748-1822), inventor of chlorine bleach, painting by J. Boilly, 1820 (Brunello)

industrialist was Cristoph Philipp Oberkampf, born in Germany but considered French. In 1755, aged 12, he followed his father to Switzerland to the prospering Rhyner family's factory (see below). In 1759, Louis XV removed the prohibitions on the manufacture of printed fabrics and the teenager set up in a shack in the Jouy valley on the banks of the Bievre, near Versailles.

Soon his new model factory employed 11,500 people. It was visited by Marie Antoinette and in 1783 was granted the title of 'Royal Manufactory'. This was presumably the occasion for the celebrated manu-

The celebrated dark blue-red coloured print 'Les Travaux de la Manufacture', 1783, shows the various processes at a calico print workshop. In the foreground the artist Huet is working on a pattern, with Oberkampf and his boy behind him to the right. At the top centre is a drying tower, elsewhere bleaching, planking of bundles of cloths on rafts, preparation of cloths, printing with blocks and engraved copper plates and dye production. And there is his wife — or is it Marie Antoinette herself — wearing a matelot hat with a Beau Brummel buckle, sketching on the top left. (Sandberg)

facturing-realist print shown here — a precursor of Futurist and Russian Constructivist textile designs.[17] The first of his most sought-after colours was madder dyed on iron mordant.

His excellent pioneering social reforms gave him no trouble with the Revolution and in 1815 he received the Cross of the Legion of Honour from Napoleon himself. One of Oberkampf's scientific friends was Claude Louis Berthollet (1748-1822), who with Lavoisier was one of the most eminent chemists in France. In 1784 he succeeded Macquer as inspector of the national dye-works. He was fascinated by dyes and by 1785 he had introduced chlorine for the bleaching of woven fabrics. James Watt visited his laboratory in Paris in 1786 and spread the news to England. By 1798 Charles Tennant and Charles MacIntosh had additionally discovered that chlorine could be

Russian Post-Revolutionary textiles: (top) V. Maslov, Jouy-style cotton print 'The New Village', 1926; (below) L. Raitser, Constructivist sateen, 'The Mechanisation of the Red Army, 1933 (Elliott & Ryan)

fixed in dried spent lime and the vastly more convenient bleaching powder (hypochlorite of lime) arrived on the market. Chlorine bleaching was the principle contribution to the expansion of the linen and cotton goods industry in the early 19th century. Agriculture also benefited by the liberation of vast areas of land previously used for open-meadow bleaching (see chapter 11).

Berthollet's funeral address in 1822 was given by Jean Antoine Chaptal (1756-1832) who is considered both the last of the great 18th-century masters of the art of dyeing and the founder of the French chemical industry. By 1782, the new professor of chemistry at the University of Montpellier had set up a factory where the process of synthesising alum was discovered (see chapter 12). More successes followed with preparation of hydrochloric acid, sulphuric acid and nitric acid.

All these essential processes not only made him wealthy, but also brought him into contact with dyers. The dyers of Rouen, where Chaptal owned some factories, were having problems with producing Turkey red and had sensibly brought over the Greek specialists from Smyrna mentioned earlier. Chaptal's curiosity was aroused and after many experiments he published *L'Art de la Teinture du Coton en Rouge*, which 'finally resolved' the method of making Turkey red in Europe. Chaptal as Bonaparte's Minister of the Interior later founded the celebrated school for dyeing wool and silk and cotton printing in Lyons; technicians trained there would one day revolutionise the textile industry, which was at the heart of the future technological supremacy of the West.[18]

J. A. Chaptal (1756-1832), Napoleon's minister and an outstanding chemist and innovator (Brunello)

Half-hearted England

In England madder-growing was less popular than dyeing. The Edict of Nantes of 1598, which was only revoked in 1685, led to the welcome immigration of skilled Hugenot craftsmen to England. In Hilton's opinion the refugees from Flanders also stimulated the replanting of madder in East Anglia. Anglo-Dutch rivalry affected British domestic politics during the 17th century and extended to plans for the the substitution of Dutch madder imports. The pioneer was George Calvert, James I's Secretary of State. Serious investigations began around 1620 linked with a Commission on Trade 'to enquire how dyestuffs [have] become dear'.

In 1621 Calvert sent his brother-in-law George Mynne, an agressively mercantile London draper and dyer, to Holland to collect slips, followed by a personal visit. He then engaged young George Bedford, the son of a Salisbury clothier who had earlier promoted woad-growing, to make a theoretical and practical study of madder cultivation in Zeeland. Bedford initially visited seven times in 16 months and fell ill with malarial fever.[19] The young man first incensed Dutch growers when they realised that he was secretly buying whole plants rather than roots and they roughly threatened and imprisoned the captain

Letter from George Bedford to his stepfather Henry Sherfield on Flemish madder and cole, [Ter]goose, February 18th, 1623 (ack. Jervoise of Herriard Coll, Hants Public Record Office)

of his ship. Bedford later also angered the London dyers by exposing the adulteration levels in imported madder and threatening a cosy trading arrangement.[20] Bedford's plans grew to include rotation of madder and rape-seed; but in between, he lost the financial prize — the exclusive patent — to Mr Shipman, Charles I's gardener, whose plantation was at Barn Elms on the banks of the Thames. Under Charles I (r. 1625-49), the cultivation of madder was a special privilege granted by the king. However there was still a margin to be had between the market price for madder in England of £3 10s per cwt, double the price in Zeeland. By 1627, the fear of prying eyes in the madder fields of Appledore in Kent reduced a sorry Bedford to personally digging up the roots at night, redolent of the 1700s tulip mania in Holland.[21]

Eleven years later a wealthy immigrant Dutch master-drainer Cornelius Vermuyden openly offered to pay an additional levy to the Crown, above the usual customs dues, to form a corporation with the sole right to trade in madder. He was refused because the existing patent still had nine years to run. In 1637 there was trouble over London farming land which was mandated for madder cultivation. Its successor patent holders, the Society of Planters of Madder of the City of Westminster, renegotiated with the Crown. New and presumably lower crown dues were agreed, with the imposition of a government surveyor. The Dutchman's plan for a corporation duly passed to the favoured Mr Shipman who was in league with Adrian Cornellis, or Corsellis (perhaps a distant ancestor of the 1851 Parisian-Dutch founder of Cornellisen, the surviving London painter's pigment firm), who had previously joined and then abandoned Bedford. They were granted the right of sole planting for four years, with import protection in the form of £10 per ton duty on the better quality and £8 on the poorer.[22] Hopes for the root were dashed by the English Civil War which bankrupted the madder corporation. But in a curious quirk of history even the war created a new demand; a rare surviving lining of an English-made Civil War helmet of the common 'three-barred pot' type was found to be dyed with madder.[23]

Madder was not forgotten and by 1660 Nicholas Crisp had set up a large plantation at Deptford along the Thames and Vermuyden had developed a large plantation near Wisbeck in the drained fens.[24] Historical studies of dyeing had been encouraged by the Royal Society in London from its beginnings in 1662.[25] Yet in 1683 John Reid's *The Scot's Gardner* still included madder purely as a 'physick' herb. James Smith a London merchant was granted a 14-year patent in 1670. He had imported foreign experts and built mills and stoves with a reputed investment of £10,000. He was in partnership with John Lilburne a London druggist and Francis Hacker, probably a Dutch expert. The madder was grown in the marshes of Walsoken and Leverington in the Isle of Ely.[26]

In spite of this apparent activity England remained largely dependent on the continent for dyestuffs, especially after the halving of Dutch madder prices in 1676, partly in the face of growing competition from Smyrna. From the 1620s after the fall of Hormuz, Smyrna had taken over from Aleppo as the western terminus for the silk trade. It was natural that locally grown madder should be exported by the textile merchants.[27] For which reasons John Houghton wrote some years later that English madder-growing had ceased, though about 1700 it was still grown in Godalming in Surrey. However, if you believe Bedford's calculation (see chapter 6), then there was plenty of profit for all who would take a longer term view, only limited by suitable acreage. Perhaps after all, it was the English speculative attitude to commerce which discouraged cultivation.[28]

Interest was reawakened with the increase in printed calico manufacture linked to the mastery of Turkey red dyeing technology about 1760 (see chapter 11) and the consequent rise in the price of madder. In 1757 the annual import of Dutch Zeeland madder was valued at £30,000 and in 1765 all Dutch madder at £150,000. From 1758 to 1765 the price of best Dutch madder increased by 40 per cent and the worst by 100 per cent, which led to its clandestine substitution with non-fast logwood dye. Imports correspondingly dropped from 20,000cwt in 1760 to 13,000cwt in 1765.[29]

In 1758 Philip Miller FRS, Gardener to the Worshipful Company of Apothecaries at Chelsea, published an illustrated 38-page treatise *The Method of Cultivating Madder, As It is Now Practised by the Dutch in Zealand: (Where the Best Madder is Produced)*. A modern Dutch authority on Zeeland madder, van der Poel considered it "undoubtably the best survey in English . . ."[30] Miller was exhorting the English farmer to return to growing madder as a substitute for Dutch imports, whose price and adulteration both increased with demand. When, from 1761 to 1766, the Society of Arts offered a subsidy of £5 for every acre planted with madder, there were 78 claimants.[31] The supreme prize of £10 from the society went to John Crow at Faversham in Kent who in 1777 achieved a yield of 18cwt 2qrs 18lbs from an acre. A tithe dispute in 1680 in the Isle of Ely had shown that 10cwt an acre was considered a good yield. But English yields were not that high when compared with other lands including Derbent, a century and more later (see chapter 5).

Miller explained that, in places such as Godalming, the cultivation of madder had fallen into decline because local vicars were successfully claiming tithes for madder which was apparently grown on lay land. More awkwardly, they wanted their tithes in kind — that is in shoots ('offsets'), which had to be dug up and laid out when ready, over a period of weeks. If the collectors appeared a few days late, the shoots had often perished. Also, according to the 1760 pamphlet, the growers were not legally permitted to take away the roots to be dried until the tithe had been collected, which meant that they could be ruined by wind and rain. The tithe collectors were not prepared to follow

Frontispiece of Philip Miller's book, 1758 (ack. British Library)

behind the farmers, as this would have cost them more than the tithes which they collected. Much litigation ensued.[32]

Partly as a result of Miller's efforts, a 14-year tithe relief was passed by the government, which limited the tithe to 5s an acre. In 1765, the anonymous pamphleteer complained "that the present modus on madder is equal to the greatest paid at this time, even on hemp and flax, which is perpetual, though it is said that those crops impoverish the ground, which must of consequence lessen the value of the tithe for some time." Moreover madder, a deep-ground plant, "enriches and prepares the land for a succession of four luxuriant crops . . . thus bearing at the rate of seven crops without an intervening fallow" — confirmed by Dutch practice, see chapter 5. The sizeable contract for madder connected with dyeing the red uniforms of the all-conquering British army was not sufficient consolation.

Scottish tartans

The famed Scottish plaids of Queen Victoria's time have a deep if dislocated history. The earliest plaid woollen cloth fragments found in the salt mines at Hallstaatt in Austria have been dated rather widely to between 1200 BC and 400 BC.[33] Others from the burial at Qizilchoqa near Hami in Central Asia have been dated between 1200 BC and 700 BC. Mid-third-century AD undyed fragments of the 'Falkirk tartan', a check herring-bone made of two shades of natural wool were found in the Falkirk Roman coin hoard.[34] There follows a long interval, punctuated by the appearance of silk, linen and cotton plaids in Fatimid and Mamluk Egypt, which were possibly imported from India or China.[35] Then another long interval before plaids were next noted by the Hallstaatters' distant Celtic cousins the Scots.

Scottish plaids also known as tartans seem to be mentioned first by Buchanan in 1582. He referred to the Scot's love of variegated garments, especially striped with the favourite colours being purple and blue. Buchanan added that some still wore

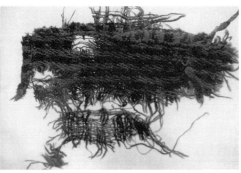

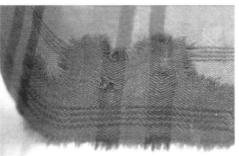

Plaid woollen twills from Hallstaat, c. 1200 BC to 400 BC (Barber, 1999)

plaids of many different colours similar to those of their ancestors. A late 16th-century chequered red and green jack lining found under the roof of Craigevar castle does not quite bear this out.[36] As the first mention of our Cumbrian farmhouse and all other Border records were from 1580, the date may be significant purely for historiographers.

The shipping lists of Dundee from 1580 to 1618 showed the continuing import of madder from Flanders.[37] During stormy voyages across the North Sea, leaking holds of ships caused sea-water damage. In 1591, two Dundee dyers were called to examine the waterlogged madder in the hold of 'The Thomas of Dundee' and they declared it totally unfit for use. Dundee was a noted centre for textiles although standards of workmanship were not high. The Rates and Valuation of Merchandise, decreed in 1612,

*Red and beige silk tartan,
?10th-12th century, Egypt (Errera)*

mention 'mader' and the now reprieved 'galles' within a long list of commodities. The Litsters of Aberdeen got into trouble in 1632 for making "filthie, defyled and corrupted" the town's water supply by washing their dyed textiles in the loch. Nevertheless, the import of madder to east coast ports continued to increase during the century. It was largely used in the Aberdeen area for dyeing cloth and stockings and between 1686 and 1696 some 100,000lbs were imported from Holland.[38]

The New Mills cloth manufactory at Haddington was the first attempt at textile manufacturing in Scotland. The enterprise, founded in 1640 and assisted by duty-free imports of wool, dyes and oils, "before 1650, was in a thriving condition, till Dundee was stormed; when their cloth was taken, and the troubles forced it to cease." It became another casualty in the suppression of Scottish Covenanting armies by English Cromwellian Reformers. Hopefully it did not affect the sale of Harry Prince's legacy, as

Late 16th-century mass-produced sleeveless padded armour jacket made of c. 1,400 small steel plates sewn into 'leather, fustian or canvas' (Eaves; Journal of the Arms and Armour Society)

the Orkney merchant who died in 1649 left *inter alia* a large quantity of madder.[39] When the mill reopened the owners tried to "save the charge of mentaineing a dyer" by appointing unskilled workmen. They gradually realised their mistake. By 1684 they had found a real dyer with "humour, character, pairts, knowledge, sobriety . . ." from Kinross. He ordered an array of dyes from Holland through Edinburgh merchants to be landed at Leith, including 1000lb of crop mather and mull madder. Crop madder was the top quality for reds, made from grinding the inside of the root. In contrast, mull was the lowest quality ground root husk, which produced a brown colour (see chapter 9).

The works were saved in 1693 by a government decree that the troops of Scotland must henceforth have uniforms of Scottish cloth "to distinguish sojers from other skulking and vagrant persons." The Act of Union in 1707 removed Scottish trade protections and the poor quality uniforms were unable to compete on the open market. The establishment that had employed up to 700 people closed in 1713.[40]

Other higher quality production continued. By 1716 Martin emphasised the fashionable aspect of plaids where "Every Isle differs from each other in their Fancy of making Plads, as to the stripes in Breadth and Colours." In Scotland the better plaids, which were carefully preserved by the wealthier families from the early 18th century, probably contained madder (and logwood and definitely cochineal). After the Jacobite Rising which began in 1745 and ended one year later in "ignoble defeat at Culloden," the Disarming Act which followed banned "any part whatsoever of what peculiarly belongs to the Highland garb." This hardly supported Philip Miller's national campaign for the reintroduction of madder to Britain, started in *The Gardener's Dictionary* in 1733.

The Scots Magazine of 1757 dryly reported that one of the Edinburgh Society's annual awards of three pounds sterling had been given to a Dalkeith surgeon for growing and preparing "the greatest quantity of madder, not under ten pounds in weight, dressed and cured for the market." The repeal of the Act did not come until 1782 and the intervening years witnessed the fragmentation of Scottish society and the decline of the Scottish dyeing industry at a time when the consumption of textiles in the rest of the world was growing fast.[41] However Wm. Wilson & Son of Bannockburn near Stirling started manufacturing tartans in 1750 and survived through 1782 and on to 1926, as the famed purveyor to the ever-growing numbers of expatriate Scots around the world. The dye lists sent to Wilson's in 1814 by Birkitt, Watson and Grainger, a London firm of Drysalters, included madder from Holland, Turkey and the East Indies.

Tourist sales followed in the tartan mania unleashed by Sir Walter Scott's novels and the visit of King George IV to Edinburgh in 1822. Scottish-manufactured high grade military uniforms were dyed with local lichen red called Cudbear (see below) as well as imported cochineal. Prices were reduced by substitute madder-dyed warp threads "as the warp is little seen and it will never be noticed."

From Hawick and Galashiels in the Borders, the woollen plaids known as Southern Tweed were manufactured from 1770 and Harris Tweed from 1844. While Southern Tweed kept up with technological changes, Harris Tweed maintained its custom by continued use of natural dyes and traditional manufacturing. In 1820 a greater variety of colours was introduced to add to the black and white checks and blues. As the contrasting colours were carded together, they produced a rich muted colour. The process was labour intensive and barely provided a living for the craftsmen and their families who were also involved upstream in dyeing. Except for imported indigo blue, they used local plants such as *Galium verum* for madder (see chapter 1). The harvesting of wild plants grew so popular that *The Oban Times* of 1915 reported in Delphic tones that "Tales are still told in the Islands about uncanny happenings while digging out 'rugh' roots during the night as no one dared do it openly in daylight." From 1695 the Soil Preservation Act had been enforced to prevent human erosion by the coast.[42] Cardon had found out that on the islands of Harris and Lewis in the

Ancestor of Bell's rotary printing machine: the rather earlier German model in Andrea Glorez' handbook, c. 1699 (Brunello)

Hebrides, so much *Galium* was consumed that the *machair* ancient communal pastures were stripped bare. Pulling out roots was accordingly forbidden on pain of death.[43]

Scottish technology & cotton prints

During the late 18th century, Scottish ingenuity turned to the exploitation of new industrial technology. The most successful rotary printing machine for cotton was patented in 1783 and 1784 by the Scot Thomas Bell. At that time English laws protected the woollen industry and only permitted printing cotton handkerchiefs. This original printing process produced the popular 'Golgas and Bandana' kerchiefs by the following method:

Many pieces of fabric were placed and held between two metal plates. The first dyeing was with Turkey red or indigo blue, over which a corrosive print produced the characteristic result.

First bandana kerchiefs produced in Scotland in 1805 (Grierson)

The first English-language manual for printing cloth was written by Charles O'Brien in 1790.[44] Amongst stories of industrial spying and the failure of Livesey & Co where Thomas Bell worked, O'Brien wrote that the most durable blacks and purples came from madder treated by iron liquor.[45]

John Wilson's rejection of Turkey red dyeing "that it did not suit his purpose" hardly discouraged others. In 1785 David Dale (Robert Owen's partner at the revolutionary New Lanark Mills), and George Macintosh of Cudbear established a dye-works at Dalmarnock on the Clyde for the sole purpose of applying Turkey red to cotton. They were in partnership with a French dyer from Rouen, Pierre Jacques Papillon. But the partnership was dissolved after just two years because, as Macintosh commented, "we could not manage his unhappy temper." Papillon left to establish his own dye-works at Rutherglen Bridge along the river. Macintosh streamlined Papillon's methods (see chapter 11) to "dye in 20 days what he took 25 to do." In 1790 the apparently ubiquitous Papillon made another partnership with Dr Black, the

Huge dye works were built north-west of Glasgow in Scotland. The Alexandria Works built in the first half of the 19th century on the banks of the River Leven. (Photo W. Kissling, Grierson)

physician and chemist, who founded the Turkey red dye-works in Glasgow. Schaefer wrote that Papillon was rewarded for his co-operation by the Scottish inspectors of dye-works. The Turkey red industry flourished and became centred on the Vale of Leven at the foot of Loch Lomond. In 1999 a museum was proposed at Renton among the ruins of one of the main dye-works in the 'Vale', west by land from Glasgow.[46] During the 19th century the Montieth and Orr-Ewing families made their vast fortunes in the madder market.

Another major technical advance was Richard Arkwright's (1732-92) spinning-jenny, which produced a strong even cotton thread and allowed plentiful cotton to become the dominant fibre. Spinning reached a delicacy

*Top left: Finely-woven 'Paisley' border band of unknown origin,
c. 1850 (Author's photo)
Top right: Late 18th century woven end band of a Kashmir shawl.
Right: Paisley shawl design brought to England by W. Moorcroft in 1823,
writing on back: "Logwardee. By order of Shah Zuman, Persia"
(both Irwin)*

whereby there were 6000 warp threads in a standard two-metre wide 'Kashmir' shawl, described below. The fineness of the threads permitted intricate patterns which in turn hastened the introduction of new Jacquard looms. In addition, the technology of the spinning-jenny and discharge printing made it possible to dye cotton fabrics as well as threads.

From 1785 fashionable 'Kashmir' shawls were reproduced in Britain — in Edinburgh and Norwich — and in other places in Europe. Though shawls were not the main textile product of Paisley, after 1800 Kashmir shawls became known as 'Paisley' shawls.[47] Taking advantage of Napoleon's blockade of British goods, in 1810 Daniel Koechlin-Schouch (1785-1871), scion of the Mulhouse dyeing family, pioneered Kashmir-style 'illuminated Merino' table-covers and wall-hangings which were produced by his new discharge printing method. Their colour range eventually extended to six main colours (see chapter 11).[48] In Europe these shawls maintained their massive popularity from 1830 to 1870, to span both the natural and synthetic dye periods.

Meanwhile, the small-scale Scottish weavers used specialist dye-houses. During the years 1830 to 1850 all the reds were the product of cochineal or madder. The reds in some pre-1850 shawls were recently analysed as alizarin or madder with alum mordant in cotton and cochineal with tin mordant in wool.[49] This was different to contemporary genuine Kashmir shawls where the red and pinks of eight examples from the Dale Gluckman catalogue were recently analysed as lac.[50]

Block and print of Blumer & Jenny 'Merino' printed cotton (Sandberg)

The industrious Swiss

Madder-growing in the mountains of Switzerland during the 18th century required even greater skill and labour than on the marshy plains. The cultivation of madder was a great leveller. The Swiss philanthropist and educationalist J. H. Pestalozzi (1746-1827) tried his hand at growing madder at Neuhof his estate in Argovia. In spite of all his efforts, and the assistance of the orphan children under his charge, Pestalozzi was unable to attain the results of his rural neighbours, who laughed at his amateur efforts.[51] One of the best cotton-printing establishments was also founded by another Swiss, Samuel Rhyner, mentioned earlier. His family imported raw textiles which were then re-exported to Holland for printing.

He understood the advantages of vertical integration and determined to learn from the Dutch and beat them at their own game. Starting modestly in 1716 the business grew slowly. His son John, later Burgermeister of Basle, wrote a *Treatise on the Manufacture and Commerce of Printed Cloth* in 1760. Soon after, the first Swiss Turkey red dye-house was set up by Johann Zeller of Zurich, who had worked in Nimes in the 1760s. By 1776, Rhyner was producing ten-colour designs, including three reds, which included colours produced by madder with different mordants.[52] Turkey red printing flourished in the cantons of Zurich, St Gall, Thurgovia and Glarus.

The old cloth, yarn and produce merchants P. Blumer & Jenny — crowned with a papal blessing in 1858 — also produced 'Merino' prints (named after the fashionable cashmere wool of indiennes) in their factories in the canton of Glarus. From 1828, they dyed their own Turkey red, which contributed to their brilliant worldwide sales. Large quantities of red discharge prints were exported to Rio de Janeiro (from 1831) the Balkans, Turkey, Russia as far south as Baku, via Hamburg to South and North America and Scandinavia, North Africa, India and the Malayan Archipelago (from 1840).[53] It was an early example of an admittedly attractive international kitsch, unwittingly designed to confound future art historians.

Other 18th-century European stories

The good news spread. Enterprising people from other relatively peripheral parts of Europe wanted to share in the growing industry.

In Spain great printing works were established by Estaban Canals in 1738. By 1760 12,000 people were employed in the Spanish industry. In the 1750s, his son Juan Pablo Canals set up laboratories and experimental workshops to apply scientific methods to the industrial cultivation and exploitation of madder. His success was rewarded by his appointment as Director-General of the Royal Dye Works and the title of Baron of Vall Roja.

The first reappearance of Venice as a dyeing centre since the black fiasco (see chapter 11) was in 1766 with the publication *Memorie di Osservazioni . . . alla Tintura* by Pietro Audino, Professor of Agriculture at the University of Padua (then within the Venetian Republic). He recommended several plants as a substitute for madder, such as *Asperula tinctoria, Asperula odorata, Galium verum, Galium boreale* and *Galium sylvaticum* (see appendix 2.3, page 317). He found out that the apothecaries from Villa del Trevisano erroneously believed that *Galium sylvaticum* was real madder. He had to admit that its red colour was finer and more vivid than that of wild madder *Rubia sylvestris*.[54] Nothing had changed.

Madder was grown in Denmark and in 1752 a certain M Lidbeck transplanted madder over the straits to Lund in the south of Sweden. He obtained an excellent crop in three years.[55] Cheaper grades of madder were grown in Breslau, Liegnitz, Ohlau and Strehlen in Silesia (see chapters 13 & 14) and in 1737 there was a government ban on export of shoots to protect the Silesian growers.[56]

North America's nascent industry

Across the Atlantic, on the eastern seaboard of North America, Europeans met the indigenous Amero-Indian dyers. Every early French chronicler since the French explorer Champlain in 1603 had admired Micmac work: "Porcupine quills dyed in red of the most vivid flame colour" — "for our scarlets have no better lustre than their red dye," "made from a little root as thick as a thread." In contrast, the first English settlers were purely concerned with functional textiles. The first dyer was one John Cornish of Boston. His modest inventory at the time of his death in 1695 included only gall, brazilwood, madder, fustic and green vitriol. Other American dyers were known from their advertisements in newspapers. The first political dyer was Samuel Wetherell of Philadelphia, a fiery patriot and supporter of independence. As a dyer he must have been particularly provoked by the mercantilist approach of the English government. Trade in colonial ports was reserved to English ships and the colonies had to buy and sell solely with England, which was exclusively in England's interests. About 1775, the regulations were tightened to prevent the rise of colonial factories which might compete with English production. Alongside the War of Independence, Weatherill was starting his own economic war of textile manufacturing. Because of the larger war, he rapidly found that imported dyes were difficult to obtain and so determined to set up local production of botanical dyestuffs, medicinal drugs and other chemical products.

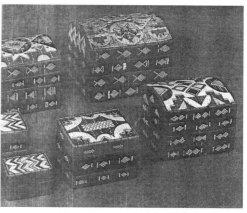

Micmac porcupine-quill boxes c. 1810-20 (Whitehead)

The Society for the Promotion of Agriculture in South Carolina offered a premium for growing madder in 1785 with little result. In 1798 Asa Ellis was the first American to publish a small yet valuable volume called *The Country Dyer's Assistant*. The book became a crusading beacon for the independent American industry when Ellis complained that all imported dyestuffs had to "pop through the hands of Spain and England"[57] He became an inspiration for American scientific innovation. Among his classic dyestuffs was madder, but other indigenous dyestuffs were also described. Both Thomas Jefferson and Dolley Madison raised their voices in favour of home-grown dyestuffs, yet could not persuade farmers to grow madder or any other dye plants.

In 1802 the American Philosophical Society offered a $150 premium for the "best experimental essay on the native red dies of the United States." The president's wife Mrs Madison's keenly awaited report never appeared, but Thomas Cooper wrote of an eight to ten acre madder plot in the settlement of Harmony, 20 miles from Pittsburgh Pennsylvania. Thomas Cooper was a political exile from England who as an early example of the brain drain, arrived with experience in cotton bleaching. He taught for many years and in 1815 in Philadelphia published *A Practical Treatise of Dyeing and Callicoe Printing*.

A May 15, 1811 entry in the lately retired President Jefferson's garden book revealed that he had imported *Galium mollugo* wild madder seeds from France, probably through his friend Andre Thouin, chief gardener of the Jardin des Plantes in Paris, sent by diplomat James Ronaldson. He planted them in the south-east corner of his garden in his beloved Monticello, which with his scientific approach became the model for American agricultural development.

That January, William Coolidge had written to a sympathetic Jefferson that "the article of Madder, is of primary importance in manufacturing . . . ," and that a "Lady in Virginia" had made a number of successful experiments in dyeing. To take matters forward there were seven sensible questions about its cultivation and treatment. In prompt reply he also recalled that it had been cultivated in Virginia for household use since before the Revolution. Col Harrison,

The earliest known illustration of an American dye-house, Hazen, 1836 (Adrosko)

a member of the First Congress, had cultivated madder successfully but found that the merchants of Virginia preferred to deal in tobacco. Jefferson finally recommended the seedsman Mr McMahon of Philadelphia's book and to buy madder seeds from him.[58]

The industry eventually took off. In 1831 madder was quoted at 18 ½ cents per lb.[59] Turkey red dyeing arrived later than in Europe and in 1840 the Merrimac and Hamilton Mills in Lowell, Massachusetts alone produced more than a quarter-million yards of cotton fabrics dyed or printed in madder colours "of a price and quality that rivalled the foreign," mainly for shawls, ginghams and table coverings.[60] However, the greater American contribution was the development of a raw cotton industry which was soon to supply the world, keeping pace with the new machines to meet a booming demand.[61]

Napoleon's legacy

Back in Europe, the peace of 1802 soon failed and the English fleet imposed the Continental Blockade on Napoleon and his empire, preventing imports from America and the East. Chemical research to substitute imports became an urgent necessity — especially dyestuffs for uniforms. As minister responsible Chaptal found that hitherto regular supplies of cochineal from Mexico were cut and so offered "a prize of 20,000 francs for finding a way of giving wool a fast red colour by using madder. It was to be a red as lively as Turkish red and similar to the scarlet of cochineal." While dyeing Turkey red on cotton had been cracked, wool remained a problem. Their madder did not give a really bright red to wool because in addition to the red-strong alizarin, dye impurities were also present which dimmed the tint. In contrast Ottoman Turkish woollen rugs never suffered from this problem. A. M. Gonin of Lyons solved this quandary in 1812 but refused the prize offered by the Société d'Encouragement in Paris as insufficient recognition of his achievement.

Eugene Chevreul (1786-1889) also responded to the challenging times. He was 'apprenticed' in the laboratories of Vauquelin who in 1797 discovered chromium and the chromates which were of great use to dyers. From 1807 he was writing about dyestuffs and later as director of the National Factory of Tapestries at Gobelins he revolutionised the understanding of fatty materials and therefore soaps. In 1839, Vauquelin's *De la Loi du Contrast Simultane des Couleurs* appeared, where he described the optical effect of juxta-positioning of contrasting colours. This effect may have been new to dyers, but actually long well-known and used by Italian Renaissance painters from Giotto to Botticelli. By 1864 Chevreul had developed the forerunner of today's colour definition system, 'Chromatic Circles', covering more than 14,400 different shades,[62] based on earlier colour wheels like Mos. Harris' 'Prismatic' in 1766, which Adrosko considered to have been the first.

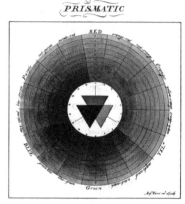

Mos. Harris' 'Prismatic' colour chart, 1766 (Adrosko)

Russia

Russian-Caucasian madder was the significant new arrival on the world market during the early 1800s. Through its effect on the Russian import market, it acted as a marginal force on the world market. The story is pushed and pulled by disparate interests both within Russia and outside which were exaggerated in the final boom years of madder as the stakes increased. In Russia, national economic asperations differed from local Caucasian colonial government tactics, and the conflicting interests of farmers, bankers and textile industrialists. Internationally, there were imports from Persia, Central Asia, Turkey and the high quality products from Holland and France and the cheap stuff from Silesia.

The Russian writers have an immediacy born of their attempts to understand the problems and suggest solutions. The tragedy was that they were too late and the attitudes of the Russian authorities were out of date. The later history of madder in the Caucasus began in the reign of the westward looking innovator Peter the Great and ended with the introduction of synthetic dyes in 1873. It followed Russia's hot and cold relations with Europe and the Ottoman empire to the west and to the east with Persia and the Russian conquests of the Caucasus and Central Asia.

During the 1700s a local industry was organised to gather wild madder roots from the marshy banks of the Terek river which meanders eastwards over the northern Caucasian steppe into the Caspian sea. For the Russians, the Terek was a favourite area for duck-shooting with the added risk of malarial infection. The first Russian factory to produce powdered madder (*krap*) was established in Moscow in 1720. In 1757 two Muscovite madder merchants Messrs Protopopov and Griaznovsky were granted the monopoly for Terek madder and they founded a second mill in Moscow. They had undertaken to substitute all madder imports within one short year, but they failed. Katherine the Great abolished the madder monopoly soon after her accession, on July 31st 1762. To help spread madder cultivation, the Russian government distributed free seeds from Anatolia to farmers in the Crimea.[63]

By 1840, Russia had finally annexed Bukhara after prolonged pressure. Russian expansion into Central Asia was part of the 'Great Game' which began during the 18th century. Russia's aim was to threaten Britain's military and trade route to India through Afghanistan and to secure a subservient buffer in Central Asia. At the commercial level, the dyers of Turkey red from Persia and Bukhara traditionally made their all-red *burlats* and polychrome *ikats* by weaving individually dyed threads (see chapter 12). The Russians wanted to substitute these popular imports and prevailed on the Bukharan Jews to introduce their textile craft to the Tatar villages of Ura and Urabashak (probably) in the Crimea. By 1790 *burlats* — known as '*kummach*' in Russian — were produced in the dye-houses of Kazan, Wiatka and Astrakhan by master-dyers from Bukhara. In 1801 the brothers Prochoroff started a Turkey red dye-works. In 1808 they were followed by Tretjakoff, and Manuiloff in 1820, Konshin in 1822 and Emile Zundel in 1825.[64]

To give a brief glimpse of Russian manufacturing and especially the textile industry, by 1812, the following factories were operating in Russia. The fur and hide industries were by far the most important:

Broadcloth	136 factories in 30 regions
Cotton	170 factories in 21 regions
Silk	105 factories in 5 regions
Hide	1150 factories in 34 regions
Rope	48 factories in 3 regions
Iron & steel	33 factories in 19 regions

In addition, there were factories producing soap, glass, candles, paper, sugar and china.[65]

At the beginning of the 19th century the Russian textile industry was weak

The venturers' legacy

and overwhelmed by foreign imports. From 1822 the Russian domestic industry established itself, but only after the Minister of Finance Count Krankin introduced a protectionist tax on imported textiles. The tax helped all Russian industries which supplied the domestic market, especially the cotton industry. From 1822 to 1832 cotton fabric production increased by 230% to 104 million roubles and by 1845 cotton fabric production was worth 132 million roubles. During the same period production of cloth, silk,

Horse-drawn carts carrying goods leaving the textile factory of E. Zundel in Moscow, passing a 1920s saloon car (Fitzpatrick)

linen and other textiles had also increased greatly. The rise in textile production coincided with growth in the consumption of madder and in its cultivation around Derbent.[66] All the madder from Derbent, Central Asia as well as the European imports were consumed by the Russian textile industry. Every year more madder was required as more textile factories opened. About 1825, the weight of Russian imports of cotton was 70,000 poods and of white cotton thread 241,000 poods. In 1860 cotton imports had risen over 35 times to 2,611,000 poods while processed white cotton thread had correspondingly decreased to 103,000 poods (appendix 4.1, page 319).

The Imperial Free Economic Society, which foresaw the great benefits of madder cultivation, established a Gold Medal in 1812 for anyone who could grow a better variety of madder than the wild Astrakhan variety from the Terek and then prove that its roots contained equivalent quality dyestuff. But it was a Persian who had settled in Derbent called Kalbalai Husein who, in about 1800, first cultivated madder there using Persian methods. His first and second attempts with Persian seeds failed. Ever optimistic, he next

The Metropolis-like pressurised bleaching vats at E. Zundel's textile factory in Moscow (Fitzpatrick)

planted seeds from Bashli in the Kaitag region in southern Daghestan.[67] He was mocked by his farmer neighbours and died in poverty in 1807. Soon after his death, though, the Bashli seeds produced an excellent crop, which sold for a good profit. George Bedford in October 1624 had recorded his similar experience in England. "For the roots digged up: every one who at the first time laughed at the project begin now to enquire of it and do believe that there is much good to be done there-on."[68] The local Derbent farmers also rushed to plant madder. By 1859 there were thousands of madder farmers in Daghestan.

The gripes of neophite farmers were universal. Philip Miller, a century earlier had also met resistance to the revival of madder cultivation in England. He

View of Derbent, c. 1700, from the shrine of the 40 Arab martyrs, (Adam Olearius, 1728; Markovin)

thought that the farmers had complained mistakenly that English land was poorer than Dutch land; that labour was cheaper, but they forgot about English productivity — an English gardener or ploughmen could do in four days what took his Dutch counterpart six; that trials had failed — usually due to the farmer's lack of skill and continual replanting without rotation, like asparagus; and that the exhausted ground would not support other crops.

When Kalbalai first introduced madder to the Derbent region to supply local demand, the price was astronomical. However the plethora of cheap Russian factory-made fabrics soon replaced the local cottage production that had used local dyes. Karpov noted that while in 1827 there were about a 100 home-installed silk-weaving looms, by 1857 only one weaver had survived.

By 1840 the Russians had also subdued the lowlands of the eastern Caucasus. With peace established, it was possible to undertake the lengthy and difficult cultivation of madder. Outside Daghestan, starting in 1835, there were several other attempts though they were mostly unsuccessful, with the exception of reasonable crops from the Crimea, Poltava and Pensa. In 1837 the Muscovite merchant Mr F. Brandenburg and the Narva merchant Mr M. Weber even attempted to float a company on the metropolitan stock exchange "for the cultivation, improvement and diffusion of various foreign plants containing dyestuffs." They were hoping to raise four million roubles, but their shares found no takers and as they were not underwritten, the enterprise collapsed.

In 1840 the Caucasian Society for the Promotion of Agriculture and Industry published and distributed a booklet in Armenian on the cultivation of madder. The wide area suitable for cultivating madder started in the south from the banks of the river Kouba, in the Kouba district, up the entire valley along the postal route, crossing the Samur river, reaching northward through Derbent, Kurinsk, Kaitag, and Tabassaran districts as far as Dashlagar.

Petrov wrote that to the south in Azerbaijan during the 19th century, madder was grown on the left bank of the river Samur, and in the Khachmasskii, Davichinskii, Kouba and Gilskii regions.

Mr Ivan Fedorovich Baranov, the textile industrialist from the city of Alexandrov (60 miles by rail north-east of Moscow) discovered that the quality of Derbent madder was far superior to Dutch madder which he was using in his textile factories. Baranov sent his manager to Derbent to buy more madder roots

Derbent: the ancient Sunday Market, selling Lezgin-made Soumak weft-brocaded, hairy-backed rugs which have been hung outside the city walls. Dr Magomedkhanov is now producing these with natural colours, using madder for red. (Author's photo)

and find ways of increasing madder production in the Caucasus. Baranov paid a good price to the farmers of Derbent. He even started to buy future crops and he invested heavily. Baranov was the first to mill powdered madder from dried roots on an industrial scale. In 1844 he established his own plantations in the Caucasus to ensure supplies for his mills. Soon other Russian textile merchants moved in, such as Messrs Zubov, Lepeshkin and Malyutin. They brought substantial investment with a sober practical approach to madder production. In many regions of the eastern Caucasus madder began to play a major part in bringing prosperity to the local population as farmers started to multiply production in response to consumers' demand. Madder prices started to climb and in some years one pood of madder roots would sell for 12 roubles and in the Derbent region local prices reached 9 roubles a pood (see chapter 13).

After 1845, cultivation had also spread to the Kouba, Baku, Lenkoran and Elisabetpol (Gengei) regions of Azerbaijan, and the Tblisi and Telavi regions of Georgia. The evident profitability of madder cultivation encouraged Russian farmers in the Stavropol region to enter the business. The Serebryakov family who were landowners in the Kizliar region even built canals 20 miles long to take water from the Terek river to their madder plantations. They produced 5000 to 6000 poods of roots a year, selling at over 6 roubles a pood and "they are keen to expand."

Baranov had larger plans beyond the Caucasus and in 1847 he decided to cultivate madder in the Vladimir region in central Russia. He purchased 242 poods 20 pounds of seed for 1,697 roubles. He was followed by a local farmer, Mr Theofan Medvedev who bought 75 poods and the next year by Mr Andrei Pineev who bought 229 poods for a bargain 1,145 roubles. In just two years just in the Alexandrovsk area 545 poods 20 pounds of Derbent seeds were bought for 3,140 roubles. However, the seeds all failed. Local farmers have always been happy to sell seeds for export rather than shoots. The centre of madder cultivation remained in Daghestan.

In 1860 Shtorkh rightly complained that "in Russia we produce too little powdered madder krap." Powdered madder was much more convenient for consumers than dried roots. From 1816 to 1844, the only customers for dried roots were some Armenians from Astrakhan and Kazan Tatars who used madder to dye cotton cloth by traditional Oriental methods. Caucasian producers only found new customers when they started to produce powdered madder. Because the price of powdered madder was higher than that of dried roots, in 1851 the governor of the Caucasus had another brochure printed for the governor of Derbent. It contained the designs and description of a mill. Russian producers of madder were very slow to buy let alone develop milling equipment which was used in the rest of the industrial world. Karpov's plea in 1857 for laboratories to be set up to measure the characteristic properties of different varieties of madder was several decades behind European practice.

Some progress was made: to combat imports, local mills were started in Kutaisi (Georgia) and in the Abkhazian and Mingrelian regions along the Black Sea coast. Other Russian textile magnates copied Baranov, first buying Caucasian product and later constructing their own mills near Moscow and Ivanovo.

Karpov noted the local economic distortions caused by the madder boom in Derbent. Because the farmers found it more profitable to grow madder, grain production dropped. In 1847 half of the Derbent plantations grew wheat, but by 1851, they had sown only 2000 poods of grain for a local population of 12,000 plus 20,000 migrant workers. The lack of wheat drove up food prices. Wheat flour cost 1 rouble 60 kopeks per pood compared to 1r 10k twenty years before in 1837, against the background of a constant rouble. The price of beef had shot up to 10k per lb compared to 1k in 1837. If madder production increased elsewhere, it would depress the price of Derbent madder, which in turn would probably restore levels of local grain production. Other farmers had also moved from their former trades, such as sheep-rearing to supply wool for carpets and sericulture.

The price of madder was volatile against a background of over-expansion of farming and consumption. The marked decrease in the price per pood of madder roots from 20r per pood in 1815 to 7r in 1832 had stabilised at about 6r from 1833 until 1844. The 1845 price of 5r per pood had dipped irregularly by up to 15 per cent before coming back to 6r in 1857 (see appendix 4.2, page 319). In August 1858 roots were selling at 8r 60k per pood and seeds at 25r per kapan.

As Khashaev the Daghestani economic historian noted, madder was easily the main crop. The Russian authorities in Daghestan became alarmed when prices dropped as investment was insufficient and some farmers went bankrupt. The 1858 crisis was caused by the imbalance of local madder cultivation with the external madder trade. In earlier years, when Baranov had started to buy the cheaper madder from the Derbent region, he was able to cut the prices of the dyed cotton fabrics which his factories produced. Other textile industrialists followed his example and started to buy an increasing quantity of Derbent roots. Demand abruptly increased, which caused prices to soar. This encouraged all the farmers in the Near Caspian region to go into madder cultivation. They often took on loans at punitive interest rates. But it took four or five years for an investment in madder production to turn a profit, and income was only realised after the crop was sold. Increased demand coupled with undersupply of Derbent madder resulted in their price overtaking the price of Dutch madder roots. In turn, the Moscow textile magnates made no marginal profit buying Derbent madder, so they forced the price down. This caused a grave problem for the more recent entrants into madder cultivation in Derbent, who had to repay their loans with interest.

From 1847 to 1862, exports of roots from Derbent had tripled and the price had doubled in constant roubles. By 1862 — after Shamil's surrender to the Russians — madder cultivation had started even in the mountains. There was much expertise among the Daghestani mountaineers. Every winter 40,000 Lezgins came down from their mountain villages for employment as labourers on the madder plantations. Since 1861 Avars and Andis started to form special labour co-operatives. They even had their own badges. Tools were available as the war had recently ended and guns were scrapped to make shovels. In 1862, 213,200 poods of madder were exported. At 7 roubles per pood, that was worth 1.5 million silver roubles (see appendix 4.3, page 320).

According to the Ministry, there was room for further growth of the Derbent madder industry. Local methods of cultivation could be improved. More information was needed about the size of the Moscow market, which depended on the import of foreign powdered madder, as well as the price levels of madder, krap and garancine. There seemed to be limited 'home' market support from Russian manufacturers who would only buy Derbent roots instead of imported processed madder if it was more profitable.

From 1856 to 1860 the price of madder had been steadily rising, but even Shtorkh realised that there were limits. The first was a financial constraint connected with levels of rent, interest rates and availability of investment capital. The second limit was related to market conditions. The textile magnates from Moscow and Vladimir, who were the main consumers of Derbent madder, had foreseen the collapse of madder prices on the European markets and refused to pay the same prices as in 1859 and 1860. In retaliation, some Derbent madder merchants started adulterating the madder roots with sand, soil and even stones to increase profits. The result was that the Russian buyers slashed the price of Derbent madder.

This was made worse by the effects of the American cotton crisis as the Russian textile industry was hit by the American Civil War. The decrease in the import of American cotton to Russia had forced some Russian textile factories to halve output while others went bankrupt. The consumption of Derbent madder had been cut too. The European textile market had been affected similarly. World production of cotton cloth had fallen causing a decrease in demand for krap. During the 1850s Britain alone had been consuming 600,000 poods of krap per annum, roughly the same amount as all the other European nations in total. The sudden decrease in demand for krap resulted in an unsold surplus of 1 million poods in Russian warehouses. Prices plummeted.

In the Caucasus, the jobs of 60,000 workers were threatened, including the 40,000 Lezgins, who might well turn away from peaceful activity back to "criminal violence." The military governor of South Daghestan, and the departments of agriculture and industry in the Caucasus region once more became concerned. In comparison, it had been more relaxed in England a century earlier, when during the 1760s boom, the more docile and perhaps less specialised agricultural workforce of men, women and children would move on to two extra months work digging up madder roots after hop-picking was finished.[69]

A white knight was required to save the industry. In January 1862 the Russian government dispatched Mr Lemkul, an engineer, to Kouba and Derbent to find out about the real state of the madder industry. Growers faced the same crisis in Azerbaijan, Daghestan's southern neighbour. His excellent report led to the decision to build mills and garancine factories in Derbent. Land was provided and considerable funds were paid to Mr Lemkul who then went abroad (this was 1862 — not the 1990s) to purchase machinery and to hire relevant specialists. In addition, a choice had to be made about when to extract the roots. Derbent roots had traditionally been harvested after four and a half years while the French only waited two and a half years. The prospect of doubling the harvest seemed attractive.

Lemkul planned a social-industrial revolution. Decades after the Jouy and New Lanark experiments, the Russian government were now to contribute to social development to complement financial and technical measures to support the industry. If education and technical knowledge were brought up to European levels, new developments in mechanics, physics and chemistry could be exploited for the benefit of the textile industry, as in France and Britain. In imitation of the Dutch and French, the Derbent farmers and mill-owners were to set up a chemical laboratory to carry out research on madder plants and soil suitability alongside Mr Lemkul's new factories. Next, a specialised commercial institute should be established to carry out market research. If he had not been too late, was Lemkul too radical for the authorities?

The terminal crisis happened in 1873 when due to nil demand for madder at the 1872 Nizhegorodsky Fair, no roots were extracted and the madder plantations were left to die. But carpet production using the new synthetic dyes continued to be the largest craft in Daghestan. In 1915, 40,000 people were involved in making carpets, about 30 per cent of all craft workers, producing carpets worth two million roubles or 31 per cent by value of all crafts.[70]

An introduction to the 19th-century madder boom

From the 16th century the Ottoman market was the largest in the world and naturally attracted European entrepreneurs. Over the years the Europeans eliminated most of the long-established Turkish cloth-manufacturing industry and bought their raw madder instead. Between 1790 and 1830, the Ottoman government had imposed a series of surtaxes for military and administrative reorganisation on trade in various commodities: cotton, sheep wool, angora wool, silk, spirits, currants, opium and madder. These stagnatory duties became the mainstay of the purchasing monopolies set up by the government in the early 19th century and were rapidly perceived to help tax farmers who bought up the leases.[71]

European textile manufacturers undermined the position of Bursa silk cloth makers by bidding up the prices of natural dyestuffs. Whilst locally produced madder was siphoned off by the higher prices prevailing in Europe, imported dyestuffs either jumped in price or disappeared from the market. In a five-year period during the 1830s imported dyestuff prices doubled.[72] Wild madder was still extracted by peasants in the 1850s.[73] Shtorkh noted that madder was then mainly cultivated in Rumelia and Anatolia, Syria and Cyprus, but the best was grown in western Asia Minor in the areas of the Bakir valley near Bergama, Kiaghir (?Çagıs near Balikesir), Demerghik (Demirci) and Gherdis (Gördes) — all not too distant from the modern DOBAG weavers in Ayvacık and Yuntdağ. Highly-rated madder roots were exported from Smyrna (Izmir) to Britain — Smyrna's largest trading partner — during the mid-19th century.[74] The share of madder roots in all Ottoman exports declined from 41.5 per cent in 1840-44 to a mere 5 per cent in 1870-4 and completely disappeared thereafter (see chapter 14 for parallel tables of Russian, British, Caucasian, Central Asian and Turkish exports and imports). Before the 1860s annual British madder imports varied between £750,000 and £1,000,000.[75] It was a substantial industry.

The warring period of the French Revolution and the First Empire (1789-1815) did great harm to the industry in Europe. For instance the high price of grain in 1816-1817 caused extensive substitution of wheat for madder within the Austro-Hungarian empire. In France, Alsace had once exported 2,500 tons a year at the end of the 18th century[76] but did not recover until Louis-Philippe (r. 1830-48) ordered the trousers and caps of the French infantry to be dyed with madder.[77] Incidentally, over the Channel, this material was highly regarded by King George V who, when Prince of Wales, had the walls of his own favourite sitting room covered with it in his newly built mock-Tudor 'bachelor's cottage' in Sandringham. His biographer Harold Nicholson did not share the King's taste for exotica, sniping that the "red covering of cloth used in those days for the trousers of the French army saddened the walls" in the already-dark north-facing room.[78]

Recovery was brisk. In 1812 John James Egg an economic refugee from Switzerland began the cultivation of Neapolitan madder at the foot of mount Vesuvius and pioneered the cotton industry in southern Italy.[79] From 1835 madder cultivation restarted in the Naples area, and by 1856, 325,000 poods of roots (5.3 million kg) were produced, which was of sufficient quality to attract Dutch and French buyers. From 1800 the Austro-Hungarian empire became a producer, with cultivation in Losdorf, Polkau, Meissau, in Lower Austria, in Moravia and in Hungary. Even after the disaster of 1816, some plantations did survive. In 1852, the Lower Austria Crafts Guild published a manual on madder and bought seeds from Avignon, to distribute free to interested farmers, provided that they reported back their results.

By the middle of the 19th century madder was cultivated throughout the world (see chapter 14 and Map, chapter 2). In Europe madder was grown in France particularly the south and Alsace, Holland, Germany in Silesia, Saxony, Palatinate, Bavaria and Baden, Belgium, Austro-Hungary, Italy particularly in Tuscany, Naples and Sicily, Spain, and Boeotia in Greece. In southern Russia cultivation flourished in the Caucasus and along the Caspian coast and in Kazan. Outside Europe madder was grown in Turkey, particularly Asia Minor, Persia, Mesopotamia, North Africa — Egypt, Algiers, Tunis, Tripolis and Morocco, Terceira on the Azores, North, South and Central America, the East Indies and Australia.[80]

World export production in 1868 of powdered krap amounted to 70,000 tons (70 million kg), valued at £3.5 millions. By the 1860s the level of production of garancine and krap in France was equal to that of Holland. They were by far the largest producers, together controlling almost 70 per cent of the market, in the following way.

In 1868 French madder exports were valued at over £1.2 millions. This included the (unquantified) bulk of the madder grown in Lebanon and Algeria which was shipped to France in the form of dried roots for conversion in the factories of the Vaucluse. France's strong position was held for some time. Ten years earlier in 1859 exports of krap were over 14 million francs. Twenty years before, in 1848, France had exported 2.2 million kg of madder roots for 1.6 million francs and 12.1 million kg of ground krap for 12.1 million francs in total 13.7 million francs equivalent to 3.4 million silver roubles.[81]

In 1858 Holland exported 4.8 million kg of krap for 2.9 million Dutch florins and (unquantified) garancine for 2.7 million florins, a total of 5.6 million florins equivalent to 3 million silver roubles. The Dutch fought back to regain market share from the French. In Holland the number of cultivation enterprises had increased from 90 to 130 between 1820 and 1870 with 13 additional new garancine factories.[82] The size of the business meant that even Italy — a minor producer — annually exported 2.3 million kg of powdered madder by 1858, over 40 per cent of total production.[83]

The largest consumer was Britain whose textile industry took about a third of world exports. In 1869 English madder imports were valued at about £1 million. In Scotland, output of Turkey red textiles was vast. Peel in his comprehensive essay on the industry, reported that in 1859 one factory in Dalquhurn dyed 18 million yards of fabric and 800,000 pounds of yarn.[84] Even the arrival of synthetic alizarin in 1868 did not signal the end of the Turkey red era. The synthetic product was actually preferred to enable dyeing methods to be further refined and cheapened without any loss of quality. In 1898 at the peak of the Turkey red industry, the firms of 'The Vale' amalgamated to form the United Turkey Red Company. Their several factories supplied the world with red cotton and only succumbed in 1936 when red naphtol dyes took over the cotton industry (see page 67).[85]

In 1869 alizarin was synthesised by Graebe and Liebermann and this discovery (see chapter 15) soon proved disastrous for the madder-producers. Synthetic alizarin sold for a quarter of the price of madder. The profits of French plantations crashed by 90 per cent, fields remained untilled and peasants starved. The growers desperately attempted to regain their former position and lodged Luddite appeals with their governments. It was all to no avail, the wheel of progress was not to be turned back. Ten years later madder-growing had been abandoned nearly everywhere in the world. Until Harald Böhmer's natural dye project (see chapter 16) reawakened public awareness throughout the world to the superior quality of madder dyes in 1983, only a fractional amount continued to be grown for high-quality artists' products and therapeutic uses.[86]

5

The care of madder from seed to sack

An uncompromising plant

WHY WOULD anyone go to the lengths of cultivating madder if they could find it growing wild? Firstly the dye content of cultivated madder was higher. Secondly perceived market demand drove the farmer to cultivate such a troublesome crop. The growing techniques were so complicated that a farmer who could cultivate madder really had mastered a mystery of nature. The expert grower was exposed to additional difficulties. The eventual rewards were great but the farmer had to survive several cashless growing seasons. The crop risked ruin by weather, disease and mistakes in the specialised methods of care. Different skilled part-time labour was required at different stages. If that labour was not available, then the crop yield was threatened. At first it had been a surprise to find such detailed descriptions of the growing methods by the Russians. As other sources appeared which explained detailed techniques of English, French and Dutch cultivation, it became clear that madder was an extremely difficult plant to grow with success. These difficulties must have been the cause of such detailed investigation.

The three Russian accounts described in the Foreword are amplified by comments from other countries. The earliest detailed critiques of madder cultivation are from the young William Bedford in the early 1620s. He wrote several letters to his stepfather and joint backer Henry Sherfield in some of the cold winters from 1620 to 1624 when he was first studying and later appropriating Dutch shoots to plant in England. Dutch scholars of today also have great respect for Philip Miller, a Fellow of the Royal Society's 38-page illustrated treatise, published in 1758. Miller had 30 years' experience of small-scale cultivation and in 1727 he had visited several plantations in Holland, between Helvoetfluys and the Brill.

De Poerck assembled some earlier information from Flanders and Artois in the form of regulations about cultivation from the 1330s to 1480s. Dates of harvest and the age of the root were controlled. For example in Lille they had to extract roots between September 8th and April 15th, to ensure that roots had a minimum of 18 months growth. In Ypres roots were 'immature' after two seasons growth and in other places it was also forbidden to extract roots then.[1]

To return to the 18th century, there is Joan Thirsk's shared discovery of an English pamphlet from 1765, whose glum remarks contrast with optimism over the Channel. The French challenge, which eventually overtook the Dutch masters, came from Jean Claude Flachat whose description of cultivation in Zeeland and Flanders was published in 1766 and who actually started a Turkey red dye-works near Lyons (see chapter 11). Peter Priester's recent book is the authoritative modern account of Dutch madder and also adds three Dutch financial accounts from 1690, 1817 and 1843.[2] All the old writers shared the same motive of stimulating madder cultivation. Shtorkh may have read the English, Dutch or French authors, but he does not seem to have copied their work — the Russian accounts were very detailed and made comparisons with cultivation in Holland and France. As such, they provide a useful basis for looking at the cultivation of madder.

Agricultural conditions

There was a lot of selection and preparatory work to be done before madder could be planted. Decisions had to be made which would affect the harvest years later.

Climate

Climatic conditions did not affect madder growth as severely as one might think, considering that the plant was brought to Russia from more southern lands. The plant did not flourish when there were sudden changes in the weather, but could survive temperature fluctuations of up to 10°C. Curiously the roots were unaffected by of elsewhere strong frosts up to -20°C, provided there was a thick blanket of snow before the frosts. The stalks and leaves would of course die back to be renewed in the

The three Russian Frontispieces (from top):
Shtorkh,1859, Karpov, 1859, & 'The Ministry', 1863
(ack. M. Shumilov; Bib. Saltikov, St Petersburg

spring. However, the root could die if winter weather was too humid or spring too humid and cold. For example, though frosts and floods in Zeeland were more severe and frequent than in England during the 18th century and earlier, Zeeland production was far greater.[3] In Russia 52° longitude was regarded as the northern limit for suitable climatic conditions for growth.

Choice of soil

Schaefer stressed that the quantity of dye contained in the root depended on the soil rather than the species of plant. In the near-Caspian region there was a wide variety of soils. In the Kouba region the soil was clay, while near Derbent it was a mixture of clay and black earth with high lime content. Karpov added that near Derbent madder was even cultivated on black clay (containing iron oxides) and on sea silt.

The question was which type of soil was best for propagating madder and which gave the highest yield of madder roots. An experienced farmer would prefer a fresh clay soil, rich with organic matter in a field with a natural drainage system. Fields without natural drainage would retain water and damage the precious roots which could easily rot.[4] Planting on heavy soil covered in couch grass would also be unsuitable. The optimal mix for madder was sandy clay with some lime and black-earth. This mix resulted in the roots producing a good crimson colour as opposed to the pale red from other soils. It was also important that the soil be sufficiently friable to allow both rain and irrigation to penetrate deeply. If the mix was chiefly black-earth, the roots were knotted and contained too little dyestuff.[5] Karpov added subtly that black-earth soil produced excellent stalks and healthy seeds but poor quality and thin roots, while clay-sandy soil produced better roots but fewer stalks and seeds. Best results were achieved from soil with some lime fertiliser, whereas too salty a soil was completely unsuitable for madder. This would appear to be qualified by his own subsequent recommendation and the experience of growers in Schouwen.

In the environs of Derbent, Kornet and Kolykhan in Tabassaran, Kejukh and Bashli in lower Kaitag and in the Kouba area they produced madder with a higher concentration of dyeing agent and better yields. Also madder roots from the right bank of the river Kouba were of lower quality than those grown on the left bank, which were of the best quality. Soil assessment was not a job for the naked eye. Only chemical and physical tests of different soils could distinguish differences in soil composition to give the characteristics of the best soils.[6] In Avignon, where excellent madder was produced, the soil contained up to 90 per cent carbonic lime. Schaefer[7] added that in Avignon two entirely different types of the same plant developed. The types of madder called '*Du palus*' or '*Palus alizari*', referred to later, had a red root which contained a larger quantity of dye than the yellow *rosée* variety which was grown in a soil containing little calcium. This was why the lime soil of the

Caucasus was considered most suitable for growing madder. For northern France, Flachat recommended low-lying humid fields, such as he found in Bergue rather than the more precious agricultural land near Lille.[8]

In Zuider Zee, grey sandy soil, preferably mixed with mud from the beds of lakes or ponds or off the town streets was best suited for madder growing. But this soil only succeeded when tilled and manured.[9] In Holland the *holders* — fields surrounded by dams — also contain some lime. It was scientifically proven that the less lime there was in the soil, the poorer the crimson colour of the dyestuff. But lime content was not the only factor involved and more research was needed. Miller added that the soft sandy loam should be 2½ to 3ft deep. In Lund in the south of Sweden an excellent crop was grown on garden soil mixed with clay.[10]

Selection & preparation of plantation

Madder should be cultivated on a flat field to provide even drainage. If the field had many pits where water could collect, then the roots would rot. When madder was grown on a dry hill, the low humidity of the soil prevented growth of the roots. It took 20 months for a significant quantity of red dyestuff to appear in the roots, but too dry soil would hinder the natural development of the plant, in which case another year's growth was needed.[11]

The madder plant did not require the best soil and could even produce a good crop on soil which was unsuitable for growing wheat. But the sandy soils of the southern parts of Daghestan could become so dry in the heat that the roots would be killed. Equally, the winds there could blow the seeds out of the sandy soil. Just as bad, the clay soils could be baked hard by the summer heat. This prevented the natural growth of the roots as well as the germination of the seeds.[12] In the Kouba region and in some areas of Derbent, madder plantations were located mainly on virgin soil which had been covered by forest for centuries. Thus the first task was to clear the trees and bushes. Experience showed that on such soils madder yields were highest, both in quality and quantity, for several years. Both tree-felling and clearing of the fields would be started in the autumn when Lezgin specialists would come down from their mountain villages, after completing their own harvests.

All the cleared timber would be burnt on the spot in bonfires and the ashes would be spread on the field. In some areas near Derbent, they planted madder on fallow fields which had been used as pastures for cattle for a few decades, but cleared forest fields were preferred. Some private farmers would plant melons in the first year after clearing, to prepare the soil, but industrial planters would plant madder straight away. In the near-Caspian area when an existing madder field was replanted, autumn ploughing was required to break up the soil which would become compacted by the winter frosts. Planting took place in winter because the frost made the broken soil friable. The main tools used were shovels and ploughs. The madder-cultivation belt could be divided into two areas: the Derbent area which consisted off small-scale farms (*la petite culture*) and the Kouba area which consisted of vast plantations (*la grande culture*). In late 17th century England madder holdings ranged from 75 acres down to 2 acres or 1 hectare.[13]

In Daghestan, methods of cultivating madder were mainly the same in both areas, but methods of soil preparation differed. Near Derbent, where there were small — typically three-hectare — farms, the farmer with a couple of hired hands would use shovels (*kizgiri*) to loosen the soil to make it friable. This would result in higher yields because the clay soil would otherwise suffocate the roots. For this reason they would turn over the soil of both old fields awaiting replanting and newly cleared fields. While shovelling, they would crush any lumps and remove stumps and stones. In contrast, on the large farms in the Kouba area they ploughed the fields with large ploughs drawn by six to eight pairs of oxen — an impressive sight. The soil was ploughed twice, once in autumn and again at the end of the year when the madder was tall and bushy. One reason for the shorter period of cropping in Kouba was that ploughing was not as effective in breaking up the soil as digging.[13]

Roughly, the depth of furrow, from 18 to 36cm, was a quarter of the width of the rows. The deeper the furrow — whether ploughed or shovelled — the longer the roots. In addition, the soil had to be friable to allow the roots to have more branches and become thicker. As every madder farmer knew, the thicker the roots, the more dyeing agent they contained.

In Derbent, the soil would be prepared in September to October. In southern Orenburg and along the banks of the Syr-Daria river June to July was preferred, as they were the hottest months. The weeds which had been damaged by the plough or shovel were duly scorched. In the Ural and north Orenburg regions, ploughing took place in autumn. During the four months of winter the temperature rarely dropped below -15°C, which allowed the soil to be broken down by the frosts.[15]

Fertilisation

"We do not use manure for madder cultivation in the Caucasus because some farmers are convinced that manure would burn the madder roots." This mistaken idea was based on several unlucky experiences of putting (probably fresh) manure into the soil. In many other areas the sad consequences of not using manure could already be seen in the 1850s. Where rich yields were produced 30 years before, yields had dropped so low that they could barely support the farmer. The first plantations of madder in the eastern Caucasus were in the Derbent area where 1850s yields were much lower than those from more recently planted areas in Tabassaran and Kaitag.[16] Sometimes farmers would start cultivating madder on unfertilised soil. If the nitrogen content of the soil was about 13 poods (or 215kg) per hectare, the dried root crop could average 106 poods with a maximum of 125 poods. But such high yields would not be achieved on second or third plantings. In France, experiments had showed that 242 poods of dried roots were grown using 7,500 poods of manure which contained 30 poods of nitrogen.[17]

Many experienced farmers found that there was indeed a connection between the richness of the yield and the amount of fertiliser used, usually manure. In the Avignon area the average crop per hectare after three years was up to 200 to 300 poods. In contrast, the crop from the eastern Caucasus after five years would be just 100 poods per hectare. The large difference was probably caused by the especially heavy manure enrichment of the soil in Avignon. The Ministry thought that more manure should have been used in the eastern Caucasus.

All soils required sufficient humus (broken down vegetal matter, but also referring to composted manure here) to prevent exhaustion, especially where the soil could not sustain the growth of a second crop after four or five years. Poor soil needed similar enrichment even for a first crop. The norm was 4,000 poods of fresh manure, to be composted, per hectare. Cattle manure was preferable to horse or sheep dung. Sodium and salt found in manure greatly improved the soil and produced higher root crops. On the island of Schouwen excellent crops were produced because of the salty soil. Incidentally, it should have been profitable to plant madder in the vast deserted salty soil regions of southern Russia.

Another positive soil additive was phosphoric acid lime produced by dissolving animal carcasses in sulphuric acid. Farmers had to beware that vegetal matter dissolved more slowly than manure. Dutch research carried out during 1824 to 1826 showed that urine from cows and other manure liquor improved the soil and the rate of growth and quantity of madder roots. Shaefer noted that during the 18th century good results were obtained in Zeeland with soil mixed with the mud and refuse from the streets of Copenhagen.[18] In Anatolia, Syria and Cyprus, farmers fertilised the dense soils to the same extent as for cultivation of wheat.[19] As a reaction, Miller[20] thought that very richly dunged land produced much haulm (stalks) at the expense of root size. Moreover, too much dung or sea-coal ashes produced darker colour dyestuff, which was similarly deleterious to growing madder (or liquorice) in the "smoak of London."

Rotation of crops

The ministry noted that there was no arable system in Daghestan. In the Derbent area, they planted madder repeatedly for 20 years in the same field. In the Kouba district they would clear out the madder fields after twelve years as by then expenditure would exceed income from the crop. Permanent planting of madder year after year could affect the content of dyeing agent in the roots. Count Gasparen, the experienced madder plant researcher, had found after several years observation that the percentage of dyeing agent diminished in the roots planted on regularly reused fields. The famous madder from Avignon had lost up to 20 per cent of its dyeing agent in later years in spite of proper care and soil enrichment. At the same time on madder plantations where planting was stopped for six or twelve years and then restarted, the amount of dyeing agent in the roots was hardly affected.[21]

Karpov considered that soil where madder had been cultivated for four years was too exhausted for immediate re-sowing and should be left fallow for two or three years. Another method of soil regeneration was to sow wheat for a single season and then replant madder. Fields which were previously vineyards gave an excellent crop of madder roots and conversely vineyards and fruit trees flourished on soil previously cultivated for madder.

While the soil would certainly be both free of weeds and friable after the extraction of the roots, it would also be exhausted of nutrient chemicals. It was therefore a good idea for farmers to next sow crops such as lucerne, maize, potatoes, wheat or beetroot or even plant fruit trees or vines. Conversely, madder flourished on fields switched from growing potatoes, beetroot, cabbage and hemp, which all required loose friable soils. In the Caucasus, farmers liked to leave wheat fields fallow for a year before planting madder. Karpov concluded that madder was a rotational crop. In Asia Minor, madder farmers would usually sow two four or five-year crops of madder in succession but never a third without a break. Soil exhaustion could be avoided by the addition of natron (see Glossary) and sodium chloride. Research over a 30-year period in the Vaucluse *département* demonstrated that constant maximum yields of madder required the field to have a 12-year respite before replanting with madder.[22] In England an interval of seven to eight years was allowed to elapse before replanting, compared to four years in Zeeland and up to ten in other parts of Holland.[23]

Miller wrote that the Dutch planted grain in rotation. In Schouwen they inter-planted cabbages or dwarf kidney beans in the first year.[24] Miller was not convinced by these "avaricious" farmers. They said that it kept the weeds at bay. He said that it actually diminished root growth. Miller might not have been aware of the farmers' cash flow problem, noted by Bedford in 1624. He wrote that the Dutch preferred the following scheme of rotation: rapeseed, madder, rapeseed, madder, followed by two or three years of wheat. If the crop was alternated on half the area, it meant that the oil crop would bring in a regular flow of cash, for the three year wait for the madder crop could be onerous. Bedford's plan was to sow 100 acres of rapeseed and plant 60 to 80 acres of madder two years later.[25] He also planted wheat and flax in the gaps in his madder field to both save weeding and help pay for the rent of the field.[26] In 1765 Mr Hutchins at Barn Elms in Surrey, where madder had been grown for over two centuries, rotated madder with barley, peas, turnips and was currently growing wheat, without an intervening fallow.[27]

The Dutch naturally thought in terms of crop rotation which implied looking at returns over a seven year period. Priester quoted the results of four different crop cycles about 1817 to 1819, which showed a range of surpluses from three guldens per hectare for a cycle of rest-rapeseed-wheat-peas-wheat-oats-*paardebonen* (horse-feed beans) to 423 guldens for a cycle of rest-winter barley-madder-madder-flax-rye-potatoes, with similar manuring[28] (see appendix 5.1, page 320).

Pre-growth

The three collected accounts of agricultural practice in the Caucasus have many different and subtle emphases, which show that there was no universally agreed method of cultivation. They also demonstrate that the authors used different informants and that the authors did not co-operate or plagiarise. Their accounts have been combined below with Miller's Dutch methods used in Schouwen.

Madder seeds

Seeds conserved the ability to germinate for two years. The dark violet seeds were heavy and dry and unaffected by mould. Before making his purchase, a careful madder farmer would put the seeds in a barrel of water. If more than a third of the seeds floated, then the seeds were unfit to plant. It was important for the farmer to know the place of origin of the seeds. Kalbala Gusein who was the first to attempt to cultivate madder in the eastern Caucasus had many failures with the seeds which he had brought from Persia. He eventually succeeded with local seeds from Andreevki village on the northern slopes of Daghestan. So farmers considered the best seeds to originate from wild madder plants from Andreevki.[29]

Derbent farmers never sowed seeds left over from the previous year, they only sowed the current year's seeds. This was probably because the old seeds were not stored properly. In Derbent certain spivs would mix last year's seeds with freshly gathered seeds. This exposed the new seeds to rot and disease. Sometimes seeds purchased from dealers in Derbent failed to produce any shoots. That was why you had to be careful whom you bought seeds from. As old and fresh seeds looked identical, it was safer to purchase seeds from the plantation field, where you kept a close watch when the seeds were packed into sacks.

Karpov would not advise sending parcels of seeds by sea, as they risked absorbing salt water. This caused the seeds to 'burn' in their packing, which ruined them. If you had to send seeds by sea, they should be packed carefully into leather sacks or wooden boxes covered in leather. In addition, as soon as possible after landing, the seeds had to be dried again. Karpov used this method to ship safely 18 poods of Derbent seeds to Orenburg in the Ural region. The Agricultural Institute in Tblisi had demonstrated that if seeds

Madder seeds (Author's photos)

were properly stored in a dry place, they could propagate successfully after several years.

In 1856, the well-respected French landowner, M. Vilmore, started experiments to find the best species of madder for quality and quantity of dyestuff. It appeared that the concentration of dyestuff varied from plant to plant, so he started selective breeding which in due time produced excellent results.[30]

Germination

In Avignon, madder seeds were germinated in wet sand for a fortnight or soaked in water for 24 hours. Near Derbent there was another local method. The seeds were 'sown' after the first snow by scattering them on the snow where they were left to absorb enough moisture to germinate during the first warm days of spring. The Caspian farmer would never delay planting till spring because he risked losing his seeds. In spring the persistent south winds dried up the soil which prevented germination.[31]

Soil preparation before sowing

Before planting, the soil had to be dug over and made friable. In October and November Derbent farmers started shovelling to a depth of 35cm. Fresh manure was harrowed into the soil during the autumn because winter manure was lumpy and required crushing. The field needed to be ploughed in the spring before sowing. Two ploughings were necessary: the first as early as permitted by the weather and the second a day before sowing. While it was satisfactory to prepare the soil by ploughing, better crops were produced after a good shovelling to a depth of 45cm. The more friable the soil, the thicker and denser were the roots.[32]

In Schouwen, they ploughed twice in autumn to help the winter frost break up the clods. In spring, they completed one or two additional ploughings just before planting between April and June, depending on the weather. The 3ft 'lands' were separated by furrows 4 to 5in deep.[33]

Growth

The farmer was now ready to decide whether to sow seeds or plant shoots.

Sowing

If the farmer could not plant madder shoots, he had to sow seeds, usually in September or October. Seeds sown during springtime were liable to be scorched during the summer and their surviving autumnal shoots risked exposure to next winter's frosts.

Where madder was regularly cultivated, new good quality seeds from Asia Minor, Derbent or Kouba were needed to avoid perpetuating undesirable traits in locally produced seeds. The farmers of Derbent also refreshed their seed stock with Caucasian wild seeds to complement the enriched soil of their plantations. In France, in 1756 and (according to Shtorkh) 1821, the government bought seeds from Smyrna (Izmir). Some of these seeds also found their way to the Gent and Tronsheim areas in Holland. Some farmers sowed seeds in a nursery plot to produce shoots for transplanting in spring or autumn, which required especial care not to damage the tender roots. Usually seeds were sown in rows to facilitate care. Shtorkh reckoned that approximately 4.5 poods of seed were required to plant a hectare of relatively dense soil against 5.5 poods for loose soil, while the Ministry and Karpov reckoned a higher 6.5 to 7.5 poods.[34] A second similar planting required 8 poods.

Madder seeds could be planted by broadcasting or in rows. Broadcasting wasted seeds, so planting in rows was preferred in the small plantations of one hectare near Derbent. The farmers placed twine on top of each row to separate the rows by 1m and planted the seeds at 16cm intervals. After planting, they covered the seeds with soil and water as required.

In 'snow sowing' mentioned above, the ploughed (but not harrowed) field was left till late autumn. After the first snows, the farmer sowed the seeds on the snow and left. The Derbent farmers explained that they needed to see where the seeds fell to ensure uniform coverage. The black seeds showed up clearly on the snow. In spring, the melting snow helped the seeds to penetrate the soil and germinate.[35]

Karpov noted that the period of sowing from October to February near

Derbent would be unsuitable in the colder climates of Orenburg and the north, where temperatures fell to -30°C, with over a metre of snow on the fields. It was sometimes difficult to find the field, let alone to work on it. The Orenburg region was vast with large variations in climate. After sowing, the seeds needed to absorb water from rain or snow, but frost was fatal for the young roots. While this schedule was suited to the Syr and Ural regions, it could be disastrous further north where it was better to sow in October and early November or next spring after the snow had melted.

Planting shoots

A plant with many side roots, called *tengels* in Dutch, was called "a well-bearded madder plant" and was rich in dye and production of shoots. To achieve this, wherever possible, farmers preferred to plant shoots to seeds, as a greater proportion survived. Roots from shoots were better and less tough than those grown from seed. Farmers separated the five or six side stalks and took care to preserve the roots of each shoot while leaving the central stalk. After two or three years one hectare of 'nursery' shoots would be replanted over two to three hectares of plantation. It was best to separate shoots during wet weather. The other method of producing healthy shoots was to bend over the side stalks of two to three-year-old plants in June and to cover them with soil. By autumn these stalks had individually rooted and could be replanted separately. They reached maturity after a further two years.

The earlier in spring the shoots were planted, the better they grew. Planting in warm rainy weather also strengthened the roots. The three popular planting layouts were in rows, beds or pits. For bedding, 140,000 to 150,000 shoots were planted per hectare.

In Derbent at the end of the first October, the whole plantation was put in order. Where the plants were too dense, they would be thinned out, and replanted to fill the barer patches. Later all the plants would be planted out in rows. In France the hot sunny climate necessitated careful watering and after one year the roots were taken up and replanted.[36]

The Dutch were celebrated as born gardeners. They observed practices hallowed by the tradition of centuries. Dutch 'peasants' were also experts in the art of irrigation. In Holland seeds were never sown: shoots or slips, called *kiemen*, were planted with an iron dibble, four in a row, 1ft apart, but never before May when the apple trees were in bloom. The parent plants had to be two years old. Immediately after planting, the shoots were skilfully watered. The roots were extracted after three years.[37] Bedford in 1624 found that '*keeme*' slips which he exported to England from Holland had to be planted within eight days, which was possible as the ship took a maximum 48 hours even without a wind. In England the problem was to find skilled labourers quickly. He explained that this was why he had also bought enough roots to plant two acres, which the following spring produced enough shoots to plant a further four acres. Export of living roots was forbidden so they had to be dug up secretly out of season in February, which risked punishment from the wrathful Dutch state.[38] Sandberg quoted the Swedish scientist Prof Lidbeck from the ancient university of Lund who visited Zeeland in 1755 and noted the following variant. One (and curiously — as the roots were re-extracted in the following paragraph of his account), two or three-year-old roots were carefully loosened from the tap root, immediately placed in a basket of earth and transplanted by placing every

Planting shoots in May 1913 in Nieuwerkerk in Schouwen-Duiveland
(ack. D. A. Zoethout; Priester)

three shoots in a small triangle, with a foot between each triangle in the row. This may well be the pit method referred to by the Russians.[39]

The English, under the tutelage of Hugenot refugees from Flanders, preferred planting 'sets' in April, in rows 18in to 24in apart at 9in to 12in intervals.[40] Miller recommended ploughing followed by digging with 3ft between the rows, similar to Caucasian rows which were 1 to 1.5m wide.[41] These differences probably depended on the desired length of roots.

Continual demands

Any relief at surmounting every one of these preliminary hurdles was tempered by the knowledge that this was only a first step before dealing with the problems of delicate care which began after planting.

Watering

One of the main conditions which helped madder grow was abundant watering at the right time. There were some places where madder did not need so much watering because of rain, for example the Kafar side of Derbent, the mountains behind the citadel above Derbent, and the wooded Kouba district villages Zeichur and Imam-Kuli-Kent. But the root yields were very low there and the main income was derived from the sale of madder seeds. Fields with insufficient irrigation were of no value to the madder farmer. All water available from nearby mountain springs, wells or rivers was used.

Louisa Chenciner, aged five, showing her madder plant, aged two (Author's photo)

On the plains of Derbent, watering was vital because of the heat of the summer sun and the lack of rain. Madder roots rapidly shrivelled in droughts. Mountain springs were the main source and aqueduct trenches were dug to deliver the water to the fields. The fortunate mountain farmer did not need to water because the morning mists and dew were sufficient. Newly sown fields needed no watering. Madder plants were watered twice and occasionally three times a year, but no more as excess water could rot the roots. As a rule, the farmers watered the young madder plants at the end of May and in August during the first year.

During the second and third years watering took place in April and in August, but in the Derbent area, they watered in winter immediately after planting. In the first year, after ploughing, the field was literally flooded, while in the second and subsequent years, watering flowed along the trenches formed between the ridged-up rows of plants.

In this way, any excess water would be absorbed by the drainage system, but this rarely happened because water was too valuable (and was quickly reused) and as any excess in the trenches might rot or kill the roots.[42] There was no need to water during the fourth year as root-rot could result and by then the taproots were deep enough to gather moisture from the water table.

In the other madder growing regions of Russia, Jaroslavl and southern

Siberia, farmers did not water their fields, to no ill effect. In the northern Orenburg region there was also sufficient regular rain. But in the Syr and Ural regions, there was less rain and watering was essential.[43]

First year weeding

A few weeks after the shoots appeared, so did the weeds. Weeding was essential for successful cultivation. In the Caucasus as elsewhere the most harmful weed was couch grass (*Triticium repens*). The weed grew in a tangle and suffocated the madder stalks, while its roots crowded and hampered the growth of the madder roots. Weeding had to commence immediately they appeared.[44]

The ubiquitous couch grass was pulled out by hand. The weeds were cleared from around each plant separately. The weeds were then be burnt in situ on the field. Several tools were employed for weeding as it was difficult to weed thoroughly by hand. Karpov had seen a special knife for getting at the roots of the weeds.

The farmers weeded the plantation twice, in April and in August, and cleared out all the grasses using a sickle. After weeding, the small depressions formed around the plants were flattened out and the whole plantation was watered.[45] In England the crop was kept free from weeds by hoeing and then allowed to grow wild for three or four seasons.[46]

Ridging-up

Six weeks after planting, adjacent soil had to be heaped up around each plant, to a maximum depth of 12cm. This was known as 'ridging-up'. In October, weather permitting, any excess growth had to be cut and another layer of soil added to the base of the plant. Ridging-up started in October and carried on throughout the autumn and even in early winter and only stopped when the hard frosts struck. The frosts broke up the extra layer of soil which enabled next year's shoots to penetrate. Ridging-up had been shown also to ensure thicker and denser roots which in turn produced more dyestuff.

Madder stalks were placed on top of the ground and covered with a layer of soil, not later than June or July, to allow the new roots to establish themselves before winter. The additional thickness of soil helped insulate the plant against the summer heat. By the following spring new shoots appeared. More rarely, some farmers would add the layer of soil in spring. However, in spring the southern wind started to blow the soil became extremely dry, which was not favourable for plant growth.[47] In Schouwen, in September or October, the green stalks were similarly spread down over the beds and covered with 3 to 4in of earth during November.[48]

The annual ridging-up gave the rows of plants an exposed castellated appearance, which was suited to Derbent where the winter temperature rarely dropped below -10°C.[49] Though covering by plough cost only half as much as spade work, the spade made a neater job, and the tops of the beds were levelled.

However, in the northern Orenburg region, the winter frosts would kill the roots, which is why a wider bed — about 180cm — was needed to provide insulation of 18cm of soil on each side of the row of plants. The trenches between the beds were also wider. The best method of cultivating madder in the Orenburg and Ural regions was to sow seeds in deep-ploughed soil and leave the plant for four years. No soil was added, but weeding was regular. Farmers who could deep-plough to 70cm could sow the entire field in one operation rather than row by row.

Second year care

In spring when new shoots came through the layer of autumn soil, more soil was added. Karpov noted that about 9cm depth was enough. In autumn when the stems and leaves withered it was time for the the rows of plants to be ridged-up with another layer of soil up to 16cm deep (4 vershka).[50] Compaction had to be avoided so that the following spring new stems were able to shoot through the soil.

Another thorough weeding was needed. The farm-labourer attacked those weeds which appeared along the tops of the ridged rows between the madder plants, which had to be removed by hand. But the lack of available labour on a family holding meant that weeding could be less frequent. During the second year the plants needed watering during April to May and again during August.[51]

Third year care

Miller confirmed that in Schouwen third-year care was generally the same as second-year care. In the Caucasus, however, weeding rarely occurred more than once as the madder plants grew strong and bushy. The weeds were then usually suffocated by the madder plants. Watering was needed as before. Before ridging-up during August and September, the farmers harvested the madder seeds, though Karpov thought that in Derbent the second year's seeds were already plentiful. An abundance of seeds was usually a sign of poor root growth.[52] In autumn in Holland another layer of soil, some 8 to 12cm deep was added to the base of the plants. Karpov had observed layers 27cm deep near Derbent.[53]

Schaefer added that in the East the plant was trained like beans or peas to increase the growth of the stem which led to a corresponding increase in the size of the root.[54] Miller[55] knew of shoots supported to a height of 10ft but thought that the cost of such supports was not economic. The reason was to allow the sun to get to both sides of the root. This was more cheaply achieved by turning the stalks over from one side to the other. In some Caucasian plantations it was not considered desirable to increase the size of the root, as it could reduce the dye concentration.[56]

Fourth year care

Except for careful watering, no extensive care was required during the fourth year. No further weeding was needed as the plants were strong enough to survive. During August, the seeds were gathered, but in autumn it was not necessary to ridge-up an additional layer of soil, as the roots would be extracted at the beginning of the fifth year. The purpose of adding layers of soil was to maximise the length of the taproots, which could in turn decrease the thickness of the side roots. The addition of layers of soil did not improve the quality of the dyeing agent in the roots.[57] In Derbent this practice was called *karamet*.

Fifth year care

Though there was considerable debate, Shtorkh and others thought that this was the best year to extract the roots from the soil, from autumn till spring. Experienced contract labourers came down from their mountain villages, who specialised in this delicate, important operation.

However, adverse market fluctuations meant that some farmers were not able to sell their roots at a profit, and so left them in the soil for yet another year. In autumn the farmers did not ridge-up the roots. Only one watering was required during the next year to increase the weight of the roots and consequently the profit per plant.[58]

Diseases & blights

The following were the more common afflictions of madder:

1. Over-wet soil caused the stalk and leaves to turn pale green.

2. The fungus *Rhizoctonia rubiae* spread like fire from root to root and destroyed the roots. The fungus turned the plant yellow at its extremities before killing it. The fungus usually appeared during the second year and killed plants during the fourth year. The fungus seemed to be independent of soil type as it was found in all soils.

3. Insects seemed to have no interest in madder. Only once in Belgium was madder selectively eaten by yellow and black caterpillars. The black ones ate the tender young shoots while the yellow ones solely consumed the roots. To save the madder, tastier potatoes were planted between the madder plants.

Moles and field mice could eat madder but they preferred insects and caterpillars so their presence was symbiotic.[59]

4. Harald Böhmer found that modern Turkish sheep and goats liked to eat madder[60] and in 1624 George Bedford's madder was prized by his neighbours 24 rooting swine.[61]

5. Perhaps the worst disease affected the farmer and that was malaria. Madder grew very well in marshy areas — the malaria from Romney Marsh which afflicted George Bedford in 1624 was worse than the attack of the pigs.

Harvest

There was endless discussion about when to extract the roots, with contrary views expressed within each country. There were three inter-linked puzzles. Which year's roots contained the best dyestuff, by quantity and quality? What was the best economic period for the farmer? What was the risk of various blights? Little scientific comparison could be achieved as any two plants were never sufficiently similar.

In 1624 Bedford boasted of the "bigness and fatness" of his root crop, which he had never seen in Zeeland for "colour and goodness." He confirmed that, unsurprisingly, the Dutch did experiment with different growth periods by his comparisons with Dutch roots which were one, two, three and four years old.

Attractions of the younger root

In Flanders madder roots were even extracted after a single year, when they contained but a small amount of pale red dyestuff. Cardon quoted a modern experiment that demonstrated that a one-year root only contained a quarter of the dyestuff of a three-year root.[62] In Germany one-year-old madder even had a name, *rothe*. Obviously one-year madder gave a quicker financial return, but it was a significantly lower return than that from the older roots. However, one-year-old roots were still worth selling and it was much easier to rotate the plantation crop.

Flachat contrasted the differing practices in Zeeland and Flanders. He thought that the eighteen-month harvest in Flanders was too early, resulting in a loss of quality and that the two to three years allowed in Zeeland was better. The Zeeland roots were dug up with a spade and fork and the rejects were replanted upright.[63] Cardon confirmed that in the Midi in France three-year-old roots were harvested. In Germany three, four or five-year-old madder was called *krap* (usually taken to mean 'powdered ground dried roots'). Karpov added that while four years' growth was considered optimal, it was also possible to extract madder roots after one or two years, but they contained inferior dyeing agent.[64] Farmers both in Derbent and other Oriental countries would sometimes leave the roots in for a fifth year, while in Asia Minor, they did not extract the roots until the sixth year. The marginal gain in weight of the roots supposedly increased the quantity of dyestuff. According to Wulff, in Persia roots between two and seven years old[65] were dug up in autumn after the leaves had fallen. The older the plant the stronger the dye. The seven-year dyestuff was of a deep purplish colour while the younger plant gave a terracotta-red colour.[66]

In Holland the shoot planting method cut down the time that the field was tied to madder cultivation to two years. When there was enough land available, it was possible to leave madder plants in the field for three years or more. Shtorkh thought that in regions where plantation land was expensive it was relatively more profitable to extract the roots after three years and plant a rotational crop. In some regions of France, the farmers left the plants in the soil for three years and started to extract the roots in the autumn or beginning of the fourth year.[67]

In addition to the diseases noted above, there was the constant risk of destruction of the crop from a variety of threats. Many Caucasian farmers agreed that if madder had been frost-bitten by winter frosts or during a cold wet spring, it was better to extract the roots during the second year. Otherwise the plants might not regain their strength and perish during the following winter. In Europe, three to four-year-old plants were more vulnerable to weather fluctuations than younger plants and four to five-year-old plants could be killed more readily by winter frosts. In addition, the farmer was obliged sometimes to dig up the roots earlier to anticipate the incubating fungal infection, described above. Schaefer remarked dramatically that in Holland within the Onrust Polder, one of the marshy areas reclaimed from the sea, the plant was only allowed to remain in the ground for two years. This prevented the roots from penetrating the soil to reach the subterranean level of the sea, which would have suddenly flooded in.[68]

With so many different factors involved, it was impossible to recommend the year in which it was best to extract the roots. Financially Shtorkh's calculation seemed to show that one-and-a-half year shoots were the best bet (see chapter 6).

Root extraction

The farmers usually started digging up the roots in late October. During the previous three to five months the October root had become much thicker and more juicy. Farmers in Derbent, Kouba and Baku applied this logic and left the roots in the soil for another winter to delay extraction until the following March and April. However, if the weather continued to be nasty, this could turn into an expensive operation. In England, the plants were raised in September.[69]

Before the roots could be extracted the stalks had to be cut, because after extraction cutting was lengthy and so more expensive, the same as in England. When madder was planted in rows it was more economical for the farmer to plough along the rows to expose a thick layer of soil which contained the roots, even though some roots could be left in the soil, especially friable sandy soils where the roots could

Dutch specialist spade for digging up madder roots, A. G. Kästner, Hamburg, 1757 (Schaefer, CIBA Review)

grow extremely long. But it was evidently cheaper to avoid paying labourers to shovel. Admittedly, when madder was planted in beds, shovels were more convenient to use. After the roots had been extracted, the soil was replaced ready for sowing.[70]

The Ministry thought that extraction of madder roots started in February and continued until May. Farmers used ordinary shovels or a local implement called *kizgiria*. Some farmers would set their entire family to work and others would hire two or three labourers as additional help. Experienced labourers, called *bel'gi*, would use a shovel to turn over the thick layer of soil which contained the roots, progressing along the row of plants. They were closely followed by boys who wielded slightly-curved wooden sticks to crush the hard lumps of soil lodged in the roots. The cleaned roots were then placed on adjacent cloths. The grassy tops of the plants were stacked separately in heaps and later burnt.

Miller preferred the deep-digging method. A trench was dug alongside the row of roots, 2ft broad and "two spits and two shovelings or two spades deep." The trench lessened damage to the roots and exposed more root and was fine preparation for the next crop. One digger worked with two or three extractors.[71]

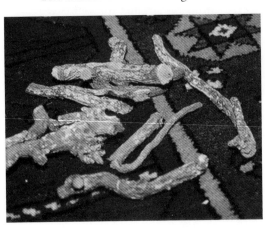

Thick madder roots from Ayvacık in western Anatolia, DOBAG Project (photo June Anderson)

Depending on the thickness of the root's beard, it could be more convenient to cut off only the side-roots. In the Kouba district and near Derbent some farmers took up the Dutch method of cutting only the side-roots and leaving the tap root of the madder plant in the soil for up to 12 years. The risk was that the slightest damage to the tap root would kill the plant. This method was called *'kaliam'* perhaps from the Dutch *keeme*,

Dutch specialist labourers extracting roots in October 1913 in Sirjansland in Schouwen-Duiveland (ack. D. A. Zoethout; Priester)

meaning 'shoots', or the Persian *kalam* meaning 'pen'. In larger farms, the plantation would be divided into one third for *kaliam* and two thirds for normal extraction. *Kaliam* brought in a quicker and longer income because harvesting selected roots began in the third year. The method of care was the same as before which made it managable to look after a mixed plantation.

Rhind was alone in saying that before drying the roots, the French divided the tap roots from the side shoots, as the tap roots when not too large were considered best.[72] In Derbent, the roots were extracted early in the fifth year during April to fit in with a ruinous market schedule. Merchants sailed to Derbent and were not willing to sail back to Astrakhan later than June to avoid bad weather. So the crop had to be sold then and there for cash. Extraction took two months which meant that steaming and drying had to take place in May. However it was well known that the roots which were extracted the following September were of far superior quality. A solution was found through building grinding mills locally. The production of storable powder allowed the farmer to sell direct from the plantation area in autumn.[73]

In Schouwen, it was forbidden to dig up roots before September 1st. At daybreak a ritual race began. The digger who delivered the first cart-load to the stove won a prize of a golden *rider* or three *ducats*.

Madder yields per hectare

The usual proviso when yields were given was that yield depended on care and watering during growth, but especially on the condition of the soil. It was confusing that yields were given as weights either of fresh or dried roots where the conversion rate was not consistent. In some areas of Derbent and Kouba district, the yield of (dried) roots could reach 120 to 150 poods per hectare. Excluding the portion left for *kaliam*, the average yield was 100 poods

(1,600kg). More recent plantations in Kurinsk district where the soil was still rich and fertile gave comparable yields between 150 to 200 poods per hectare, which was higher than Shtorkh's figure. Madder root yields per hectare varied from plantation to plantation:

Caucasian estates	450 poods undried
Gasparen	720p
Metzger	625p
Sprengel	1,080p
Pabet	450p
Einel	750p
Reider	680p
Betsgold	1,560p
Gartuch	580p
Belgian estates	430p
Algerian (Shir, Constantin)	1,500p
Average crop of above:	803p or in dried form 160p

Count Gasparen's yields for undried roots varied from 585 poods from unfertilised, dry soil to 1,360 poods from fertilised, rich soil. The French record yield was 1,925 poods (385 poods dried) and the Dutch record from the island of Schouwen was 2,095 poods (419 poods dried). Miller's calculation for Schouwen was a more average year's upper 227 poods dried per hectare, but when grown in 'light' soil, it decreased to less than a half.[74] While these average yields assumed good weather, it was still possible to achieve average undried yields of 500 poods under variable conditions. One-year-old madder roots yielded a lower 320 poods undried of less fast yellow-red dyestuff.

In England the average dried yield was lower at between a half and one ton per acre. That is 70 to 140 poods per hectare.[75] The supreme prize of £10 from the Society of Arts went to John Crow at Faversham in Kent who in 1777 achieved a yield of 18cwt 2qrs 18lbs from an acre. A tithe dispute in 1680 in the Isle of Ely had shown that 10 cwt per acre was considered a good yield, which looks lower than elsewhere.[76]

Rhind described an experiment near Tours, which yielded 496 poods of fresh roots per hectare though a half to three-quarters of the yield was more usual.[77] Variation in drying yields as described in chapter 6 made yield comparisons yet more misleading. In addition, yields did not include the ancillary cultivation of grass for hay and seeds which required special expertise too.

Harvesting madder grass

There were differing ideas as to the effects on the roots of cutting the grass. While rotten stalks retarded growth, Miller warned that cutting the stalks in summer reduced root size by a third. Shtorkh thought that in the Caucasus it appeared to have no effect. Schaefer in contradiction wrote that in France the tops of the plants were cut three times during the course of the third (I think) year which greatly increased the growth and the weight of the roots.[78]

Madder stalks and leaves had equal nutritional value to lucerne (purple medick, *medicago sativa*, resembling clover, cultivated for fodder, first mentioned in 1626, often as *la lucerne* in 17th- and 18th-century agricultural books) and were considered to make first-class cattle fodder. Starting in June of the second year, the stalks and leaves would be cut two or three times during the summer depending on their rate of growth.

As soon as the stalks were cut, the roots had to be covered with soil to protect them from sunlight. The 'grass' could be fed direct to animals or dried into hay. In a thirty-month growing period, it was possible to produce 100 poods of dried roots and 150 poods of hay per hectare. Cows fed on madder stalks produced a yellow shade of milk and their bones became red[79] (see chapter 4) or according to Schaefer,[80] a reddish shade of milk and a yellow tinge to butter — all harmless effects. Schaefer also noted that the colouring action became more pronounced when roots were mixed with the feed.

Harvesting madder seeds

Instead of harvesting madder 'grass', the farmer could wait until the seeds appeared. Some farmers would select the most vigorous plants and plant them out separately to gather the best seeds. They then cut off most of the stalks, leaving the best four or five, so that all the nutrition would be concentrated in those stalks. As the stalks grew they were supported vertically by wooden sticks stuck in the soil. When the seeds were ripe, the farmer cut off the entire stalks and dried them so that their seeds were easy to gather.[81]

In Derbent, madder plants produced significant quantities of seed during the second and third years, whereas in France the black seeds were gathered at the end of the second year.[82] Flowers appeared in June and seeds from the end of July and August.

When the seeds turned violet-black they were ready to be gathered. The stalks were cut at the base of the plant with a sickle and then left to dry on the rows, so the seed pods could be easily detached from the stem. The stalks were then threshed and burnt. The seeds were dried and put into sacks. It was important to harvest the seeds before they dropped to the ground as ripe seeds were only lightly attached to the stalks.[83] Both too much rain or too long drought could result in damage or destruction of the seeds, but more perilous were the combination of devouring locusts and the south winds which easily broke the stalks.

A normal yield of madder seeds doubled the weight of seeds sown. There was much variation in weight for a crop of seeds. The crop could be as high as 45 poods per hectare or as low as nothing. A rough average was about 18 poods per hectare. The best seeds were of the same size, rounded and black. A test which showed that a seed was good for sowing was if a white inside was revealed when the seed was cut in two.

Though it was possible to buy a pound of seeds for 25 kopeks direct from a farmer in the south of France, a foreign seed dealer's price in Russia was four or five times as much. In 1846 there was a very poor crop of seeds and the price soared to 2 roubles per pound. It was much cheaper to buy Russian seeds at 12.5 kopeks per pound. The price varied in other years. Some citizens of Alexandrov (some 60 miles by rail north-east of Moscow) paid 7 roubles for a pood of seeds, or 20 kopeks per pound in 1847, 1848 and 1851. But there was a good living to be made from growing seeds. A farmer could plant these Russian seeds and harvest 15 poods of seed per hectare, making an income of 150 roubles in two years.

6

The farmer's rewards, banks & bankruptcy

The farmer & the accountant

EVERY AUTHOR who has written about madder became convinced that it was one of the most profitable crops known. The variety of calculations set out below may have more relevance to agricultural and social conditions than financial disciplines. The accounts bear witness to the popularity and ingenuity of different methods used in the Caucasus, France, Holland and England. Most methods separate cultivation from the heavy capital requirements of the drying, crushing and grinding processes. Paul Rix, of Deloitte & Touche's agricultural accountancy division, appropriately based in Cambridge, kindly sent me a modern bench-marking method for a parallel crop — asparagus — which has a 12-year life. The problem is to assess crop efficiency in terms of both return per acre and return on capital.

But the available information is incomplete. While the calculations enable one to admire the size of surplus, they all leave out a formal balance sheet, listing fixed assets, current assets, short-term liabilities and borrowings, and long-term loans. The price of land is irregularly mentioned, as is the rent and the tithe, a fixed tax on production rather than consumption. The farmer and his family's work are also thrown in at a notional zero worth. So, it is often not possible to convert a surplus figure, which is a sort of gross profit margin, into a directly comparable net profit. Double entry bookkeeping may have been invented by the ancient Romans, but highly profitable businesses were reticent about publishing full accounts until this century.

Rix also showed how start-up expenses for asparagus are split up or amortised into 12 equal charges over the 12 years of the crop. While this is correct and fair, the madder grower was most concerned with cash flow or rather the lack of it. He had to take the start-up costs on the nose, as the money was spent, and there was no direct income from the roots for two or three years, until extraction. Some intermediate income could be generated by selling slips, seeds and rotational crops or other crops planted between individual madder plants.

Return per unit area, usually per hectare or acre is the traditional agricultural reckoning method. In contrast, with the Caucasian figures, I have attempted to calculate a return on capital to decide which method of cultivation and cropping is 'best'. These calculations bring into focus the problem of dealing with loans. Rix would correctly remove the loan and interest from the reckoning, and include land values to give the owner-occupier's capital. This is just one method of investment appraisal and is one which he would use to compare a number of farms as it puts them on a 'level playing field'.

The modern banking practice of 'prudent' lending judges, through long and hard experience, that lending up to 60 per cent of net asset value is 'safe'. In previous centuries, the higher risk was accompanied by higher and increasing interest rates. As can be seen in our time, 'prudent' lending does not always protect banks (such as London & County) from failing when their security, such as property, drops in market value. There have been several madder price slumps too (see chapter 15). Hungry modern banks also lend against stock and 'work-in-progress' and this was also the case with madder-banking. The difference is that stocks are usually sold in a few weeks and ongoing capital projects customarily receive quarterly stage payments, neither of which was the case with madder.

So, it can be appreciated that the speculative madder adventurer-farmer — if he was a good talker — could have very little of his own money involved and achieve an astronomic return on it. For this reason, I have calculated the returns on total capital employed, which would have been of more relevance to a potential lender.

There seem to be several reasons why the English never exploited madder cultivation to the same extent as Holland, France, Ottoman Turkey or the Caucasus, in spite of being a major consumer from the 18th century. There was the short-term attitude of the English venturer, which is still evident in today's 'venture' capitalism. This was reflected in the English preference for the manufacture of printed textiles for a captive empire market, rather than the cultivation of the upstream dyestuff, when there were several sources of supply. Another reason was the lack of skilled labour in England coupled with the increase in wages from the 1730s as English industrialisation took labour away from the land. As early as 1731 Jethro Tull published his *New Horse-Houghing Husbandry*, introducing his labour-saving seed-drill and horse-hoe inventions in a fury at his labourers' increased wage demands and resistance to new methods.[1] The skills necessary for madder cultivation also required years of training and continuity of labour, which was a long-term investment in an unreliable work-force. Thirdly, the lack of expertise of farmers recently converted to madder-growing and an unskilled work force meant that English yields were significantly lower than elsewhere, as was shown above.[2]

Profit & loss farm accounts

Karpov's tale: some quick-rouble entrepreneurs take out a high-interest loan to start a plantation and ask for another loan in the second year, then another and so on. When they extract the roots in the fourth year, they find them poor and unfit for sale and the result is bankruptcy and ruin. It was always thus.

Our short historical review of available accounts of madder-farmers starts in 1622 with Bedford's wondrous exponential projections for cultivation in England based on his Dutch experiences. Next an English tithe dispute provided figures applicable to Micawberesque profit and ruin on either side of the halving of the Dutch benchmark price for madder in 1676. By the 1730s the optimistic Miller was back with Dutch figures to prove that madder could be grown profitably in England. But in 1765 the continuing tithe, joined with insufficient government assistance, failed to cheer up the grumbling English pamphleteer. He used his numbers both to show how profitable cultivation could be, while at the same time prophesying doom when madder-growing became consequently more popular and prices dropped.

The Russian quantification of doubtless dissembled secret Caucasian calculations must have required much ingenuity. Shtorkh's earliest figures of 1833 from Derbent (appendix 6.1, page 321) give expenses only. At 109 roubles for a four-year-crop from seeds the expenses per hectare are about a third of his more detailed figures from the 1850s, though in line with Karpov's contemporaneous four-year figure of 137 roubles — both excluded allowances for manuring (appendix 6.2, page 321). Shtorkh's contribution was to demonstrate the best method of cultivation by like-for-like comparisons of five methods of growing madder. Eighteen-month shoot cultivation came a long first against six-month shoots and three-year seed crops from virgin, loose and tough soils. Two other accounts of further methods were unable to match the winner. The Ministry's five-year seed crop (appendix 6.3, page 322) was a long way behind Karpov's surely over-optimistic four-year seed crop.

The Dutch had made similar calculations centuries before and the figures for cultivation of shoots in Zeeland in 1690 and in Schouwen in 1817 and 1843 complete a more regular timespan with Bedford, Miller, the pamphleteer and the Russians (see appendix 6.4, page 324).

Bedford's frightening experience with the Dutch, who were unenthusiastic towards his clandestine purchase of shoots and young roots for replanting, must have been repeated in Derbent. There the active market was in questionable quality seeds rather than inspectable shoots. A wise grower would use his own slips, and his own seeds. There was a more formal government prohibition on the sale of shoots in Breslau in 1737 to protect local growers.[3]

*George Bedford's undated accounts of expenses of Netherlands journeys, c. 1623
(ack. Jervaise Herriard Coll., Hants Public Record Office)*

The farmer's rewards, banks & bankruptcy

A. The first calculation must be the grandmother of pyramid selling schemes:. Young George Bedford's figures from Holland for an English project, February 1622:[4]

> Secretly buying a *mett, mete* or *meate* of one-year-old madder roots for 2 acres, which produced enough slips in the following spring to plant a further 4 acres. One-year roots produce the same slips as older roots and are therefore relatively cheap at £14
>
> Secretly buying a mett of keeme shoots to plant 4 acres which the next year will plant out to 16 leaving the 4 acres still good, £ 7
>
> Income:
> A *mett* of three-year-old roots digged up £30-£40
>
> Expenses:
> All cultivation expenses less than £5 per acre

Bedford omitted the further more exciting calculation in his letter:

> 1 *mett* of roots for 2 acres = 6 acres after one year, and = 18 acres after two years
> In year 2, 2 acres (= 1 *mett*) can be harvested, against £14 purchase and £10 cultivation expenses, making a surplus of £6-£16
> In year 3, 4 more acres (= 2 *mett*) can be harvested, against £20 cultivation expenses making a further surplus of £40-£60
> In year 4, 12 more acres (= 6 mett) can be harvested, against £60 cultivation expenses making a further surplus of £120-£180

and so on — in exponential progression, only subject to suitable land being available.

B. Next, English 1660s-70s figures per acre, gathered in connection with tithe disputes, providing a glimpse of bankruptcy:[5]

Expenditure per acre:	
Cultivation costs	£12 to £15
Stoving and drying	£ 2 to £3
Total expenditure	£14 to £18
Income	
A good crop of 10cwt per acre	£32
Surplus	£18 to £14
Income, after the crash of 1676	£16
Surplus	£ 2 to £ 2 loss

C. The authoritative and optimistic Philip Miller's 1730s figures for Schouwen, to encourage English cultivation, given in mixed currencies (see Glossary):

First year expenses per *gemet* — 4100 sq m:

1.1 Buying shoots	15-20 Glrs	£3 11d Flemish
1.2 Planting; 6 planters, 2 rakers @1 Glr/ day		
5-6 'carpers' women or		
boy shoot-pluckers @ 2 Sch/ day	16-20 Glrs	
1.3 Weeding		£2 Flemish
1.4 Ridging-up soil by plough:		
ploughing	2.5 Glrs	
levelling	1.5 Glrs	
or ridging-up by spade	8-10 Glrs	

Second year expenses:

2.1 Weeding	3 Sch
2.2 Ridging-up soil by plough:	
ploughing	2.5 Glrs
levelling	1.5 Glrs
or ridging-up by spade	8-10 Glrs

Third year expenses:

3.1 Extraction, specialists @ 5 sch/ day	36-100 Glrs	
Extraction in 'light' land		£9-10 Flemish
3.2 Drying roots		
mull	2 Glrs/ cwt	
better grades	3 Glrs/ cwt	
3.3 Pounding roots		
mull	15/- per cwt English	

D. 'Calculation of the Expence of planting One Acre with Madder, being the lowest Estimate yet Obtained from the different Planters', from the anonymous English pamphlet of 1765.

To make government look more kindly on the grower who is not shown to be doing too well:

Expenditure:

1. If after turnips, when the Ground is supposed in good heart and clean, two Ploughings, 18 inches deep and harrowing sufficient   £2 2s 0p
2. 12,000 Plants sufficient though 20,000 recommended @ 10s a thousand
    £6 0s 0p

3. Planting   £0 12s 0p

4. Six times hoeing the Crop in the Three Years	£2 0s 0p
5. Pronging and gathering up the Crop at a Medium	£9 0s 0p
6. Three Years Rent, at a Medium throughout the Kingdom for such land @ 30s	£4 10s 0p
Total expenditure:	£24 4s 0p

Income:

A good crop will produce 8 tons of green roots which will dry to 1 ton. The Price now asked by the Planters, from £50 to £60 per ton, dried and cleaned and fit for manufacture. Mr George Rutt, the present only Manufacturer (ie the processor of dried roots), accounted that the Plantations have rendered from, on

an Average	£40 to £45 per acre.
Surplus per acre	£15 16s to £20 16s
Less tithe of 5s per annum per acre	£ 0 15s
Net surplus	£15 1s to £20 1s
Annual surplus	20.7% to 27.6%
If the price of madder halved the farmers faced ruin with losses of	£4 4s to £2 6s

"NB: The present high price is owing to the small quantity now cultivated here and that the Relief expected would encourage more cultivation and result in a reduction in prices."

E. The Russian figures glossed over quality control by the farmer and market fluctuations which were obviously beyond his control. They did attempt to answer the questions of optimal growth, depending on harvest method and timing and whether to harvest seeds for resale or stalks for cattle fodder.

Nowadays, a good computer model could provide a multi-factor solution optimiser, but when this was written in 1860 calculations were cruder. All attempts to measure the various quantities and the attempt at scientific analysis must be applauded. It was a good start.

The purpose was to encourage Russian peasant farmers to become smallholder madder producers, alongside continuing subsistence farming. As they mainly grew hemp, it was demonstrably more profitable to switch to madder. With a steady supply of manure and the leisure to attend to watering and weeding, it was calculated that a quarter of a hectare plot was optimal. This small-scale production could bring in relatively high annual income of 45 roubles to a peasant family.

This assumed the ability to grow good quality madder and to collect and sell it at market. That in turn implied technical training, literacy and a co-operative selling organisation which was both utopian and futuristic in 1860.

Shtorkh's comparative Caucasian figures, 1850s:

1.   Planting seeds for three-year yields

If the soil is loose and friable, madder roots can reach 70cm in length.
If the soil is tough, madder roots can only reach 50cm in length.

Soil type:	Loose		Tough	Virgin
First year expenses				
1.1 First ploughing; @ 1r/day	10.00r		30.00r	60.00r
1.2 Second ploughing	1.00r		2.00r	2.00r
1.3 Harrowing; @ 1r/day	0.50r		1.00r	1.00r
1.4 Delivery of manure	7.00r		7.00r	-
1.5 Spreading manure; 4 women				
@ 20k/day	0.80r		0.80r	-
1.6 Harrowing manure into soil; 10 days	10.00r		10.00r	-
1.7 Sowing; 8 men @ 50k/day,				
4 women @ 20k	4.80r		4.80r	4.80r
1.8 5.5 poods seed @ 5r/pood	27.50r	4.5p	22.50r	22.50r
1.9 Hand weeding x 3	30.00r	x 2	20.00r	20.00r
1.10 Ridging-up soil x 3	9.00r	x 2	6.00r	4.00r
1.11 Autumn ridging-up soil; @1r/day	10.00r		6.00r	5.00r
1.12 4,000 poods of manure @ 2k/pood	80.00r		80.00r	-
Subtotal	186r		190r	124r
Second year expenses				
2.1 10% interest on loan for				
first year exp	18.56r		19.00r	12.43r
2.2 Hand weeding x 2	20.00r	x 1	10.00r	10.00r
2.3 Ridging-up soil x 2	6.00r	x 1	3.00r	2.00r
2.4 Cutting grass	5.00r		5.00r	5.00r
2.5 Autumnal ridging-up soil	5.00r		6.00r	5.00r
Subtotal	55r		43r	34r
Third year expenses				
3.1 Interest on loan	24.00r		23.30r	15.87r
3.2 Cutting grass	5.00r		4.00r	5.00r
3.3 Extraction of roots	35.00r		45.00r	25.00r
3.4 Drying roots	25.00r		25.00r	25.00r
Subtotal	89r		98r	71r
Total	329r		331r	240r

2. Planting shoots for 18-month and 6-month yields

Period		18-month	6-month
First year expenses			
1.1	First ploughing; @ 1r/day	10.00r	10.00r
1.2	Second ploughing	1.00r	2.00r
1.3	Harrowing; @ 1r/day	0.50r	1.00r
1.4	Delivery of manure	7.00r	3.60r
1.5	Spreading manure; 4 women @ 20k/day	0.80r	0.40r
1.6	Harrowing manure into soil; 10 days	10.00r	6.00r
1.7	145,000 madder shoots	50.00r	50.00r
1.8	Planting shoots	10.00r	22.50r
1.9	Hand weeding x 3	30.00r	30.00r
1.10	Ridging-up soil x 3	6.00r	6.00r
1.11	Autumnal ridging-up	5.00r	-
1.12	3,500 poods of manure @ 2k/pood	70.00r	40.00r
1.13	Extraction of roots	-	15.00r
1.14	Drying roots	-	15.00r
Subtotal		200r	181r

Second year expenses			
2.1	10% interest on loan for first year exp	20.03r	
2.2	Hand weeding x 2	20.00r	
2.3	Ridging-up soil x 2	4.00r	
2.4	Cutting grass	5.00r	
2.5	Extraction of roots	35.00r	
2.6	Drying roots	25.00r	
Subtotal		109r	

| Total | | 309r | 181r |

Income

1 Seed method: Income in 3rd year

Soil type		Loose	Tough		Virgin
Hay	300p @ 15k/pood	45r	45r		45r
Dried roots	140p @ 5r/pood	700r	700r	120p	600r
Total		745r	745r		645r
% profit		126%	125%		169%
annualised		42%	42%		58%

2 Shoot method:	Income in 18 months		6 months		
Hay	200p	30r	60p		9r
Dried roots	140p	700r	55p		220r
Total		730r			229r
% profit	136%			27%	
annualised	96%			54%	

It could be more profitable not to cut the hay, but to harvest the seeds instead. In one year a hectare could produce 15 poods; seeds sold @ 5r/pood (?net of harvesting expenses which are relatively low); so two years' seeds could sell for 150r compared to 45r for hay.

Surplus and annual rate of return in per cent

1   Seed method

Soil type	*Loose*	*Tough*	*Virgin*
Average capital employed per annum = year 1 + year 2 + year 3 / 3 (ACE)			
ACE	252r	251r	174r
Surplus - hay	416r - 55%	414r - 50%	405r - 78%
Surplus - seeds	521r - 69%	519r - 69%	510r - 98%

2 Shoot method:	18-month	6-month
ACE	254r	181r
Surplus - hay	421r - 110%	48r - 53%
Surplus - seeds	466r - 122%	n.a.

Shtorkh averaged out all surpluses, the farmers' measure. I have added the bankers' measure of the annual percentage return on the average investment (assuming that the value of the land is written off). The 'average capital employed' is used because increasing amounts of capital are borrowed each year, for the whole year, to pay expenses incurred. Accordingly, the average capital employed was a lower figure than the total capital invested for year three, which means that the rate of return on ACE was higher. Both bankers' and farmers' reckonings agreed that the most profitable method was to grow shoots for 18 months.

This seems reasonable if the risks of seed planting, disease and future market fluctuations over a three-year period are equal or relatively higher than the risks of shoot planting, disease and future market fluctuations in the shorter eighteen and six-month periods.

If the availability of bank lending was also considered, more virgin land could be developed for the same loan. However there was a greater probability of a credit squeeze over the three-year period than the 18-month or six-month periods. Calling in loans before the end of a growing period and taking the crop as security when the farmer could not pay has always been a profitable venture for a bank, especially if the banker had prior knowledge of a forthcoming increase in the crop value. This nasty trick is still practised in some Mediterranean countries on property developments.

Shtorkh also appears to have his timing of interest payments a year late and to have ignored the final interest payment completely, whether for the third year for the seed method or for the second year for the shoot method. This would have the effect of reducing the seed method surpluses by about seven per cent and the shoot method surpluses by about the same amount. The further effect was to reduce all the ACE returns by about two per cent, which was another of the many factors in the risk assessment between cultivation of madder, rye and wheat.

If it is assumed that the farmer only had a fixed area of land for growing madder and was in the business for a number of years, then it is also significant to know how exhausted the land became over a period of several re-plantings, using the different methods. As we have seen in chapter 5, exhaustion happened gradually, year by year, and took two forms both of which affected his income. Firstly, the weight of roots harvested decreased and secondly, the quality or strength of the dyestuff diminished. This meant that every six to twelve years the field had to be left fallow or the crop rotated. There was an opportunity cost lost with the former method which may however have been unavoidable. Also, did the seed methods exhaust the soil more than the shoot methods and was virgin soil more resilient than enriched soil?

Shtorkh with his persistent averaging, calculated that the average annual income per hectare from madder was 134r which he compared favourably with 20r for rye and 30r for wheat. But the capital invested (ACE), the risks of damage during growth and the risk of the banker's trick must have been lower for rye or wheat, which obscures his comparison.

When giving the cost per pood of dried madder roots to the farmer Shtorkh omitted to mention that six-month roots did not contain as high quality dyestuff as the others and virgin soil probably produced the best quality dyestuff. This was significant if the market price dropped for various grades of root. There seemed to be a greater safety margin in virgin or six-month roots:

1. Seed method; soil type:	Loose	2.35r/ pood
	Tough	2.37r
	Virgin	2.00r
2. Shoot method:	18-month	2.79r
	6-month	0.71r

If we look at price-quality spreads for Caucasian madder between 1846-1856, it seems that significant amounts ranged in price from top quality at 6.00r to bottom quality at 3.00r, which supported the above remarks about percentage safety margins.

The Ministry figures (appendix 6.3, page 322) in the 1850s for five-year yields from seed on virgin soil and two-year yields from shoots showed profits of 300r per hectare for five-year roots from seed, equivalent to 75 per cent or a meagre 15 per cent annually and 134r per hectare for two-year shoots equivalent to 111 per cent or a better 56 per cent annually. Again the two-year shoots were the best earners by far, with the margins dangerously low on the seed crop.

The Ministry made a further proviso. The five-year net profit would only be gained by farmers who were landowners with sufficient capital. Those who rented land and borrowed from the bank would have a much lower income. Average rental for one hectare in Kouba district was 8r per annum or 40r for the five-year period. Average annual interest on a bank loan could be 18 per cent rising to 24 per cent at harvest time. If we consider the lowest interest rate to be 12 per cent, the total interest over the five year period was 100r. So the net profit for a tenant without capital was reduced to 124r or 27r per annum per hectare. As a large number of farmers had little capital and would make the lower profit, they were hit relatively harder by falls in the market price. As Shtorkh explained, "it is easy to understand why the *kaliam* method is so popular with the farmers of the area near the Caspian Sea. The same average figures could apply to the Derbent region."

In contrast, Karpov's figures (appendix 6.2, page 321) in the 1850s for four-year yield from seed seem too good. The surplus was 1200r per hectare or 307 per cent profit or 77 per cent annual profit. His yield was far higher than the Ministry, 180 poods compared to 80 poods plus seeds from shoots or 100 poods from seeds. The reason was partly because he was using better seeds and partly better land as the annual rent was 24r per hectare compared to 8r quoted by the Ministry. His labour costs were far cheaper as well, for example extraction cost him 90r and the Ministry 170r. He may have been given high figures or had found favourable local conditions.

Financial roundabouts

Return on capital is a bankers' measure. In general, farmers preferred to measure return per acre. When land was plentiful and therefore of little value and labour was scarce, the measure of success was the return per man-day's work.[6] However Deloitte's, as agricultural accountants, "use return per acre only when bench-marking an ongoing business. They would not use return per acre in isolation to appraise an investment and would not advise clients to do so either. Return ratios alone are not adequate to appraise projects — insufficient cash-flows are what causes bankruptcy. A project may have excellent ratios but if there is no cash, the business will fail."

Because madder had to be rotated with other crops such as wheat or rapeseed, it might have been more meaningful to give average returns over a cycle of say seven years, which is what the sophisticated Dutch growers were doing and examples of their calculations during the 1820s are given in appendix 5.1 (page 320). But in reality farmers must make a return every year. Throughout history, the risks and rewards of agriculture, to paraphrase Thirsk, attracted adventurers who with their family and friends borrowed on a shoestring to make the most of a fleeting chance.[7]

7

The purer the colour:
ground krap and garancine

Dealing with the fat roots

PROCESSING THE extracted roots was no simpler than their cultivation. Steaming, drying and crushing processes varied from country to country with Holland as ever providing the technical expertise, though the more outdoor Caucasian methods produced a better dried root. Nor did the European dyestuff producer rest after the powder had been prepared. Different methods were devised to purify and concentrate the powder. These developments eventually led to the manufacture of the top quality concentrate garancine.

Schaefer reckoned the dye-bearing root to be approximately the same size as a quill with many branches. The Persian roots used by Winsor & Newton were slightly larger, whilst the small bundle of wild roots from the banks of the river Terek which I bought in Makhachkala in Daghestan in 1994 were pen-sized — somewhat fatter. Grierson had them up to 3cm in diameter and Böhmer's Anatolian roots look older and bigger too.[1]

Field steaming

Before drying the roots were improved by steaming. The roots contained sugars and resins which caused internal fermentation, which helped convert the original yellow dyestuff into the desired crimson. This property was exploited by the Caucasian farmers who steamed their roots outdoors in special underground pits for ten to twelve hours to obtain the best possible colour from the roots. The yellow colour of the raw roots also changed to dark red during steaming. The appearance of the tap root when cut was similar to a pale-yellow carrot. After twelve hours' steaming, its colour changed to dark-cherry red. A Micmac-style test of excellence of dyestuff was to chew the root, spit and see the dark-red colour of saliva (see chapter 17). Unsteamed roots, dried naturally, would keep the yellow colour of fresh roots.

To make his oven, the farmer would dig a truncated conical hole, with a smaller diameter at the bottom than the top, in the field or near the shed. This hole was called *tondyr* (possibly the same word as *tandir*, the local bread oven), with a depth of 175 to 213cm. Another, larger trapezoid shaped pit was about 6m long, 54cm wide at the top and 35cm at the base. The walls were lined with clay, sometimes supported by an internal wall of bricks or stones — presumably the yellow Derbent clunch. Two batches of roots could be steamed in a day. The entire steaming process was carried out by highly paid specialists. While the wood was burning inside the pit, the madder roots were heaped beside the opening in a pile up to 2m high, and generously sprinkled with water.

Bundle of roots bought by the author in Market No2 in Makhachkala (Author's photo)

Dry wooden twigs, branches and trunks were burnt inside the oven until the outer walls turned white with heat. This meant that the internal temperature was right for steaming. Then as many roots as possible were put into the oven and pressed down underfoot and the remaining roots were heaped directly over the opening in a one-metre-high pile.

The pile was again abundantly watered and covered with five or six layers of thick blanket, pressed felt or home-made carpets to keep the steam inside. Steaming reduced the volume of the roots to a third. After steaming the roots were taken out of the pit with a pitch fork. The oven was then heated up again for the next batch of roots.

Drying & shrinkage

The roots were only dried after steaming. The three methods of drying were in sunlight, in the shade or in special sheds. "The more bitter the taste of the fresh extracted root, the less weight it will lose in drying," Miller noted elliptically.[2]

During drying the roots lost up to four-fifths of their weight.

There appeared to be no simple optimal moisture level. The younger the roots, the more they dried out and the more weight they shed. Mountain-grown roots which had not been watered only lost half their weight.[3] Shtorkh quoted experiments which showed that the variation in loss of weight in drying roots actually depended on the moisture of the roots which depended on the moisture in the soil:

Moisture in the soil:	*Moisture in the roots:*	
%	% actual	% theoretical
56.5	77	77
51.3	68	70
48.4	60	66
43.6	57	60
32.6	42	45

Another moisture analysis showed that the age of the root affected the water content. The freshly extracted madder root which had grown in the soil for thirty months had 72 per cent water content, slightly down from 74 per cent after eighteen months. As a top limit, in wet soils, the root water content could be as high as 80 per cent.

The effect of water content on dried yields was another factor. For example, the lime-rich soil of Avignon retained moisture throughout the summer (with average temperatures varying by 5.1°C), and yielded 272 poods of dried roots per hectare. In contrast excessively dry neighbouring soils (with average temperatures varying by 3.2°C) only yielded 197 poods per hectare.

Natural drying

The steamed roots were spread in a shallow 10 to 15cm layer to dry. The farmers moved the roots about two or three times a day to allow them to dry evenly. With the help of good weather, drying could take two or three days, while the roots lost up to 70 per cent of their weight. When the roots were dry and brittle, they were packed in great hemp sacks called *kharals*, one of which could hold 7 to 9 poods (102 to 144kg) of madder roots. The sack was fastened to crossbars supported by four pillars, so that it would not touch the ground even when stretched. A labourer stepped into the sack and crushed the roots with his feet. Then the sacks were packed full and tied and left under the sun for some time for final drying before sale.[4]

There were problems. If the weather was bad, the roots needed to be stacked in a shed and brought out again when the weather improved. When roots were left to dry in the sun, they lost a lot of weight and the quality of the dye could be diminished. When the roots were dried in late autumn, there was danger from early frosts which peeled away the outer skin of the root and exposed the central part which contained the dyestuff. The dyestuff then risked being spoiled.[5]

Shade drying

This method seemed less of a risk. Extracted roots were left to dry on flat mats in the shade. After a few days they withered. With regular rearrangement, they dried evenly. However, the drying roots could still be spoiled by excessive moisture, sunlight or frost.

Petrov wrote that in 1938 in Azerbaijan some farmers who still grew madder had formerly dried outdoors using heated pits. They had changed to drying in the open attic for one and a half to two months. But the quality of the dye had suffered.

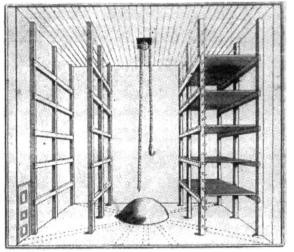

Shed drying

The Dutch as usual led the way. In Holland the northern sunlight was not strong enough for outdoor drying, so the roots had to be dried in drying houses. The temperature needed to be kept constant between 24° to 26° Reamur (30° to 32.5°C), which dried the roots in ten to twelve hours. They were sufficiently dry when they became brittle. (Incidentally, Reamur the 18th-century French scientist also researched into cochineal dye.)

The capital cost of the

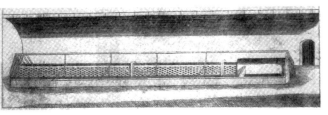

Top: Dutch madder-drying room. The roots were spread on the shelves accessible by climbing the rungs. A. G. Kästner, Hamburg, 1757 (Schaefer, CIBA Review)
Bottom: Dutch madder-drying furnace. The roots are dried spread out on the roof above and off-picture. Georg Krünitz, Berlin, 1818 (Schaefer, CIBA Review)

purpose-built shed and equipment was high and the plant was either shared between several farmers or rented out by the owner. In October 1624 George Bedford found himself at the end of a queue of 27 Dutch madder farmers and had to wait until Christmas week to be overcharged.[6]

More than a century later, Miller described the drying process in Schouwen with drawings and plans of the special plant and equipment. The fresh roots were taken to the 'cold stove' an air-drying barn-like building, where the labelled parcels of roots were laid in heaps separated by wicker hurdles. Each farmer's part-dried roots, called *relzyn*, were then carried separately to the 'hot stove'. The drying tower was heated by 15 brick flues under the floor which was covered in low-burnt tiles. Some of the tiles could be removed to moderate the heat by diverting hot air to different parts of the tower. There were four or five lofts, about 5ft above each other.[7] The oven which usually burnt turf and sometimes coal was situated at the base of the tower in the 'glory' where the workers slept. The plant was staffed by a foreman dryer who looked after the tower

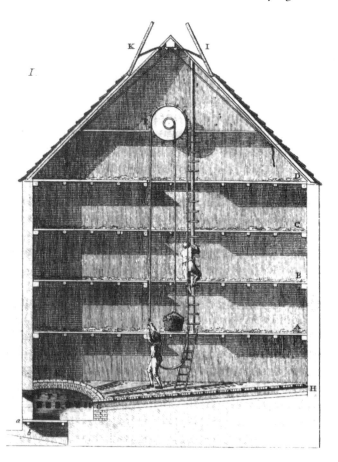

Dutch drying tower, attached to the complex of processing buildings on page 128, De Kanter, 1802 (ack. Priester)

and the kiln. He was paid piecework at five stivers per cwt of prepared madder. His assistant was paid up to 19sch a week. There were some 20 heating towers in Schouwen which during the season from September to February produced 10,000 'weight' of madder each, or two million lbs in total.

Loading began at six in the morning because it was cool and the damp air reduced the dust. The roots were hoisted in baskets by ropes into the heated tower where they remained for roughly 20 hours. Then the roots in the hottest part of the tower were exchanged with those in the coolest. All movements were made at night so the master could work uninterruptedly in the cool. This was all considered conducive to production of better quality madder. This stage of drying continued for up to five days until the roots were dry enough to be taken out and threshed on a clean stone floor to remove any dirt. The roots were then taken to the horizontal 'hog' kiln, heated by Friesland peat which produced an even and moderate heat. The kiln was stoked from one end and heated its flat barrel-vaulted roof on which the roots were spread upon a hair cloth.

There was no chimney and the smoke was let out of a small window. The roots were dried over the kiln for 20 hours under the supervision of an experienced dryer, who finely adjusted the temperature to suit the thickness of the roots and the outside weather conditions. Flachat thought that drying in front of an open fire, as practised in Zeeland, was too rapid and harmed the dyestuff and so preferred shed drying *"comme on fait à Lille."*[8] He was probably referring to a variant of the 'darry' method of drying which was prohibited in 1494 at La Brielle and in 1516 at Zierikzee. Roots were dried in the fumes of a fire fuelled by fresh peat, salt and sulphur, which must have dulled the dyestuff's colour.[9]

In northern France, the best drying houses were those of Lille, where clean hot air from the ground-floor furnace rose naturally by convection through passages into the first-floor drying room. To avoid risk of deterioration through mould, regulations stated that

The Lille drying-house, Duhamel de Monceau, 1762 (Schaefer, CIBA Review)

the roots had to be put in the stove before May 15th. A similar regulation was in force from the 14th century in Bruges and probably in the other production areas of Flanders and Artois.[10] In southern France, the hotter climate permitted part-drying the roots on paved ground in the open air, though they were never exposed to the sun. This process took three or four days. The roots were then placed in a baker's oven after the bread had been removed. In Alsace and Silesia the roots were laid on drying frames in heated rooms, which had to be aired frequently to get rid of the fumes.

In England the anonymous pamphlet of 1765 complained of "the great Expence of Buildings found necessary to dry the Crop, at least £100 for a plantation of 20 or 30 acres, the Roots not being Marketable until thus dried, nor can they be moved any distance . . . being subject to mildew which would greatly damage them." A Dutch-style solution was grudgingly put forward, which actually enabled the tithe to be reinvested for further profit: "Unless a sufficient number of the Parishioners constantly cultivate Madder, it cannot answer the Clergyman's Purpose to erect proper Buildings for drying the Tithe-Roots . . . and must perish if remaining long in the State they are when taken up." Someone must have heeded this advice, for an observant French traveller to London in 1773 — after the slump in prices — professionally remarked on the madder ovens he saw at Mitcham in Surrey and Stratford in East London.[11]

Miller[12] proposed the following cheaper conversion of existing English farm buildings. The 'cold stove' could be a covered barn slatted at the sides, using sheep hurdles on the floor, where the roots dried for three to four days and were turned once or twice. When the earth had crumbled away, the roots were dried in kilns normally used for malt or hops — also recommended by Flachat.[13] The dried roots were taken to corn threshing floors where the mull husks were sold for 15s per cwt which defrayed the costs of drying. The threshed roots were re-heated taking care to use a thermometer to avoid overheating which would spoil the dyestuff. It was 1758 and the Industrial Revolution had arrived.

An assessment

The advantage for the madder growers of the Orient was the enhanced value of their dye from roots dried in the open in dry and pure air. In contrast, their European competitors had to dry their roots in drying rooms with moist and impure air. Edward Bancroft (1744-1821), in his time one of the greatest authorities on dyestuffs, considered that the difference between European madder and that of the Levant was as great as the difference between a European and an Angora goat.[14]

Pounding

In the Caucasus until 1938 there was a steam mill in Kouba for grinding madder roots. During grinding, they were losing up to 20 per cent of the madder as dust so they started sprinkling the roots with kerosene. This formed a sticky powder and the losses were cut to five per cent. Near Aphurja village in the Konakhkent region instead of kerosene the farmers used naturally occurring crude oil, found in pools on the ground. Petrov

Dutch horse-powered pounding-house: the powder was sieved in the right-lower corner shed hung with cloth. The dying house is top right. A. G. Kästner, Hamburg, 1757 (Schaefer, CIBA Review)

mentioned M. E. Skorobogatov who was trying to cultivate madder in Central Asia. He experimented to prove that adding raw oil to madder to improve grindability also reduced the quality of the dyestuff. [15]

In Holland the technology had long been more sophisticated. A water-mill for grinding madder was recorded at Hesdin in 1342 and contemporaneous mills were recorded at Lille.[16] Horses were also used as the motive force. The dried roots, which were never allowed to be 'burnt', were taken to the

'pounding house', resembling a 'grist mill', turned by three horses. The horses directly rotated a large toothed wheel above their heads, which drove a smaller bevel on a long horizontal mounted shaft. Redolent of a pianola, the shaft bristled with a balanced line of pegs which raised and released a row of tilt-hammers, vertical stakes made of wood shod with iron, which dropped into hollowed oak log mortars.

Flachat noticed that some wood stampers were bound around their bases with thick iron bands "framed like the points of a star" to prevent the roots from adhering to the stamper. He also cunningly suggested using existing tobacco mills in France. The pounding

Another Dutch pounding-house, pre-1800, Georg Krünitz, Berlin, 1818 (Schaefer, CIBA Review)

was regarded as the most important part of the process of refining madder and an experienced craftsman was put in charge. The pounding master was presumably paid about the same as the dryer who was paid piecework at five stivers per cwt of prepared madder. The horse driver was paid some nine stivers per cwt which included hire and feed of his horses. The master had five

A see-through drawing of a rural Dutch madder processing building, 1811. Roots are stored on the left, next to the drying tower, with its furnace to the right. The building on the right houses the horse-powered tilt-hammers for pounding the roots. During the succeeding decades, the French may have surpassed the Dutch because the Dutch farmers continued to use their own or shared processing buildings, while the French farmers delegated the skilled work to large-volume specialists.
(Gemeentearchief Schouwen-Duiveland; Priester)

other assistants, with their wives and sons to fetch and carry, who were paid 10 stivers per 3000lbs of prepared madder. The master had to constantly agitate the madder with a special shovel fitted to the cavity of the pounding block. They worked at night by candlelight because they were convinced that sunlight would destroy the lustre of the pigment.

Delicate pounding

Simple pounding of the complicated roots was found to waste the precious dyestuff. The centre of the root contained three times the concentration of dyestuff of the rougher outer layers. To exploit this, carefully controlled pounding and grinding produced a more profitable mix of dyestuffs, with the top quality commanding a premium price. The first pounding pulverised the husks and thin roots, producing the inferior '*mor mull*'. The valuable residue was called '*oor onberoofde*'. The second pounding pulverised about a third of the roots, producing '*gor gemeens*' and the third produced the best '*kor kraps*'. The sweepings were also collected and sold as '*den beer*'. As soon as the dye powder was ground, it was sifted over a tub to fill a wooden cask, while any sunlight was kept out.

George Rutt, "the present only manufacturer" known to the English pamphleteer during the 1760s followed Dutch practice and separated the madder into four different classes:

Mulls	2/16	*price from*	£5 to £9 per ton,	*average*	£ 7 10s	£0 18s 9p
Gemeens	3/16		£12 to £30		£21 0s	£3 18s 9p
Umberoes	5/16		£80 to £95		£87 10s	£27 6s 11p
Crops	6/16		£110 to £140		£125 0s	£46 17s 6p
Crops can only be sold at this price when kept three years after gathering						
Total						£79 1s 11p

He was buying at £50 to £60 per ton, so with a revolving stock of 'crops' he made a gross surplus of £19 to £29 a ton. However, interest on capital expenditure for plant and equipment, and the percentage of total capacity used for a ton of dried madder and changeover time ('down-time') between different farmers' batches were not given, so we cannot calculate the manufacturer's profit.

De Poerck confirmed that similar practice was well established some four hundred years before during the fourteenth and fifteenth centuries in Flanders and Artois. The dyers of Ypres used five grades of ground madder, with familiar names such as the better *crapmede* (*garance-grappe*) and *goede ongheroofde mede* (*bonne garance non-robée*). Small roots gave *garance 'courte'*. *Mul* from the outer husks contained little dyestuff and much earth and was banned together with the enigmatic *blomme*. In Bruges in 1460 they called *garance non-robée* '*ghoede ghemeene meede*' and *mulle* was again forbidden. In Saint-Omer '*corte mede*', as it was called in Flemish, was forbidden by statute, as was another unidentified product, '*tizeke*'.[17]

Flachat agonised over the way of obtaining the best dyestuff from the root. Though green or dried, the skin had to be removed to obtain the best colour and this was easier when dried. But he feared the loss of dyestuff or parenchyme in drying and preferred older plants, though 'true' roots reduced more than others during drying, which concentrated the dyestuff. He recorded experiments carried out by one Sr Guerin from Corbeil en Gatinois who was attempting to match the Zeeland roots.

It was more profitable to separate the components of the root. The best dye came from the parenchyme where 3oz 2 gros dried to 5.5 gros, followed by the heart which contained little dye, where 6 gros dried to 2.5 gros and the skin which was for brown dye only, where 0.5oz dried to 1 gros. He took a similar root and found that without drying there was 3.5oz of parenchyme, which was harder to separate and produced a visually weaker dye, while the 0.5oz heart and 0.5oz skin were the same as when dried. To Flachat it proved that the root must not lose more than seven-eighths of its weight in drying or it would lose its parenchyme. He also dismissed other methods of making madder into a paste, which was then reduced to a half by semi-drying, as it adversely affected the distribution and concentration of the dyestuff.[18]

From the 1790s, Dambourney (see page 55) began cultivating *Rubia peregrina* which he found growing wild among the rocks of Oissel in Normandy. As he had no nearby drying facilities, he used the root fresh and found that the dyestuff from 4lbs of fresh root was equivalent to that from 1lb of pulverised dried roots, which seemed to double his yield. He also preserved the fresh roots by laying them in a pit 3ft deep in alternate layers of roots and earth, which avoided the mildew that dried roots were prone to develop.[19]

Purifying the powder

Thanks to continual natural fermentation, madder powder stored in barrels for one to two years gained up to six per cent in weight and the concentration of dyestuff also increased.

In some areas of Germany, the Netherlands and France, there was an additional modification to add more value. The rough powder produced by the initial surface grinding was cleaned in water solution and then squeezed in a hydraulic press to get rid of the soluble sugars present in the roots which debased the colour of the dyestuff. The residue was re-dried and reground to produce additional top quality powder.

Though the *lizari* of the Levant held all the advantages, when imported into Europe it was never able to compete with local powdered product. This was because the European dyers, who were less skilled than those of the Levant, could not process the roots to get rid of the outer skin and so preferred the albeit inferior European powder. The ground roots were much easier to pack into sacks or barrels.

Abroad, with the Dutch in the lead, sophisticated mills produced ground krap of about 86 per cent by weight of the dried roots while in the southern Caucasus the conversion yield ranged from 75 to 80 per cent.[20] Good practice was confirmed by its absence when Skorobogatov noted the causes of the decline in modern madder. Apart from poor methods of cultivation, traditional steaming had been discontinued. Grading had also disappeared, where once textile manufacturers had used only special fine grade to dye silk and cotton and 'grain-ground' grade for wool.

Added brightness

There were various treatments of dried madder to enhance its brightness. The Persians had traditionally obtained a particularly bright red called *dugi* from the roots by adding dried yoghurt (*dug*) to the extraction water, which presumably caused fermentation.[21]

The madder industrialist M. Gautier devised another method, which was similar to pit steaming. He cleaned madder roots in water-filled vats. Undried roots were left submerged for two days and dried roots for three days to encourage natural fermentation. The water would then be drained off and the vat refilled with boiling water and left for a further 20 hours, when the water would be drained off. Next, the roots would be half covered with water and left again, after which the water would be drained off and the roots placed in a powerful press to remove the remaining liquid. This process removed all the fermenting agents and so stopped further natural fermentation, which restricted any further oxidization which would worsen the quality of the dyestuff. The pressed roots would then be dried in a stream of hot air to convert the yellow dyestuff into bright crimson by saturating the yellow dyestuff with oxides.

M. Steite, another madder industrialist, also devised his patent process. He put 100 poods of undried roots into a 1,600:7 solution of water and ammonia (urine) and left them submerged for 34 hours to dissolve all unnecessary and harmful impurities. The roots were then washed in water, dried, ground and screened into a powder.[22] Another similar French method was to treat dried, threshed, but unground roots in a mixture of potash and cow-dung which had been kept for a year. The treatment lasted for three to four days according to the grade of the madder.[23]

From krap to garancine

Madder was best-known in Europe in its powdered form as 'krap'. In the Russian textile industry krap was widely used to dye, in order of importance, cotton fabrics, wool and silk and then hides and skins. Ground krap was always more expensive than roots, with a sole exception in 1851. (Perhaps pre-purchase had created a shortage and a later shipment of roots was needed to top-up supplies?)

In 1828 Messrs Robiquet and Colin bought the patent to produce garancine from madder roots,[24] but garancine only started to be widely used in 1839 in Rouen and Alsace. Garancine (a French word) was a natural concentrated refined powder of madder roots which had been produced by a patent process. It was both of excellent quality and being less bulky it was easier to store, transport and use. One pood of garancine equalled three and a half poods of madder roots. Schweppe[25] put it more precisely, that 100 parts of madder yielded 30 to 40 parts of garancine with four to five times the colouring strength of the original madder. However the Dutch used the conversion ratios of 3kgs of ground madder for 1kg of garancine and 0.8kg of ground madder for 1kg of roots.[26]

Garancine derivatives lit up the market. In 1845 Leonard Schwartz from Mulhouse bought a patent to produce garancine from by-products of the production of krap by treatment with sulphuric acid. He called this dyeing agent '*garanceux*'.

In the same year Mr Steiner started producing garancine in England while Messrs Parise, Gastar and Fock, textile industrialists from Rouen were the first to start using a dyeing agent called kolorin which was better quality than krap. Messrs Girarden and Grellei started to produce kolorin on an industrial scale. Their kolorin was sold in Rouen for 40 francs per kg (it was 40 roubles per pood c. 1859, implying that the franc had dropped too low). By 1847, there were 15 factories in Avignon and one or two factories in Alsace producing garancine. During this time about half of the French textile industry switched from krap to garancine. *Fleur de garance*, 'madder flowers', was introduced in 1852 by Messrs Julian and Roquer in France[27] The colour of the madder was not much changed but the strength was doubled.

Pincoffin, also known as '*alizarine de commerce*' or 'commercial alizarin' was introduced in 1854 by Mr Pincoff and traded by the Mancunian company, Pincoff, Schunck & Co. Its strength was less than madder (1:4) but it gave a beautiful pure violet. Kopp's purpurin appeared in 1864 with 50 to 55 times the colour strength of madder. Pernod's madder extract from Avignon also produced brilliant and beautiful shades from garancine which was used directly for textile printing after 1867.[28]

The plethora of products described above encompassed manufactured garancine and virtually all its derivatives. There seemed to be a great range of quite similar products on the market, a sign of the birth of modern marketing. It was also evidence of frenetic and secretive competition to profit from the growth in both demand for madder and developments in technology. A modern parallel is the price of computers that each year roughly halves as their power doubles. The next chapter outlines the chemical processes which fulfilled the demands of a hungry market. Chemical formulae are excluded in favour of tracking the entrepreneurial hunt for improved technology both in manufacture and in convenience for the mass-producer customer — the textile manufacturer who had industrialised and taken over the dyers' work.

8

Inside the vat: the hunt for the dyestuff

A maze of analyses

THERE WAS more money to be made if more dyestuff could be extracted from what was discovered to be an increasingly complicated root. Chemists rushed to analyse the root, attacking different aspects of its composition. The incompliant roots were all slightly different. Research results were also slightly different. The process is still going on. Helmut Schweppe, the modern chemist, has got furthest with his uncompleted analysis of 25 colour components in madder (see Glossary — hydranthraquinones). The Russians, driven by the textile magnates who saw huge increased profits, were rightly curious and assembled all the existing knowledge about the composition of the root. The root contents varied considerably according to Dr John, or to Dr Buchholz (in brackets). After correct drying, the root contained:

43%	(22.5%)	wood fibre
20%	(39.9%)	readily extractable red dyestuff
8%	(8%)	dark-coloured glue
5%		oxide of dyestuff
3%	(1.2%)	tar-based red dyestuff
1%	(1.9%)	dark-coloured waxy substance (soluble in hot spirit)
8%		potassium and lime, ?potassium carbonate
7.5%		phosphorus lime and magnesium, ?magnesium phosphoric carbonate
2%		phosphorus and sulphuric acid and potassium, ? potassium phosphoric sulphate
1.5%		ferric oxide
0.5%		silica
0.5%		others
	(0.6%)	acrid easily extracted substance
	(12%)	water-soluble substance
	(4.6%)	potassium-soluble substance
	(1.8%)	lime-soluble substance

Kuhlmann had also made another differing analysis. To Shtorkh this confirmed continuing uncertainty. This was either caused by inaccurate analysis or by a variety or combination of differences in the samples of root: their age, origin, soil composition and treatment and the subspecies of plant. Even from a single root, the thickness of root, skin and amount of skin analysed was not constant.

Several chemists from different countries were busy analysing madder in different ways to discover its secrets. According to Payen's analysis, the correctly dried root contained 1.33 per cent nitrogen, compared to 1.24 per cent usually found in roots for sale. Also after combustion, 9.78 per cent of ash was produced, well over Schweppe's 6 per cent adulteration limit, described below. Girardin discovered that roots which had been correctly dried at 100°C and powdered produced only 5 per cent of ash, which implied that the tough outer skin of the root with small particles of earth accounted for 4.78 per cent by weight of the root.

Girardin and Labillardiere then found that Provençal madder yielded 8.8 per cent ash, while Alsatian madder yielded 7.02 per cent ash. Schlumberger found that Avignon madder gave 8.77 per cent ash and Chevreul combusted Levantine roots to find 9.80 per cent ash. Analysis of the ashes of Alsace madder, according to Koechlin who burnt two samples and of Dutch madder, by May, who burnt one sample, all showed different compositions (see appendix 8.1, page 325)

The mineral salts present in madder ash, as identified above, showed that madder could absorb the mineral salts found in the soil. For example in Zeeland, natron was substituted by different combinations of alkaline salts, including silica which increased the fastness of the dye and in Alsace, by lime, with similar effect. It was as though madder was a living organism — which of course it was.

The 'soft substance'

Schaefer[1] told how early scientific research was stimulated by the fact that madder dyed bones red, as mentioned earlier. The phenomenon was first recorded by 16th-century physicians Mizaldus and Lemnius and rediscovered in 1736 by the English surgeon John Belcher (1706-85). While Belcher was dining with a cotton printer in Surrey he was surprised to find that the bone in his pork joint was bright red — this led him to publish a learned treatise.[2]

At that time great interest also existed in France for all matters connected with the dyeing of madder. The agriculturist, physiologist and botanist Henri Louis Duhamel du Monceau also studied the red bone puzzle. He was convinced that he would thus be able to discover the secret of the mordant by means of which Turkey red, the most brilliant of all scarlet dyes was produced in the East (see chapter 11). Duhamel made exhaustive tests with the bones, claws and beaks of pigeons and turkeys which had been fed on a diet containing madder.[3]

He discovered that neither all the bones of the same animal, nor corresponding bones of different animals were dyed equally. From these experiments Duhamel concluded that it was the calcium in the bones that bound the madder and that it must be calcium mordant which the Oriental dyers used to fix the pigment to the fibre. Though this fact had already been recognised by others, it had never been turned to account and even Duhamel's attempts to utilise the results of his research for the French dyeing industry were unsuccessful.

The same search was on, on the other side of the Channel. In 1803 when England was feeling the force of Napoleon's blockade, the Society for the Encouragement of Arts, Manufactures and Commerce offered a large number of prizes for inventions to substitute for former imports. In the June issue of the *Gentlemen's Magazine*, Prize No 103 was a Gold Medal or 30 guineas offered for "the cheapest and most effectual method of printing or staining cloths with a red colour . . . equally beautiful and durable with the red colours now generally procured from decoctions of madder."[4]

The fragile dye

Natural dyes were delicate substances. High temperatures could evaporate, disintegrate or char dyes. Both hot and cold water could dissolve so-called easily extractable dyes. Spirit could dissolve tar-based dyes. Powerful oxidisers such as hydrogen peroxide, chromic acid, or nitric acid could degrade dyes, turning strong reds into grey. Sulphuric acid charred most dyes, but dissolved madder and indigo.

The madder tap root and side-roots were covered by a thick layer of tough skin called *l'écorce* in French and *die rinde* in German. The outer layer contained little dyestuff, which though not red, was usually removed and converted to a bright red dye by dissolving in alkaline solution. Beneath was the soft substance or red mass called *l'aubier* in French and *der splint* in German, which surrounded the woody heart fibres called *les ligneux* in French or *die holzfaser* in German. The dye was present in the form of glucosides (see Glossary), which could be separated comparatively easily.[5] The most important of these was ruberythric acid, which was split up into sugar and alizarin, the principal dyeing agent.

Bastet investigated the relationship between the age of the root and the percentages of soft substance and wood fibres:

% Soft substance in root after	10 months	18 months	30 months	42 months
Freshly cut root	86.0%	93.0%	100%	100%
Dried root	22.0%	25.0%	30.1%	36.4%
In fresh wood fibres	7.5%	14.0%	31.0%	66.3%
In fresh soft substance	78.5%	79.0%	69.0%	30.7%
In dried wood fibres	3.3%	6.1%	13.6%	29.1%
In dried soft substance	18.8%	18.9%	16.5%	7.3%

This provided a qualitative reason for cropping after 30 months. Depending on the ease of separating the soft substance from the dried wood fibres, there was no doubt that 42-month roots were significantly larger than 30-month roots.

One-year-old madder contained mostly a yellow dyestuff and the red dyestuff appeared during the second year. It was known that Derbent madder contained the highest concentration of dyestuff, which explained its preference by textile industrialists. Derbent madder had a dye concentration 1.4 times that of French or Dutch madder.

Alizarin was the principal dyeing substance. The method of extracting alizarin from powdered krap was complicated. First the krap had to be boiled in water for several hours. Later some hydrochloric or sulphuric acid was added to the brown liquid. The denser thick brown substance at the bottom of the vessel contained the dyestuffs as well as other impurities. The brown matter was separated and rinsed in cold water to remove any traces of acid. It was then treated with boiling alcohol which only dissolved the dyestuffs.

The alcohol solution was then boiled with water alumina or silica solution, which also dissolved dyestuffs, until the solution became colourless. Alumina absorbed ruberythric acid, which could be removed by treating the solution with alkaline carbonic salts. The dark-red alkaline solution was rinsed away with water, leaving the valuable brown residue containing alazarin and alumina or silica. The residue was dissolved in a solution of hydrochloric acid, leaving alumina or silica in solution, isolating the neat alizarin in the form of a yellow-red crystalline powder. The alizarin powder could then be dissolved in alcohol and conveniently stored until the alcohol was vaporised to leave the concentrate ready for use.

Obtaining pigment from madder roots

Shtorkh credited the chemical researches of Drs Schunck, Gillins, Schtrekker, Rokhleder, Schlumberger, Debus, Wolf, Schwartz and many others with the identification of the dye matter from the madder root. They also described its impact on chemistry, which affected the study of different acids, salts and other fundamental substances. Shtorkh was bowled over by the swift technological progress which combined practical experience and research with a deep understanding of the laws of inorganic chemistry. Grierson explained the chemical reasons why the drying stage was most critical. Within the root an enzyme — erythrozyme — existed and during the drying stage (and again if the dyestuff was heated very slowly during drying) this enzyme hydrolized the alizarin glucoside which released the colouring agent and so created a stronger dye. The enzyme was destroyed by strong heat during the dye process. This was why the Oriental method of air-drying in the sun produced better dyes than the kiln drying which was obligatory in the north.[6]

The freshly dried grown root was not useful as a dye. The root had to be matured and only then the dyestuff extracted. It needed one to three years, depending on the climate and soil, to release its dyestuff. Fermentation and action of sulphuric acid were needed to convert the ruberythric acid into alizarin, the colorant. Alsatian madder fermented naturally in sealed barrels, where a certain portion of the glucoside present was separated by the action of the erythrozyme contained in the root. In the Caucasus, Schaefer[7] thought that fermentation was brought about by storing madder in pits for six months after harvest. There was Dambourney's method of storage of fresh roots by burial, but Schaefer may have confused this with the steaming process described earlier or the storage of the roots in large canvas sacks. While natural fermentation did some of the job, it was only some 20 per cent and further chemistry was necessary for full release of the dye.

Daniel Koechlin in 1804 noted that to strengthen madder dye in textiles it had to be added to a solution of potash, soda or lime. In 1823 Kuhlmann's research into the madder root determined its component parts, subsequently partly confirmed by Buchholz and John, whose tables are on page 133. Robiquet and Colin in August 1826 experimented on the infusion of powdered krap with cold water, and were first to obtain the pigment in pure crystalline form, by sublimation from powdered krap, which was named 'alizarin'.

At the same time the researches of Gaultier de Chaubry and Persoz succeeded in revealing the chemical secrets of the red and rose dyestuffs in madder. Soon after in 1827, Kuhlmann, while verifying the research of Robiquet and Colin, discovered 'xanthin', the yellow dyestuff in madder. These two chemists next found another method of extracting the dyestuff from madder with the help of sulphuric acid. Their work had been prompted by Koechlin's analysis which had attributed dyeing qualities to alizarin and purpurin. In recognition, the rose pigment in madder was called 'purpurin'. In 1828, Lagier, Robiquet and Colin took out a patent for the process for a concentrated madder dye named 'garancine', described below. According to Runge, in his work of 1835, madder contained five different dyestuffs; Schunck in Manchester isolated three: alizarin, rubiadin and xanthin. Following all these experiments, the chemist Schwartz deduced that madder consisted of one dyestuff which contained all the well-known tints obtained from krap depending on the dyeing process.

Enough theories . . .

Refining garancine from madder

Garancine was a chocolate-brown powder, which dissolved in cold water giving a yellow colour, in mineral acids greenish-yellow, and brownish-red to red in alkalines. It had no smell or taste.

In 1828 Robiquet and Colin were working in collaboration with a group of French merchants, with whom they had already begun production of garancine under the name of *charbon sulpherique*. The process was as follows. Powdered krap was wetted in five or six times its weight of cold water and left overnight, in order that the dissolved dyestuff precipitate gradually. It was gathered in a canvas filter, strained and the sediment forcibly compressed. This operation was repeated three times. After these thorough washings the extract produced from the madder contained sugars, slimes and other substances:

> Fresh grape skins i.e. tannic acid (? to start fermentation) were briskly pounded into this mixture and then sulphuric acid was poured on. In addition, half the amount of the acid of the solution was added to the original powder. To the (? remaining) acid was added a roughly equal amount of water, or more as required. The diluted acid was poured onto the compressed sediment and transferred to a lead-lined vat and vigorously mixed together. Mixing continued for some time, while the blend was heated over a hearth to remove its hot vapours. Heating continued for half an hour, as the temperature increased to 100°C. After cooling, water was added and all the insoluble matter — garancine — was collected in a filter, and washed repeatedly with water until it did not contain any residual acid.

In 1829, the Avignon mercantile house of Lagier and Thomas bought the patent. At first they encountered problems stemming from their own technical experience, which they took three years to overcome. A further setback was the change of current fashion towards dark thick materials which were not especially enhanced by bright dyes like garancine. However, in spite of these problems of ownership, production and marketing, by 1835 garancine was finally recognised in the trade and became a deserved success.

The garancine factory in Avignon only used local madder. In Alsace they mixed local madder with some from Avignon, to improve the quality of the dye. In 1839, the enterprising Rouenais factory of Schlumberger-Rouff began to manufacture garancine by their own method:

> Powdered krap from barrels which had been more or less compressed

into lumps was broken down on a worktable by a wooden implement and converted into a powder which was loaded into a lead-lined vat, where it was soaked in a little water. Then sulphuric acid was added in the proportion of half the weight of the powder. Two labourers without pause mixed the paste with shovels. After some time they poured out the mix into a vat, added water, similarly washed the vat out five or six times, filtered the solid residue, heated it in an oven and finally reduced it to a powder. This type of garancine was always acidic and could not be used to dye material violet.

From that time, the number of factories producing garancine significantly increased. While several different variants were developed, the fundamental process remained the same. As well as factories in France, others started in Britain and Holland, which all produced excellent garancine.

By 1859, even in the Moscow and Vladimir districts of Russia many factories had been built, both under Russian and foreign ownership. They were not only establishments for the conversion of Russian and Caucasian madder into marketable powdered krap, but even for conversion of krap into garancine. From a host of establishments — Shtorkh became poetic — the best garancine came from the houses of Malyutin, Lepashkin, Shipov, Rebevek and Aschenbach. Of all these manufacturers the first place was awarded to the honoured citizens of Moscow, the brothers Malyutin, for their production of the best quality and largest quantity of krap and garancine from Derbent madder. The most recent significant factory to open near Moscow in 1852 was in Pushkin Selo, established to make garancine from Russian and Asian madder.[8]

Schweppe's version of the old recipe for garancine was slightly different:

The madder roots were boiled with dilute sulphuric acid. The ground madder was washed with cold water and then cooked with a mixture of water (one part, equal in weight to the madder) and sulphuric acid (one-sixth part) for approximately one hour, after which the liquid was filtered and the residue washed to neutrality and then dried. Concentrated sulphuric acid could be used in place of dilute.

In addition, Schweppe gave the recipes for the four other purified madder derivatives mentioned earlier. There was evidently intense activity just before the appearance of synthetic alizarin.[9]

'Madder flowers' (*fleurs de garance*) was introduced in 1852:

Ground madder roots were treated with 12 parts of water containing 0.5% sulphuric acid and the mixture was allowed to stand for a few days until fermentation started. Then the madder was filtered off and rinsed with water until it was neutral. It was then packed in cloth sacks, pressed in a hydraulic press, dried in a hot room at 50° to 70°C and packed in barrels. Madder flowers had been cleansed of various acids and salts, lime, magnesia, pectin and sugar.

'Pincoffin' (commercial alizarin), introduced in 1854, was manufactured as follows:

Carefully washed and neutralised garancine was treated with superheated steam at 150°C. It no longer contained purpurin.

'Kopp's purpurin' was introduced in 1864:

It was manufactured from ground madder that had been thoroughly soaked with water, saturated with sulphurics acid and then allowed to stand for 12 hours. The residue was then filtered off and it was once again treated with cold sulphuric acid. The combined filtrates were acidified to about 2% with sulphuric acid and heated with steam to 40°C. Kopp's purpurin then formed in large flakes. It was filtered off, and finally the filtrate was heated, causing another product — green alizarin (with resinous impurities) to precipitate. Rubiadin dyestuff was found in the filtrate and the green alizarin produced supplied good colour and had 18 to 20 times the strength of madder.

'Madder extract Pernod' was developed in 1867 in Avignon to improve their famous product, garancine:

Garancine was treated with boiling 0.5% dilute sulphuric acid until all the colouring matter was dissolved. The extract was allowed to cool and a reddish-orange sediment formed. The sediment was filtered off, washed to neutrality and after addition of a thickener was used direct for textile printing.

To a non-chemist, these recipes sound like endlessly varying mantras. They provide a glimpse into the obsessive minds of these chemist-businessmen, driven by the inspirational combination of scientific discovery and financial reward, like latter-day alchemists turning relatively base matter into gold.

The next chapter describes the opposite of purification — adulteration, which destroyed reputations far swifter than quality controls could rebuild them.

9

Almond husks, brick dust & 'super-fine-fine'

The penalties of adulteration

EVEN IN THEORY, the specification of different parts of the root was complicated. In practice, misrepresentation of the grades together with adulteration by external substances forced the merchants to be vigilant. Shtorkh could say that "we believe that Russia can export the excess quantity of madder from the Caucasus, especially as the quality is superior to both French and Dutch madder. The initial reactions of French and Dutch textile industrialists has been to confirm its excellence."[1] But the reality was extremely modest. European merchants had accumulated centuries of experience of quality assessment of powdered madder. Virtually none was sold to Europe because the quality could not be guaranteed. Small export orders were completed southwards to Ferabat and Zinzili in Persia from Baku, where from 1853 to 1856, between 56 and 6 poods of cheap madder were sold per annum.

The rewards of reputation

The very act of defining different grades indicated quality control and the desire of the producer to protect the reputation, reliability and price of the top quality product. Unfortunately, the opposite was also true for a commodity whose quality standards were not defined. Ingenious adulteration materials included inorganic substances such as brick dust, ochre, yellow clay, and yellow sand, while burnt sienna and copper ferrocyanide have been reported in samples of madder brown. The inorganic content was determined by burning a sample of madder. If it yielded more than six per cent ash, it was contaminated with inorganic substances. In Flanders and Artois during the 14th and 15th centuries detailed regulations specified the proportion of earth allowed in different grades of ground madder.[2] In 1630 George Bedford was granted his official London post of inspector and sealer of imported madder after he had demonstrated by simple weighing that Dutch madder contained between 2 and 30lbs of sand and earth per cwt![3]

Mineral substances were less harmful than vegetable adulteration which could dull the colour. During the Middle Ages, the use of brazilwood was strictly limited by weight to 1lb and 1 *quarnon* per stone in Audenaerde, Douai and Malines and other localities including Leiden. Brazilwood gave a 'false' scarlet which was not fast, but dyers liked to it to brighten madder. Strictly speaking, brazilwood was a dye-bath or post-dyeing additive in contrast to the contaminants which were mixed in with the dye powder.[4] Other similar organic contaminants included oak shavings, logwood, redwood, old fustic wood, sandalwood, almond shells, mahogany shavings and clover. These impurities could be determined by a comparative dyeing test against a known sample of madder. The dyed textile samples were drawn through a weak solution of bleach and then through a soap solution and then treated with a tin chloride solution which destroyed all the wood dyes, except for the madder. If samples treated in this way were compared, the quality of the madder was determined with relative accuracy.

Pernod devised the following test to discover the type of wood contaminant. A piece of paper was impregnated with a tin chloride solution of 1 part tin : 2.5 parts nitric acid : 5.5 parts hydrochloric acid : 20 parts water. The madder powder was sprinkled on the treated paper and after 30 minutes, all the spots where wood particles came to rest changed colour. Redwood gave carmine red, logwood — violet, and old fustic wood — yellow dots. Pure madder displayed only a light yellow. Tannic contaminants could be similarly displayed, using a paper impregnated with iron chloride solution in ethanol. Tannic impurities displayed randomly spaced black dots.[5]

A particularly attractive buff pigment appeared on the market during the 19th century, sometimes called 'Egyptian brown', which can still be seen on view as an historical curio at the Winsor & Newton private museum in north London. In contrast to respectable merchants, at the bottom end of the market there were mountebank colourmen, such as the notorious Miss Provis, who during the 1790s duped seven or more artists into parting with ten guineas each for copies of her 'authentic' manuscript of Titian's secrets.[6] It is possible that some such unscrupulous colourmen passed off some stale stocks of mummy pigment as being a specially mordanted rose madder, which therefore commanded a higher price.

The Napoleonic Wars had marked a renewed interest in archaeological discoveries in Ancient Egypt, which inspired the Neo-Egyptian style in architecture and furniture. Decorated mummy-cases were highly prized and still grace the great museums of the world. This possibly led to the grotesque practice of grinding their contents — the mummies — to make the warm-coloured buff pigment, which became rather popular with artists, even though Field remarked on its "strong smell resembling garlic and ammonia." Around 1800, instructions for its preparation included in *A Compendium of Colours*[7] recommended that "the flesh of mummy be ground up with nut oil very fine and may be mixed for glazing with [madder] lake [*inter alia*], and needed a little drying oil mixed with the varnish . . . it may be used . . . without fear of its changing." In the late 19th century the true and shocking identity of the pigment became known (once again) and artists immediately ceased to use it.

Mumia had been traded earlier. In 1424 the Wali of Cairo questioned some tomb robbers to discover the source of their fortune. Under torture they revealed that they were boiling up mummies until the flesh fell off. Then they skimmed the oil off the top or the morbid waters and sold it to the Franks — foreigners — for 25 dinars a cwt. Mumia was considered to have medicinal value and fetched a good price in Europe. Sir Thomas Browne in *Hydriotaphia: Urn Burial* — a 17th-century masterpiece — referred scathingly to "Pharaoh sold for balsoms."[8] Harley also noted that since the late 16th century mummified bodies had been imported from the more lowly "momia" caves, a massive necropolis near the pyramids.

Back in London, the blackish stuff was for internal medicinal use and, as was frequently the case with drugs, the raw material was tried out as a pigment. As late as Carter's 20th-century excavations of the tomb of Tutankhamen, the long-believed aphrodisiac potency of the mummy's organ led to its mysterious disappearance.[9] Whilst export of mummies was *"contrabanda"* during the 16th century, and the pigment accordingly rare, in 1586 John Sanderson, a young English gentleman adventurer, assisting William Shales, the factor of the Turkie Company during the time of William Harborne's embassy to the Sultan, observed that Shales found that, "with words and money the Moors will be entreated to anything."[10] Perhaps this explained why mumia was described by Vladimir Dal in his Russian Dictionary as "English earth."[11]

Derbent versus European madder

Even though Derbent madder was 40 per cent 'better quality' than the European, it sold for less and the price included a hefty 75 kopek per pood haulage charge. In addition, Shtorkh's assertions about the undervaluation of Asian and Caucasian madder depended on his assumptions of the quality and consistency of the product for which he produced little evidence. In fact there were complaints of adulteration of Derbent madder. Schaefer[12] thought that in the East there had been so much falsification of madder powder that dyers insisted on buying only roots.

Of course, there was no evidence either of consistency of European madder, nor indeed were there over-frequent complaints of adulteration. But the size of the French and Dutch madder industries and their widespread continual export over long periods implied greater quality control than could be expected from the nascent Caucasian industry. In fact, the wide range of the European trade's quality bench marks described below implied the existence several admittedly intricate (even arcane) systems of quality control which were notably absent from Asian or Caucasian production. There should however be some evidence of quality standards in the Ottoman empire, as this was the case with several other commodities.

For these reasons, the raw figures from primary sources such as customs' ledgers were more useful to describe what is a confused picture, than Shtorkh's compounded figures which did not separate the amounts of non-garancine from garancine.

Quality control

It must have been very confusing to buy madder on the international market. Different numbers and names were given to product grades from each producer country. In another twist, products from the same country had different market names when sold in different countries. To add to the potential misinterpretation, all grades were not sold in all markets. The Russian price lists from about 1860 give an accurate impression of the chaos.

According to the St Petersburg price lists, there were several sorts and qualities of foreign krap: Dutch krap — 1st, 2nd and 3rd class; Breslau krap: Ordinary and Red class; and French krap: S. F. F. and E. X. F. Shtorkh noted that: "In France, the most expensive krap is Cyprus at 7r per pood with Provence at 4.75r per pood. The best powdered kraps are Dutch, rated at '240 points', next Alsace at '150 points' and then Avignon at '125 points'."

The medieval regulations of Flanders and Artois set out the permitted impurity levels for different grades of madder. In Reimerswaal in 1480, the best grade *grappe* could contain 1 to 2 per cent earth, the next *garance non-robée*, 2 to 4 per cent. *Commune* powdered madder could have 4 to 7 per cent, *garance courte* 7 to 10 per cent and *baeillioen* or *mul* 10 to 16 per cent. In unwitting anticipation of current European Community regulations, in Ypres, Lille and Arras — and elsewhere — the different grades of ground madder were compressed into regulation-sized pseudo tennis-balls for sale. Mercifully, these rules were enforced with tolerance and neighbouring figures showed slight variations. In Lille they only distinguished between milled products called *ravenelle, paillin* and unmilled called *en croche*.[13]

Their Dutch successors continued to bring order to the market by standardisation. In Holland, excellent garancine was produced which was exported in large quantities. Dutch garancine had a strong unpleasant smell and a bittersweet taste and a colour ranging from red to brown, which depended on the type. The best quality powder was produced if the outer layer(s) of the madder root were removed before grinding. The dyestuff was called *crop* or *krap* in Dutch, *garance robée* or *garance grappée* in French, 'crop-madder' in English, or *beraubter krapp* or *feiner traubenkrapp* in German.

Statutory Dutch assayers over the centuries checked that the madder had not been 'burnt' in drying and that the quality was constant in every cask. Purity statutes passed by the governments in 1662, 1671, 1699 and 1735 regulated that the highest *tare* (dirt) allowed in krap was 2lbs per cwt, in *onberoofden*, below, was 8lbs while in middle quality *gemeen* or *fatt*[14] was 12lbs.[15]

The middle quality product was produced if the rough outer layer was not removed. It was called *gort gemeen, gemeen* or *gemeens* in Dutch, *garance non robée* or *mirobée* in French, or *unberaubter krapp* in German. The browner colours were usually of a lower quality called *mullen* in Dutch, 'mull' in English, or *bil(l)on* or *garance courte* or *garance mulle* in French, or *mullkrapp* in German. It was greasy in feel, hygroscopic and changed colour from bright orange to bright red. This product was not handled by reputable merchants — it was sometimes even thrown away in 18th-century France.[16]

The best quality was of an excellent bright colour while the worst could only be used one year after grinding and gained its full concentration of dyestuff in three years. Dutch krap was also called *nizhnii grozdovoi krap'* in Russian, presumably referring to the Nizhegorodsky Fair described below. The dust from madder mills was also in demand among the Dutch dyers and was known as *beeg* or *den beer*.[17]

There were additional more complicated subdivisions of quality. Customary trade-names of various kinds of madder indicated the ratio between *gemeen* and *crop*. Thus *onberoofden* meant one-third of *gemeen* and two-thirds of *crop*; or expressed in figures *'twee en een'* was 2:1 and *'een en een'* was 1:1. Inspectors were appointed to examine the tubs after filling. If the goods were passed as fit for sale, the barrels were sealed and marked in black ink with the arms of the place of origin and the mark of the manufacturer.[18] In the early 18th century German merchants would only buy casks marked 'Zirksee'. Writing in 1702 Sir William Petty gave two qualities of Flanders madder as bale or crap madder being the finer and pipe madder the coarser. Baillie John Steuart a merchant in Inverness complained in 1721 to his suppliers in Rotterdam about a mix-up:

> "The two Hhds. (hogsheads) mader you sent me by the 'Majory' is not of a right quality for this country; will not sell here at any price, and must be returned p. first occasion, being Crust mader (mull) instead of best cropt (krap) which I called for."

He had probably paid the lower price too.[19] In the 1850s and 1860s exclusive brands such as 'Soeters', 'Rijkmakers' and 'Willemstadse' were introduced to regain market share.[20] In the 1850s, krap from Alsace and the Palatinate replaced krap from Holland on the French market. One reason was that in

Alsace refining was in the hands of a specialist enterprise separate from the growers, whereas in Holland each grower did his own refining.[21] Alsatian krap had the following characteristics in comparison to Dutch: a stronger (peculiar, according to Schaefer) smell, and a less sweet taste, but with the same bitterness. Alsace also absorbed atmospheric moisture and changed colour from pale-yellow (saffron according to Schaefer) to dark-red. It was very sensitive to light, so it was kept in closed barrels for up to four years.[22] During fermentation in the barrel, it became greasy to touch and developed an unpleasant smell. When stored in sealed barrels, the dyestuff gained full concentration in two years, as opposed to three to five when stored differently. In barrels the powder solidified as hard as stone.

In Alsace, they never sold powder made only from the rough outer layer of the roots. Alsace quality levels were: 'O.' = *mull*; M. F. = *mittelfein* or relatively fine; 'F. F.' = *feinfein* or very fine; 'S. F.' = *superfein* or super-fine; and 'S. F. F.' = *super feinfein* or the finest. 'F. F.' was the most popular grade, with 'S. F. F.' very seldom used. The great mills were in Strasbourg, Gagenau and Heisselbrun.

After the Napoleonic Wars finished in 1815, French krap from Avignon became very popular. In Avignon every krap manufacturer had his own grading system, which was why the term 'S. S. F.' could mean finest or least fine, depending on the producer. When buying Avignon krap it was best to take a sample rather than to deal by the label. Characteristics of Avignon krap were a pleasant smell, a bittersweet taste and a pink, red or brown colour. The finely ground powder had a dry feel.

Around Avignon, famously on the shores of the Isle-sur-Sorgue[23] madder plantations were situated in former marshland, called *palud* in French. These plantations produced excellent madder, with bright red roots, compared to the usual pink roots. When powdered, *palud* krap was not as bright a red as the others, but after about a year, the colour turned into a distinctive blood-red. Relatively little *palud* krap was needed to produce the same red as the more common pink krap. On the market, much krap contained a 50-50 mixture of *palud* and common kraps, which produced a most efficacious dye. The quality of grinding was extremely sophisticated in Avignon and a wide range of grades were produced after removal of 3, 5, 7, 10 or 12 per cent of the root, that meant the rough outer layers.

It was possible to use Avignon krap immediately after grinding, but its quality improved after a year. It was easy to store in barrels as it did not petrify and the dyestuff lasted for several years. While some time earlier there were two colours of Avignon krap on the market, red and yellow, by 1860 there was only the red. In former times, the grades were *mull*, 'F. F.', 'S. F.', 'S. F. F.', as marked on the barrels. In 1860 there were the following types: *palud*, pink and a mixture of *palud* and pink, with the following grades: *Mulle*, 'F. F.', 'S. F. F.', 'S. F. F. F.', 'E. X. T. F.', 'E. X. T. F. S. F.', 'E. X. T. S. F. F.'; *Mulle* would have other abbreviations on its labels and for other sorts the abbreviation 'P.' for '*palud*' or 'P. P'. for 'pure *palud*'; 'R. P. P.' for 'red pure *palud*'; 'R.' for 'pink krap'; and more commonly 'F. X. T. S. F. R. P. P.', meaning 'especially good pure red *palud*'.

There were two sorts of Breslau krap from Silesia. One was harvested in spring and the other in September. The sacks were tested and sealed. In, perhaps, a veiled statement about the church and state, the cheaper quality was marked with a cross, and the finest with a crown. Silesian madder preserved its powdered form better than other European varieties and was made up in linen sacks for transport and sale. Silesian madder contained much less pigment than Dutch or French madder and was used for ordinary cotton printing or wool dyeing. It was therefore only marketed in the adjoining districts such as Prussia, Bohemia, Saxony and the Nizhegorodsky fair in Russia.[24]

In Britain home-produced industrial ground madder was of two grades: 'grape-madder' and 'bunch-madder'. Grape-madder was the heart of the root whereas bunch-madder consisted additionally of the bark and small fibres from within the root. For grape-madder the finest roots were selected, the bark separated at the mill and the cleaned roots kept in casks for three or four years. It was claimed that this process made the roots more suitable for dyeing and that, unless the casks were kept closed, the madder tended to lose its dyeing properties.[25]

10

Leonardo's choice madder lakes

Colour & medium

THE SHADES of colour of madder lakes vary through scarlet, carmine red, red with a bluish tint and pink (see Glossary). Since classical times painters have used madder lakes as part of their repertoire of reds. This is confirmed by modern analytical methods which have developed greatly in the past 40 years and especially during the last 15. The combination of limited equipment, funds and time available has resulted in the analysis of only a small proportion of the paintings in the great museums and galleries of the world. Madder pigments have however been analysed in over twenty paintings — some famous — from Europe (15th to 19th centuries), Russia (sixth to seventh centuries) and Tibet (15th to 19th centuries). The list in appendix 10.1 (page 325) must be incomplete but it shows how wide a range of artists used the lakes.

Winsor & Newton's rose madder pigment, quill sized Persian madder roots and tube of Rose madder water-colour (Author's photo).

Early painting methods combined pigments with waxes or gum. In Roman Egyptian Mummy portraits the binding medium was replaced with egg tempera, rediscovered by the Early Italian School painters of the 13th century. The artist's studio where the master had assistants and apprentices came into being about 1290 in Sienna. The introduction of vegetable oils — usually linseed, safflower or sesame — was often credited to the Van Eyck family who used maple oil during the late 14th century. However the use and formulation of oils, which were more convenient than tempera, must have developed over the preceding centuries.[1] The 1950s saw the addition of quick drying, minimal colour-shift acrylics to the continuing use of oil and water colours. In 1994 Winsor & Newton introduced the more light-fast synthetic 'Permanent Alizarin Crimson' to supplement 'Alizarin Crimson' introduced c. 1860 and 'Carmine' from kermes.

Ancient madder pigments

The earliest madder lake yet analysed is dated to the eighth to seventh century BC. The pottery and votive figurine shards, found in the Amathous area in Cyprus, with reddish-purple decoration on white slip have been tested to contain madder pigment. There were five shards all of which contained alizarin. Purpurin appeared in four shards and probably pseudopurpurin, xanthopurpurin, and munjistin in one each. Foster and Moran identified these colorant substances (see Glossary, 'anthraquinones') of madder by light and UV spectroscopy, electron impact ionisation and X-ray analysis. This indicated the now-indigenous *Rubia tinctorum*, which grows wild near springs and streams.

Quantities of the anthraquinones were too small to indicate which other subspecies of madder were used. Iron was also found in the pigment, an extraordinarily early isolated use of iron mordant.

There are many earlier Cypriot ceramics, but none decorated with madder pigment. By visual comparison, five per cent of all later bichrome-ware in the Lanarca museum are decorated with madder pigment. This suggested to them that either madder or the technology was imported from Greece or the Middle East at that date. Foster and Moran, who must know their material, added that "visual inspection suggests that madder was used as red pigment on pottery since Neolithic times

'The Painter's Craftshop' by Johann van der Straet called Stradanus (1523-1605), a Flemish designer who worked in Italy, Nova Reperta, c. 1600 (ack. British Museum, Winsor & Newton)

in Israel . . . peaking between the twelfth and eighth centuries BC" — a possible earlier source.[2]

Higgins identified rose madder as the brilliant pink with a slight purplish tinge on a Greek terracotta figurine after 330 BC. The change to a naturalistic hue followed the earlier lurid colouring of red ochre and chalk. The figurine was dipped in white clay solution and then fired, after which pigments were applied with a brush over the white slip.[3] Wallert identified wild madder from 320-280 BC in the purple pigment from the painting inside the basin of a grand carved marble ritual foot bath. The artist painted three swirling nereids riding on hippocamps, which referred to an episode during the Trojan War. Vitruvius[4] in the first century BC had described that as well as from molluscs "purple colours are also manufactured by dyeing chalk with madder root and with hysginum . . ." which Wallert confirmed matched the spectra of wild *Rubia peregrina* (and *Galium cruciata*, bedstraw) with dominant purpurin and pseudopurpurin but no alizarin.

Analytical methods used by Wallert were UVS, FS and TLC, and for the chalk XRF and XRD (see appendix 10.1, page 325).[5] In 1951 Farnsworth identified purpurin as an alumina lake painted on a bowl found in Corinth dated to 146BC.[6] In 1809 Chaptal reported on various pigments found in a paint shop in Pompeii, one of which he decided was an alumina lake, whereas his description suggested a madder lake to his modern counterpart Schweppe.[7] Russell in 1892 examined the pigments in six first-century AD Egyptian paint pots found by Flinders Petrie in Hawara and analysed the pink pigment as madder on a substrate of gypsum.[8] A memorial portrait-bust of a Woman in tempera on wood said to be from er-Rubayat dated AD 160-180, showed her draped in a pink tunic which was found to contain pink madder lake.[9] In 1815 the British scientist Sir Humphrey Davy recognised the presence of pink pigment on a ceramic vase fragment found at the Baths of Titus in Ancient Rome but was unable to identify it.[10] These examples of ancient pigments indicate widespread use of madder lakes.

Standing woman in outdoor dress, Tanagra style, 330-200BC, 180mm height (ack. British Museum; Higgins)

The Getty basin, with inside decoration of three painted nereids on hippocamps, Greek 320-280BC, 565mm diameter (Wallert)

Incunabulae

Napoleonic Neo-Classicism had passed into history when, thirty years later, Mary Philadephia Merrifield went to northern Italy with her sons on commission from Her Majesty's Government to collect or copy ancient manuscripts about artists' pigments. The two following manuscripts mentioned madder.

Merrifield dated Eraclius' manuscript to the 12th century by following up some detective work on pertinent details in a recipe for dyeing Cordovan leather with madder. Cordova was taken by the Moors in AD 711. Eraclius, who appeared to be a composite author, alluded to the later Saracen and Arabic leather trade. In the recipe No. XXXII for Cordoban leather, the northern and western European medieval name for madder, '*warancia*', was used. *Garancia* also appeared in No. LIII, by

Petrie's Hawara paint pots, one containing rose madder pigment, 1st century AD (ack. British Museum; Walker et al)

Isidore, the seventh-century bishop of Seville. Both occurrences implied that the compilation was after the date of the expulsion of the Moors in 1236, which ended the effective monopoly of the Cordoban leather industry. '*Sandis, id est garancia*' was the term also used in No. LIII, while '*rubea*' was used in No. LV, which suggested other different authors.

Gotting and Kühn have confirmed that madder lake is present on the marriage document of the Empress Theophanu in AD 972, where it was applied on the back of the parchment and on the front in the red areas of the medallions as the top layer over a base of red lead.[11] The late Middle English 13th-century term 'rubric' did not refer to madder. It meant the heading of a chapter or the title of a law, written in red ochre, which grew from form to content, into a term for the law itself.[12] In other Christian Orthodox lands, madder was listed as a red colour used for manuscript illustration in Russia and an Armenian text had it as a component of purple, but without further modern corroboration.[13] Further east, the modern Chinese painter Yu Feian mentioned that madder, safflower and lac were used in modern and traditional Chinese painting and Feller suggested that madder was available for Japanese woodblock printing — again without corroboration.[14]

Portrait of a woman in tempera on wood, c. AD 160-80, said to be from er-Rubayat (ack. British Museum; Walker et al)

Merrifield seemed to have missed that *rubia* was mentioned as a component of *pandius* in the colour recipes of the 12th-century *Mappae Clavicula*. *Pandius* referred to a number of complex mixtures of pigments, several of which are red.[15]

Merrifield also translated the 63-year-old Parisian notary Jehan Le Begue's 1431 manuscript. It too was made up of other texts collected by Johannes Alcherius in 1410-11, added to the earlier *Catholicon*, a Latin dictionary compiled in 1286 by Fra Boldi from Genova. The introduction mentioned that before printing block techniques were common in England, linen cloth was painted with figures, flowers and patterns to imitate embroidery. *"Rubea radix est de qua rubeus color fit, miscendo cum creta alba, id est, gipso"* — "From madder roots comes the colour *rubeus*, which needs be mixed with white

The noxious mercuric sulphide process,
engraving from Agricola, De re Metallica, 1556 (ack. University of London Library; Harley)

creta," i.e. chalk, gesso.[16] This appeared to contradict recipe LII, where "the juice of dragon's blood or cinnabar (see chapter 2) and *sandis* — madder — is used either pure or with red chalk; other juices of a similar kind are also mixed with green or yellow earth."[17]

Recipe LV for lakes for purple colours provided a primary method of straining boiled madder roots to which Cardon appended her recommendation to add chalk to the dye-bath.[18] Roosen-Runge wrote that madder lakes were mentioned in workshop treatises of the early Middle Ages as components of pigment mixtures, but not as colours to be used on their own and that madder lakes have not been identified in coloured miniature manuscript illustrations of that period.[19] Laurie (1913) found evidence of madder lake in a book illustration of c. 1465-89 in the Advocates' Library in Edinburgh.

Sealing wax & kings

On a more ephemeral note, Brannt[20] indicated that madder lake was used in sealing waxes.[21] However, King Stephen's 12th-century seal and other later red beeswax seals from the Public Record Office in London were analysed by the Glaxo laboratory who found mercuric sulphide, made by a particularly noxious process. The earliest red wax seal in the Public Record Office in London is attributed to Afric Earl of Mercia in 1007.

Earlier royal seals were made of lead and ancient seals from the Middle East were made of clay. Later seals used shellac sticks or Spanish wax, which was clear resin and cinnabar.[22] Winsor & Newton think it unlikely that madder was used as it was too expensive. They have no records of making sealing wax from their catalogues, but they think that it is very likely that they produced some for private orders.

High Renaissance luxury

One of Merrifield's Venetian informants said that the contemporary Venetian painters made much use of madder-lake, and that the old Venetian school had also used locally grown madder. She doubted this, as in 1565 — actually 1548 (see chapter 3) — madder was being imported for dyeing from Flanders.[23] Her informant had taken off some of the colours with a knife and *inter alia* lakes of kermes and madder "were analysed by a very skilful chemist (now dead)."[24]

The fact that madder is barely mentioned in 14th to early 17th century recipes partly reflects the possibility that cloth shearings were also the source of this dyestuff for painters. It may also reflect the chance survival of early sources and the research still to be done into sources in difficult Flemish, Dutch and German dialects. It seems certain that there were strong links with the textile dyeing industry at that time. From the late 16th century the availability of cochineal from the New World led to a decrease in the use of textile shearings. By the 19th century, the most important sources for artist's pigments appear to be cochineal and madder, lac and kermes being hardly mentioned.[25]

Many surviving luxury textile fragments from church vestments show how the thick cut-and-uncut silk velvet gold brocades were chopped up and joined to form the traditional shapes of the vestments. The intricate patterns which decorated the textiles frequently seem to have been ignored by the cutter. The huge prices paid for these textiles meant that even small swatch-like fragments have survived. It is also understandable that shearings and clippings were reused as a source of dyestuff, not only for pigments but also in dyeing.[26] They were called *vlocken* in Flemish or *bourre* in French sources. For example, a recent analysis of Titian's Venus and Adonis, c. 1560, in the J. Paul Getty Museum in Malibu seemed to confirm this. Microscopic examination of a cross-section prepared from a sample of the red glaze of the cloth draped over Venus' seat revealed the presence of a few textile fibres within the lake pigment. The fibres contained both madder and cochineal dyestuffs. While there are other explanations, including the use of a piece of fabric to apply the paint or to level its surface, the use of shearing in the preparation of the pigment is more likely.[27]

By tradition, this cope, made of a patchwork of two of the best red silk velvet brocades, was part of the Burgundian booty captured at the battles of Grandson and Murten in 1476.
The cross was embroidered later. It shows the high value of these silks and that sumptous colour could be more important than design
(Schmedding B, 1978,
Mittelalterliche Textilien in Kirchen und Klöstern der Schweiz)

Lake pigment recipes describe how alkali was used to dissolve the dyestuff out of the textile waste. Alum was then added to the solution to precipitate the pigment. In 15th and 16th-century recipes from the Netherlands and Germany, it appears that the alkali used was sufficiently strong to reduce the shearings to an amorphous, even gelatinous consistency. The test was for the alkali to dissolve a feather. Seventeenth-century recipes for *bourre* seem similar, with the final pigment containing much textile matter, which was not necessarily recognisable. Not so in Italy, where from Merrifield's[28] 15th-century Bolognese manuscript — *Segreti per Colori*, "the alkaline dyestuff solution was pressed out of the textile fibres and the clearly weaker alkali poured through again to extract more dyestuff."[29]

Broadly speaking, Kirby observed that painters working in Italian city states in and about Florence, Sienna, Venice, Ferrara and northern Italy tended to use lake pigments prepared from scale insects, whereas artists working in northern Europe tended to use madder lakes, with later addition of kermes, and New World cochineal during the 17th century. The sample of analysed paintings is too small at present to be more definite. However, this development reasonably seemed to have paralleled the use of dyestuffs for textiles (see chapter 4).[30]

Few mentions

Eraclius merely lists madder among the colours for painting[31] as does the Table 3 of *Synonymes*.[32] From then silence until 1612, when Neri, translated by Merret, gave a recipe promoting an "especially very beautiful and pleasing to the eye" madder lake to undercut "chermisi."[33] He recommended that with both less alum and more dyestuff than for cochineal, madder produced "a very fair Lake for Painters, and with less charge than from Cochineel, and that from Madder in particular will arise most fair and very slightly." However, madder neither appeared in an English 1606 to 1612 price list from *The Art of Lymnynge* manuscript[34] nor in a colour sample board probably compiled by Edward Norgate about 1630 for Sir Theodor de Mayerne, the Genevois scientist and physician to Charles I. Strange, for the king's gardener, Mr Shipman had been granted the charter to grow madder (see chapter 4).[35]

Further silence until 1733 when madder lake was included among the lakes at the end of *Abecedario Pittorico*. Decades after the French publications about Turkey red for textiles (see chapter 11), the anonymous author of *Traite de la Peinture au Pastel* in 1788 observed that while madder of all the local plants gave the most durable reds, the addition of juice of poplar made it still more permanent, while juice of white beech bark was still better. Constant de Massoul, the colour-maker, confirmed the superior fastness of madder lake, though in his list he only mentioned the word 'lake' omitting 'madder'.[36]

Page of colour samples accompanying Waller's paper in Philosophical Transactions, 1686. Madder does not appear in the reds on the lower part of the table (ack. University of London Library; Harley)

Impressionism & the toothpaste-tube

Hoofnail in the early 18th century suggested a method for making a good, reasonably cheap scarlet. Two oz of crop madder were placed in one pint of alum water, heated gently for two hours and allowed to stand for 24 hours. It was then strained and precipitated with a solution of salt of tartare. His dilemma was that the same quantity of madder did not regularly produce the same quantity of colour. The quantities and other details make this the source for Englefield's recipe, described below.[37]

From the mid-18th century, with the increased popularity of the British Grand Tour of classical Greece and Rome and the appetite for classical outdoor scenes, amateur painting became fashionable, the equivalent of superior holiday photographs 200 years later. William Reeves was the first in 1766 to make useable watercolour cakes by adding honey to moisturise and preserve the pigment. This must have appealed to Isaac Smith, midshipman on Captain Cook's voyage to Australia, who took his water-colours with him. Reeves may have got the idea from a rather awful tale picked up on the Grand Tour. Abd al-Latif al-Baghdadi, an Iraqi

Trade card of W. & T. Reeves (ack. Winsor & Newton)

doctor who visited Egypt at the beginning of the 13th century wrote of a gang of workmen who discovered a jar of honey from ancient times but perfectly preserved. They were contentedly dipping into it when they found a mummified baby also preserved in the midst of the honey.[38]

From 1775 to 1828, the uncertainties of the French Revolution, Napoleon and industrial and political reform inspired the Golden Age of Satire. More than 10,000 different hand water-coloured satirical prints were sold on the streets of London. James Gillray (1756-1815)

'Fashionable Contrasts — or The Duchess's little shoe yielding to the Magnitude of the Duke's Foot' satrical cartoon by James Gillray, 1792 (ack. Andrew Edmunds)

was the greatest satirist. Among more than a thousand prints, his 'Fashionable Contrasts' shows the central emphasis which a nice deep madder wash could lend to 'The Duchess's little shoe', redolent of the symbolic association of red with passion (see chapter 17). It nicely captured the mood of the time when such great changes were taking place.[39]

By 1800, there were about 200 artists' colourmen in Britain. Today there is effectively one, Winsor & Newton, who finally bought out the other survivor W&R Reeves Ltd in 1982. There are a few other firms in Europe. Sir Henry Englefield may have won the Society of Arts Gold Medal in 1804 for his carmine-like madder lake and first mention of the mechanical press in the manufacture, described below, but the leading colourman's chemist at the time was George Field, who won his gold medal in 1815 for his pressure percolator for filtering lakes.[40] In his obituary, Field was said to have turned his attention to madder when supplies were blockaded by Napoleon.[41] The blockade was short-lived as madder continued to arrive from Holland, Turkey and Italy and even from France by foreign ships.

George Field (c. 1777-1854) — mezzotint by Lucas after Constable (Harley)

The problem with paint colours had a different complexion. Sir Joseph Banks, president of the Royal Society, refused in 1789 to have his wife portrayed in oil by Sir Joshua Reynolds, president of the Royal Academy, or any other oil painter, and plumped for John Russell's pastels instead: "Being of the opinion that the oil pictures of the present time invariably fade quicker than the persons they are intended to represent." There was clearly a crisis in British painting technique during a boom period for painters. The number of paintings shown at the Academy Exhibition alone increased from 340 in 1779 by more than four

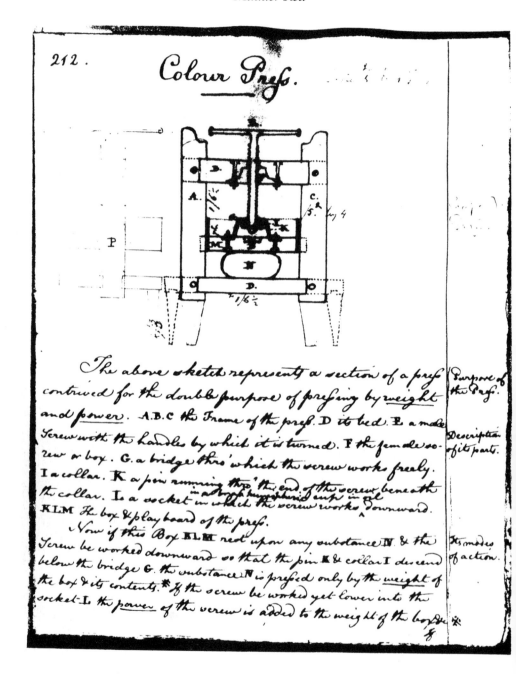

Field's 'Colour Press', Practical Journal 4 (ack. Courtauld Institute)

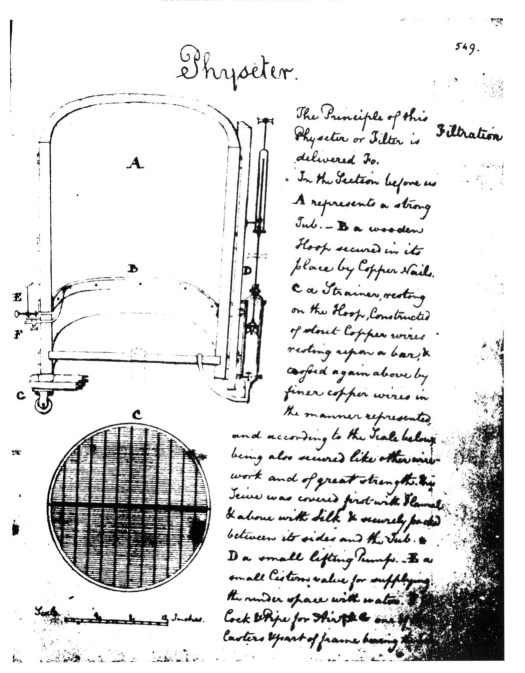

Physeter.

549.

Filtration

The Principle of this Physeter or Filter is delivered To.

In the Section before us A represents a strong Tub. – B a wooden Hoop secured in its place by Copper Nails. C a Strainer, resting on the Hoop, Constructed of stout Copper wires resting upon a bar, & crossed again above by finer copper wires in the manner represented, and according to the Scale below being also secured like otherwise work and of great strength. This Seive was covered first with Flannel & above with Silk & securely packed between its sides and the Tub. D a small lifting Pump. E a small Cistern valve for supplying the under space with water Cock & Pipe for this C one Casters & part of frame having

Scale   3 Inches.

Field's 'Physeter', Practical Journal 5 (ack. Courtauld Institute)

times to 1500 in 1855.[42] This must have influenced Mrs Merrifield's expedition to find and translate ancient recipes, mentioned above.

From 1804 to 1825 Field crammed ten volumes of octavo notebooks with his experiments to improve his colours, starting with madder lakes. Each notebook acted as an ongoing file. The first — *Practical Journal 1* — started in 1804, with title pages such as 'Rubric Lake and Colours Experiments Continued 800 to 835', had 835 entries solely about madder. Madder also appeared regularly if randomly in the other Practical Journals, excepting 9 and 10 when Field's later attention turned to ultramarine. In addition to his Leonardoesque drawings of complex machinery, bristling with curiosity, he elegantly painted a picture of a Dutch madder plant, the origin of his roots, bound with a pink bow, painted with his own madder lake pigment. Field was seriously interested that his pigments were light-fast. For example, he considered his 'madder yellow' insufficiently light-fast so he dropped it from his list, while the likes of Ackermann's

Above: Internal title-page from Field's Practical Journal 1, started in 1804 and which contained 835 experimental observations on madder (ack. Courtauld Institute)
Below: George Field's painting of a madder plant tied with his own dyed pink bow (ack. Courtauld Institute; Fairbairn)

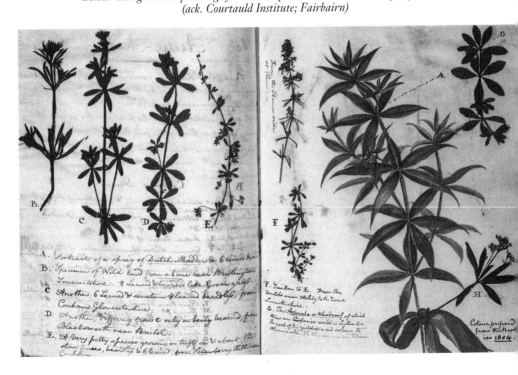

gall-stone and quercitron pigment was puffingly sold as 'yellow madder'. In this, he was most unusual among 'colour-makers' as pigment manufacturers were known and 'colourmen' or makers of artists' colours, who combined pigment with medium.

His first lake-making Colour Manufactory at Conham in east Bristol began production in 1808 and founded his fortune. He moved back to the metropolis. From 1813 Field manufactured madder lakes at his home 'elaboratory' at Heath 'Cottage', Hounslow Heath, on the site of the present A4 trunk road west of London. He supplied several of the best colourmen such as Roberson's, Ackermann's, Emerton and Manby and probably J. Varley as well as directly to painters.

In 1826, he moved onward and upward to Syon Park House in Isleworth where he built his third 'elaboratory' in the grounds in Syon Hill Cottage, in the lovely 'Marlbro' Park otherwise Syon Hill Park. Later Field also supplied William Winsor, a chemist (1804-65) and his contemporary, friend and partner Henry Newton (1805-82), an artist, who founded their soon-to-be world-famous firm in 1832 working from 38 Rathbone Place — appropriately in the heart of the future bohemian Fitzrovia in London. At the sale of Field's effects soon after his death in 1855, Winsor & Newton bought his notebooks and reproduced his three-tier rose madder lake manufacturing method described below, a version of which continues in production to the present day.[43] By the time Field's classic *Chromatography* was published in 1835, he was manufacturing rose, brown and purple shades of madder

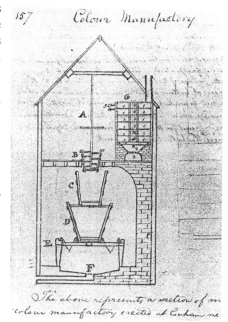

George Field's Conham Colour Manufactory
(ack. Courtauld Institute; Harley)

*Three examples of madder lakes made by George Field,
Practical Journal, 1809 (ack. Courtauld Institute; Harley)*

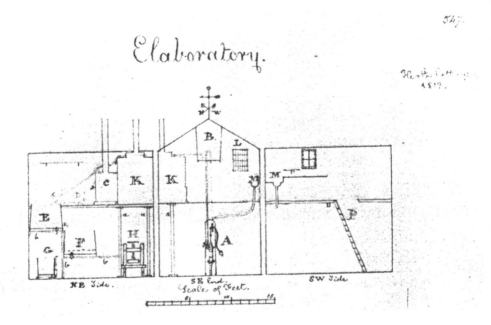

Above: Heath Cottage Hounslow, Field's Elaboratory for lake-making in 1813 — long demolished, Practical Journal 5 (Harley; ack. Courtauld Institute)
Below: Emerton and Manby, Colourmen trade card, 1796, showing horse-driven rotating pigment grinders, similar to madder pounders on page 128 (ack. British Museum; Winsor & Newton)

pigments, and madder carmine which was superior in texture and transparency, and a water-colourist's concentrated madder called 'liquid rubiate'. His madder lakes were indeed easier to apply, faster to light and more beautiful than others. This reputation was borne out by the list of distinguished artists beginning with Sir Thomas Lawrence, and including Constable, Turner, Mulready and Wilkie, who in the 1820s all subscribed for his publication. He had after all been one of the three founding directors of the British School in London which was created to provide an exhibition gallery for the display and sale of British art.[44]

Every artist's problem was how to get pigment to the studio or outdoors without leakage, spillage, drying out or the need to add solvent until the paint

Leonardo's choice madder lakes

LIST OF COLOURS.

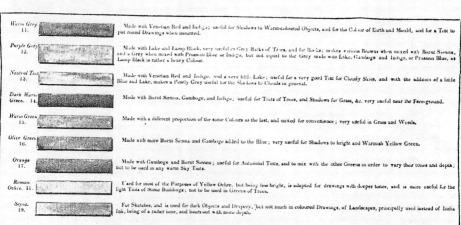

Cobalt Blue. 1.	Usefull as a Substitute for Ultramarine in its' Brightness of Colour, and Superior when us'd in Skies and other objects, which requires even Tints, us'd occasionally in retrieving the Brightness of those Tints when too heavy, and for Tints in Drapery &c. Capable by its' Superior Brilliancy and contrast to subdue the brightness of other blues.
Prussian Blue. 2.	For the Blue part of clear and fine weather Skies at all times of the day, make a Purple, when mixed with Lake, useful for distant Mountains and Drapery; makes a bright Green when mixed with Gamboge, and is permanent but rarely used for the green of Trees; makes a good pearly Grey for Clouds, &c. when mixed with Lake and a little Gamboge.
Indigo. 3.	For Twilight and Evening Skies but not sufficiently bright for Skies in clear days; is useful for the green of Trees when mixed with Burnt Sienna and Gamboge; useful when mixed with Lake and Gamboge, to make Greys and Neutral Tints with; washes smoothly much easier than Prussian Blue, and probably on that account often used, where Prussian Blue would be most proper.
Lake. 4.	For Purples when mixed with Indigo or Prussian Blue, which last should be principally used for distant Hills and Mountains; this mixture is useful for the shadows of nearer but yet distant Hills; makes a Grey or Neutral Tint when mixed with Gamboge and Prussian Blue, and not to be used for the warm Horizon Tints of the Sky, which in redness should generally not exceed the Tint of light or Venetian Red; the Purple Lake is more permanent than the Carmine or bright Lakes, the Madder Lakes excepted.
Gamboge. 5.	For Green when mixed with the Blues, to be used in Trees and Grass, and to make Greys and Neutral Tints when mixed with Lake and Indigo or Prussian Blue, but most frequently with Indigo, not to be used in the Horizon Tints of Evening Skies. Yellow Ochre being a mellower Tint, and preferable in tone. Gamboge will make a good Orange Colour, when mixed with Burnt Sienna, useful for Autumnal Tints and faded Trees; makes a pure Green when mixed with Indigo or Prussian Blue.
Burnt Sienna. 6.	For rich Banks of Earth in Sunshine and Evening Tints, and for glowing Tints on Buildings, not to be used in the Horizon Tint of Skies, but particularly useful in making Green of various degrees of warmth and depth when mixed with Indigo and Gamboge, and when mixed with Purple Grey, easily converted into different degrees of Warm or Sober Brown.
Yellow Ochre. 7.	For Stone Buildings or Plaster, Corn Fields and Yellow Lights of the Sky towards the Horizon, mixes well with Venetian Red, for warm Lights on Buildings, &c. but never to be used in the Green for Grass or Trees, it not being transparent enough, and liable to be washed off too easily.
Venetian Red. 8.	Useful for the Red Horizon Tint of Skies, and to make a Neutral Tint when mixed with Indigo and a very little Lake, and is most excellent for its quality of mixing well with all Colours, (Indian Ink not excepted) and laying even and smooth on Paper with less trouble than light Red, for which it is a valuable substitute and is preferable to Indian Red, (which is too heavy and purple) and is very good to mix with Yellow Ochre for general Tints. Used in Bricks, Tiles, &c.
Vermillion 9.	For the brightest Reds, is useful in Flesh and Drapery and in painted Objects, such as Flags, Boats, &c. being of that degree of brightness which will by contrast send back many other reds in to distance
Burnt Umber. 10.	Used as Shadow to warm Tints of Earth, and Burnt Sienna, and near Fore-grounds, and for the colour of Earth; useful for small dark touches of Shadow to Pebbles, &c. in Fore-grounds.
Warm Grey. 11.	Made with Venetian Red and Indigo; useful for Shadows to Warm-coloured Objects, and for the Colour of Earth and Mould, and for a Tint to put round Drawings when mounted.
Purple Grey. 12.	Made with Lake and Lamp Black, very useful in Grey Barks of Trees, and for Rocks; makes various Browns when mixed with Burnt Sienna, and a Grey when mixed with Prussian Blue or Indigo, but not equal to the Grey made with Lake, Gamboge and Indigo, or Prussian Blue, as Lamp Black is rather a heavy Colour.
Neutral Tint. 13.	Made with Venetian Red and Indigo, and a very little Lake; useful for a very good Tint for Cloudy Skies, and with the addition of a little Blue and Lake, makes a Pearly Grey useful for the Shadows to Clouds in general.
Dark Warm Green. 14.	Made with Burnt Sienna, Gamboge, and Indigo, useful for Tints of Trees, and Shadows for Grass, &c. very useful near the Fore-ground.
Warm Green 15.	Made with a different proportion of the same Colours as the last, and mixed for convenience; very useful in Grass and Weeds.
Olive Green 16.	Made with more Burnt Sienna and Gamboge added to the Blue; very useful for Shadows to bright and Warmish Yellow Green.
Orange 17.	Made with Gamboge and Burnt Sienna; useful for Autumnal Tints, and to mix with the other Greens in order to vary their tones and depth; not to be used in any warm Sky Tints.
Roman Ochre. 18.	Used for most of the Purposes of Yellow Ochre, but being less bright, is adapted for drawings with deeper tones, and is more useful for the light Tints of Stone Buildings, not to be used in Greens of Trees.
Sepia. 19.	For Sketches, and is used for dark Objects and Drapery, but not much in coloured Drawings, of Landscapes, principally used instead of India Ink, being of a richer tone, and bears out with more depth.

These Colours which are considered as Permanent, are sufficient for the general purposes of Painting in Water Colours, and by which great depth and purity may be obtained; but in order to retrieve parts of Drawings, which may have too much heaviness; and for Historical, Portrait, or Flower Painting in Water Colours, many other Colours may be found useful and particularly valuable. Such as Indian Yellow which is very brilliant, and being Transparent, is useful in Glazing over Greens, which are too dark or heavy, and to give them richness, the with gall-stone which is by some Colourmen now rendered Permanent, is superior to Gamboge in every thing except that they are by no means so well adapted to make the Greys or Neutral Tints with, nor to express pale Yellow or Green lights. In addition to these are the Iron Yellow, the Madder Lakes, and Brown and Purple, which last is particularly deep and rich, and useful for Drapery &c. with many other Reds, Browns, &c. which are found useful for various purposes of art, but which would be too numerous to be here described.

For colouring from Nature, thick Paper with rather a rough texture, such as Cartridge, is preferable. Likewise for Drawings of Buildings and Castles. &c. but for the best finished Landscapes, the Paper best adapted to the purpose is, Extra Wove Imperial, or Royal, or Super Royal, either hotpressed, or as it comes from the Maker. The smooth is best adapted to small Drawings and to Alterations, as the washing with a Sponge will not create too much roughness. If the thin Wove Papers be used, it will be best to mount them two or three thicknesses first, as they are more liable to wrinkle than the thick Paper. A very little of the Mixture of prepared Ox Gall with the Colours will prevent any thing like greasiness in working them. These Colours are most convenient for Sketching, when in tin boxes.

London: Published 1816, by J. VARLEY, No. 44, Conant Street, Hanover Square

J. Varley's List of Colours, 1816, in which red, brown and purple madder are cited but not illustrated
(Harley)

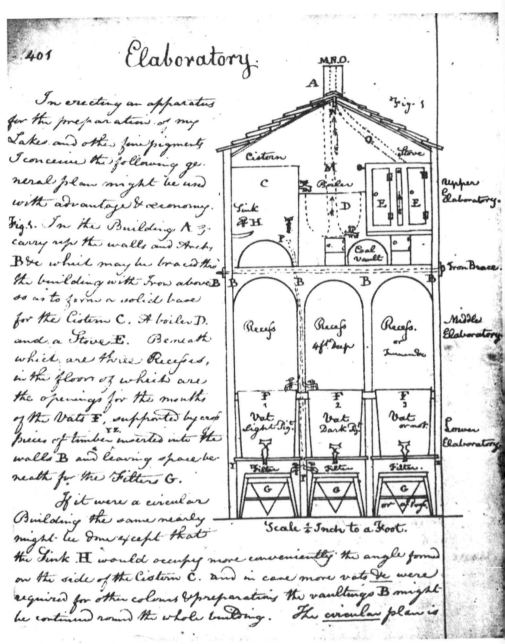

Elaboratory.

401

In erecting an apparatus for the preparation of my Lakes and other fine pigments I conceive the following general plan might be used with advantage & œconomy. Figs. In the Building A 3. carry up the walls and Arches B &c which may be braced thro' the building with Iron above B so as to form a solid base for the Cistern C. A boiler D. and a Stove E. Beneath which are three Recesses, in the floors of which are the openings for the mouths of the Vats F, supported by cross pieces of timber inserted into the walls B and leaving space beneath for the Filters G.

If it were a circular Building the same nearly might be done except that the Sink H would occupy more conveniently the angle formed on the side of the Cistern C. and in case more vats were required for other colours & preparations the vaultings B might be continued round the whole building. The circular plan is

Figures labelled within the diagram: M.R.O. · A · Fig. 1 · Cistern · Stove · C · Boiler · Sink H · D · E F · Upper Elaboratory · Coal vault · Iron Brace · B B B · Recess · Recess 4ft deep · Recess or Furnace · Middle Elaboratory · F2 · F3 · Vat Light Pig. · Vat Dark Pig. · Vat or mst. · Lower Elaboratory · Filter · Filter · Filter · G G G · Scale ⅛ Inch to a Foot.

Above: George Field's three-tier elaboratory or Lake Laboratory, Field Practical Journal 9, 7 (ack. Courtauld Institute; Fairburn)
Right: Winsor & Newton's North London Colour Works, 1841 (ack. Winsor & Newton)

was applied. Newton's 1833 notebooks show how they first improved the moisture-retaining qualities of water-colour blocks by the addition of glycerine.

They next looked at the inconvenient traditional containers for oils. Oil paints had been carried about in squash-ball-sized chamois-leather pig's bladders, which were pierced with a tack to let squeeze out the oil colours. The bladders were soft and leaked messily. So by 1840

Oil paint stored in pig bladders, Winsor & Newton glass syringe, Rand's collapsible lead tube and Winsor & Newton's modern tube (Fairbairn)

Winsor & Newton were using a cunning syringe glass tube of about ½ inch diameter, but the plunger got stuck when the smeared pigment dried out and the glass broke. In 1841, John Rand patented the lead screw-top paint-tube, which was sold by Thomas Brown to Winsor & Newton and filled with mass-produced pigment at their North London colour works in Kentish Town. This was immediately rewarded by royal custom. Both Queen Victoria and

Prince Albert bought oil tubes and improved water-colour cakes, and issued 'by appointment' warrants. Indeed, the royal paint-sets, though later discovered to have been barely used, raised amateur painting to the epitome of fashion. Winsor & Newton became the suppliers of madder lakes for oils and water-colours for the painters of the Empire. At the 1851 International Exhibition at Crystal Palace, the sole Gold Medal for the chemistry of artists' pigments was awarded to Winsor & Newton.

It can be said that the paint-tube played a significant part in allowing artists to escape from their studios and paint outdoors and that this was one stimulus behind Impressionism. The improvements in methods of extracting madder dyestuffs which resulted from the work of Colin and Robiquet in France and Field in Britain made madder, together with cochineal, the artists' choicest reds from 1830 to 1900.[45]

Above: Miniature portraits of Messrs Winsor & Newton (ack. Winsor & Newton)
Below: 'The Secret', painting by W. H. Fisk, 1858, featured an enigmatic micmac quill-work purse (ringed). (Whitehead)

The palettes of the precursor of Impressionism, J. W. M. Turner, contained madder lakes with unusual copper substrates as did many of his oil paintings and water colours during his productive years from c. 1792 to c. 1850.[46] Both he and Constable used Winsor & Newton watercolours. William Holman Hunt and John Ruskin were also customers. It could not have been entirely a coincidence that William Henry Fisk in his painting dated 1858 'The Secret' elegantly placed a Micmac quill-work purse in the right lower corner, whose 'Micmac red' had not long been equalled by the English colourmen (see chapter 4).

Extruded annealed aluminium-alloy tubes which were both lighter and more flexible came in during the 1920s and are still in use today. The inside of the tube is painted with golden-coloured varnish to stop possible reaction between the pigment and the tube. The seal is completed at the bottom by half an inch of latex which is spun-in to provide a seal when the base of the tube is rolled closed. The outside of the tube is painted with cosmetic white enamel which acts as a suitable background for the label on which the accurate colour of the contents is printed. A photoelectric dot even lines up the label with the tube so that all tubes are similar.

Secret recipes

At Winsor & Newton's, the modern version of George Field's three-tier method still takes 13 weeks. Damp fresh madder from Iran (formerly from Holland) is converted to cakes of madder lake on the premises in Wealdstone in north London by his traditional method. Field invented a wooden press with a weighted lever arm for squeezing out the dye, which is still in use. The madder

was held in a bag under pressure while water ran through the bag carrying the dye to a vat below, where it was filtered and the precipitate was washed many times. The filtration rate slows as the sediment falls and the fluid thickens. The man-sized vats are made of wood, pine or oak, bound with iron hoops. They are always kept wet. Stirrers and other implements which contact the dye are also made of wood and the sieves are made of thick linen sewn onto 50 cm square wooden frames.

Field's three-tier 'elaboratory' drawn in his 1809 *Practical Journal*, consists of a boiler and cistern on the top, the steeping vats in the middle and the filters on the ground to drain away the water. It is very similar to Winsor &

Winsor & Newton's triple roll mill for grinding rose madder pigment (Fairbairn)

Newton's present-day set-up on two levels with a pump instead of the third level. One of Field's recipes for madder lake produced pigment that was about 20 times the concentration of the original powdered madder, which also roughly corresponds to Winsor & Newton's current secret process:

> I now took the 52lbs of madder from which I had obtained the foregoing colour, having first washed it with much water I turned it from the filter bags into 4 tubs after the water had drained from it. I now took 18lbs of powdered alum, dissolved it in about two tubs full of hot water —

precipitated it with near 10lbs of salt of tartare dissolved in hot water — filtered in three cotton filters — edulcorated (freed from soluble particles by washing) the precipitate during the day with about 20galls of water, next day re-dissolved the precipitated alumina in 9lbs of muriatic acid — diluted the whole until it measured 54 quarts.

I then added this fluid to the above 52lbs of madder in the tub in the proportion of 1 quart to a pound of madder, stirring them at intervals during two days.

The above madder some of which had been in the bags six weeks, tho' washed daily by pouring water through it in the bags and stirring, smelt very strong and the bag which had been longest wet had bred a number of small worms on the outside (yet this madder does not seem to yield less beautiful tincture than the latest, if any difference, is rather deeper coloured — [presumably desirable fermentation had occurred]. The wet madder appeared at the top of the bags of a deep chocolate colour verging on black but near the bottom of all the bags it appeared a much lighter brown or nearly of its original colour; I therefore suspect where it appeared of this latter colour, the water and the stirring had not reached it.

The madder and the mordant having macerated (softened by steeping in a liquid) two days as above, I strained the red tincture therefrom thro' the flannel (loosely woven wool) bags and muslin sieve into a clear tub — let it rest, elutriated (separated the lighter from the heavier particles by washing) it, precipitated it with a clear solution of alkali not in excess — edulcorated the precipitate in cotton filtered during a day — pressed off the moisture and dried it in the sun where it yielded about 2lbs 9oz of pigment.[47]

Field's professional rival, the "ingenious, scientific and worthy baronet" Sir Henry Englefield, also published his domestic-scale madder lake recipe, "there being no pigments in use, of a nature sufficiently permanent":[48]

Two oz of the finest Dutch crop madder, is enclosed in a bag of three or four times that quantity, and beaten in a marble mortar with a marble pestle, and about a pint of cold soft water, which when rendered very opake by the beating, should be poured off, and fresh water put on; about five pints of water, in this manner, will extract all the colour. The tinged water is then to be put into a copper vessel well tinned, or one of earthen ware (the use of iron should be carefully avoided in the whole process) and heated till it just boils, then poured into an earthen vessel, and an oz troy of allum, dissolved in a pint of boiling soft water stirred well into it; after this an ounce and a half of a saturated solution of mild vegetable alkali is to be poured gently in, and the whole well stirred during the operation; it is then left to settle, and when cold, the clear yellow liquor above the colour may be poured off; a pint of boiling soft water is then to be well stirred in, and when cool the liquor separated by filtration in the usual way. Boiling water should be poured on it in the filter, till it passes through of a light straw colour, and free from an alkaline taste. The colour is then to be dried quite gently and will when quite dry weigh ½ oz or a fourth the weight of the madder used.

Water-colours need maximum permanence, brilliance and transparency. Gum Arabic increases brilliance, gloss and transparency. Ox gall improves wetting on papers. Aquapasto provides water-colours with a texture that can be scratched out and art masking fluid acts as a masker.

It is hardly surprising that the following ten later recipes for various madder and alizarin lakes were of varying exactness, even though they were accurately assembled by Schweppe. Some give quantities and/or temperatures or details of the process or warnings, while others do not. Winsor & Newton commented that compared to their process, these recipes produce pigments which are harder, weaker and duller and less light fast than their own.

Pubetz in 1872 described the manufacture of madder lakes which could be produced from madder or its derivatives such as garancine or Kopp's purpurin. Sugar is first removed from the madder by an alcoholic fermentation. Since alizarin and purpurin the main dyestuff components of madder are insoluble in cold alkaline sulphates, the following pre-treatment is required. Water soluble impurities are removed by treating 1kg of madder or its derivative with a solution of 1kg sodium sulphate in 12 litres of water for 12 hours at room temperature. The residue is pressed on a filter cloth and washed with cold water until no sulphate ions are present in the water. The treated madder or its derivative is extracted by adding a boiling solution of 1kg of alum in 12 litres of water, allowed to stand for 20 minutes, and then filtered or decanted. The residue is washed with hot water.

It is then precipitated with a soda, potassium arsenate or borax solution. Alternatively, better results are obtained when 1kg of warm lead acetate at 50°C is added to the filtrate and the mixture is agitated intensively until all the sulphate is changed into lead sulphate. The deep-red liquid is removed from the lead sulphate deposit and later decanted. The lead sulphate is washed with hot water and this wash solution is used instead of pure water for the next preparation. The washed garancine residue can be extracted a second or third time, using 25% less alum and lead acetate. The entire deep red solution is heated to just below boiling until a purple-red sediment separates and then cooled to obtain the best madder lake. So-called crystallised madder lake forms dark-red shiny facets.

The quality of the colour depends on the alum extract being precipitated hot. Otherwise the free alizarin, which separates as a brown material from the alum solution during cooling, will colour the madder lake brown. Overcooking the madder or garancine will create decomposition products which will dull the intense colour of the lake and if overheated to 66°C 'burnt' madder lake also loses its water and is thus darkened.[49] So the alum solution must be kept hot but not allowed to boil during the laking process. Excess alum solution is to be avoided too, as it forms a dull lake.

De Puyster in 1920 gave three recipes for different qualities of madder lake. For a fine quality lake, ground madder is allowed to stand in water for one day at 27° to 38°C, then an alum solution is added using one part alum to one part madder and the mixture is heated to 71°C. The liquid is filtered and the lake precipitated with sodium carbonate. The usual caveats about overheating apply.

A moderate quality lake can be manufactured by modifying the previous process. 100lbs of ground madder is put into a fine mesh cloth bag in a tank to which 250galls of water are added in small amounts until the colouring matter is all extracted. The solution is filtered, brought to the boil and a solution of 100lbs of alum in 150galls of water is added, followed by 75lbs of potassium carbonate in 60galls of water under constant agitation. The solution is allowed to stand for 12 hours and the precipitated lake filtered off to avoid the subsequent extraction of the dreaded brown products and tannins. The lake is dried at 'moderate' temperature.

A similar method is employed to produce madder lake from garancine. 100lbs of garancine is boiled for 3 hours with 250galls of water, to which is then added 100lbs of alum dissolved in water and the combined solution is boiled for 2 hours. It is then filtered hot through a flannel cloth and a solution of 1½lb of tin chloride in water is added to the filtrate. A solution of up to 75lbs of soda crystals in water is added, sufficient to ensure complete precipitation of the alumina lake, which is then filtered off through a flannel cloth, the residue is rinsed well and dried at a 'moderate' temperature.

Madder carmine is a more brilliant madder lake, which has been improved by adding an ammonia alkaline solution of cochineal carmine during the precipitation of the madder lake with soda crystals.

Steiner lake and Van Dyck red are cheap madder lakes manufactured from inferior grades of madder producing less brilliant colours.

Purpurin (see Glossary) madder lake is prepared from one part purpurin or Kopp's purpurin combined with one part alum. The beautiful red lake is not very light-fast. Firstly, the purpurin is finely pulverised and washed in cold water. A yellowish-red liquid runs off which yields a rose-red lake at 80°C with the addition of a small amount of soda. The extracted residue is treated with a 5% alum solution, the resulting solution is filtered boiling and is then saturated with magnesium carbonate until red flakes appear.[50]

Rose madder or pink madder lake, with excellent light-fastness, is prepared as follows. Powdered madder is extracted for one day with cold 3% to 4% sulphurous acid. Two per cent strength sulphuric acid is added to the extract which is heated to 55°C. The purpurin carboxylic acid (pseudopurpurin) which precipitates in flakes, is re-dissolved in alum solution. The lake is precipitated from the liquid, which has been warmed to 70°C, by the addition of one part soda to six parts alum. If the precipitation is performed on chalk a brighter shade of pink madder is obtained. To concentrate the lake, dissolve the pseudopurpurin in sodium hydroxide solution and precipitate with aluminium sulphate.[51]

Alizarin lake is made as follows, according to Wagner.[52] Dissolve one part aluminium sulphate in ten parts of water at 60°C, then treat with a solution of ½ part anhydrous soda in one part water. The precipitated aluminium hydroxide is rinsed with water. To this hydroxide is added in sequence ⅕ part sodium phosphate dissolved in two parts water, ³⁄₁₀ part calcium chloride dissolved in three parts of water, and a paste of two parts alizarin mixed with ⅖ part of Turkey red oil (sulphated castor oil, a surfactant) and two parts of water. The mixture is diluted to 50 parts with water and boiled for six hours, replenishing the water. After cooling the alizarin-alumina-calcium lake is filtered off and dried at the lowest possible temperature.

A very light-fast pink alizarin lake is manufactured as follows. Mix water containing aluminium hydroxide, aluminium phosphate, calcium salts, sulphated castor oil, and alizarin. The mixture is boiled, keeping the acidity between pH 3.2 to 5.5 (see Glossary).[53]

Substitutes — with the advent of synthetic dyes, attempts were made to replace madder lakes with synthetic organic pigments. This was to save the costs of the laborious preparation of madder lakes and to improve on the lack of light fastness of rose madder lakes containing purpurin. Soon after the synthesis of alizarin in the 1870s, synthetic alizarin lakes were made and later 'azo' lakes also provided excellent substitutes (see Glossary). Today Winsor & Newton supply both synthetic and madder lakes. Winsor & Newton's 'alizarin' was an abbreviation for 'alizarin crimson', the most popular red invented c. 1860. It was not sufficiently permanent by today's more exacting standards, so a 'permanent' anthraquinone pigment was introduced recently. 'Madder carmine' is a madder lake improved with carmine.

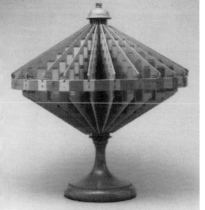

The 1930s Ostwald Colour System from a Winsor & Newton brochure (ack. Winsor & Newton)

A perennial problem is that few printers can print reds accurately. This is noticeable especially in photographs of textiles with their variegated surfaces and light absorption. The colour charts which painters use for buying pigment are never as accurate as the paint manufacturers would wish. It was therefore a pleasant surprise to find that digital photographs put on the Internet seem to give accurate reds.

Testing for madder lakes in paintings

Madder lakes have been identified in paintings by Leonardo,[54] van der Weyden, Vermeer, Rubens, Dürer and Fantin Latour, as well as in a Late-Egyptian tomb painting, Russian ikons and Tibetan thang-kas. The list below cannot be exhaustive as only a fraction of paintings have been tested and this list does not even attempt to include all the painting which have been tested: it merely shows how widely madder lake was used (see appendix 10.1, page 325). Description of the highly technical tests used in pigment analysis is beyond the scope of this book and can be found in accessible specialist publications.[55]

Leonardo's Last Supper: detail of St Simon, showing where old deterioration made Helmut Kühn's non-destructive analysis possible (Kühn)

The technology of analysis is constantly developing and earlier results are frequently cross-checked against more modern techniques. Kirby and White's qualitative remarks confirm that between 1400 and 1890, recipes for red dyestuffs most frequently mentioned are those extracted from brazilwood, madder, and the scale insects, kermes, cochineal and lac. Of the 62 paintings (65 including two earlier analyses, one mentioned in Schweppe, and the painting by Larkin) which they analysed from the National Gallery, London, less than a fifth — only 12 — contain madder, of which three are 'probably' madder. As a first step, there is a simple visual test. On the aluminium-containing substrates widely used up to the 19th century at least, madder gives a more orange red than the others, while lac and cochineal can give quite blue-toned crimsons.

Three main difficulties in analysing a lake pigment dyestuff need to be overcome. Paintings are usually analysed only when they come in for conservation. The small size of the sample can be inconvenient. The sample may have crumbled from around a hole or a crack or the edge of the canvas hidden by the stretcher or the frame. There may be no sample available in a painting in good condition or where red does not appear on the edge. In a traditional lake pigment the dyestuff is often present in quite low concentration. One example of a modern intense pigment 'alizarin crimson' prepared in the laboratory to a typical recipe yielded 30 per cent by weight of alizarin dyestuff in the total pigment. Whereas some 15th-century samples such as one from the robe of St Paul in 'The Virgin and Child' with Saints Peter and Paul by Dieric Bouts (NG774) are much less intense in colour.'

'Secondly, a paint sample may consist of several layers of pigment bound in paint medium, only one of which may contain lake pigment. As traditional lake pigments are translucent they were frequently used as glazing pigments, which were very effective and perhaps deceptive in exaggerating the amount of pigment which they contained. In the case of oil medium, a large amount of oil is necessary to produce a workable paint, in other words lake pigments have a high absorption and often little pigment may be present in samples.

It can also sometimes be difficult to separate the lake from the other pigments, which could include other lakes. So the equivalent of background radio 'noise' can appear with signals from other nearby pigments obscuring or confusing the information which could identify the lake. The colorant must also be extracted from the pigment for most analytical methods. This can prove difficult where the pigment is securely bound in the medium. Madder and cochineal appear as two lakes in a painting by Larkin, c. 1610. In contrast, madder and kermes appear together in one pigment by the Master of St Giles, c. 1500 (NG1419) and another attributed to Provoost, early 16th-century, (NG713). These pigments were probably produced by a mixed-colour textile shearing, such as the 16th-century Italian *mezza-grana* dyeing described by Rosetti and the *demi-graines* or *demi-cramoisis* of 17th-century France, or by a combination of different coloured shearings. It has not been possible to resolve if the painting by Rubens, 1629 (NG46) used distinct madder and (probably) cochineal lakes or a mixed pigment.[56]

The secret of the Penny Red

'Rainbow' Penny Reds (ack. Simon Beever, Sothebys)

Another secret recipe to achieve a rose madder pigment was the printing ink for the Penny Red postage stamp. The Penny Black postage stamp was postmarked in red which could be removed. As a result of the Rainbow Colour Trials, the Penny Red was introduced in 1841 because the black postmark was more permanent and it was easier to see in poor light than the Penny Black.

The ingredients were kept a state secret by the first postage stamp printers, Perkins Bacon of London. "If it got public it might facilitate the discovery of some mode of successfully removing the obliterating stamp (which is now impractible), so as to use it again, & thus defraud the revenue." There was a cocktail of three reds and other chemicals in the formula. 'Rose pink', which must have meant madder, was the principal of the ingredients and accounted for 16/53 by weight of the pigment. Next among the reds was 'Venetian red' which meant kermes (see p. 56) in proportion 12/53 and then 'cochineal' 2/53. It was probably not the same red pigment as was used from 1712 until 1870 for tax stamps on newspapers and almanacs, because that oxidized to black, which was not a property of madder though it could be the effect on other chemical additives to the ink. This has been repeatedly observed by Harry Dagnall, author of *The History of the Stamp Office*.[57]

11

The secret recipes
of Turkey red

A short history of dyeing with madder

THESE TWO chapters might appear to be about the noxious stinking dyeing process, with limited appeal to those who feel equally at home in the kitchen and the cow shed. Cardon quoted an 18th-century French traveller in Greece, in the village of Anibelakia, on the hunt for the secrets of Turkey red. He noted that the stench was so bad that its only inhabitants were the dyers and their families.[1]

But there are other wider implications. It is remarkable that no two of either the old or the modern numerous recipes are the same. Su Grierson, who has been distinguished both as a textile historian and a dyer, thinks that this is largely because dyers have an unrecorded and therefore unrecognised practical lore which corrects and improves during the stages of the dyeing process. She cites the example of a battalion of chemists and other experts being defeated by the mystery of obtaining the ancient Phoenician purple from molluscs, until — quite recently — a practising woad dyer, John Edmonds, broke the secret using his practical know-how (see chapter 17). There seems to have been a body of knowledge and skill which is almost lost nowadays.[2]

The problem of how the dyer arrived at a complicated successful method which seems to have no clear chemical logic can partly be resolved by his employment of an accumulated practical dexterity which bred its own innovation. In addition, a new theory is described in chapter 17. It is based on a reconstruction of the landscape of an ancient dyers' thought, which was a combination of folkloric symbolism with the various philosophic attributes of colour put forward by the medieval Arab writers, derived from the Ancient Greek texts.

Ancient European dyeing

Evidence of dyeing comes from a variety of sources. Discoveries of dye vats confirm the location of the dye-works and traces of dyestuff about the vats tell us what dyes were used. Rules and regulations to maintain the quality of dyes or to protect public health were also often preserved. Then there were manuscripts and printed books containing dye recipes, which help to locate a technique from the language of a region or people. Surviving dyed textiles are only useful if they can be dated and the dyestuffs analysed.

Adrosko suggests that the first Western dyers were probably the Swiss Lake Dwellers mentioned above who lived about 2000 BC.[3] Penelope Walton Rogers is sure that there are likely candidates for the earliest occurrence of madder in Britain among late Iron Age textiles although none have been analysed yet. She generously drew my attention to the earliest madders which have been analysed. They are late first century or early second century AD ancient Roman wool fragments from the Flavian site in Vindolanda camp on Hadrian's Wall. Of the 100 fragments of British sheep's wool, from over 50 separate textiles, nine were dyed. Eight of those fragments were dyed with madder or a close relative. These textiles appear to have been part of a Roman army contract and would seem to confirm the Hollywood and Pinewood film versions of Roman soldiers dressed in madder red. Another contemporary leather strap apparently painted with madder was found in Birmingham.[4]

Other similar Roman finds have appeared in northern Europe. I was reliably informed that two mislaid *Journal of Danish Archaeology* papers include the identification of madder in textiles from Norwegian and Danish graves of the Roman Iron Age, which were probably imports. Curiously, London has never been rich in Roman textiles, so a recent find has caused much excitement. I was kindly allowed to look through a microscope at a small fragment of yellow solid gold-wrapped thread from the later fourth-century Roman coffin, which contained the remains of a young

Two folios from the Stockholm Papyrus: top: a fake-purple receipt (Brunello); bottom (Sandberg)

woman, at the Museum of London. The thread which is awaiting analysis was dyed deep-red, and the gold-wrapped cloth was probably imported.

If my argument based on the Berber adoption of *rubia*, the Latin word for madder in chapter 12 is valid, then the 1950s Berber recipes are the same as the Roman empire recipes. There is a long tradition of Europeans trying to copy the magical dyes of the Orient. In the third-century AD Stockholm Papyrus (see chapter 3), there were 70 recipes for fake purples — the mysteries of *murex* were impenetrable — which included the vat-dye method (see Glossary) described below, which used madder.[5]

The medieval vat

Wulff thought that madder went out of use in Europe at the end of the Roman Period and only came back "during the crusades" as Turkey red.[6] There seems to be some evidence (see chapter 3) to cast doubt on this general statement. However, if he was referring solely to the Turkey red dyeing technique rather than the simpler dyeing methods, then it hard to say one way or the other.

The first evidence of local dyeing with madder in Britain is much later. Although Walton found no vats or utensils to dye the madder most commonly found on cloths from Coppergate in tenth and eleventh century York, there are madder-stained late Anglo-Saxon potsherds from London,[7] Thetford,[8] late Anglo-Saxon and Norman Winchester[9] and medieval Norwich.[10] These potsherds come from relatively small containers, which would have held at most two litres of dye liquor.[11]

Mrs Merrifield, who translated several early texts on dyeing during the 1840s, thought that the Jews were the principal dyers in Italy until the eleventh century. The Jews were settled in both the Christian and Islamic worlds and so able to benefit from both technological heritage and industrial progress. While there was evidence that Jews were dyers and had bought the monopoly for dyeing in some towns, as in other areas of industry, there are insufficient surviving records to construct an overall picture. In addition, Merrifield noted that from the frequent occurrence of treatises on dyeing in old manuscripts from monasteries, it seemed probable that this art was also practised in monasteries alongside painting and medicine. These various arts were frequently inter-linked.

For instance, John Mills has studied carpets in European paintings, which testify to the painters' fascination with carpet designs and colours. While most of the medieval carpets represented appear to have been made in Turkey, there is no direct proof as inventories never describe carpets or other textiles in sufficient detail, especially with regard to their designs. As the Europeans were able to weave finer silk brocades, it is puzzling that there was no medieval manufacture of knotted-pile rugs in non-Islamic Europe (see page 204). Mills reasonably argued that the taking of Constantinople after the diversion of the Fourth Crusade in 1204, when the Venetians were able to send back the Horses of St Marco, must have been when Oriental carpets were also sent to Italy.[12]

However there are few records, survivals or painted images before the

infrequent 14th-century paintings and richer material of the 15th century. As the Seljuk Turks reached Anatolia about 1041 and later Turkish village and Turkmen nomad rugs (but not Ottoman court carpets) regularly used madder for reds, oranges and violets, I suppose that some of these rugs would have had bright madder reds and pinks. Later examples include the probably late 13th or early 14th-century carpets which survive from the Seljuk Turkish mosque of Ala ad-Din in Konya, the 14th-century octagon animal rugs in European paintings, the elaborate octagonal knot design rug now in the Türk ve Islam Museum in Istanbul and the 16th-century so-called Damascus carpets.

Italian taste for quality madder red dyes must have been stimulated by the appearance of Turkish rugs. Julian Raby cited several examples. In 1461 an order was passed that every Florentine galley-captain who had made the journey to the Levant, specifically to Romania, pay 12 florins towards the purchase of rugs to decorate the Casa della Parte Guelfa. Close to the madder fields in the entrepôt island of Chios, the Chian notary Antonio Gallo also purchased 50 western Turkish rugs for export to Italy in 1492. Further rugs in the Vatican inventory of 1489 are described with typical Turkish Kufic borders as being "in the manner of the knot of Solomon."[13]

Florentine School Madonna and Child Enthroned, first half 14th century, with carpet with splayed eagles, Stat Mus Preus Kult, Berlin (J. Mills; Sylvester, Mills & King)

This was contemporary with their depiction in European paintings from the fifteenth century, with for example, the popular madder red ground with yellow arabesque so-called 'Lotto' design and interlaced octagons, the so-called 'Holbein' or 'wheel' rugs. The admiration of the artists for the small stunning madder-brick-red field carpets is often shown by their position at the centre of studio paintings, for example at the feet of the Virgin Mary and other temporally distinguished sitters.

It is puzzling that the Italians who dominated trade with the Levant during the 14th and 15th centuries and who bought so many rugs dyed with madder

Some export rugs were named after the Italian artists who painted them: (left) the Bellini Ushak prayer-rug c. 1500 (Stat Mus Preus Kult, Berlin; ack. Sylvester, Mills & King); and (right) a Lotto from about 1600 from Medias church in Romania (Author's photo)

Other export rugs were named after trade towns: (left) a Yomut Turkoman carpet popular with the British 19th century burgeoning middle classes, miscalled 'Bukhara' (Lefevre Catalogue, December 1977) ; and (right) a 16th century so-called Damascus checkerboard carpet (ack. Michael Franses)

were not interested in dyeing with madder but preferred kermes. Italian recipes for madder were scarce. While Merrifield's older manuscripts in Lucca and the *Mappae Clavicula* contained only leather-dyeing methods, the manuscripts in Bologna were richer in providing additional methods for silk and wool. The Sloane MS No 1754 contains *'De Tincturis'* where the dyeing of the dresses worn by monks is described. There were generally accompanying recipes for removing stains.[14]

In contrast the northern Europeans dyed with madder. From the 14th-century quality restrictions for powdered madder were in force in Ypres, Saint Omer, Reimerswaal and Lille. Dyeing rules were strict for madder red produced in Bethune, Douai, Bruges, Valenciennes, Aire, Ypres and Leiden and for topping with Brazilwood to add a tinge to the reds of Audenaerde, Douai and Malines. Rules were concerned with quantities and qualities of dyestuff and water used in the dye-bath. Additives were also controlled, such as copperas and wood-ash or wood-ash and urine, or cream of tartare, or wood-ash and lime, or copperas and lime or the bad lime and urine. The quantity of cloths allowed in a dye-bath was limited. A used dye-bath had to be seen to be thrown out into the river so that it could not be used again. The regulations build up a picture of widespread high standards in many

A member of the guild of tapestry weavers handing the statutes of his guild to the Doge for confirmation. The Doge puts the local weaver in his place, showing off his Ushak Turkish rug which would typically have a madder red ground, anonymous 15th century painting (Leix, CIBA Review, 328)

busy dye-works in the region.[15] Alum was the most common mordant used to prepare wool and other fibres to take on the full brilliance of the madder dye. Regulations for aluming survive from different local authorities from the 1330s to 1460s in Flanders and Artois, from Valenciennes, Douai, Bruges, Bethune, Aire, Malines, and Ypres.[16]

It was no coincidence that the first printed book on dyeing appeared in Brussels in 1513, *T' Bouck van Wondre*, 'The Book of Marvels'. Among other matters, it gives iron compound mordants for dyeing blacks. Brunello thinks this odd, as there were ordinances at the time in Flanders and Holland prohibiting the use of iron compounds.[17] In Leiden in the late 14th century, the only officially recognised method for dyeing black wool was first to dye with woad and then topping with madder on an alum mordant. This process was often done in two dye-houses. In six rule-books of 1436 to 1568[18] it was written that the standard was enforced by wardens who were assisted by other officials such as madder-testers and scrutineers.

Madder appeared but obscurely in Italy during the 15th and 16th centuries when the Florentine silk industry was predominant in Europe. The guilds took great care to ensure

Van Eyck, Madonna of Canon van der Paele, seated on a checkerboard rug, late 15th century (ack. L. Trench)

that all raw materials were of the finest quality. The dyes were divided into three classes, with the red dyers of scarlet (kermes) and madder being elevated to the *tintori d'arte maggiore*. The dyers had their own workshops and were obviously highly skilled which gave them independence from the monopolistic Calimala and the Arte della Lana guilds. They even briefly formed an independent guild in 1342-3.

King Edward VI, standing on a small-pattern Holbein rug, c. 1550, artist unknown (ack. National Portrait Gallery London; J. Mills; Sylvester, Mills & King)

In 1400 there were 40 dye-houses in Florence, usually worked by a master, his family and one or two assistants. In the *Trattato*, a technical manual of the textile industry, hank-dyeing of wool was described in detail. There was a rare recipe for madder.[19] One method for deep purple shades consisted in placing prepared wool for half an hour in boiling water, after which it was treated in the dyeing vat for eight minutes with woad, potash or madder. The wool was wrung out, plucked, washed and the water removed by stamping it with the feet. The process of dyeing was then repeated, different cauldrons being used for the various wool-bundles. Finally the wool was packed into sacks and washed in the waters of the river Arno.

Madder and some other dyes were also mixed with blood. No chemical reason for this has been found, so it seemed to have had an alchemical function. The blood was initially red and acted as an animalising agent for the vegetable dye to produce a 'balance'. A

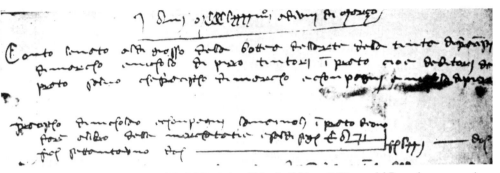

Extract from the 1395 accounts of the M Datini and Nocolo di Piero di Giunta del Rosso dye company in Prato near Florence (Brunello; ack. Datini archives, Prato)

law promulgated by the Great Council of Venice on September 21st, 1413 forbade dyeing with blood within the city limits, while exempting established dye-works in the swamps on the outskirts of the city: "The dyeing with woad and blood, which makes mortal putrefaction and pollution of our air as our renowned doctors have clearly decided." The penalty was "imprisonment for six months in the petty prisons, and to be banished from Venice for five years," without pardon or remission.

Blood reappeared in 1548 in Rosetti's *Plictho* in a formula for making a "fine scarlet," where the recipe had ox, cow or bull's blood overlaid with madder.[20] Burani's theory in his late 18th-century writings was that the Venetian dyers "of the lesser art" (*picigaroli*) in the 15th century, had applied madder on a fat mordant according to

The law forbidding the use of blood within the city limits, Venice, 1413 (Brunello; ack. PRO Venice).

the methods later described as Turkey red. Blood from cattle and goats was mixed in with the madder.[21]

In *Plictho* about a third of the 107 formulae dealt with red and several others with blacks. The Venetians were expert in producing these fashionable and sought-after colours. Because the only red dyestuff mentioned for linen and cotton was brazil-wood or *verzino*, S. M. Edelstein deduced that the preparation of Turkey red made from madder was still an Oriental secret at that time. However wool was dyed with kermes and madder, singly or in mixtures.[22] Written about 1500, *The Lisle Letters*[23] confirmed that carpets were luxury goods and virtually unobtainable in England. Arthur Plantagenet Viscount Lisle was one of Henry VIII's most important courtiers and was given charge of Calais. His wife could only find Turkish carpets in the king's possession and was obliged to ask him to borrow some to decorate her chapel for the christening of their expected baby.

The venturers' treasure-hunt

Almost a century later, Turkish rugs still held many secrets for the English. Richard Hakluyt, the venturous merchant of the Middle Temple gave the following instructions to Morgan Hubblethorne, an English dyer who was sent to Persia in 1579 on a mission of industrial espionage:

The same the world over: a 16th century Dutch customs officer, wood-cut from Dramhouder, Praxis rerum criminalum
(H.G., CIBA Review)

In Persia you shall find carpets of coarse thrummed wool, the best in the world, and excellently coloured: those cities and towns you must repair to, and you must use means to learn all the order of dyeing of those thrumms, which are so dyed as neither raine, wine nor yet vinegar can staine . . . For that in Persia they have great colouring of silks it behoves to learn that also.[24]

The English wool-weaving and dyeing industry duly recovered from the Black Death. Parliamentary statutes of 1489, 1512, 1515 and 1536 forbade the export of undyed cloths, though the Crown was pleased to sell licences to flout the regulation. Elizabeth I supported the merchant venturers rather than the manufacturers, who nevertheless in 1566 slipped through an Act saying that one cloth in each bale of ten had to be dyed before shipment. The merchant was given additional work and the dyed piece sold for less than the unfinished. In 1601 the queen revoked the act, but by 1614 the merchants were reorganised into a company which was to exclusively export dyed and finished cloths.[25]

In the 1670s, English west-country red 'Glosters', thick but finely-woven woollen broadcloths, attractively packed in bales of four or five pieces, were the most popular colour in a significant export business to Smyrna through the Levant Company. They were bought by Thomas Palmer in England who made a modest two per cent, for Jacob Turner to sell in Smyrna. Each piece had been cut into two lengths from 15 to 32 yards, but generally the shorter the length, the cheaper the quality of fabric and dye used. The popular medium-priced reds sold at £11 to £12 a piece, which price included all the English overheads: dyeing, hot pressing, mantling, imbaling, cartage, wharfage, portage, boat hire, impositions and customs.[26]

A similar 19th century souvenir red leather pouch decorated with the Sultan's 'tughra' on dazzling madder leather (Author's photo)

A contemporary reverse tourism goodie is the red morrocco-leather envelope-sized pouch in the Victoria and Albert Museum London, with floral designs embroidered with silver and gold wrapped threads and blue silk thread, forming the inscription: "Constantinopol 1676/Willm Whitmore." He was probably the son of Sir George Whitmore, Lord Mayor of London (d. 1660).[27]

The name 'londra' for cloths given by Italian merchants at the beginning of the 17th century was still actively used in the 'darkest months' of 1738-9 when the cheap now Yorkshire-made madder-red (rather than the expensive cochineal) broadcloth had found a stable market among the fez makers of Aleppo and other Turkish cities. Yorkshires had taken over from the Venetian export trade of similar 'red caps', where the bonnets of Genova and Marseilles were manufactured 'in imitation of those from Tunis."[28] To barter reds for silk, wrote Arthur

Serpent cum winged creatures at the end of tendrils suggest the wak-wak tree, Indian cotton, mordant-stamped red-brown c. 15th century, found in Fustat (ack. Textile Museum, Washington 6.151; Gittinger)

Radcliffe, who ran the Levant Company from his London mansion in Devonshire Square, in 1732, was the same as paying money for silk, since reds themselves were so readily convertible into cash.[29]

The voyages of merchant adventurers to India brought back to the West the knowledge of Indian chintzes, which Hobson-Jobson derived from the

Sanskrit word *chitra*, meaning 'variegated' or 'speckled'.[30] 1400s Indian cottons, resist-dyed brown-red by stamped mordants have been found in Fustat in Egypt.[31] In the opening years of the 17th century, England and Holland followed Spain and Portugal in setting up East India companies to establish their trade legally. Among the early trade goods desired by the

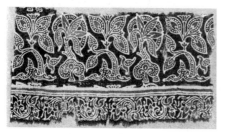

islanders of the South China Sea in exchange for spices were the painted fabrics of India, picked up in transit on the Coromandel and Malabar Coasts in the south of the subcontinent. In due course some of these cloths were brought to Europe, where their bright, fast colours and beautiful designs made them into desirable curiosities.

Early 15th century Indian blue and red-brown cotton, decorated by trees with elaborate outlines, produced by stamped resist, painted mordant and dyeing, found at Fustat (ack. Textile Museum, Washington 73.200; Gittinger)

'Calico' derived from the Persian name *kalamkari*, or *qalam-kar*, meaning 'pen-work'.[32] Printed cottons were the luxury end of the extensive Indian and Persian production of painted and printed materials. They were made by a series of processes which involved painting the outline of the design on the cloth in mordant solution and then using batik techniques to colour in the design; further details were added by painting the cloth with dye solution. This complicated process was first revealed with part-dyed textile

A Kashmir wooden printing block (Haller; CIBA Review)

swatches as illustrations by M de Beaulieu, who found it in Pondicherry on India's east coast, c 1734.[33] Most decorated Indian cottons, however, were produced by printing mordants and colours using blocks.[34] The principle dyes were indigo blue and a range of madder-related reds. Dr G. W. Taylor analysed the reds as chay root, madder, *munjeet* and *Morinda* root,[35] which confirmed the contents of an early Indian medical treatise which listed 45 shades that were the results of 77 dye processes.[36] Indian silk, wool and cotton carpets, in contrast, rarely used madder for reds.

Samples of printed fabrics produced by two reserve methods. In the upper pattern the background was covered and in the lower the design was covered (Juvet-Michel; CIBA Review)

Sandberg, who is a practising dyer, favoured the French traveller Jacques Savary's account of how Indian calicos or *zize* were produced in India, first published in 1757 and in German edition in 1811, with contributions by the highly-placed Prof Hermbstedt of Berlin. The process highlighted the problems faced by European imitators both in finding the unobtainable Indian ingredients and cheap skilled labour. For example, the best cadu shells, about the size of a nutmeg, come from Malabar and had superior contracting and tanning qualities than gall nut, pomegranate rind or sumac:

> The cloth was prepared by bleaching to half whiteness in a gall bath prepared with dried pulverised shells of cadu fruit and buffalo milk, followed by alternate drying in sun and shade and repeated baths. Glazing was achieved by folding the cloths into quarters or sixths and laying on a surface made of Indian date tree planks. The

Border of a Persian or Indian printed calico with inscription, c. 1750, from Daghestan (Author's photo)

folded cloths were beaten with hard round wooden catapouli mallets until a uniform surface was achieved. The pattern design was applied by sprinkling a small bag-full of charcoal powder through a perforated paper stencil. The dots were then joined with a pen dipped in ferric ink which reacted with the tannic acid to produce a black line. The ink was prepared by allowing iron foundry cinders to stand in palm or coconut vinegar for several weeks. Too much iron gave a red line. The pen was a proto-felt-tip, made of a bamboo stick with a metal tip surrounded by a ball of hair or plant fibres. If a woodblock stamp was used, the ink needed to be thickened with starch or flour.

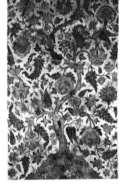

The tanning chemicals were excluded by immersing the cloth in a bath of fiercely boiling river water, immediately followed by animalisation in a similar boiling bath with additional sheep or goat dung. The cloth was left in the bath to cool overnight, then rinsed repeatedly and dried in the sun. The Indian dyer said that animalisation was necessary for the blue colour, which Savary said was true as if any tanning chemical remained, the indigo turned black. The cloth was then painted with the felt-tip pen or printed with a mixture of beeswax diluted in resin in a negative of the pattern to resist the indigo dye.

Indian export chintz for the British market c. 1700. Palampore (bed cover) fragment from the Coromandel Coast. The tree-of-life large-scale design was derived from 17th century English embroidered crewel work (Victoria & Albert Museum London, I.S.119-1950; Gittinger; Skelton)

The chay root (see chapter 1) — or sometimes *Galium triandrum*, called *madra* — provided the red dye which was applied after the blue colour, but only when the resist wax had been removed from the calico, which was then bleached. Next the cloth was prepared for the red dye by repeated vigorous boiling and animalisation as before. The cloth was then worked by hand with fatty buffalo milk, which was most important for the final

Above: Indian and Indonesian substitutes for madder: Morinda citrofolia (top) and Oldenlandia umbellata (bottom), called 'chay' (Gittinger)

185

result. The cloth was then sent to the red dyer who was located near a rare hard-water well. The dyestuff roots had to be pulverised in a stone mortar, while hard-water was judiciously added. Depending on the desired result, more or less alum was also added. The calico was dipped into the red dye-bath which was heated until the hand could not stand it, when the cloth was taken out and dried. The colour flakes which appeared when the dye was painted onto the cloth were then removed and the cloth returned to the bath and boiled for an hour. This puzzled Sandberg who thought that other wax resist areas for yellow would melt, so he suggested partial painting on of a thickened dye. However, it seems to me that as the red dye only takes on the mordanted cloth, it was the mordant that was painted onto selected parts of the pattern (see top illustration on page 184).

Mixing the red chay dyeing solution with the black iron solution and rice vinegar produced a violet red, ranging from weak grey violet to dark brown violet depending on the mix. Different red colours could also be made, presumably from chay in a warm bath and other *Morinda* dyes in cold baths, but they are not described by Savary. Finally a non wash-fast yellow dye was painted on with starch gum, either as a yellow or to turn the blue leaves green. The yellow was a mixture of flowers from the cadu bush, pomegranate rind and alum. Secret fixers unfortunately also dulled the yellow.[37]

Indiennes mania

The Restoration brought Dutch mania to London by 1683: "You cannot imagine what a great number of chintzes would sell here, they being the ware of gentlewomen in Holland . . . 200,000 of all sorts in a year will not be too much for this market."[38] The prolific Daniel Defoe chastised the calico craze rather late, if 1708 was indeed the first edition, but that does not affect his delicious style:

> These people's obsession with products from India has now reached the painted calicos, which were formerly used for quilted blankets and the clothing of lower class children. Today they are even used by our finer women. The power of fashion is so great that we have seen persons of rank wearing Indian cloths even though only the maids were allowed to use them before. The queen herself has been seen in Chinese silk and calico . . .[39]

The English bans on importing calico in 1700 and 1727 and similar French and German decrees were completely ignored by fashion-conscious women. Public calico burnings even took place in Berlin and Paris. The French government had cause to regret their forebears' expulsion of Hugenot dyers who never returned.[40] Home textile industries were under threat. Resulting bans on imported calicos were imposed in France, followed by William III's decree against printed cloths in 1700 reinforced by a ban on all calicos in 1727.[41] These bans must have been hard to impose because not only did wilful women encourage widespread smuggling but there were so many Indian names for cotton textiles — well over a hundred names and variants[42] — that it would have been difficult to define what the material was, and if, indeed, it was banned. Economic forces were in place for the development of the European calico printing industry, though coupled with imperfect technology.

Not all producers benefited. The Venetians, perhaps as a reflection of the economic power shift from city-states to national economies, not only lost the fez market but also the long-profitable manufacture of their celebrated black cloth. One reason for the decline of the Venetian dyeing industry during the 18th century was the following protection racket. Venetian black was traditionally obtained by topping dark blue woad with madder and re-topping with an extract of nut gall or of valonia oak combined with vitriol of iron.

However, in 1713 the dyer Alessandro Ceroldi of Padua obtained a peculiar deal from the Venetian Senate by which the recipe was forcibly changed. His method, using logwood from Jamaica, was neither new nor his own. It did not even produce the best black colour and it furthermore was not as fast as the old black. Ceroldi gained the right for his lifetime and twenty years thereafter to receive a royalty of two coins on each piece of cloth dyed black by his so-called Dutch and English method which was to be enforced on all the other dyers. Most dyers left and set up elsewhere.[43]

Northern Europe was more prepared to meet the challenge, but slowly. Because Indian calicos could not be matched in Holland, in 1678 two merchants from Amsterdam and a Turk founded the first European cotton print works in Amersfoot where the water was suitable for dyeing with madder. The venture did not take over the world.[44] The indiennes fashion peaked in France in 1685.[45]

> **TERMINAZIONI**
> *Degl' Illustrissimi, & Eccellentissimi Signori*
> **PROVEDITORI**
> **DI COMMUN.**
> In proposito della nuova Tintura in negro all'uso d'Olanda, e d'Inghilterra.
>
> 1 7 5 9.
>
> Stampate per li Figliuoli del qu: Z. Antonio Pinelli Stampatori Ducali.

The Venetian Regulations of 1759, still authorising Ceroldi's blacks of 1713 (PRO, Venice; Brunello)

The French discover the secret

In France too, enterprising men tried their uttermost to penetrate the secret. Yet Colbert and later enthusers for madder seemed to have ignored the writings of a French nun in Eastern Maritime Canada, which followed repeated written praise for Micmac red, which had begun with a letter from Champlain in 1603. In 1670 Mère Marie de l'Incarnation described how the Micmac Indians dyed porcupine quills by boiling them in *tyssa-voyana* or *Galium tinctorum* roots, "which makes them as beautiful as cochineal makes scarlet in France."

About 1747 a simplified process was developed in France. There are several claims to credit the first French dyers to imitate that beautiful, fast red on cotton using Turkish methods. Sandberg — presumably from a mention in Le Pileur's *L'Art de la Teinture* of 1776 — named Messrs Fraquet and d'Haristoy at Darnetal near Rouen.[46] Cardon gave credit to Messrs Goudard and Eymar at Aubenas and Nimes in Languedoc.[47]

But who was 'Le Pileur d'Apligny' — 'The Pulveriser of Flatness' — and was he a single author? 'He' was the first to publish precise information on dyeing cotton the colour called Turkish red — at that time, 1765, called 'Adrianopolis red.'[48] It was an exact copy of the title and chapter from Jean Claude Flachat's book published the following year (see below). Le Pileur was also named as author of *L'Art de la Teinture* published in 1776. This Pileur sounds more like Diderot, intimately referring to *"et dans l'Encyclopédie"*[49] and to the appended volume of engravings.[50] He only mentioned Flachat once, in order to criticise him for confusing *'garance-grappe'* and *'la robée'*, as *'mirobée'*. In contrast he cited the work of Dambourney, Lesbros, Duhamel, Tschifelli, Dupuy and Althen. In the chapter on *rouge d'Adrianople* he mentioned Darnetal and "other manufactures in France."[51] Diderot's massive *Encyclopédie* had a relatively short entry on madder and a longer entry on the whole of dyeing, but mentioned no names.[52]

Seated man hand crushing madder roots between rollers; on right two 'arçonneurs' (thrummers) and a 'divideuse' (winder woman), fluffing up cotton with a bow and mallet, dye vat in the background, Flachat (ack. LSE Library)

Flachat had lived for several years in the Levant and studied the commerce and arts — even the poetry — of the Ottomans. He returned to France and according to Schaefer set up a Turkey red dyeing factory in St Chamond, near Lyons in 1748: "Charles 'Slachat' (Schaefer misread 'F' for 'S' in 18th-century script) journeyed to Adrianople (Edirne) in 1748 and returned with a master-dyer to set up a Turkey red factory in St Chamond."[53] Flachat himself wrote that his somewhat larger team was made up of two dyers from Adrianople, two tin-smiths — *étameurs* from Constantinople, one of whom made top-of-the-range *caffetières* (coffee-pots), a Persian spinner and a thrummer or *arçonneur*, who specialised in fluffing up cotton with a longbow and mallet, from Smyrna, an Indian *brodeur au tamis* or sieve-maker who refused to come but taught Flachat his expertise and two Armenian vitriol makers from Cyprus.[54] Soon after, other Greek dyers settled in Marseilles and Turkey red dye-houses mushroomed in Rouen, Nimes, Marseilles and Normandy.

Flachat's book, sponsored by Henri Bertin, the minister of finance was published in two volumes in 1766 in Lyons. In addition to his account of Turkey red cotton dyeing in Adrianople, he also described cultivation of madder in Zeeland and Flanders, *'Culture de la racine de garance'* (see chapter 5) and Turkish cotton cultivation and conversion before he turned to bleaching *'Procédé usité en levant pour Blanchir le coton file'* (see below).[55] He had wide interests and *tome I* also has engravings of raki stills and a macaroni extrusion press, accompanied by long advice on how to do business in the Levant. Curiously this is not too distant from other subjects tackled by Le Pileur such as 'Historical essays on morality' in 1772, 'Music' in 1779, and 'Beer-making' in 1783.

In the frontispiece to *tome II*, Flachat described himself as *"Directeur des Etablissments Levantins & de la Manufacture Royale de St Chamond, Associé de l'Académie des Sciences, Belles-lettres et Arts de Lyons."* Was this the price for giving his account of cotton dyeing to Le Pileur which was also published by the French government

'Memoire contenant le procede de la teinture du coton rouge-incarnat d'Adrianople sur le coton file', by J. C .Flachat, 1766 (ack. LSE Library)

a year earlier with an identical title, or was it an exotic alias?

Several other Europeans also wrote about Turkey red, if in less detail. The German-born natural scientist S. P. Pallas who had travelled in the Caucasus in the 18th century confirmed that cotton dyeing with madder had been successfully carried out in 'Astrachan' before the method was known in Europe.[56]

Convoluted recipes for Turkey red

Books did not solve the problem of achieving the 'right' Turkey red. It was not enough to acquire some knowledge of the method or even secure possession of a recipe. The process was so delicate and intricate that even the differences of climate, the air and the water in Europe and the East meant that any method had to be adapted repeatedly. After several trips to Turkey to buy madder roots and initiations in Greek to the secrets of Turkey red, J. B. De Beunie in his *Mémoire sur la Teinture en Noir*, published in 1777 in Rotterdam, observed that the Turkey red of European cotton printers was much less fast than the real thing. De Beunie invented a chemical test which destroyed all the imitation Turkey reds but did not affect the real dye. He then indulged in the pleasure of naming a list of distinguished dupes, starting with Hellot.

Though the process was developed empirically by the Oriental dyers, it was

1600s painting of cloth bleaching at St Gallen, Switzerland, showing the fields of whiteness (Sandberg)

later analysed scientifically by Claude Berthollet (1748-1822), Edward Bancroft (1744-1821) and J. A. Chaptal (1756-1832). More recent research has indicated that the Turkey red pigment may be described as a lake (see Glossary) for whose formation aluminium and calcium must be present.

The European recipes for the Turkey red dyeing process were made up of a number of distinct stages. The first three — oiling, sumaching and mordanting prepared the fibre, while the fourth was the actual dyeing and the fifth was the clearing process. Ordinary madder dyeing, in contrast, only used an alum mordant. It might have been simpler to describe only one method but it would have been misleading. Instead, a combination of methods and comments on their peculiarities follow which attempt to form an impression of the complexity of the 'secret' process.

Preparation of the fibre was more lengthy than the dyeing. After the weavers' dressing had been removed from the cotton fabric by repeated bleaching on grass or by fermentation in diluted lukewarm potash together with frequent boiling, the fibre was oiled with a fatty oil. The oil was combined with sodium carbonate to ensure an even distribution of the oil over the fibre. Chaptal noted that the soda should be caustic and that its corrosive action should on no account be based on the addition of lime as this would endanger the workmen. Only vegetable oils were used, especially rancid olive oil ('Gallipoli' or *huile tournante*), which formed a milky emulsion with the sodium carbonate. In Italy 'Gallipoli' oil was produced in cisterns filled with olive oil. Impurities sank to the bottom and the pure oil was taken off the top leaving behind the dyers' oil. Oxidation products of fatty acids were also suitable. Good results were obtained with palm-oil. But rapeseed oil which was always used in Germany was regarded as inferior. Drying oils like linseed oil had the effect of blackening the red and so could not be used.

It was almost an invariable custom to prepare the fibre with dung — cow-dung in Europe and sheep-dung in Turkey. It could have been that the process was meant to change the nature of vegetable cotton fibres into that of wool. Schaefer added that this was influenced by alchemical notions of the significance of putrefaction. The active constituents were believed to be the gastric and intestinal juices of the ruminants, as well as their gelatine and albumen. Bancroft thought that this 'animalisation' alone was the key to the transformation of ordinary madder red to brilliant Turkey red. At Rhyner's Basle dyeworks in the 1770s, the non-dyed parts of the cloth had to be cleaned with a wash of animal manure and bran followed by several days drying on grass.[56]

'Sumaching' with sumach or 'galling' with nut-gall are equally puzzling to the modern chemist. The purpose was to subject the fibre to the action of tannic acid before dyeing. Early writers associated this too with 'animalisation'. The animal character of the gall-nuts, the tannic acid and the oil were said to unite to form the required fast and brilliant combination with the madder pigment.

Three similar German wool-dyers, anonymous pen & wash, c. 1500, 1505 & 1545 (Nuremberg State Library, Brunello; second two; Leix, CIBA Review)

Aluming was the next indispensable process. Mordants were originally applied with a brush and later by means of wooden printing blocks bearing the required part of the pattern. For dark red a mordant consisting of eight parts of alum (see chapter 3), two parts of carbonate of soda and one part of white arsenic dissolved in water was used. For lighter shades of red, the mordant was made of equal quantities of alum and cream of tartare. As the mordant was colourless it was slightly tinted with brazilwood to detect that the mordant had really been transferred. After this treatment the fabric had to dry for 12 hours and was then rinsed in running water, to remove the mordant's strong salts. The cloth was rolled into bundles and planked on rafts to press out the liquid.[58] These processes were often combined and some were repeated. Lavoisier and other distinguished chemists got around to examining Le Pileur's 1765 ten-step method in 1778, with Flachat's quantities and terms appended:[59]

1. Deep cleansing of the cotton, usually as thread, with lye of Alicante ashes (or other), sometimes followed with other washings using quicklime. 100 lbs cotton to 50 lbs ashes in 700 litres of water measures in 50 litres buckets (*sapin*).

2. Animalisation by treatment in baths containing a mixture of sheep dung and animal intestinal fluids, to give the cotton the nature of wool. The *premier appret*, called *sikiou* in Adrianople, using 25 lbs of *crottin de mouton*. Cardon added options of cow or dog excrement.[60]

Andi woman dyeing black with Chechen willow-bark, Daghestan. She was the last traditional natural-dyer until Magomedkhanov revived madder dyeing in 1998 (Author's photo)

3. Immersion in a soapy bath of rancid sesame seed or olive oil together with wood ash lye. The cotton is taken out after 12 hours, wrung out and dried. The immersion process is repeated twice more. The second *appret* used 12½ lbs of oil. Cardon had found that suet (*suif*) of whale oil or fish oil was used in different regions.[61]

4. More wood ash lye is added to the remaining immersion solution and the thread is passed through the solution three times to remove remains of loose oil.

5. Treatment with a decoction of nut galls or sumach extract. 25lbs of *galle epineuse* in 600 lbs of water.

6. Fixing with alum — *alum de Rome*, consisting of repeated applications in baths containing alum and wood ash lye. This requires several days, after which the whole previous treatment is sometimes repeated.

7. Washing to eliminate the loose alum.

8. Dyeing in red with Smyrna madder called *lizari* — Flachat stressed 'not Dutch' — together with ox blood and sheep blood, bringing the bath to the boil and boiling for one or two hours. 50 lbs of madder and only dye 25lbs of fibre at a time.

9. Rinsing in river water and washing in soap and wood ash lye to remove loose dye. *Avivage*, 150lbs of ash in 1,000 lbs of water and using *sapon de marseilles*, still the best soap.

10. '*Rosage*' or treatment with a boiling bath containing soap, a little tin salts and nitric acid to lend the colour brilliance.

Recipes often differed. One says that dung mordanting should be repeated seven times, that it should contain *huile tornante* and mixed with a solution of potash; the oil-bath should be repeated twice and followed by three washings in a solution of potash. The gall-steep was reinforced with sumach and quercitron bark. Before aluming, the fifth stage, the fabric was dried and was finally chalked with powdered chalk. Another recipe had 13 steps. The fabric was boiled and then mordanted with cow-dung and oil, followed by three oil-baths. Next there was a succession of four sodium-carbonate baths, followed by washing, galling or sumaching, aluming and a final clean.

After lengthy preparation, the fabric, which varied in colour from white to grey, was dyed with madder which contained a variety of extra ingredients. The strangest was oxblood perhaps another aspect of 'animalisation'. Schaefer added that the superstitious Oriental dyers believed in some magic power of the blood, while the rational Europeans used it as a fixative, though they too might have thought that the colour of the blood would enhance that of the madder. As late as 1840, a London chemist Thomas Packer's recipe for Turkey red includes addition of "not coagulated sheep blood [that] must be mixed with the water in the dyeing kettle right after the madder is added."[62] The American 19th-century novelist Nathaniel Hawthorne alluded to this in *The Scarlet Letter* where Hestor Prynne, the unfortunate persecuted adulterous mother is punished by being forced to wear a penitent's shirt marked with the letter 'A' the same colour and smell as blood.

Detail of Oberkampf's Jouy print (page 58) showing the rafts of bundles of cloth to press out the liquid at the end of the aluming process (Sandberg)

The 'clearing' process brightened the colours by removing unwanted tinges and cleaned up the non-dyed parts of the cotton cloth after dyeing. After the first dye there were frequent repeat treatments and re-dyeing.

The final stage was called 'clearing'. The oldest method was to boil the red threads or fabrics in soap baths containing potash. After boiling the cotton was spread out on the grass and exposed to strong sunlight. To get rid of the faint reddish tinge on the undyed parts of printed calico, the cloth had to be bleached on grass for five or six days, being watered seven or eight times a day to keep the cloth damp and to keep the colours bright. May to September was the season for bleaching to

Women washing at the river, woodcut by Hans Franck, ?-1526 (Schaefer; CIBA Review)

benefit from the early morning dews. Sometimes the fabric was then treated with stannous salts and nitric acid before a second clearing.[63] Papillon considered that soap was an essential element in Turkey red dyeing. His soap bath was the last operation of his highly complicated dyeing process, after the caustics and madder had been applied. White soap was said to dissolve the yellow-brown element of madder and thus remove its brownish-red hue and liven up the red, equivalent to the best and more expensive cochineal (see page 199).

In 1785, two French chemists, Louis Avers and Dr Saint-Everon, discovered that fabrics dyed with madder required treatment with stannous oxide added to the clearing soap to gain the Bukharan lustre. Berthollet in 1824 noted that

View of a French Turkey red dye-house, 1780: several dyeing vats, aluming vats on right, fresh water on left, hank-drying apparatus behind water (Roland de la Platiere; Haller; CIBA Review)

English dyers turned madder dyes away from yellow by top-dyeing with lichen purple.[64] In Europe it was also discovered that the dye was brightened if, after oiling, the fabric was dried hot at 60° to 70°C. Next it was found that for better results the fabric needed to be boiled, preferably under pressure in sealed metal cauldrons. During the 19th century steaming was introduced which had long been used in England as a fixing agent in wool dyeing. The process was constantly being improved.

20th century Swiss Turkey red dye-house Schwanden, Glarus (photo Dr P. Tschudi; Schaefer; CIBA Review)

Turkey red dyeing was a lengthy process, which could take a month. There were many accidents and the results were rarely the same. Reputable dyers were obliged to place only the very best of their products on the market. It need hardly be added that only the finest quality cottons were able to survive the treatment. This fostered their reputation of indestructibility.

Industrialisation & bleaching

French laboratory to mordant cotton yarn to dye Turkey red, c. 1800, J. A. Chaptal, L'Art de la teinture du cotton en rouge, 1808 (Brunello)

While these practical applications were known on the continent, in England, in 1756, the Society of Arts was offering a prize to anyone who could discover how to dye cotton fast red. This was of especial interest to the industry in Manchester, which from 1750 was taking over world leadership from India. The decline of the Indian cotton industry was due to British trade policy influenced by the development of machinery and dye technology married to new building techniques and the captive markets of the empire. Changes in fashion in Europe and natural disasters in India indirectly boosted the British textile industry. There was also the opportunity to make domestic economies. Manchester textile manufacturers were obliged to import from Turkey threads dyed in Adrianopolis

Red or have raw cotton shipped from the East Indies to Turkish dye-houses, which dented their profits.[65]

A certain Charles Steiner is credited with the introduction of Turkey red (from Russia according to Schaefer) which was perfected in 1818 by the chemist John Thompson. However the French artisan Louis Borelle moved to Manchester earlier and duly collected the English prize in 1786, with his *rouge des Indes* which straight away became a key item in an Anglo-French commercial treaty.[66]

Vegetable fibres vary in colour and are not white. Consistently brilliant-coloured prints required a suitably prepared bleached white fabric. Edinburgh's dyers were more sophisticated. At the request of the city's bleachers, Dr Francis Home (1719-1813)

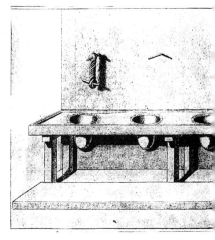

Detail of mordant appliances for Turkey red dyeing, c. 1815, J. B. Trommsdorff, 1819 (Haller, CIBA Review)

published the first scientific explanation of bleaching in 1756.[67] He explained the action of alkalis, distinguished the effects of various ashes and lime and suggested ways of measuring the alkalizing strengths. He saved money by the introduction of dilute sulphuric acid (see Glossary) to speed up neutralisation after bleaching. At the same time the Irishman Joseph Black (1728-99) wrote how to safely caustify lye ash by an exact addition of lime. The ability to measure exact proportions resulted in the repeal of the draconian capital laws prohibiting the addition of lime to lye ash, which further speeded up the process of bleaching.[68]

J. G. Dingler's steaming apparatus for clearing Turkey red textiles, J. B. Trommsdorff, 1819, (Haller, CIBA Review)

In 1774 the Swedish pharmacist Karl Wilhelm Scheele discovered Chlorine. Berthollet as a follower of Lavoisier was against the Phlogiston theory (see Glossary) and so it was natural that he wanted to study the composition of chlorine. During his experiments, he found that when an aqueous solution of chlorine was exposed to sunlight, oxygen was produced leaving hydrochloric acid, which he called "oxygenated muriatic acid." By 1785 he had tested its discolouring action on vegetable fibres and so discovered bleach, which was rapidly put to industrial use.[69] Milk was traditionally used in the bleaching process. When it became recognised as a valuable food, its price increased, which gave additional impetus to investigating alternative methods of bleaching.[70]

The old process comprised of alkalizing, rinsing, twisting, squeezing, beating and spreading out in sunlit fields. All these processes were repeated scores of times over weeks or months. The hot lye was tested with the end of the tongue and the temperature of the baths by finger. Additives encompassed lime water, cattle dung or pigeon

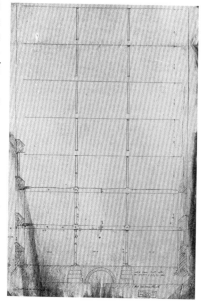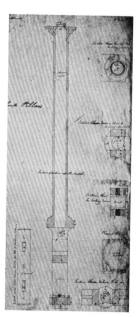

Philip and Lee's cotton mill, Salford, near Manchester, 1801: Watt and Boulton's working drawings for the first seven-storey mill with cast-iron beams and columns (ack. Birmingham Ref Lib; Giedion)

droppings. In Holland specialists immersed the linen which had been washed in hot lyes in sour milk, which both neutralised the lyes and produced a finer white. Before placing the linen on the fields, the grass had to be of sufficient height to allow free circulation of air underneath. The linens were was repeatedly sprinkled with water, so that the action of air, light and moisture destroyed the natural coloration of the linen which could then be washed out.

The method of bleaching was vastly improved by the introduction of chlorine. Far less time was required compared to the following thorough 30-day bleaching method from the Levant, described by Flachat:[71]

1. Mix 100 lbs ash of green wood and 25 lbs of slaked lime and throw in a bucket of water (50lbs) and put the paste in a wooden or earthenware vat and add a further 12 buckets of water. Leave for 24 hours and replenish.

2. At the same time, dissolve 25 lbs of soda in 12 buckets of water and stir 12 times during 24 hours with a wooden paddle.

3. Sew 100 lbs of spun cotton into skeins and wet them in the above mixed waters and tread in the cotton (by foot). Drain off the excess water and leave for 2 hours.

4. The wet cotton is placed in a sealed vat and boiled for 4 hours and then allowed to cool. The cotton is next taken into the river where it is trodden again for 1 hour. Then it is wrung out and dried in the sun.

5. The cotton is washed in a wooden vat. It is then covered with a cloth onto which is added 50 lbs of green-wood ash and 25 lbs of tobacco stalk cote ash. Heated river water is continually poured through for 36 hours.

6. After cooling, the cotton is left in the sun for 16 days and turned every 4 days and then re-washed in the river as above. The cotton is then put on poles to be exposed to the sun for 10 days and turned each day.

Turkey red in Scotland

Turkey red cotton dyeing took off in Scotland after 1790 when a Frenchman sold the Scots the secret. A different expertise in dyeing was available from the long-established woollen industry.

Wool dyeing maintained traditional methods. A good name in the traditional Scottish plaid industry, Wilson's of Bannockburn the tartan manufacturers in 1783 used the following two dye recipes for madder on wool:

Madder — take 1½oz alum, 1½oz argale (scrapings from inside wine barrels, see page 297 for similar scrapings) and near 1oz waters (meaning unclear) to the preparation. Boil them 2 hours. Then synd them. Next day finish with 6oz madder to the string and a little brown.

Dark red for fine coats — take 1½oz alum, 1½oz argale to the string. Boil them 2½ hours. Then synd them. Then do them off with 6oz madder and as much wash as you wish to make them dark.

Grierson interprets 'synd' as the practice referred to by Partridge in 1823, that after mordanting, the yarn or cloth should be rolled and left until it smells and tastes sour "let lay to sour." Also his explanation of "as much wash as you wish to make them dark," means "if the red should prove too yellow, put a small quantity of urine into the liquor, run the cloth again for ten to fifteen minutes, and it will be red enough." This was of course the same as the Highlander's technique.

How to dye 'common red' on wool was recorded in a report from Locheil Estate in Lochaber in 1772: "They boil the yarn in alum and water and after they have steeped the madder, they boil it and the yarn in a pot or kettle, and when it is half boiled they take it off the fire and put in a little stale urine."

Cardon also assembled some ground rules for dyeing wool with madder[72] (appendix 11.1, page 328).

The secret recipes of Turkey red

Stunning Turkey red gowns from the Renton dye-works north-west of Glasgow: roller and block-printed English cotton round gown, c. 1825 (left), printed cotton dress, c. 1837 (right) (The Herald, Dec, 21, 1998)

The French dyer Peter Jacob Papillon helped found the Scottish cotton-printing industry. An abstraction of his Rouenais method for dyeing Turkey red cotton was published in the *Philosophical Magazine* in 1804 :[73]

1. Cleansing — cotton was washed in a 'ley' of barilla, pearl ash and quicklime, strong enough to 'float an egg'.

2. Bainbie or Gray Steep — 2 pails of sheep's dung was soaked in 10 pails of strong barilla water, to this was added oil of vitriol, gum Arabic, sal ammoniac and olive oil. Tramp, steep for 24 hours, wring and dry. Repeat two or three times.

3. White Steep — as above but without dung.

4. Gall Steep — steep 24 hours in gall solution.

5. First Alum Steep — 24 hours steep then dry.

6. Second Alum Steep — as before but finish by steeping for 6 hours in the river then dry.

7. Dyeing — For 10 lbs of cotton, the dye-bath contained 2 gallons oxblood, 28 pails of milk-warm water and 25 lbs dried madder. Raise the temperature to boil over 1 hour, boil for a further hour, wash and dry.

8. Fixing Steep — Cotton steeped for 6 hours in dung and alkali. Wring and dry.

9. Brightening Steep — The dyed cotton was boiled for 2 hours in a strong solution of soap and barilla water.

For these operations vessels of copper and wood were used, they were also hooped with wood or copper, 'not even a nail of iron' being used.

Discharge dyeing in Mulhouse

The complexities of dyeing Turkey red meant that it was never possible to apply as part of a cotton printing process, so it was not long before a suitable method was developed. By 1810 Koechlin-Schouch of Mulhouse had developed the method of 'discharge dyeing' on a Turkey red cotton ground (see chapter 4). To destroy selected parts of the Turkey red 'lake', he exploited its ability to withstand the effect of lime chloride, in conjunction with its vulnerability to free hypochlorous acid. He printed tartaric acid — later arsenic acid — on to Turkey red fabric and then passed the fabric through a solution of lime chloride. The liberated hypochlorous acid destroyed the printed designs, without affecting the remainder.

Next he found that if the tartaric acid was omitted, blue could be superposed on the red ground, making black. In 1820 a new method of achieving yellow on a Turkey red ground was discovered by Jean Louis Lassaigne (1800-59) which Koechlin immediately employed. Lead acetate was printed on the Turkey red ground and then exhausted in a solution of sodium bichromate. By overlaying yellow with blue, green resulted. That provided the necessary range of six major colours and ensured consequent riches for Koechlin. As late as 1865, a British calico printer named Thomas Hoyle carried on a flourishing business in Turkey red discharge printing.[74]

Su Grierson's outdoor Highland dye-vats with the results of two dyers working for four days (Grierson)

Globalisation of Turkey red

European entrepreneurs filled the geographically distant lacunae in the Turkey red dyeing industry. Although Robert Asplund had established a Turkey red dye-works in Stockholm in the 1780s, only Wilhelm Rohs' 'Levanten' dye-works started near Goteborg in 1827 survived until the 1850s. During the 19th century the German dye cities of Barmen and Eberfeldt increasingly supplied 'genuine

Turkey red' cotton yarn to the Scandinavian textile factories.[75] In 1835 a Leiden calico printer was the first European to export to India, thanks to the British Free Trade policy. 'Selling coals to Newcastle' also appealed to the Dutch, who, in the steps of the Swiss export house Blumer and Jenny, were making fake Javanese batiks using madder dyes in the 19th and early 20th centuries.[76]

The Boston Tea Party had been a protest by American settlers against having to buy exclusively through English merchants. The same grievance applied to textiles which the Americans wanted to import direct from India. The next step in their economic interests led to the gradual establishment of an American home industry. John Rauch an American whose dye book was published in 1815 gave the following directions for Turkey red.[77]

He believed that the dyer of such yarn had to have a specialised Turkey red dye-house. It was necessary to have 4,500 to 5,000lbs of yarn on hand, so that with the assistance of eight to ten helpers the dyer could finish 100lbs a day. It took him 16 actual working days with one drying day allowed after each day's work. A total of 40 to 50 days were required to complete the process. Basically cotton was prepared by soaking in soda, after which the cloth went through several days dippings in oil and sheep-dung solutions. Then it was dipped in soda and nitric acid, next in nut gall solution and finally in alum solution. The first three-quarters of the processing mordanted and prepared the yarn. The actual dyeing in madder solution took only three hours. The remaining dips were in oil and soda solutions, concluding with (? another) final alum, nitric acid and water bath, followed by a rinse and shade-drying.[78]

Among the spoils of French colonial conquests in North Africa were both excellent cultivated madder and ancient dyeing methods. Following the defeat of the Ottoman navy at the battle of Navarino in 1827, the Magreb north coast of Africa lay open to the subtleties of English and French gunboat diplomacy. When the French took possession of Algeria and Tunisia from Ottoman Turkish suzerainty, over the years from 1830 until 1845,[79] the more business-minded of the 105,000 non-military settlers would have found an existing original tradition of dyeing with madder, which doubtless encouraged them to cultivate the plant to their great profit.

During the previous century the *abbé* Raynal (1713-96) had enthused of *"un rouge eclatant et durable"* from the Djerid oases near Tozeur in maritime southern Tunisia.[80] To the west, the banks of the Oued Tensift river which flows from the Atlas mountains to the Atlantic passing near Marrakesh were famous for their madder, which was also sold in the oases of Djerib, where the annual market was the occasion for trade between nomads and sedentary peoples. Djerib is inland, nearest to coastal Gabes and Djerba island off the east coast of southern Tunisia. Madder was also bought in Tripoli, further east round the gulf.[81] The French profited from North African cultivation but unlike the 13th-century Hohenstauffens from Sicily, they were probably too late to appreciate the dyeing skills of the Berbers (see chapter 9).

In Europe progress towards the synthesis of madder did not discourage development of concentrated purer madder products. For example, 'Madder flowers', (see chapters 7 and 8) the cleansed madder product with double the strength of madder was introduced in 1852. It was used for dyeing by addition to the dye liquor. The colour exchange required less time than

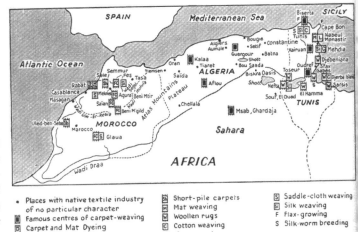

- Places with native textile industry of no particular character
- Famous centres of carpet-weaving
- Carpet and Mat Dyeing
- Fleecy carpets

- Short-pile carpets
- Mat weaving
- Woollen rugs
- Cotton weaving
- Linen weaving

- Saddle-cloth weaving
- Silk weaving
- F Flax-growing
- S Silk-worm breeding

Traditional Berber madder red weaving centres in Morocco, Algeria, Tunisia and Libya (map by Schaefer; Galotti; CIBA Review)

madder and the madder flowers were removed after each exhaustion of the dye liquor. 'Madder flowers' produced beautiful pink and violet shades.[82]

Morris & Co continued printing fabrics with natural dyes in the early 20th century and had 'rediscovered' the following simplified method, which was given in their catalogue. Most of the cloths printed were plain-weave cotton and linen, but some were also printed on velvet or velveteen:[83]

> The cloth is first dyed all over in an indigo vat to a uniform depth of blue, and it is then printed with a bleaching reagent which either reduces or removes the colour as required by the design. Mordants are next printed on the bleached parts and others where red is wanted and the whole length of material is then immersed in a madder vat calculated to give the proper tint. This process is then repeated for the yellow (welds), the three colours being superimposed on each other to give green, purple or orange. All loose colouring matter is then cleared away and the colours are set by passing the fabric through soap at almost boiling heat. The final treatment in the process is to lay the cloth flat on the grass, with its printed face to the light, so that the whites in the designs may be completely purified and all fugitive colours removed in nature's own way.

Exotic red leather

From before the times of the Ancient Romans leather was dyed red. In the Middle Ages Cordoba and later Morocco were centres of luxurious soft thin leather production (see chapter 3). During the 19th century and after, exclusive leather gloves were still dyed by the 'English' process, using very small quantities of acids and lyes.

To 130gms of potash add drops of sulphuric acid until the fizzling solution is neutralised. The solution can then be used for dyeing the rinsed and buffed skin, previously rubbed with alkaline solution, with various colours, such as madder-red and sandal with indigo.[84]

An intractable process

As a modern chemist, Haller echoed Schaefer's sentiments that Turkey red dyeing still remained a mystery with regard to explaining how the various heterogeneous treatments of the fibre were united into a process.[85] He put forward that only six processes in strict order were necessary to achieve a satisfactory Turkey red. They were oiling, mordanting, fixing, dyeing, steaming and clearing. To squeeze out more profits, great efforts were made to reduce the number of essential steps by combination, but all such economies failed. Only in

*William Morris
'Medway' design 1885,
printed cotton
(Fairclough & Leary)*

direct printing was the 'one-bath' method possible, because the printing colour contained the necessary metal salts and oil, already modified to suit the process. Also both dyeing and printing have the two hour steaming process in common. Modern craft methods were more concerned with quality of colour definition and fastness than the economies gained by cutting down the process (appendix 11.2, page 328).

The mystery engendered some charming later ideas. Scottish chemist and textile printer Walter Crum (1796-1867) in 1863 left an almost final mark on the theory of what happens during the dyeing, with the most beautiful and dreamlike microscopic colour drawings.[86] These images were meant to confirm his Mannerist theory that 'dissolved metal oxides in the mordants enter the pores of cotton fibres and are then precipitated during decomposition as insoluble powders which are trapped in the fine, filter-like structure. His

*'Morocco leather' glove sweatshop in New York
(photo Three Lions; Latour; CIBA Review)*

early influence on Science Fiction or his late development of the Phlogiston theory have not yet received due recognition. Another intriguing more modern theory was put forward by Barber who, discarding the colours of heraldry, thought that the reason why the flags of most countries which became political entities before 1856 (surely 1869) were coloured red, white and/or blue because those were the most wash-fast and light-fast colours.[87]

These quirky theories may be isolated examples of misconceptions about dyeing. But they draw attention to the more serious mutual misunderstandings between the Western and Oriental worlds, which were also manifest both in the methods of dyeing and in their absence. After the fall of Rome, classical science survived in the Arab Muslim empires in Egypt, Baghdad and Spain as well as in Orthodox Christian Byzantium until 1453. The Arabs and Jews were expelled from Spain in 1492 and as I have said elsewhere, the expulsion lost Europe the secret of Turkey red dyeing. There appears to have been a fundamental difference in how the western and eastern mind understood dyeing with the Jews usually providing a bridge by their presence in both worlds. The

Walter Crum's beautiful drawings of how he thought madder dyed cotton, 1863 (Journal of the Chemical Society, London; photo CIBA Review)

Western religious and secular traditions of painting as mural decoration replaced the Oriental carpets and other portable textile hangings derived from a nomadic tradition of tent-dwelling. In addition to paintings and textiles, glazed ceramic tiles were developed for stone city buildings in both worlds. Glazed tiles originated and were more predominant in the Muslim world, originally perhaps as a substitute for glass mosaics. These cultural differences may explain why so much care was lavished on textiles and associated dyes in the Orient.

Wool is easier to dye with madder than silk — both were dyed identically by Eleanor Matthews and the silk (right) came out streaked while the wool (left) was perfectly dyed (Author's photo)

It has been argued both ways that the Arabs declined and that the West exploited the Muslim world at a bewildering variety of dates from the Crusades to the end of the Ottoman empire in 1945. In the light of this general 'decline' it is ironic that when it came to dyeing the magical Turkey red, the Oriental secrets were both far better that western knowledge and also quite independent of later European advances in scientific chemistry.

12

An Oriental tradition

A western view

THE ABOVE ARGUMENTS may well be tempered by the chauvanism of history, and so it seemed natural to divide Oriental dyeing history from that of Europe. This merely reflects the broader misunderstandings between Occident and Orient whose occasional close links were interrupted by a history of conflicts – not forgetting their respective regular internecine wars. The nation states of the West as the more recent imperial colonial powers have been more comfortable collecting Oriental Art than the Islamic world in amassing European Art. Sometimes it happened in a different way. For example the Ottomans absorbed French Rococo into their already diverse cultural vocabulary. As already mentioned, early Arab rulers did collect Western libraries and more recently Japan as an economic superstate has provided the exception in Asia, with its large purchases of Impressionist paintings.

But the reality is that overall the artistic traditions were separate. It was simpler to write the Western history of dyeing first as it seems to be documented more fully than the more ancient Oriental tradition where no less information has come through later survivals and indirect sources.

Dating the earliest vats

It would be convenient to be able to determine the earliest date for madder dyeing from adjacent technologies. As George Taylor the distinguished dye authority and practitioner has found, it is possible to dye madder cold without a mordant in a wooden bucket, so the introduction of iron technology would not indicate an *ante quem* date. However, iron derivatives did contain important new elements for varying colouring agents, so the dates are of some importance. The secret of smelting iron — discovered about 2500 BC — was only used for practical products from about 1400 BC in the south-east Caspian region and dispersed by the fall of the Hittite empire about 1200 BC.[1]

It would be useful to identify the oldest dye-works, but frustrating if there was no trace of the dyes used. It would be tempting to extrapolate which dyes were used by working out if the vats were heated and if the layout would suit direct dyes or vat dyes using mordants. Adrosko referred to a Chinese chronology dated c. 3000 BC which mentions dye-workshops. The earliest facility that has been tentatively identified as a dye-works is on a windy hill at a Minoan site near Myrtos in southern Crete, dated to the Early Bronze II Period, c. 2500 BC.[2]

Brunello's assumption that the Hebrews practised dyeing on a vast scale was based on the number of purported dye-works found in Israel. However, with the exception of Tel Mor where there are mollus-can royal purple dyeing installations and a few other coastal instal-

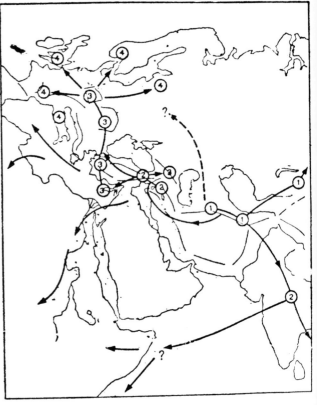

Map showing diffusion of metallurgy — could this apply to madder? Originating in Mesopotamia, numbers show the different stages of the spread (Forbes, 1958)

lations, no dyestuff remains have been found. The stone dyeing equipment at Tel Beth-Mirsim dated 589 BC has grooves around the rims of the stone vats to catch the overflowing dye when the skeins are immersed.[3] Also the dye could run back into the vat through a connecting hole when the dyed skein was removed. Traces of lime and potash were found in the pots, which implied to Barber[4] an earlier practice of mordanting, unless of course the potash was solely used for making soap.[5]

Informed historical alibi can be added to technical discussion about dye-works. Dye-works do not appear from nowhere. Forbes mentions the "Magdala of the dyers" on the river Jarmuk. In addition, the vats in Gezer which, like the above, were not built to be heated — unlike those at Pompeii — could only have been used for 'cold-dyeing'. Still Gezer was really an important dyers' centre in Hellenistic times as were Beth-Asbea, "the town of *byssos*" and Luz — mentioned centuries later by Benjamin Tudela.

However well informed, the circumstantial evidence of history is weak when uncorroborated. For example, the art of dyeing also has a long Jewish connection. Robinson has conjectured, though without proof, that the Jews may well have learned the art of dyeing during their time in Egypt when they were tanners and fullers.[6] Long after, Abba Hoshayah of Tarya, the saint, was a fuller.[7] The tribe of Zebulon were believed to have acquired the art of dyeing purple from molluscs and glass-making from the Phoenicians.[8] Unfortunately the Biblical scarlet referred to the colour from kermes, not madder.

It would be elegant to date the earliest madder dyeing from the oldest texts which used the word for colour — or better, for madder. The Akkadian *birmu*, from Old Babylonian and later meaning 'colour', also means 'many-coloured textiles', which must have included red.[9] Stephanie Dalley the Akkadian specialist at the Oxford Oriental Institute has not come across any textual references to madder before the Late Bronze Age, c. 1600 BC[10] (see chapter 3).

Dated textiles provide good evidence as shown in chapter 3, but only if analysis is possible or convincing. To the west of China, the mummified so-called Indo-European-featured, over six foot tall, Cherchen man, carbon-dated by the Chinese to c. 1000 BC, from Urumchi may appear to be wearing a madder red woollen cloak — but Barber was unable to obtain any samples for analysis.[11]

The technique found in the textile itself can give clues. Though there is no proof, Forbes thought that textile printing was discovered in India from where the Chinese obtained it about 140 BC. Carter pointed out that the Indian method of textile printing differed from the less expert European method which grew up during the time of the later Crusades. While the early European printer actually impressed treated pigments on the fabric directly from his block onto only the surface, the Oriental dyer had learnt the secret of allowing the colour to penetrate fully by impressing the negative of the print with a mordant or wax resist.

The wax resist kept the printed portions white when the fabric was later dipped in the dye-vat. In contrast, the mordant print alone took and

Cold-dyeing installations cut into the living rock at Tirath Yehudah, east of Tel Aviv (top & middle), and Kfar Ata (bottom) — (Arch dept Min Ed & Cult Jerusalem; Horn; CIBA Review)

held the dye in the vat, after which the dye could be washed out from the rest of the fabric.[12] The earliest resist-painted cloth is now dated to the early fourth century BC. The original cloth was used as a sarcophagus cover from Kurgan 6 of the Seven Brothers, near Kertch in the Crimea.[13] The sophisticated work suggests that this technique was well-developed and as several of the designs are repeats it seems likely that either a stencil or block was used. According to Strabo, these prints were imported to Alexandria from India too. Fourth-century AD finds at Achmin (Panapolis, Egypt) included stamps and printed textiles. The oldest European finds of these exported prints were in the grave of St Caesarius at Arles (d. 543). More calicos in red and black designs were found in sixth to seventh-century sites at Achmin and at the same time the Sassanian Persians employed printing as a major technique for decorating woollens, linens and silks.

Cherchen man, c. 1000 BC: Barber was 'baffled' by the red, which she puzzlingly compared to henna (The Guardian, Barber 1999)

Harder Roman evidence

Combinations of these identifying techniques are more convincing when applied to the later textiles of the Roman period. Pliny linked the Latin name *rubia* to the Greek "with which they dye wool and finish leather."[14] Dioscorides mentioned the use of madder in dyeing but without more detail.[15] Cardon obliquely transferred Pliny's quote to Dioscorides, 3.160.[16]

One ancient dyers' workshop has survived at Anthribis in Egypt (present Schaq) discovered by Flinders Petrie before 1908.[17] In addition, several fuller's establishments have been found in Egypt, some of which also dyed cloth. For example a *fullonica* was discovered in 1935 at Tebtunis by the Italian Archaeological Mission.[18] In Pompeii, the dye shop was located on the Via dell'Abondanza and several surviving pictures advertised their trade and products. An inscription about a dye-shop survived in Aquilea, and Aquinum, Tarentum, Ancona, Calabria, Baiae and Sicily were known for their dyes. These must have varied greatly in fastness, as was indicated by the different words for the Roman dyers who re-dyed faded clothing *offectores*, as opposed to dyers of new

DYERS WORKSHOP

Plan of dye-house at Anthribis (Forbes, 1956)

cloth called *infectores*. The almost complete absence of *tinctores* and *infectores* in Rome, though so common in other Italian towns, led Forbes to suggest that the metropolitan dyers called themselves the superior *purpurarii*, 'purveyors of purple'. In the later Roman colonies, there were, *inter alia*, dyeworks in the Balearic islands and Silchester in Britain.[19]

Several classical authors mentioned the exotic 'dyed sheep', which were mordanted live and came out sporting luxurious purple, scarlet and crimson fleeces. Virgil[20] stated that the wool was coloured red when the sheep ate the plant *sandix(s)*, which has been interpreted as madder.[21] However, Michael Ryder the modern authority on sheep, as an experiment, was entirely unable to colour even one hair of his pet mice by diluting their drinking water with madder.[22]

Remains of Pompeii dye-house (photo A. Maiuri; Brunello)

From Ptolemaic Egypt (332 BC to 30 BC) there are several papyri with references to the business of dyeing.[23] There was loose government control over dyers and fullers who were members of guilds which sometimes obtained government concessions to ply their trade for which they paid an annual fee. While in the days of Ptolemy Epiphanes, dye-works were leased by dyers' guilds instead of the temple, by the third century AD, the same dyers of Arsinoite *nome* were no longer required to lease the right to dye and instead paid normal sales tax — an early form of VAT. Private dyeing businesses were even sold, such as one at Oxyrhynchus.

Because of favourable local conditions, there are many textiles from this period which have survived. Purple-dyed woollens only seem to have appeared in the fourth century AD in Byzantine Upper Egypt. Sandberg illustrated one such — an aubergine Coptic panel — which Dr Ekroth-Edebo of Goteborg had analysed as madder without indigo or woad.[24] Cardon referrred to Schweppe's

Examining cloth, a Roman stone relief found near St Wendel in Germany (Faber, CIBA Review)

analysis of a similar lilac, called
'Egyptian purple' in a sixth-century
Coptic woven textile. The lilac was
originally obtained and recently
reproduced by top-dyeing madder red
onto indigo blue. Schweppe's analysis
by chromatography showed purpurin
with no alizarin which indicated wild
madder such as *Rubia peregrina*.[25] No
purple silks were in evidence in the
sixth century. A late Coptic papyrus
probably referred to mordanted
dyeing with madder when it mentions
that dyeing with "the *sekht* stone
(kaolin) is a red purple, the *djedi* stone
(iron or copper) a black purple."[26]
Cheaper purple imitations for wool
were sometimes concocted *inter alia*
"from a root."[27] Reinking translated

Coptic woven panel with the cardinal animal design in monochrome lilac madder, 4th century (Sandberg)

the many dyeing methods described in the third century AD *Papyrus
Holmiensis*, which included the following for dyeing purple with madder:

> A reddish hue is achieved this way. As the wool is taken from the indigo
> vat, spread it in a circle, strew it with ashes and tread it well. Then
> unloosen it, stir fuller's earth with water and wash the wool with this
> earth until it is clean. Then the wool is rinsed and mordanted with alum.
> The sign that the wool is sufficiently mordanted will be if you observe
> that it sinks down in the vat and that above it the liquid is clear.
>
> Then heat rain water until you can no longer hold your hand in it.
> For every pound of wool take half a pound of dried, crushed and sieved
> madder and half a pound of beans and add sufficient vinegar to form a
> porridge. Put this porridge in the vat and stir. Then immerse the wool
> and stir it constantly so that it is dyed evenly. When you see that the
> bath has been sufficiently depleted, take the wool out and rinse it with
> brackish water. If you want the colour to be vivid and fast, treat the wool
> again with alum. Then rinse again in brackish water and leave it to dry in
> the shade, protected from soot and dust.

In this recipe the flour of beans is added to counteract the lime compounds in the
water, which in Egypt was always somewhat brackish, even from the ordinary
wells used by the dyers. Wool was dyed before spinning whereas linen and cotton
were dyed as yarn or after weaving. The surviving recipes are for dyeing wool.[28]

Many Hebrew words associated with dyeing appear in Jewish texts. The
(not identified and therefore) Babylonian Talmud edited about 500 AD[29]

recorded that during the second century, the Jewish dyers and carpet-weavers 'guilds' in Heirapolis in Phrygia had counterparts in the cities of Palestine and Babylonia. The emperor Diocletian made membership of 'guilds' compulsory and dyers even took out a version of professional liability insurance, or was it 'protection money'?[30] After a two and a quarter year apprenticeship,[31] the trainee dyer knew how to control the matching of colours by immersing small samples of the cloth, known as the 'taste'.[32] He wore special gloves to protect his hands.[33] He ground the dye ingredients with a special hand-mill.[34] In the smaller Jerusalem Talmud, compiled about 425 AD, the Mishna, which was assembled c. 200 AD,[35] commented that when they went abroad, dyers hung red and blue threads behind one ear and green and pale blue threads behind the other, in what appears to be an early form of advertising. It should also be recalled that the Talmud and Mishna were compilations of earlier oral material.

Jewish and Syrian dyers appeared to have had a good reputation in Imperial Rome which continued to the Middle Ages. Akhissar, the ancient Thyatira, a Jewish stronghold in Asia Minor, seemed to have been connected with dyeing in the early centuries and even in modern times, the crimson fez was manufactured in the locality.[36] In Asia Minor, Galatian red wool was also famous in antiquity. During the Mishnaic period, Migdal Zevaya on the eastern bank of the Jordan, Haifa and Luz were known as dyeing centres and after the Bar Kochba War 132-135 AD, Lydda and Beth-Shean — both important weaving centres — also established dye-shops.[37]

Oriental mystique

In medieval Europe, madder dyestuff yielded a remarkably fast and cheap dye on wool, cotton and silk. The colour was however disappointing, as it varied between a dull brown and terracotta, and was nowhere near the brilliant scarlet of the kermes shield-louse (*Coccus ilicis*), which was the popular scarlet dye of the Middle Ages. After the discovery of America it became customary to add a touch of yellow-wood to the madder dye which made the colour lighter with an orange tinge, though it did not increase its lustre.

This was in marked contrast to Turkey red, which was made in the East using a secret process, and which yielded a brilliant and lasting shade of red. In France this was known as *rouge turc*, *rouge d'Adrianople* or *rouge des Indes*. In spite of their exorbitant prices, yarns dyed with Turkey red, mainly from Asia Minor and Greece, were sold in large quantities in Europe during the 17th and 18th centuries. The yarns became indispensable both for embroidery and for the developing cotton and linen industries. In Greece, both madder cultivation and Turkey red dyeing took place in Boeotia, the plains of Thebes, and the marshy region of Copais and Adrianople. Between 1650 and 1690 it flourished in villages on the slopes of the Ossa and the Pelion, in the Tempe valley and near the towns of Larissa, Baba, Rapsaria, Turnavos, Pharsala, Arta, Kaphanii, Janiza and Saloniki, making it one of the most remunerative industries in Greece's history. The favoured trade routes were by sea from Smyrna to Marseilles and Venice and by river, up the Danube to Vienna.[38]

The Persian tradition

Persia is said to be one of the places where madder dyeing first took place, so Wulff's fine account of a traditional Persian dyer's polychrome workshop is probably close to an early method:[39]

Shipping on the Rhine, 16th century, German wood-cut. Water transport was preferred to road transport, which was unprofitable because of high cartage costs, unreasonable frequent tolls, risk of robbery and accidents on disintegrating roads (Leix, CIBA Review)

In the two main madder centres of Persia, the dyers, in the absence of a modern water supply system, are obliged to have their dye-houses near water. In Shiraz there is a water supply canal and in Isfahan the river Zayandeh-Rud. Most dyes require boiling for the preparation of the extracts as well as for the actual dyeing. The dye-houses usually have a long row of built-in boilers along one wall. They are made from either copper or cast iron depending on the requirement of the dye. Each boiler has a fireplace underneath. Opposite the row of boilers is a similar row of vats of glazed earthenware for the preparation of the dyes and the cold rinsing or soaking of the fibres. The tall fermentation vats for the indigo process are placed together each one being secured by a wooden stand. These vats are covered with basketry lids, to ventilate the vats.

Most of the dyer's work is dyeing skeins of wool; there is hardly any piece-dyeing. The natural fat in wool fibres has to be removed before dyeing. This is done by rinsing the wool in a solution of potash in warm water. The wool is then transferred to the dye vat for boiling to apply the dyestuff. The skeins are dipped into the vats or boilers and turned over with wooden rods. Heavy wooden pegs are let into the wall above the vats. The skeins are hung on the pegs to drip out and for exposure to the air, where the process requires oxidisation. The largest vats are those for rinsing, from where the wool is finally taken out into the yard and hung there to dry on heavy poles. The dyers work on contract for the weavers. The price per skein depends on the weight of the yarn dyed but varies for the different colours.

More rough and ready were the methods of the nomadic Qashqa'is, of Fars province in southern Iran:

> They first wash the wool on the hoof. After shearing, the wool is scoured in boiling water to which potash or carbonate of soda has been added to remove excessive natural lanolin. The wool is then mordanted for 12 hours in cold water usually mixed with ammonium alum, mined in north-west Iran which can be bought in the bazaar. Yoghurt or iron vitriol are other fixing alternatives, all producing different colours. The uneven thickness of the hand-spun wool causes uneven dyeing which gives an attractive lustre to the colours.[40]

Like the Persian red-dyers mentioned by Barbaro in 1471,[41] a medieval Persian dyer from Tabriz who worked in India took a book of recipes with him which included the following mixture for a rose colour:[42]

> Take *ratanjot*, a sort of cochineal, madder or a very little lac colour and cinnabar. Add water, soak them for 12 hours, put in wool and steep for 36 hours, boil for three hours, then bathe the wool in alum and wash well, afterwards dry in the shade.

The Persian word for dyer is *shabbag*; the Talmudic Hebrew word is *zeba* in Judges 5:30. One indication of the number of Jews who were still dyers in the 19th century is the surviving surname 'Zebag' or 'Sebag'.[43]

Posh dyes

Several authors think that from late Roman until medieval times the Jews had an effective monopoly of dyeing around the Mediterranean. The evidence below supports this as far as it goes, but it is like an attempt to reconstruct a tree from its leaves. As already mentioned, the Jews were thought to have acquired the various skills in antiquity from the Phoenician cities of Tyre and Sidon, located next to Palestine and from the Ancient Egyptians as an extension of the fullers' trade.

The literature provides a unique and vivid insight into the social position of dyers. Jewish dyers were granted a variable place in society. This could have arisen partly because of the difference in social and economic standing between the artisan and the merchant.[44] In the Babylonian Talmud, compiled about 500 AD, dyers were described as of the best social class and as skilled craftsmen the dyers enjoyed higher social acceptance,[45] while in Alexandria they were later equated with oyster-gatherers and cobblers.[46] About 1150, an admiring biographer of Archbishop Nicetas of Chonai described his abhorrence of Jews: "Wherefore they were ejected from their residences and like hungry, leather-gnawing dogs, they prowled about the towns, as tanners and dyers of old clothes." The stink of tanners and parts of the dyeing process gave rise to a regulation that Jewish wives could exceptionally sue for divorce if they found the smell unbearable.[47]

Dyers met with unexpected dangers. A Jewish dyer from Byzantium was almost tortured to death, having been accused of spoiling a precious fabric. In pre-emptive retaliation his two children had been taken hostage and he had to travel to Cairo to raise their ransom.[48] Egypt was flooded with Syro-Palestinian dyers during the eleventh and twelfth centuries because of the permanent state of warfare in the region, which caused local artisans to complain about the competition. The lists of the poor in Old Cairo contain names of dyers who were refugees from the wars about Rum (Konya).

In medieval Egypt, Jewish dyers' names were followed by the sobriquet *tavag*, derived from *tsava*, the Hebrew for dyer, the same word as the Talmudic *zeba*, mentioned above.[49] Under the Abbasid Arab dynasty in Cairo (from 923), Palestine was a fertile and flourishing country. Dyeing was a traditional skill and during the tenth century there was prosperous trade at the September Fairs in Jerusalem. Goitein[50] quoted accounts from 11th-century Cairo where 63lbs of silk cost 474 dinars of which 129 dinars was for dyeing and the dyes cost four times the dyer's wages. At the top end of the textile market, a gold-thread *badanah* manufactured for the Caliph cost 1,000 dinars a piece.[51] Yet in 1260 in Mamluk Syria, a lowly status was accorded to Jewish dyers.

Jewish dyers were active all around the Mediterranean. In the Hohenstauffen Empire of southern Italy, they were first recorded in Gaeta near Naples in 1129. The three Jews of Arles in 1138 contracted with Abbot Pontius of Montmajour for the entire output of kermes in Miramar.[52] In 1147 Roger II attacked Byzantine Thebes and evacuated all the Jews to southern Italy. In the 1160s Benjamin of Tudela wrote that he met dyers in the following towns who were largely the only remaining Jewish inhabitants: in Benevento, one dyer who lived in St George the ancient Luz, twelve in Bethlehem, two in Bet Nuba, one in Jaffa, one in Karyaten Binyamin and one in Zer'in, the ancient Jezreel and ten dyers in Brindisi. He also spoke with four families in Jerusalem who paid a small annual rent to King Baldwin III (r. 1151-1163) for the dyeing monopoly.[53]

Jewish dyers remained in Palestine under Crusader rule in 1187. From twelfth-century Cairo, an order has survived for four pairs of small prayer rugs, of which two were red. In it the writer pleaded that "please, my lord, the red should be as red as possible!"[54] In 1231 Frederick II charged the Jews of Trani with the administration of the state dyeing monopoly, and commanded them to sell at 33 per cent profit for the treasury. In 1245 dyers were recorded in Trani and Cosenza and Sicily and there were 25 dyers' families in Malta. Salerno was also an important dyeing centre, while the *tincta judaeorum*, or dyer's tax was recorded in Benevento and Agrigento. The Saracens had started cultivating dye plants in Sicily as a result of which a group of Jews from the favoured island and entrepot of Djerba in the Bay of Tunis were prevailed on by the Normans to settle near Palermo in the early 13th century. They must

The mantle of the Holy Roman Emperors, Palermo, 1134 (Talbot & Rice; ack. Kunsthistorisches Mus., Vienna)

have had something more to offer than their fellow-dyers to the north. Djerba was the eastern trade junction for the Berbers.

The fascinating range of dye methods which survived among the Berbers until the 1950s may well indicate what the Norman emperors of the Two Sicilies were interested in, more than 700 years earlier. The Hohenstauffen's had uncommonly lavish taste in textiles. The magnificent red (but not madder) silk coronation mantle of the Holy Roman Emperors, made for Roger II in 1134, was embroidered with a pair of huge pearl-encrusted addorsed lions, subjugating camels. This survives as part of the Hapsburg treasury in Vienna. The brilliant Palermitan silk brocades also testify to their luxurious style.[55]

Mediterranean Jews & Berbers

Through information about the Mediterranean Jews and their links with the Berbers and Sicily, it is possible to argue that the Berber recipes date from the Roman period, perhaps from the Phoenicians. A simple reason is that the Berber words for madder are derived from Latin or Spanish *rubia* (see chapter 2).

Penelope Walton Rogers reasonably countered that the recipes were more likely to have come from from Islamic Spain, but that implies that they arrived after the expulsion in 1492 as the Arabic word *firwah* or Hebrew *pu'ah* would have been used in southern Spain from the time of the Islamic conquest of Toledo in 711. If the 13th-century Jews of Djerba possessed these earlier recipes, it would change the following excellent ethnographical descriptions into a unique historical document.

The Berbers of Morocco, as Galotti recorded, made rush mats of palm-fibre or esparto-grass or mat-weed, dyed red with madder:

> Twenty pounds of alum were dissolved in a large earthenware vessel filled with water, in which the rushes were soaked for 14 days. They were then exposed to the sun for a day and re-immersed for a further fortnight in the same bath to which a further 5lbs of alum had been added. Groussin thought that they used an abnormally large amount of alum — 25% of the weight of the wool. The rushes were removed from the bath and placed upright to drip. Water was then boiled in a tinned cauldron to which the juice of 20-30 lemons was added. Two handfuls of pounded madder were added and a layer of rushes added to the cauldron, followed by more madder and another layer of rushes and so on. The cauldron was kept over the fire for two hours.[56]

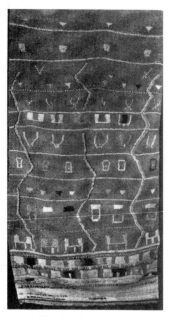

Uled-ben-Seba rug with wandering dreamy design on a madder ground (Galotti, CIBA Review)

Madder also appears in loosely knotted rugs from southern Morocco. The rugs from Uled-ben-Seba have wandering dreamy designs on pink and red madder grounds and flat rugs with spaced-out rows of knots known as *tellis* on dark red madder or cochineal grounds were used as pack-covers or beds.[57]

Moroccan leather, called *filali*, was a specialty of Marrakesh and above all Tafilalet. The leather was dyed with a rose madder glaze from roots ground with date pulp or oil and alum.[58] Lacroix described how the mountain Berbers of the Ouarzazate region, in the Atlas range in southern Morocco, dyed wool dark red and bright red using madder grown at Ait Zineb:

> The dark red dyeing process was standard with white alum or a little less powdered locally mined grey alum mordant, but the bright red was achieved by adding the bark of crushed apple-tree (*pommier*) to the mordant solution and a little black ash to the powdered root dye-bath.[59]

In the Saharan Atlas mountains, in the Djebel Amour region of south-eastern Algeria, the Ksouriens, notably

Mats of esparto grass, Tunisia (photo J. Galotti; CIBA Review)

from Touila, dyed wool bright chestnut with local madder. The wool was used entirely for mixing with camel hair to weave high quality *burnouses*, the hooded capes of North Africa. Touchon noted that the wool was dyed before it was spun:

> The wool was dyed with 25% alum mordant by weight and then with 30-40% hand-crushed madder roots and no tartare is added.

Madder was also used in some Douars, Oulad Ali Ben Ameur, notably by the Ghementas group, to dye dark brown wool in woven decorated tent bands. Standard dyeing was followed by browning in ferrous sulphate.[60] Near the north Sahara in central Algeria, in the Ghardaia region madder was found in Ghardaia, Djelfa, Laghouat, Tadjemout and Ain Mahdi. Bonete found that it was almost too hot to grow madder:

> The garden plantations of Ghardaia have enough water. But even after a rainy spring the merchants of Laghouat could save only a few months' supply. The wild drought-starved roots could only be gathered in spring and gave a mediocre colour, used by the nomads for their decorated *flijs* or bags. The wool was mordanted in 30-40% by weight of alum and dyed in 50-100% madder. The town dwellers of Laghouat found that it was necessary to mix the madder with henna to obtain an orange red and to add both walnut skins and pine bark to obtain the chocolate-maroon colour called *bidi* to dye wool for their *burnouses*. The wool was mordanted as above and dyed in 70% by weight madder, 100% henna, 10-20%

walnut skins and 80-100% pine bark. The inhabitants of Ghardaia obtained a beige called *ubar* from the same mixture plus 50-70% cloves.[61]

In South Tunisia, in the eastern coastal area, madder was once cultivated in the palm groves of the Aradh, in Gabes, Methouia and Oudref, in the groves of Djerid, in Tozeur, and perhaps among the palms of Nefzaoua, in Mansourah. Coustillac noted that in the 1950s all the dyers on the island of Djerba were Jewish women. The madder dye called *bedoui* was used in domestic dyeing of all clothes and other useful textiles:

> The skilled women dyers of Oudref boiled their wool for a day in a weak mordant solution of 10% alum with optional tartare. They used a few barley grains as a telltale in the 100% madder dye-bath, where the wool was stewed for four hours. When the grain burst the temperature was right. The desired hue was controlled by the time — from three to 15 minutes — that the dyed wool was immersed in a 15% chalk finishing-bath.[62]

Inland, south of Gabes in the arid Jebel Dahar or the Matmata hills with its celebrated underground houses, Barnaby Rogerson has recently found a variety of traditional red rectangular woollen shawls. They are sparsely decorated with

Sorting and pounding madder roots in Oudref, south Tunisia
(Coustillac; Cahiers des Arts et Techniques d'Afrique du Nord)

interwoven white cotton stripe motifs and white cotton and natural dark wool end stripes. Rogerson was told of their unusual 'mordant resist' dyeing technique. He understood that only the fine-spun white wool was mordanted, so that when the whole cloth was dyed red with madder, the cotton and natural dark wool kept their colours. The indigo blue shawls were similarly decorated. The shawls were called *'ketfiya'*, *'tajira'* and *'bakhnug'* in ascending order of size.

To the north, over the Straits of Gibraltar, the Jews of Aragon, Seville and Saragossa were known as dyers in the Middle Ages. Their activities expanded to Safed, the wool-weaving centre, during the 16th century.[63] Toledo was the Jewish garment production centre in Castile and in 1290 dyers were also mentioned in Avila and Segovia. Al-Jahiz, in his *Handbook of Commerce*[64] wrote that the best crimson (kermes) was found in Spain and that only a certain group of Jews knew how to obtain it. He also wrote that Jews predominated in the dyeing and tanning industries in Egypt, Syria and Babylonia.[65] In the south of France, the notary's registers of 1293/4 give several names of dyers in Montpellier, Avignon, Marseilles and Perpignan.[66]

Ian Bennett considered that in the Islamic world dyeing was carried out by the village or town dyer who was often Jewish and that their craft was kept a closely guarded secret. Many of the Islamic and Jewish formulae and practical knowledge for dyeing and fixing were lost when the Moors and Jews were expelled from Spain in 1492 under the Catholic domination of Ferdinand and Isabella.[67]

The Ottoman empire

It is easy to overlook the size of the Ottoman economy, which during several centuries was equivalent to the whole of Europe. The crowded map of the dye-works in Anatolia, which, however important, was only a part of the Ottoman empire, and the annual levies they paid to the Sultan or his tax-farmers during the 16th century, both show that the industry was highly developed.[68] During this period, Jewish communities in Salonika and Constantinople were involved in the dye industry, which subsequently declined due to competition from Venice and Ancona.

Turkish knotted carpets were luxury exports as well as being made for home use and the domestic market, whereas beautiful flat-woven *qelims* and bags were only for local use. Godfrey Goodwin calculated that there were well over 100,000 mosques in the Ottoman empire. While the majority of floors were covered with straw until the 19th century, the congregation brought their woollen knotted-pile mats to prayer and many gave rugs to their mosques. Many mosques were filled with layers of carpets.[69] In addition, military requirements for the expansion of the longest-lasting empire in modern history were vast. Innumerable tents were made of felted wool or cotton, frequently dyed madder red.[70] The infantry and *sepahi* cavalry went to battle bearing mass-produced coiled cane small circular bucklers. These were often discarded

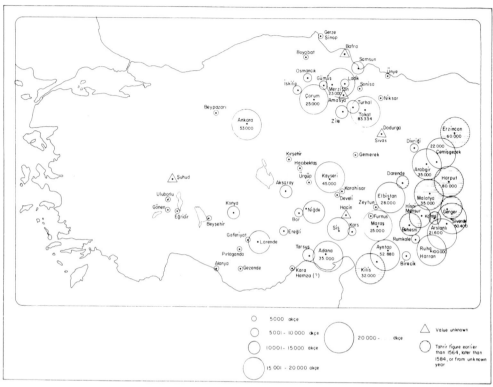

16th-century Ottoman dye-works in Anatolia (Faroqhi)

in the heat of battle. The solid wooden shock-absorbing centre on the inside was strapped onto the left arm for sword fights. The outward-facing, slightly flexible cane was strengthened and decorated in intricate patterns by tightly wound dyed woollen and cotton threads, where one section of red was sometimes dyed with madder and the next with cochineal.

There are at present no comprehensive figures for madder red or indeed dyeing in the Ottoman empire. The massive and excellent records in the Turkish archives in Istanbul may one day yield up this sort of detailed information. Until then, there are only a few random facts extracted from larger surveys to hint at the size of the industry. In 1529 the annual revenue estimates *mukataas* in the entrepot city of Damascus included 20,000 *para* for dye-houses, quivalent to a third of the value of revenues of spices from pilgrim caravans, a third of the estimate for the mint and a tenth of the estimate for customs.[71] In 1551, the revenue of the large dye-house of Basra was 262,000 *akces.*[72] The widespread traditional dyeing industry continued throughout the six hundred years of the Ottoman empire. For example, in Damascus in the 1850s, 70 of the 5,000 Jews were dyers.[73]

Not for export: two village rugs from western Anatolia; 17th century animal skin rug (Türk ve İslam Museum, Istanbul); and a rug from Sarkişla with the best madder range: brick-red, apricot, pink, deep purple, orange and brown, c. 1800 (private collection) (Author's photo)

Grossgeim's Caucasian dyeing techniques

The Ottomans controlled Derbent from 1579-1602 and held Baku during the same period. Both before and after that time there were strong trade links between Turkey and the Caucasus. There was influence from Ottoman textiles as is strikingly shown in a range of close copies which appear in Kaitag embroideries from Daghestan and in architecture in the Eastern Gate in Baku.[74]

Earlier this century, Alfonsin Grossgeim of Baku indulged in a learned love for the plants of the Caucasus. He recorded that "in the original carpet weaving areas of the Caucasus the inhabitants have centuries of experience of preparing dyes for wool, with traditional methods of dyeing and of post-dyeing treatment." Many of these recipes had been discarded and forgotten, apparently for ever. This emphasised the value of the recent work of V. A. Petrov and I. P. Grunskaia-Petrova in Karabagh and Kouba, the traditional carpet-producing regions of Azerbaijan, where they studied local methods of dyeing wool for carpets. All the three consecutive processes — pre-dyeing, dyeing and post-dyeing — were very complex:

The dyeing substances of the roots provided, by themselves, a knotty mixture of pigments. The recognisable red colours are obtained from the interaction of all these pigments and can vary from dark-claret to rose-red, as well as orange-red. In addition, the colour is often subjected to further action from minerals in the water. This occurs first while using an alum mordant and then while dyeing the wool.

Before mordanting, the wool is treated by wetting, either by simple [spring] water or by water with added elm ash or putrefied urine of long-horned cattle and camels. The latter method was considered rather accomplished. After the pre-dyeing work the mordant alum is added. The prepared yarn is next treated with a dye extract. Then the pigment extracts are treated with metallic acid fixative compounds, the so-called 'lacquer'. In local dyeing, an aluminium mordant is obtained from alunite (see page 231), while, for a ferric mordant, iron filings are treated in an extract of Carnelian cherries with ground barley grains.

Detail of 16th-17th century slit-woven tapestry kelim, called 'kosak', from Antalya, southern Anatolia, 4.5m long (private collection). Josephine Powell linked the stepped design with Central Asian 'chii' reed screens, found around the inside of yurts, decorated with wrapped threads, similar to Ottoman bucklers (see page 224). (Author's photo)

In addition, the material of the utensils in which the mordant is produced is very important. Some vats are made of untinned copper, others of tinned copper, or with a tin lid and so on. In the dyeing process, during the transference of the dye in solution, tannic substances undoubtedly play a large role. During dyeing they lay out the yarns, either interlaid with the appropriate dyeing plants or immersed in the previously prepared dye extract. The post-dyeing treatment is to fix the dye and occasionally to modify the colour tone. This process is carried out by various methods, one of which is practised high in the mountains where the dyed material is dried, spread out in the sun for a long period, and finally, the processed carpet nap is fluffed up with hens' egg-yolks.

O. V. Marggraf is an ever-respected Russian ethnographer who wrote about Caucasian handicrafts *inter alia* at the end of the 19th century. In his opinion:

Late 17th century Ottoman military tent, felted cotton or wool appliqué on a madder red background (Curuk; ack. Askeri Museum, Istanbul)

The art of dyeing woollen and leather objects in the North Caucasus was at a much higher level and much more widespread than in Russia. Except for indigo, the dyes were of local origin, the most popular being madder. They recently started to use a dye called fuchsin. Alum — *kvastsy* in Russian — and iron green vitriol — *kuporos* (see Glossary) — are used as mordants, as well as lime, lye from ashes and ferriferous clay. In Dal's dictionary, curiously *mumiya = zhelezistaya glina*, ferriferous clay and also = '? English earth' ('mummy') (see chapter 9)[75] and ochre. At certain times of year local people collect raw dyestuffs, load them onto their horse-carts and take them to market, especially those in the regions which are famous for their wool and carpet-weaving. Local dyers buy their supplies at these markets. In the Chechen-Kumyk areas in northern present-day Daghestan cloths and floor carpets are dyed with bright yellow, red-brown, crimson and black with few ornaments. But the best dyeing is in southern present-day Daghestan, where

Painting by Levni of Sultan Ahmed III's encampment on the Okmeydani in Constantinople, where archery competitions took place, for the festivities celebrating the circumcision of his sons, 1720; from the 'Surname' ('Book of Festivals') of Vehbi for Ahmed III (Curuk)

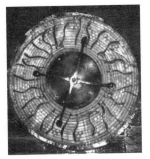
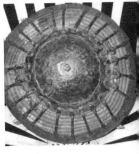

17th-century mass-produced cane bucklers. Madder and cochineal dyed threads wrap the coiled cane held in position with wrought-iron clips. (diam c. 300mm). (Author's photos)

they even dye yarns and make (mosaic) designs on felt cloths, called *arbabash* by the Kumyks or *yistang* by the Chechens. They produce a good range of colours and their dyeing is faster, finer and more even than elsewhere in the Caucasus.

Mr Zolatariov, Marggraf's informant, "met families in north and south Daghestan who were dye specialists to whom others brought wool and cloth for dyeing. They owned special ovens, cauldrons and dyeing ingredients. They received payment in kind, with the customer leaving a portion of the dyed textile for the dyer to keep. It seems that the southern dyers, who were Lezgins, Tabassaranis, Kaitags, Azeris and Mountain Jews, had learnt their art from the Persians from the south. In turn, they passed on their more advanced methods to the northern dyers, who were Kumyks, Chechens and Avars."

Kaitag embroidery with an outstanding c. 1600 Ottoman brocaded velvet design with a central ogival medallion, carnations, saz leaves and end floral lappets. The red was analysed as madder by Harald Böhmer and Recep Karadag. (Chenciner, 1993)

Indeed, the Sassanian Persians ruled Derbent from the fifth to seventh centuries AD before the Arab conquest and one of their rulers was King Khosrows who was famous for his great garden carpet. The Kumyks were a branch of the Kipchak Turkic nomadic tribal confederation and came south and settled during the 14th century. They were certainly sheep-rearers, felt-makers and weavers.[76]

Marggraf continued: "They mostly dye cloths rather than yarns or wool. In south Daghestan yarn is only dyed for carpet production and in Cossack regions to the north where women knit coloured stockings (he may have meant mountain Daghestanis such as Bezhtins). Dyeing and all wool working is done by women throughout the North Caucasus:

"All the local dyeing methods are similar. The article to be dyed is left to soak in a solution of alum. At the same time the dye-containing substance — tree-bark, roots or bushes — is boiled in water for some time and then filtered. The article is then submersed in the dye and stirred occasionally.

"After dyeing, if the article was not bright enough, it would be dyed again. Sometimes the article would be immersed in a lye made from ashes or green vitriol solution to brighten the colours. The most popular local colours are black, brown, cherry-brown, yellow, beige and red. Dark green, pink-lilac and lilac are rarely used and only by the most advanced dyers. Whilst blue, dark blue and bright green are not found by locals. Red is achieved by dyeing a cloth in a decoction of madder roots. Dark red is achieved by putting the cloth into a decoction of sandal wood after it has been soaked in alum mordant for some time. Madder is widely used in the south of Daghestan and the Kumyk region."

Magomedkhan Magomedkhanov, my friend and collaborator, who is leading the natural dye revival in Daghestan, discovered that the Dargins (who are related to the Kaitags) bought their madder roots (*khuna* in Dargin) from Terekeme near Derbent. First they dried it in the shade and then they

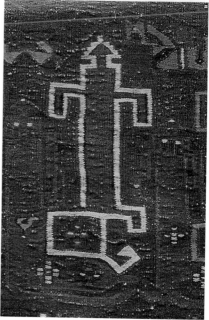

Top: Kumykh 'arbabash' felt mosaic from Daghestan, 19th century.
Bottom: Detail of Daghestan Avar 'davaghin' with dragon and simurgh design, 19th century (Author's photos)

ground it by stone hand-mill. Next they boiled it. When the liquor became cool they added cow urine or vinegar with the local thyme called '*chabrets*' — "you know it, we add it into tea." And only after all this do they they dye wool. "Good smell. *Parfum à la France. Aromat Argentina.*"[77]

Marggraf's 'table XXV' mistakenly identified the Lezgin tribes as Dargins,

Stone hand-mill for grinding madder roots DOBAG project, 1990s (photo H. Böhmer)

also listed were Lakis, Avars, Kurins, Tabassaranis and Andis, which left out the Lezgins themselves, who were famous as carpet weavers. However, he added that all the Lezgins were involved in hardy and fine broad-cloths, carpet, textile, felt and silk production and products; the Chechens with felt capes (*bourkas*);[78] and the Mountain Jews with leatherwork, carpets, cloth and gold thread work.[79]

Ikats of Central Asia

On the other side of the Caspian Sea, the 19th-century dye-workshops remained unchanged from ancient times. Cauldrons of clay or metal were set into the earth and only a rough stick was used to manipulate the articles in the dye-baths. There certainly were old links with the Caucasus and Russia. The Silk Route passed through the northern Caucasus, confirmed by finds there of 14th-century Luccese silk brocades, now on show in the basement of the State Hermitage in St Petersburg. At the same time religious teachers from Daghestan (called 'al-Dagestani') enlightened the Sufi schools in Bukhara.[80] The control of 19th-century madder imports from Central Asia to Russia (see chapter 14) were but one of several reasons for Russian annexation in the 1830s. Evidently there was a local tradition of madder-dyeing there, long practised by both Jewish and Muslim dyers.

The characteristic feature of the silk *ikats* of Bukhara is the pattern which is usually very colourful with diffuse transitions between different coloured areas. This blurring is intentionally caused by the 'space-dyeing' method. Yarns were tightly bound together at specific places which followed the design, before they were put into various dye baths. Careful dyeing could produce multicoloured yarns. Usually the warps were dyed in this way to produce a vibrant longitudinal flame-like result, now known as 'warp-pattern *ikat*'. Wefts were sometimes treated similarly, to produce a 'weft-pattern *ikat*'. The extremely complicated designs of 'double *ikat*' were produced by combining space-dyed warps and wefts. Further colour variation resulted from 'mordant *ikat*' where specific bindings were used to mordant yarn unevenly. The bound yarn where the mordant had not penetrated made the colour paler. Looser or tighter binding gave differing intensities of colour. Also colours were over-dyed to produce rich tones. This was recently discovered by Jan Wouters who analysed madder — usually mixed with predominant cochineal, indigo and *isparak* yellow — in yellows, greens, blues, turquoises as well as the expected reds, violets, browns and oranges.

Late last century Krauze and Oglobin found the following recipes:[81]

Silk 'ikat', 19th century (Tashkent Museum; Author's photo)

To dye silk gold, Krause wrote that 6lbs *isparak* (yellow delphinium), 1½lbs madder and 3oz alum, boiled together "for quite a long time." For red silk, sandalwood and madder were used. Oglobin noted that cotton was dipped in alum solution, wrung out and dyed with madder. 1 pood, or 16kgs of cotton took ½ *funt*, or ½lb of alum and 3lbs of madder.

Neighbours in the Russian empire

Marrgraf's comments on the poor standards of traditional Russian dyeing highlighted the differences between Asiatic dyers, Jews and Russian peasants who lived side-by-side. This was hardly surprising in view of Russia's historic practice of exchanging raw materials such as precious stones, furs and hides, mica, timber, fish and honey for manufactured or finished goods. The poor peasants had to make do with home handicrafts.[82] In contrast, according to Errera,[83] the Jews of Russia created the linked industries of dyeing and preparing furs. Probably the Russian Jews had connections to the west with the Jewish dyers of Brest-Litovsk in Poland and Lithunania, and further into Europe with the Jewish dyers of Prague who were noted from the 17th century.[84] In 1844, after Bukhara had been annexed by Russia, there were 10,000 Jews there who were mostly dyers and silk merchants and who had monopolised the trade.[85]

The sophisticated Asiatic and Jewish methods had no influence on the conservative Russian peasants, many of whom Karpov remarked were completely ignorant of their neighbours' skills — "in all areas of Russia where madder grows, the local peoples use the roots to dye their home-produced textiles. For example in the Ural region, the Kirghiz dye their pressed felts with madder roots, while the Russians are ignorant of the unique properties of madder and never use it."[86]

In various parts of Russia peasant women would dig up wild roots for home dyeing. They extracted the roots when the plant started shooting and during blooming. They knew that the thicker the taproot, the stronger the dye and also that younger roots produce a brighter colour than older roots. After the roots were dried, they were crushed and boiled from dawn to dusk in a cauldron to obtain a red-coloured solution. The dyeing agent would then separate itself in the lower part of the cauldron. They dyed cloth by simply dipping it into the solution.[87]

A Pre-Columbian recipe

There was ancient migration and settlement over the Bering Straits all the way to the southern extremity of the Americas, which may have involved transfer of dyeing.[88] However the amazing and pre-eminent standard of Pre-Columbian weaving, which drew from over a hundred different techniques would suggest that they developed their own dye technology. In Pre-Columbian South America, while insect dyes were more widely favoured as a source for red, it is surprising that madder-type methods of dyeing had also developed (see chapter 3):

> The Araucans or Mapuche of Central Chile, the only Indians in Chile whose language was independently preserved, boiled the roots of *Relbunium hypocarpium* for a couple of hours and added them to a bath of alum and *culle* (*Oxalis rosea*). The bath was boiled to prepare the *kelu* dye. This technique is used in modern dyeing.[89]

South East Asia – the longest dye

Turkey red dyeing arrived relatively recently in South and South East Asia by the Islamic cultural route from the Near East via British India, further-India and Indonesia, for it was not noted by the thorough Dutch botanist Rumphius writing at the end of the 17th century. Though the process remained essentially the same, local ingredients were substituted. Mineral alum was replaced by plants containing alumina, for example the bark of various species of *symplocos*; madder by the *chay* root or *Morinda citrofolia*, both containing alizarin (see chapter 2). Different oils were used for Turkey red dyeing in the Orient with excellent results. In the Levant, as in Europe rancid olive oil was used; in Asia Minor — sesame-seed oil and even lard instead of oil; the dyers in Masulipatam and Pulicat on the Coromandel Coast of India and the Batak tribes of Sumatra also used lard; in the Far East oil-bearing seeds were pounded and mixed with ash-lye; the Jews of Bukhara and the Armenian refugees in Astrakhan even used fish oil. Hot dye baths were more common in the western regions of the South and South East Asia.

A. Bühler (via Theo Maier — the painter from Basle) gave perhaps the longest-duration recipe from Tenganen in Bali where, like the red from Flores in the lesser Sunda Islands, the whole process took six years:

Wood ashes from the kitchen, consisting of the ashes of coconut-palm leaves, are mixed with cold water and strained through a bamboo sieve into a clay bowl. Then *Curcuma* rhizomes (see Glossary), which contain a yellow solid dye, are pounded and mixed in with the lye.

After the addition of coconut oil, the mixture is left for three days until the liquor begins to smell of peppermint and has assumed a vivid ochre colour. Boiled and dried hanks of yarn are placed in a clay basin and sprinkled with the liquor, carefully spreading it evenly. The hanks are then worked vigorously and hung up outdoors for a day and a night. The process is repeated three times with three-days pause between treatments. Vigorous foot-stamping aids absorption in the second and third treatments. After that it is hung up for ten days, rinsed in a lye of pure ashes and dried. It is particularly important that the yarn is exposed to the night-time dew and thoroughly dried in the sun. The preparation process can be repeated as often as ten times.

The dye is extracted from the root of *Morinda citrofolia* which is mixed with *symplocos* bark. The plants are crushed and pounded and the liquor is prepared with water. The yarn is left in the dye-bath overnight and allowed to dry for three days. Dyeing is repeated up to ten times, for red and for deep fast red up to 30 times, with an interval of 15 days between treatments.[90]

Alum mordant

Because alum mordant was used with madder and other non-red dyes, its mention or presence in red textiles is partial evidence of the root. Schaefer wrote that madder dyeing was complex because the dye, extracted as an aqueous solution from the root, whether it was whole or powdered, imparted no lasting colour to the textile fibre. Accordingly, it was necessary to subject the textile to a preparatory treatment before dyeing. This was traditionally done by means of a mordant known as 'red liquor', which consisted of alum with a certain content of clay. Alum is a kind of corrosive substance which if applied to the fabric fixes madder there at a molecular level.

The earliest textile evidence is as follows. At Mohenjo-daro on the Indus in India, the presence of alum mordant in cotton fabrics of about 2000 BC has apparently been analysed,[91] and according to Barber possibly earlier for an Ancient Egyptian polychrome textile at the pyramid of Unas (Saqqara), built c. 2350 BC. The textile, which is now in the Museum of Fine Arts Boston, is decorated with 'two baby-pink and two pale powder-blue stripes and a blue fringe'.[92] Aluminium salts were found in the Tutankhamen fabrics, 1350 BC[93] and in some seventh-century BC textile remains from Karmir-Blur in Armenia.[94]

The earliest textual evidence is somewhat later. The Assyrian 'chemist's

Klausen on the road to the Brenner pass, etching, Albrecht Dürer (Leix, CIBA Review)

manual' mentions alum as a mordant.[95] In Egypt where alum was mined, according to Lucas and Harris[96] "there is textual evidence which may indicate the use of alum as a mordant during the New Kingdom," 1450-1200 BC. Trade records have survived from c. 700 BC. Neo-Babylonian tablets from Uruk record the importation of alum from Egypt along with dyes and wool.[97] Then there were records of alum mines. Pliny listed further sources of alum as Spain, Armenia, Macedonia, Pontus, Africa, Sardinia, Melos, Lipara and Strongylos.[98] The mines seemed never to run out. Over the centuries, the continuing use of alum as a mordant was familiar to the Greeks and three alum pits are known to have existed in Turkey in the 15th century, one near Constantinople, the second at Phocaea[99] near Smyrna and the third in Sebin-Karahisar in eastern Anatolia.[100] The Italians obtained their supplies from them. Alum was also imported from north of the Alps to Basle from 1400 and Italian 'ice' alum — or *'allume di ghiaccio'*, a variant of rock alum — was specified in Como.[101] Alum used in Flanders and Artois during the 14th and 15th centuries was similarly differentiated as 'ice', but also as 'Castille' and 'Bougie', from present-day Algeria.[102]

The Genoese, who also boasted a considerable dyeing industry,[103] held the valuable alum monopoly during the 15th century. Its enduring worth was confirmed in 1547 when the Venetians bought the monopoly for three years for 25,000 gold ducats. At that time, one Bartholomew Perdix, who had learnt about alum in Syria, proved the existence of volcanic alunite on the island of Ischia near Naples. This may have stimulated interest for further prospecting in Italy and the famous alum pits in Tolfa near Civitavecchia were soon opened in 1462 by Pope Pius II. The production of alum was regarded as the monopoly of the Holy See, which soon led to the price of Italian alum exceeding that of Turkish. During the early 1500s, the Italians opened more pits at Cartagena in Spain and large quantities were exported via Antwerp to Holland, France and Germany. In Germany the production of alum by heating, slaking and washing

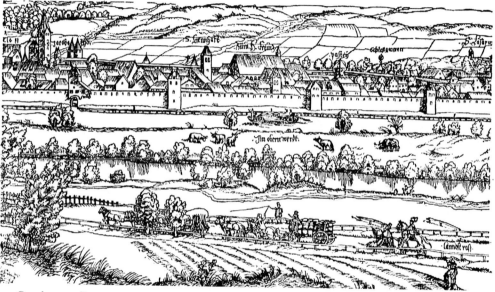

Cavalry guarding transport carts on the highway bypassing Ratisbon, Germany, 16th century woodcut
(Leix, CIBA Review)

alunite was begun after the 1550s at Oberkaufungen in Hesse, Commatau in Bohemia and Niederlausitz in Glatz. At the beginning of the 17th century an Englishman called Thomas Challoner brought some Italian workmen from Tolfa to Gisborough in Yorkshire to extract alunite. The idea of post-Reformation England becoming independent of papal alunite provoked the Church to pronounce an anathema against the hapless Italian contractors.

Alum was evidently too important a substance to escape the attention of chemists. By 1782, Jean Antoine Chaptal, the brilliant new professor of chemistry at the University of Montpellier had set up a factory where the process of synthesising alum was discovered.

13

Fashionable prices

International slumps & product developments

THERE WERE AT LEAST six booms and slumps in the price of madder from the 17th century interwoven with the growth of international mercantilism, until the final slump in 1873 with the introduction of synthetic alizarin. Records are more complete from the 1800s and Shtorkh's Russian figures give an indication of the international market.

The causes of slumps were wars, overproduction of madder, interruptions in the supply of cotton, fashion change and technical change. These causes were frequently combined. To simplify the reasons, the main slumps were in 1631 caused by the English Civil War and the Thirty Years War from 1618 to 1648; in 1671 when the imported indiennes craze was at its height, and c. 1750 when European fashions replaced Indian prints; and the Seven Years War in Europe c. 1745. There was an intermittent depression from 1765 to 1810. At the beginning of this period overproduction of madder was caused by French government encouragement and good prices.[1] Later there was the French economic slump which led to the French Revolution, and the prolonged disruption caused by the Napoleonic Wars. Around 1855 the Crimean War affected manufacturing and about 1860 the American Civil War cut cotton supplies.

There were several Indian cotton slumps especially c. 1750. In addition, great famines affected Indian textile producing regions when thousands of people died in 1630-1 and 1647. Indian wars disturbed production in 1565, 1712, 1725, 1741 and 1755 when a Dutch factor estimated that 400,000 people were killed in Bengal and Bihar. Extortion by local rulers forced whole weaving communities to move.[2] Finally British imperial trade policy used India for its own purposes. Indian textile production, even when under British ownership, was dropped for the more attractive prospect of industrialised production in England combined with a captive market in India.

It may well be that wars increased demand for uniforms and tents, that trade frequently continued throughout wars (for example Ottoman-Venetian trade) and that wars were localised. On balance, the destruction caused by wars and their cost, with resulting disrupted supplies, decreased demand for textiles. The price drops caused bankruptcies as the following selection illustrates:[3]

1621	66fl per cwt for best Dutch pounded madder
1622	75fl
1623	21fl
1624	16fl; Bedford gave £3 10s per cwt in London and half that in Zeeland[4]
1627	57fl
1640	28 *akces* per *oke* (pounded); 24 *akces* (roots) — Ottoman prices. The implication of state price-fixing was that there was a price crisis[5]
1660s	up to £4
1676	down to £1 10s[6]
1733	25fl
1739	50fl
1765	40% for better -100% for worse quality — increases on 1758 prices[7]
1861-5	Crash caused by the American Civil War
1868	30s
1870	8s, the effect of synthetic alizarin

The above theory looks rather selective when considered against the graphs of Dutch madder and wheat prices from 1580 to 1910.[8] The smoothed fluctuating price of madder appears to have followed that of wheat — that is, the agricultural price cycle. However, the fluctuations in madder price are so irregular that several conflicting factors must have been involved. The apparent contradiction is somewhat explained if we take a slump to mean a short-term relative decline in prices. This could have been caused by lack of cotton supplies in wars, economic depressions after the end of costly and exhausting wars or a glut of madder chasing rising prices in peacetime. Price jumps could have been caused by jumps in production of textiles due to fashion changes or cheaper manufacturing thanks to industrialisation or to greater prosperity through peace and industrialisation. The demand for red military uniforms, battle tents, sails or other military textiles would have modified slumps in wartime.

Examples of local price factors are illustrated by Russian records. The Ministry found that until 1854 imported krap sold for between 1½ and 2½ times the price of local roots, even though Shtorkh reckoned that Derbent roots contained 40% more dyestuff than Dutch roots. This seems to have been rectified from 1857 when Dutch and Derbent prices became roughly equal. Russian imports were nearly all ground powder with roots coming only from Turkey. Garancine first appeared on the Russian market in 1846 and steadily increased its market share. Its higher price — roughly three times the price of krap — was a reflection of its higher quality and greater ease of use (appendix

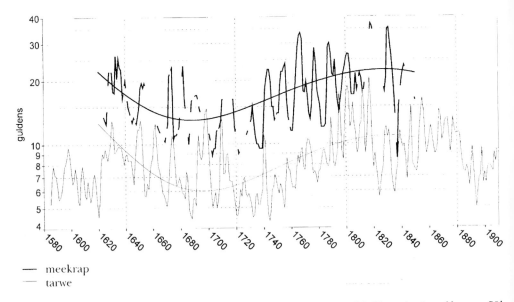

Dutch prices of madder (meekrap) and wheat (tarwe) from 1580 to 1910. Madder prices in guldens per 50kg and wheat prices in guldens per hectolitre. The vertical log scale diminishes the fluctuations in the price of madder and emphasises the similarity to the fluctuations in the price of wheat. Both smoothed curves show a decline from 1620 bottoming out around 1690 and then coming back again around 1830. Among the different grades of madder, the price selected was of 'gemeene', a relatively poor quality. (Posthumus; Priester)

13.1, page 334). Quite rapidly a balance was established between the prices of krap, garancine and roots, because one pood of krap corresponded to 1.33 poods of roots and one pood of garancine corresponded to 3.5 poods of roots. (i.e. the price of garancine was about 3.5 times the price of roots).

The Nizhegorodsky Fair

The Nizhegorodsky Fair or *yamarka* ran for about six weeks of the year from July 15th. It was the greatest semi-open-air trade fair within the borders of Russia, of equal importance to Moscow's markets, five hundred miles to the west, and a match for the Fairs of Eastern Europe. '*Nizhegorodsky*' is an adjective for the region near Nizhnii Novgorod, whose name was changed to 'Gorkii' in the post-Revolutionary fervour of 1932. The chronicles of 1366 mention that the sizeable market sited on the peninsula formed by the meeting of the Oka and Volga rivers near Nizhnii Novgorod was looted and destroyed by Novgorodian river raiders, called *ushkuiniki*. From the fifteenth century to the early 16th century, the oldest market at Arskoe field (*pole*) near the residence of the Kazan Khan became the most important of the middle Volga

Fairs since its beginnings in the mid-13th century. Muscovite colonial expansion eastwards led to the market being banned to Russians by Grand Prince Basil III in 1524, following the total massacre of the Russian merchants there. An alternative eastern Muscovite market, of questionable success, was established at Vasilsursk where the rivers Sura and Volga joined.

For practical reasons, trade gradually shifted to a one-day annual market which commemorated the death of St Makarius on July 25th, near the rebuilt Makarev Monastery, about 88km south-east of the Oka junction, on the principal commercial route along the Volga river, used since Viking times. Though the market was said to have been founded in the 1550s, the completion of a new cloister in 1624 marked the regulation of the relatively modest market into long rows of temporary wooden booths, without the monastery walls. From the 1620s the Makarev Fair together with the Moscow Fair made up the central Russian commercial market, linked to the Svensk Fair in the Ukraine. Basic goods marketed at the Fair were fish, down, metals and metal products, grains and groats — or crushed grains such as *kasha*.

In 1641 Tsar Michael authorised the monks to collect a duty from the traders in addition to rents.

Map of European Russia in the 19th century (Fitzpatrick; E.W. Fox, Atlas of European History, 1957)

Early 19th century view of Nizhnii Novgorod, 1824 from I. Gurianov (Fitzpatrick; Lib of Congress)

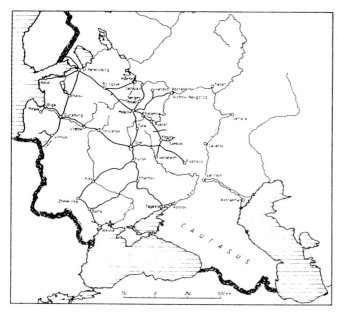

Map of the rail network in Russia, 1870
(J. N. Westwood, A History of Russian Railways; Fitzpatrick)

By the 1660s, the duration of the Fair had extended to two weeks. Its success attracted the interest of Tsar Alexis, who declared that the state would take-over the levy of duties after the first five days of 'free trade', setting the pattern for the future. As well as Russian merchants from the far-off Arkanangelsk and Vologda ports handling imports from Europe, and others from eastern Siberia, the market was a centre for merchants from the Transcaucasus, Central Asia, Iran, India and China, who shipped their goods by river barge from Astrakhan.

After 1691, Peter the Great took over all duties and licensed the monastery to maintain transport across the Volga. The government also paid for a police force of 300 lay brothers. In 1718 the Fair was put under the Department of Commerce, in recognition of its size. By the end of the 17th century, the annual volume of goods at the Fair had reached 80,000 roubles, in 1720 — 300,000 roubles, and in 1741 — 490,000 roubles, when the Fair became the property of the government and overseers of collection of duties were imposed. By 1755 the state had erected 830 wooden booths (*lavki*) for traders. Stall rents rose from 15,000 roubles a year in 1790 to 24,000 roubles in 1800. By 1790, according to Fitzpatrick[9] or 1800, according to Russian encyclopaedias,[10] the Fair's business had boomed to 30 million roubles.

At this time the Fair

The Makarev Monastery c. 1800, from J. Holman, 1825
(Fitzpatrick; Library of Congress)

Map of 19th century western Russian empire changes 1801-1900
(R. Harrington; Fitzpatrick)

had expanded to 3,200 government and private commercial buildings. In 1804 a visiting physician, Dr O. Reman, reckoned that the 'modest' Fair with its two mosques, was more important than urban fairs at Frankfurt and Leipzig, which must have been the case for Russian and Eastern traders. The more numerous Ottoman Balkan fairs lend a perspective to the size of trade. In the 1830s when up to 40,000 visited Leipzig, including an increased number of women, a far greater 150,000 people were said to be in daily attendance at Nizhnii Novgorod, where they were offered both better value and choice of goods.

A 19th century caravan from the East in Russian territory (Fitzpatrick)

About this time inadequate facilities were choking the burgeoning market. A Kazan Jewish merchant Evreinov offered to build a *gostinyi dvor*, or Ottoman-style bazaar, of agreed design, in return for a 20-year lease of the Fair dues from Tsar Paul. A crisis followed when the tax-farmer allegedly increased the duties and the traders sales decreased, 'forcing' Tsar Alexander I to cancel the agreement. In spite of the 'crisis', by 1809 the government, in partnership with other merchants, had completed 32 two-storey buildings, which contained more than 1400 new shops. Their investment of 600,000 roubles produced attractive gross rents of 21 per cent a year. There were an additional 1800 temporary stalls built along the outer roads by the merchants.

The river-bank on the monastery side of the Fair was overcrowded and flooded each spring. As early as the 17th century the Fair spilled over to Lyskovo village on the other side of the Volga and disputes arose with the monastery who owned the rights to passage over the Volga. Lyskovo became the livelier part of the market alongside the main unloading sites for the bulkier cargoes, such as leather, wood, iron and glass. Some cargoes remained on the barges while others were distributed on both sides of the river, which created chaos. During most of the 18th century the Lyskovites both raided and distributed forbidden alcohol to the monastery's market, until Prince Georgii Alexandrovich Gruzinskii took control. He maintained that he

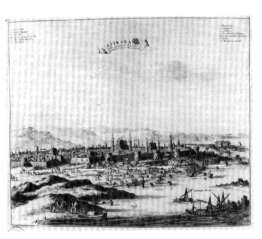

View of Astrakhan made in 1637 (published by Pierre van der Aa in Leiden in 1727, from Adam Olearius' (1599-1671) Voyages en Moscovie, Tartare et Perse; Chenciner & Magomedkhanov)

was descendant of the old kings of Georgia, (who had recently in 1801 deposed themselves by seeking Russian 'protection'), and direct descendant of King David and of Jesus Christ.[11]

Prince Georgii usurped the Lyskovo market and river passage. The monastery-side authorities were afraid to confront him as he provided much-needed discipline which halted the traditional raids. If he caught a trader swindling, he punished him by selling his goods for next to nothing. The state wanted Prince Georgii's monopoly of the market and the great fire in 1816, that caused losses of the order of 2 million roubles might well have been arson. It followed the visit of the tsar's *Kantsler* N. P. Rumiantsev, who had a personal disagreement with the Prince which began over the Lyskovo revenues which no longer went to the State.

In 1817 the government transferred the market to Nizhnii Novgorod, 88km northwestwards up

Pre-railway Eastern trade routes of the Ottoman empire (Inalcik, 1973)

the river. Situated at the strategic east-west junction of the Volga and Oka rivers, Nizhnii Novgorod was founded in 1221 by Prince Vladimir. The city, perched on the promontory hill, overlooked the river bank that from the 16th century had acted as a depot for river-borne goods from the Volga region and all of the East. Barges arrived in the spring to await an armed escort-boat from Moscow for the southern leg of their journey (see page 241).

From at least the 16th century the heavy river boat or *kolomemka* was joined by lighter rowed craft called *strug* and *pauzok*. Goods were reloaded into river boats at Astrakhan from Caspian seafaring *zebeks*. In between the rivers, the passage continued by porterage, both by cart and pack-caravan. While a loaded horse could carry 50 to 60 *batmans* or 3 to 3½cwt, a camel could manage half as much again and a mule 300 to 400lbs. Ittig quoted larger Persian 'mule-loads' called *khaira*, of 100 *batmans* or 650lbs. Depending on its definition, a 'bale' weighed between 213 and 276lbs. The strongest human porters in Port Petrovsk, (now Makhachkala and the older Tarki, behind on the hill, see page 255) the northern Caspian port of Daghestan were the Persian stevedores who could carry seven 20kg boxes of fruit at a time on a Turkish-style back saddle. In two Kizliar customs-ledger entries, northbound madder was mentioned. *"Alidzhai"* presumably *alizari*, the Levantine word for madder was part of a long list of goods arriving in Kizliar from the Persian town of Kouba on January 4th, 1812 and in November later that year 203 units — perhaps *kharal* bags — were carried by a Persian merchant Baba Inal Oghlu, resident of Derbent, from Derbent to Kizliar on the way to Astrakhan.[12]

Derbent trade ledger from 1726
(Chenciner & Magomedkhanov; ack. Daghestan Archives)

New Fair buildings were needed and a Spanish engineer A. Bekantur forthwith undertook the 6 million *assignat* rouble (3.5 *assignat* = 1 silver rouble) government project. The first 1.5 million rouble tranche had to be found by Tsar Alexander I from his Winter Palace renovation fund. The new bazaar, *gostinii dvor*, was finished in 1822 at a price of 9 million roubles. It offered 1,000 more booths than the *gostinii dvor* at Makarev. Remaining construction which included a pontoon bridge over the Oka was completed in 1827, three years after the engineer's death for a further 11 million *assignat* (3.15 million silver) roubles. There was even a sewage system with underground public toilets which were constantly flushed by water from adjacent canals.

The Fair lasted officially from July 15th until August 15th, which was soon extended to August 25th. The Fair was an immediate success, with commerce valued at 26 million roubles in 1817, which grew to 243 million roubles by 1881. The main goods traded included furs, hides, metals and metal products, wheat, fish, tea, wood, cotton goods, wool, linen and silk cloth. By 1822, the 2,500 stalls in the inner core were insufficient and high value merchandise was increasing housed in the shanty outer districts of the Fair, which had sprawled over 734 acres by the 1860s. The temporary stalls numbered some 3000 to 4000

View of Astrakhan by J. B. Homann, Nürnberg, 1727
(Hotz collection; ack. Royal Geographical Society)

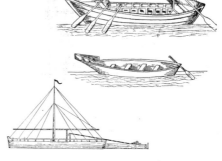

Clockwise from top left: 17th century view of the Oriental vegetable bazaar in Astrakhan; View of Ormuz; 16th-17th century Russian freight river boats, the light 'strug' above and the ferry or unloading craft 'pausok' middle, the 'kolomenka' for heavy freight below; a 17th century Caspian ship from a Persian glazed plate (all Fekhner); serf haulage on the Volga by Repin (Fitzpatrick 28a)

in 1858. The merchants made them of wooden planking, covered with cheap cotton printed awls. They were removed in the autumn as they would otherwise be washed away by the spring floods. In spite

Engineer Bekantur and his new building
(Fitzpatrick; Library of Congress)

of a ban on stoves or candles in the outer south-west and north-east areas, fires ravaged the Fair in 1857, 1858, 1864 and 1872. The last destroyed 500 river barges and damage was estimated at 2 million roubles From 1870 the shops outside the *gostinyi dvor* were steadily rebuilt in stone, but by the 1890s 2000 temporary shops were still made of wood.

At the rival Kursk Fair, in 1834, sales were 22 million which was equal to the combined sales of the four large Ukrainian markets. In 1865 there were 6,500 monthly markets in Russia, of which 35 boasted turnovers in excess of one million roubles. The second largest *yamarka* was at Irbitsk in Siberia and the third at Melornichsk near Orenburg, where madder from the East was traded. There was no security of continuing business, which gave the Nizhegorodsky Fair its edge as noted by Laurence Oliphant who was a Scottish visitor in 1852: "Here fortunes were to be lost or won in a few short weeks. The rich merchant had brought valuable wares from distant lands at an enormous expense. Both he and the peddler had staked their all on the results of their transactions in the allotted time, and were in no humour to trifle with it."

During the 1840s steamboats replaced the slower rivercraft. The Fair prospered there until 1917, though the new Russian railroad system dampened its contribution. Trade volume was down to 152 million roubles in 1893, but recovered to 167 million roubles by 1914. The Fair was briefly resuscitated as part of Lenin's New Economic Policy from 1922 to 1929. The Nizhegorodsky Fair rapidly grew in importance for imported madder, handling 1.4% of Russian imports in 1844, 8.5% in 1849 and 28.9% in 1853 (appendix 13.2, page 334).

A plan of the new Nizhegorodsky market
(Adres-Kalendar; ack. Library of Congress, Fitzpatrick)

*Above: 19th century Nizhnii-Novgoroksky market:
fire-risk from wooden temporary stalls (left)
and safer newly built stone permanent stalls (right)
(Fitzpatrick; ack. Library of Congress)
Below: Compare Bekantur's new building (far left,
facing page) with the later Washington Stores,
New York City, 1845, where a row of stores were
all under one roof (Giedion)*

European import prices

Large profits were made trading
madder, as implied by the large price
variations inside and outside Russia.
While the average price at the Fair
from 1845 to 1856 was 8r 29k, the

average price in France and Germany was only 3r 56k. The best krap came
from France, Belgium, Holland, Great Britain, Italy and Portugal. (appendix
13.5, page 337) Count Gasparen calculated that the average price of madder
abroad (i.e. outside Russia) between 1813 and 1843 was 3 roubles 25 kopeks
per pood (16kg); Sprengel's was priced at 4r; Einsel's at 3r and Gazzi's at 4r.
However in Russia, according to Mr Dulvetov, a landowner in Feodosia, the
price was 7r and from Mr Gartuch of Poltrava, the price was 6r.

Average prices per pood of European krap between 1844-1856 were:

Abroad	3.56r
By land via the west*	4.98r
Nizhegorodsky	8.29r
Major Russian cities	6.77r
Western imports	6.23r
Roots	4.05r
Baltic ports*	6.15r

Black Sea & Azov*	5.49r
St Petersburg	7.60r
Moscow	8.09r
Riga	7.08r
Odessa	5.27r
Astrakhan	5.15r
Average*	5.74r

see appendix 13.3, page 335

Not surprisingly, prices in landlocked Moscow and Nizhegorodsky were highest, and lowest at the Asian ports of Astrakhan and Odessa. The lowest price 3.50r was in Astrakhan in 1853 and the highest price 14r in Moscow in 1844. The average low was 5.34r and the average high was 8.00r. Prices of krap madder in other major cities in the Russian empire were recorded in customs ledgers from 1844 to 1856 (appendix 13.4, page 335). Average prices decreased by 28 per cent from 1845 to 1850, due to increasing Asian imports and then rose back by 31 per cent in 1856, because the Crimean War hampered maritime imports, as overland shipment was more costly. During 1854 and 1855, the Crimean War prevented any madder arriving at the Fair, excepting small amounts from Prussia and Austria, but prices were only 10% higher the following year.

There was the phenomenon of rapid price changes as the Fair progressed. For example the price of Dutch and Breslau krap at Nizhegorodsky Fair varied wildly, almost doubling during the Fair, from 1845 to 1848, but calming down from 1849 to 1853. This may have been caused by indirect variations in demand. At other times prices could also have been affected by the fires of 1857, 1858, 1864 and 1872. The last destroyed 500 river barges and damage was estimated at two million roubles. In normal times, all the madder-producing countries exported to Russia (appendix 13.6). The average prices of European krap imports from 1844-1856 were:

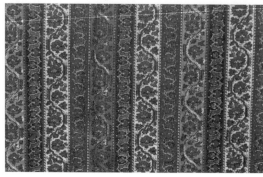

Russian cotton prints, probably Turkey reds — far left: French-rococo garland style; left: Persian small floral stripes (Author's photos)

Fashionable prices

Prussia	5.43r
German *landern*	6.59r
Holland	6.67r
France	6.95r
Belgium	6.36r
Great Britain	7.37r
Italy	7.11r
Austria	6.43r
Turkey	4.79r
Portugal	7.31r
Average	6.70r

The large local price fluctuations were further affected by world prices. Price fluctuations were set against a background of huge increases in European, American and Russian textile production. There was a trough from 1848-1856, average prices per pood were:

Year	average	average price of imports
1844	6.62r	6.59r
1845	8.85r	9.74r
1846	7.73r	8.24r
1847	6.97r	7.23r
1848	7.01r	6.50r
1849	5.49r	5.67r
1850	6.14r	6.13r
1851	5.26r	5.77r
1852	5.38r	5.86r
1853	4.94r	5.43r
1854	4.93r	5.60r
1855	3.98r	3.25r
1856	6.09r	6.75r
Average	6.10r	6.36r
General average	6.23r	

It may seem strange that there were such erratic price fluctuations against a booming background of continual expansion of the linked textile and madder industries described in the next chapter. In addition to obvious factors which have been discussed such as wars, the explanation may lie in the imperfections of the markets. Irregular and slow communication of information and orders were compounded by dislocated transport to cause erratic real and perceived changes of conditions which affected prices. Improvements were brought about gradually by the development of railways, telegraph and postal services which started in Britain as early as the 1840s and later in other parts of the world.

14

The 19th-century
madder boom

A worldwide boom

THE MECHANISATION of the textile industry, advances in dyeing and printing on cotton and American intensive cotton production all made cheap popular products available. Industrialisation had spread spending ability as never before. The world market responded strongly. By 1868 world madder exports had reached £3,500,000.[1] After long Dutch domination of the market, France caught up in 1848. If the substantial Russian figures are typical of world trade, the two countries controlled about 90 per cent of the Russian and world markets. From the late 1840s French settlers began to cultivate the extra raw material from her newly subjugated Algerian and Tunisian colonies.[2] The excellent and plentiful madder roots were shipped to France for processing. France's industry had become massive, exporting over £1,200,000 in 1868, yet this was only a fraction of the roots that were used in her domestic textile industry.[3]

Of this 0.42 million poods were exported to Great Britain, Switzerland, Prussia and the USA. Cardon wrote that the departments of the Midi in France in 1881 produced 25,000 tonnes (25 million kgs or 1.6 million poods) of madder.[4] Shtorkh wrote that in the Vaucluse or Avignon region of France, the annual production of 1.2 million poods of madder roots was ground into krap by 500 mills at 50 factories. Cardon confirmed that in only one of the regions where madder was produced, la Fontaine de Vaucluse, during the late 19th century, 50 water-mills turned night and day for eight months of the year to grind 40 million kgs of roots into 33 million kgs of powder.[5] French specialist garancine factories overtook the grower-owned facilities in Holland. In 1858 Dutch exports were 5.5 million florins or 3 million silver roubles. Ottoman exports peaked in 1856 at a freak £1,300,000 — though the amount was around £1,000,000 for several preceding years. Britain took 55 per cent of Ottoman exports, though in the following 12 years Britain's take dropped to an average of about 15 per cent, against total Ottoman exports dropping to £398,000 in 1868[6] (see appendix 14.1, page 339).

The cotton mills of Manchester, the north of England and Scotland made Britain the largest importer. Before 1860 annual British madder imports varied from £750,000 to £1,000,000. Average annual imports of madder of all kinds between 1858 and 1864 was 318,700cwts. In 1864 the average price of ground madder was 42s per cwt and roots 45s. 94,000cwts of ground madder were imported from Holland, France, Spain and America and 191,000cwts of roots from France, Italy, Turkey and the East Indies making a total of about £627,000. 11,000cwt of an inferior kind of madder known as *munjeet* was imported from the East Indies at 26s 3d per cwt. The weights were up from 84,000cwts of ground and 180,000cwts of roots in 1852.[7] It is not clear if these figures only refer to *Rubia tinctorum*. Cardon wrote that from the second half of the 18th century, when Britain took over from India as the world's leading cotton print manufacturer, Indian madders, including *Rubia tinctorum*, *Rubia cordifolia* — 'munjeet', *Rubia sikkimensis* and *Oldenlandia umbellata* — 'chay', were increasingly imported to Britain.[8] Ottoman Turkey was a major trading partner from 1840 to 1868. In 1870 Britain imported 38,000cwts (133,000 poods) of ground madder and 133,000cwts (466,000poods) of roots of which 43 per cent came from Izmir,[9] which together with the effects of the Crimean War prevented serious Turkish exports being available for Russia.

Aerial view of the International Exhibition, Paris, by Frederic Le Play, 1867 (Giedion)

Apart from the excellent Dutch combined graph of madder production and exports from 1815 to 1910, there appear to be no convenient tables showing the history of the madder trade or of the dye. The nearest equivalent is Prof Traian Stoianovich's graph of European exports to the Levant of pieces of cloth from 1600 to 1800, by quantity, for England, Venice, France and all Europe.[10] This represented a significant part of world trade and is indicative of the increase brought about by industrialisation, until the Napoleonic Wars which changed the map of the Ottoman empire. Even if the values were known they would be meaningless over so long a period.

The following detailed figures for the Russian madder market eloquently illustrate the dramatic world expansion.

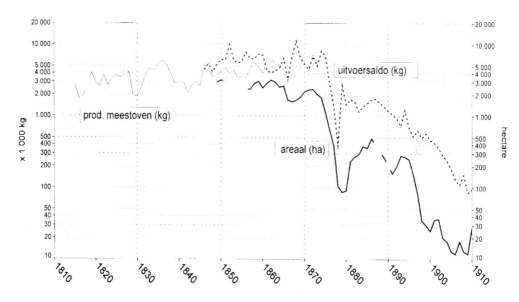

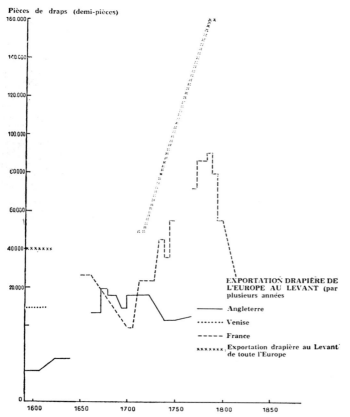

Above: Production from Zeeuwse, the area cultivated in Zeeland, and total Dutch exports, on the vertical log-scale. The steady level of full-capacity Dutch production during the 19th century masked the increase in Avignon and Alsace production. Dutch production only gave way with the introduction of synthetic dyes. The apparent recovery from 1885 to 1895 is exaggerated by the log scale, but does reflect the early unpopularity of poor quality synthetic dyes. Weights are for ground madder or equivalents, 3kg ground = 1kg garancine and 0.8kg ground = 1kg roots. (Priester)
Left: European exports of cloth to the Levant, 1600 to1800. Note the magnified scale below 20,000 to accommodate pre-Industrial Revolution quantities of pieces of cloth. (Stoianovich)

The three-cornered competition for the Russian market

Shtorkh, writing in 1859 during the boom years, thought that the Russian textile industry would never have got started and flourished in the 19th century without protectionist tariffs. The 'Ministry' concurred that 'the period from 1822 to 1848 saw our cotton fabric manufacturing industry increase under 12 protectionist taxes, while madder which had only been established for ten years, became a significant trade commodity and supported its home market strongly'.

While madder imports to Russia were steadily increasing during the half century to 1856, they still represented a relatively modest and decreasing part of total imports — which had been increasing — for about ¼ per cent, but which were still of taxable size. All Russian imported madder was subject to tax and there were five convoluted tariff impositions (more according to Karpov) during the period 1819 to 1857. The tariffs differed for European dried roots, powdered krap, garancine by sea and garancine by land, for Black Sea and Caucasian ports of entry and for Asian roots. As ever, they appear to be arbitrary, based on a vague 'golden egg' principle of not depressing trade too much (see appendix 14.2, page 340). All packed goods bore an additional tax regardless of content: boxes 10 per cent, barrels 10 per cent, single sacks 2 per cent, double sacks (on mules) 4 per cent, single bales (*pletevki*) 5 per cent, and doubles bales 8 per cent. In addition there were inland local sales taxes levied on madder. Moscow charged 2 per cent; St. Petersburg 2 per cent (to fund construction of the new stone bridge over the Neva river); 0.5 per cent in Archangelsk, Taganrog and Mariupol. The treasury tax receipts on European madder reached 281,000 roubles in 1856.

Six merchants: a 16th-century Ragusan, a 16th-century Jew, a 16th-century Greek, an Armenian c. 1800 (Stoianovich); a 17th-century Russian, a 17th-century 'Oriental' (Fekhner)

The rise of the Russian textile industry was reflected in the consumption of madder. Shtorkh estimated adjusted annual average weights for imported madder roots, krap and garancine during:

1800-1814	27kp
1815-1821	40kp
1822-1826	46kp
1827-1831	57kp
1832-1836	80kp
1837-1841	134kp
1842-1843	113kp
1844-1848	163kp
1849-1853	293kp

The 1850s registered an eleven-fold increase compared with 1800-1814. In a three-cornered struggle, European imports gradually gave way to Asian and Caucasian competition:

Russian cloth market at the Nizhnii Novgorod Fair,
second half 19th century
(ack. Library of Congress; Fitzpatrick)

	European	%	Asian	%	Total imports	Derbent	Other	Cauc tot
1844	73kp 377kr	93	5kp 15kr	7	79kp 392kr	0kp	0kp	1kr
1845	124kp 947kr	90	13kp 30kr	10	137kp 978kr	0kp	0kp	1kr
1846	134kp 862kr	95	8kp 19kr	5	142kp 881kr	61kp	8kp	289kr
1847	161kp 951kr	88	21kp 61kr	12	182kp 1012kr	41kp	6kp	212kr
1848	94kp 501kr	88	13kp 49kr	12	107kp 550kr	45kp	6kp	272kr
1849	187kp 936kr	88	26kp 74kr	12	213kp 1011kr	67kp	9kp	295kr
1850	161kp 865kr	85	28kp 81kr	15	189kp 946kr	67kp	9kp	366kr
1851	152kp 767kr	86	26kp 72kr	14	178kp 838kr	76kp	10kp	330kr
1852	156kp 767kr	83	32kp 81kr	17	187kp 848kr	146k	19kp	561kr
1853	120kp 522kr	78	35kp 92kr	22	154kp 614kr	126kp	17kp	553kr
1854	32kp 180kr	56	25kp 81kr	44	57kp 261kr	132kp	34kp	745kr
1855	9kp 28kr	26	25kp 76kr	74	34kp 105kr	107kp	10kp	450kr
1856	30kp 202kr	66	15kp 36kr	34	45kp 237kr	141kp	31kp	928kr
Average					132kp 667kr	78kp	11kp	385kr

There was no reliable information of the amount of madder annually produced in European Russia, but Shtorkh estimated it to be about 20k poods worth 100kr, which is the figure he added to form the total consumed in the following tables:

The 19th-century madder boom

	Total imports		%		Caucasian total		%		Total incl Russian excl garancine	
1844	79kp	392kr	100		0kp	1kr	0		79kp	493kr
1845	137kp	978kr	100		0kp	1kr	0		157kp	1079kr
1846	142kp	881kr	75		69kp	289kr	25		211kp	1270kr
1847	182kp	1012kr	83		47kp	212kr	17		249kp	1324kr
1848	107kp	550kr	67		51kp	272kr	33		177kp	922kr
1849	213kp	1011kr	77		76kp	295kr	23		308kp	1406kr
1850	189kp	946kr	72		76kp	366kr	28		285kp	1412kr
1851	178kp	838kr	72		86kp	330kr	28		284kp	1269kr
1852	187kp	848kr	60		165kp	561kr	40		372kp	1509kr
1853	154kp	614kr	53		143kp	553kr	47		317kp	1268kr
1854	57kp	261kr	26		166kp	745kr	74		231kp	1105kr
1855	34kp	105kr	19		117kp	450kr	81		171kp	655kr
1856	45kp	237kr	20		172kp	928kr	80		241kp	1265kr
Average	132kp	667kr			89kp	385kr			220kp	1054kr

During the continual struggle between Caucasian and European madder to dominate the Russian market, average European import prices decreased by 28 per cent from 1845 to 1850, due to increased Caucasian substitution, which confirmed Shtorkh's choice that the winner was Caucasian madder.

Evidently Caucasian madder played a more important role, but the figures excluded garancine the concentrated high quality product, which also became increasingly popular. Karpov was right that the Caucasian industry needed downstream processing facilities and skills to grind krap and process garancine. After 1858 the annual value of garancine imports exceeded the total annual value of krap before the introduction of garancine in 1842 to 1846 by 50 per cent and increased beyond 150 per cent in 1861.

The American Civil War (1861 to 1865) stopped imports of American cotton to Russia and stagnated cotton fabric production. The consequent decreased imports of garancine through St Petersburg for the year to November 1st, 1862 was 37,600 poods from 70,100 poods in 1861. Bankruptcies and hyperinflation followed in the Caucasus.

European madder imports

Ninety-four per cent of imported madder from Europe came in through the Baltic ports, with the remaining four per cent by road and two per cent through the Black Sea. The growing value of the trade attracted government attention as a source of potential tax revenue. The majority of imported madder arrived in Russia through the seaport of St Petersburg, where 85 per cent of duties were collected. It was then transported to Moscow, where the remaining duties were paid, and thence to Nizhegorodsky Fair and other industrial centres (appendix 14.3, page 340).

According to published figures which covered 1799 to 1861 (appendix 14.4, page 341),[11] after the 1822 protectionist taxes, the largest imports of madder roots was in 1840 at 166,000 poods, and the least in 1854, which was a year of exceptional military activity. Before the 1822 tax, Shtorkh's average figures in thousand poods for the import of krap from Europe were:

1800 to 1814	23.4 k poods p.a.
1814 to 1824	38.9
1824 to 1834	55.2
1832 to 1836	79.7
1837 to 1841	133.6
1840	166.4
1842 to 1846	101.5 @ approximately 8r/pood, 800 k roubles
1847	107.4
1848	74.0
1849	111.8
1850	87.9
1854	32.3 (The missing years were absent from the library in Tblisi)
1857	76.2
1858	55.6
1859	66.6
1860	73.7
1861	50.2 @ approximately 7r/pood, 350 k roubles

The decrease in imports of krap was due to both the increase of Derbent madder production and the increase in parallel imports of more expensive garancine from 1858:

1847	7.0k poods	174 k roubles	i.e. 25 roubles a pood
1848	4.5	181	i.e. 40.5
1849	12.9	290	i.e. 22.5
1850	14.3	326	i.e. 22.8

Unfortunately the above tables were discontinued — though there are muddy figures from 1851 to 1856 (appendix 14.5, page 342) — because in later statistics garancine is included with other dyeing agents, while representing the majority value in the grouping:

1857	8.3 k poods	135 k roubles	i.e. 16.3 roubles a pood
1858	82.9	1,183	i.e. 14.3
1859	101.3	1,625	i.e. 16.1
1860	98.6	1,587	i.e. 16.1
1861	120.2	2,069	i.e. 17.3

The Ministry five-year totals of imports of krap to Russia by country of origin and weight in thousand poods during the pre-garancine period:

Exporter	1827 to 1831	1832 to 1836	1837 to 184	1842 to 1846	1844 (Shtorkh) to 1856
Holland	33.7kp	50.5	73.6	51.9	40
France	13.1	17.2	43.0	38.2	31
Prussia	7.6	3.2	3.7	0.8	3
Turkey	1.1	6.5	6.7	0.8	1
Other countries	1.9	2.2	5.8	3.2	2
Total	57.4	79.7	133.6	101.3	77

Shtorkh's averages for 1844 to 1856 show that the krap market was in the hands of Holland with 50 per cent and France with 42 per cent, together accounting for 4.5 out of 5 million roubles of payment over this period. Prussia and Great Britain were far behind with 2 per cent each. German *lander*, Belgium, Italy, Austria and Portugal also exported minor amounts (see appendix 14.6, page 342).

The Caucasian Trade

The ledgers of Derbent bear witness to the significant development of Daghestani trade at the beginning of the 19th century.[12] There were 420 shops belonging to 80 merchants and three caravansarais. There were 25 foreign merchants. Common currencies in use were Dutch ten-rouble banknotes, Russian silver roubles, and small copper coins and banknotes from Shirvan and Kouba *abazi*. From S. Bronevskii's accounts for 1807,[13] trade from Derbent and Shirvan to Kizliar included the following commodities: wine, rice, walnuts, fresh and dried fruit, honey, oil, fish, madder and other goods of total value 182,000 roubles. In the 1820s good quantities of madder came from Derbent. Madder cultivation began first in the Tarki shamkhalate.[14] O. Evetskii[15] wrote that the madder sent to Kizliar was sold for 40,000 silver roubles and further north to Astrakhan, for 65,000 roubles. Kizliar was on the road north to the Nizhegorodsky Fair and in the 1830s out of 9,000 inhabitants, 1,000 were merchants. In 1834, Russian and Persian goods traded through Kizliar were valued at 1.1 million roubles, 73 per cent of which were cotton textiles. In 1844 the Amir-Adji-Yurt customs post at the exit from North Daghestan counted among other commodities 21 camel-loads or sacks (*chuval*) of madder. The *Kavkazkogo Kalendaria* in 1850 published that 58,000 poods of madder were gathered in Derbent and 20,000 mountain villagers were employed.

The statistics of the Derbent military government from 1845 to 1854 show the importance of madder, between three and ten times the weight of the next most important commodities, dried pears and walnuts, which passed through the port of Derbent. Madder accounted for 32k roubles in 1845, 260k roubles in 1846 and 399k roubles in 1850. In the 1850s Port Petrovsk and Temir-Khan-Shura had grown to equal Derbent as trade centres. Temir-Khan-Shura had 117 commercial buildings and 108 shops. [16]

Derbent madder had to compete with the handicap of transport costs of 80 kopeks a pood for the Derbent-Astrakhan-Nizhegorodsky-textile factory in Ivanovo or Moscow route. From 1849 to 1854, there were 157 irregular deliveries of less than 100 poods to more than 4000 poods. Caucasian madder was usually delivered in large sacks called *kharals* and sold by weight. A pitfall for the unwary buyer was that depending on its place of origin a so-called '*kharal*' contained differing weights, ranging from 6 poods from Baku to 8 from Khiva (appendix 14.7, page 343).

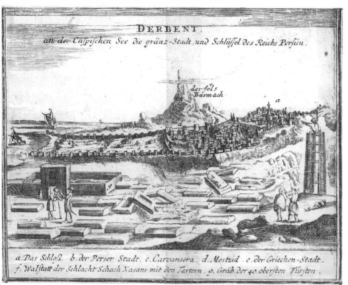

View of Derbent c. 1720, J. B. Homann, Nürnberg,1724
(Hotz collection, Royal Geographical Society, London)

Sales at the Nizhegorodsky Fair appeared to show that Derbent madder accounted for 65 per cent in 1849, while Asian exports from Bukhara, Khiva and Persia accounted for 29 per cent from a total 25,000 poods. In 1855 during the Crimean War, Derbent madder had gained 90 per cent of the market against the Bukharan 10 per cent, from a larger total of 94,000 poods. Dutch and Silesian madder were squeezed out of the Fair. Although the figures left out French products and may be incomplete as the European sales seem too low, the sales of Derbent madder relative to Asian appear correct (see appendix 14.8, page 344).

The market structure was complicated with textile industrialists doubling as both cultivators and traders in madder, which worked well when the market was expanding. In 1856, the first lot of madder from Kizliar was sold at Nizhegorodsky Fair, part of the 120,000 pood shipment from the Caucasus. The lot included 60,000 poods which had been pre-purchased by a group of textile industrialists — Messrs Molchanov, Lepeshkin, Milyutin, Baranov and Aschenbach. In 1857 the madder trade at the Fair was less of a success. 150,000 poods had been delivered of which 63,000 were sold at 6.50 roubles per pood for Khiva and 10.75-13.50 for Derbent and Kouba. At the end of the Fair, the remainder was unsold and prices dropped by 40 per cent to no avail and the unsold 87,000 poods had to be returned to Moscow. In a single year as well as over longer periods, Caucasian, like European madder varied greatly in quality which was reflected in market prices. While from year to year price fluctuation could depend on supply and demand, within a single year price variation would more closely reflect quality, as was recorded in the price of different contracts for Caucasian madder from 1846 to 1856 (appendix 14.9, page 345).

The American cotton crisis caused the price of madder to crash to 4 roubles per pood in 1864 from levels of 7 to 9 roubles in 1857 to 1859. The Kavkaz and Mercury Company which owned

Russian troops approach Tarki, on the hill behind present-day Makhachkala, previously Port Petrovsk, named after Peter the Great's first landing and occupation of the Caucasus in 1723 (Markovin)

riverside wharfage at Nizhegorodsky Fair had scheduled 230 sailing to leave Derbent. It was in vain. That year madder for sale from Derbent amounted to 1.1 million roubles and goods sold to merely 52,000 roubles. In 1864 In Derbent 8 million roubles had been invested at high interest rates ranging from 24 per cent to 100 per cent per annum.

Borrowers faced bankruptcy. Food prices soared. For example in 1848 a pood of pears in Derbent cost 30 kopeks, and in 1864, 1.20 roubles, while a pood of walnuts costing 55 kopeks in 1858 had jumped to 1.26 roubles in 1864. Agricultural land prices also crashed. In the highlands of Daghestan in 1864 one *sabu* (1/12 *desiatin*) of land under cultivation cost between 30-50 roubles. A meadow producing hay for 100 cattle cost 70-75 roubles. In southern Daghestan a *sabu* had also fetched 50 roubles. In the southern part of the Kurin region a *sabu* dropped to 16 roubles, while in some prime villages of southern Daghestan, a *sabu* was only worth 3 roubles.[17] Not much earlier Shtorkh had enthused: "Since 1846, madder imports have risen significantly and show every sign of continuing to rise in the future, proof that the trade is highly profitable."

Persian & Central Asian trade

Persian and Central Asian madder also benefited from the mid-19th century textile boom. Derbent madder was of higher price and quality than Bukharan madder which came from Khiva, Persia and Tashkent. Asian madder was frequently gathered from wild plants and in the Caucasus one pood of wild madder roots could fetch up to 7r. In contrast, the Derbent area was well-known for its huge madder plantations. Prices of Asian and Caucasian madder imported to Russia via Astrakhan, according to the Derbent, Petrovsk (Makhachkala), Nizovsk and Baku customs ledgers were steady between 1844 and 1856, averaging at 4.75r, 4.01r, 3.43r and 2.98r, respectively (appendix 14.10, page 347). Non-Caucasian Asian madder was imported to Russia at Astrakhan and via Orenburg and Siberia.

While Astrakhan prices varied between 5.49r and lows of 1.55r in 1849 and 2.0r in 1854, Orenberg prices were steadier averaging 2.78r (see appendix 14.11, page 347). Persian prices ranged from 1.55r to 2.11r; Khivan from 2.00r to 2.41r; Bukharan at 2.00r and Tashkent madder about 1.59r, a quarter of the price of Western madder. At place of entry to Russia the price of equivalent European madder was 20 per cent higher than Khivan and 30 per cent higher than Persian. This partly reflected the lack of modern grinding equipment and partly quality control. In addition, transport costs and profit-taking meant that Nizhegorodsky Fair prices for Asian madders had increased to 3.31r. The average price of madder from Khiva was 4r per pood and from Persia 3.5r.

The Persian madder trade was long established. The Venetian traveller, Barbaro, who visited Persia in 1471, wrote that the Persian dyers journeyed to India with large quantities of madder, where they exercised their craft as red-dyers. Shiraz and Isfahan were traditional trading centres for madder.[18] However, exports to Russia were small compared to European exports. A modest 1,000 poods traded in Astrakhan in 1844 rose to 12,000 poods in 1852, while from the Orenburg and Siberia route 4,000 poods in 1844 increased to 28,000 poods by 1850 (appendix 14.12, page 348). The average total from 1844-1856 was 21,000 poods.

Roughly speaking the weight and value of Asian madder more than doubled during the second half of the 12-year period to 1853. 26,000 poods were exported from Khiva and 6,000 poods from Persia and 2,000 poods from Tashkent. Madder from Khiva accounted for 75 per cent of all Asian madder imports to Russia. The remainder was mainly from Persia, which included a small amount from Tashkent and Bukhara. Derbent, Kizliar, Kouba and Baku had become part of Russia and therefore their trade was excluded from import statistics (appendix 14.13, page 349; and see map on page 237).

Ministry figures listed 'various dyes' which were mainly madder but included indigo and 'ink-nut' from Persia. They showed approximately a three-fold increase from 1850 for 1854 and 1857 to 1861 which reached 94,000 poods in 1858. Exports from Bukhara suddenly rose to 47,000 poods in 1849, dropped away completely and again rose to 37,000 poods in 1860. It was these increased exports that prompted Karpov's study (see appendix 14.14, page 349).

Persian madder took on a new lease of life in the 1860s when the Ziegler company manufactured large quantities of rugs in Sultanabad (see chapter 16). Leonard Helfgott confirmed that this increase was reflected in the larger Persian-owned carpet enterprises.

15

Coal tar reds & the death of madder

Tragedy beckons

THE LATER tale of madder turned into a Classical Greek tragedy. When European dyers and chemists found out the Oriental secret of the beautiful Turkey red in the mid-18th century, the world opened at their feet. The energy released into chemical research during the Industrial Revolution resulted in the understanding of the chemistry of madder, the dyeing process and the nature and isolation of alizarin, the red dyestuff. The proud chemists found that they were playing god. Similar forces led to the discovery of a range of cheap synthetic chemicals to replace natural products. Perkin's synthesis of mauve in 1856 was inevitably followed by Graebe and Liebermann's synthesis of alizarin in 1869. Within a few years the world-wide madder industry was destroyed.

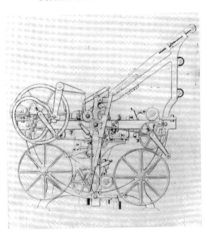

The 'perrotine' cloth printing machine invented by Louis Perrot in 1834 (Brunello)

If the following account appears as an apotheosis of chemists, then it reflects what was happening.[1] Their work founded the modern chemical industry. By the 1850s, the new mechanisation of the textile industry which had caused vast growth in production, in turn created a similar demand for detergents, bleaches and dyestuffs. The introduction of chlorine bleaches, Leblanc's soda and the perfection of cleansing soaps enabled the cotton mills of England and France to speed-up different phases in the finishing of textiles.

The second great leap forward in printing fabrics occurred in 1834 when Louis Perrot (1798-1878) invented the famous *perrotine*, a new machine without rollers, but capable of mechanically printing in up to five colours.[2] While chemists had been able to supply the increased demand for ancillary hypochlorites, sulphuric acid and sodium carbonate, there had been no such progress with natural dyes. The only change had been the more extensive cultivation of madder in Provence and other regions.

Earlier chemists had indeed stumbled upon some of the intermediate discoveries, but their significance would only be appreciated later. Woulfe in 1771 treated indigo with nitric acid to obtain a yellow substance that dyed both wool and silk. In 1779, Welter had reproduced it by nitrating silk. Without knowing it, both had prepared 'picric acid', which was applied by Guinon to dyeing in 1845. Scheele, the discoverer of chlorine, had noted in 1776 that a reddish residue resulted from treating uric acid with nitric acid and then evaporating the product. Since this dyed the skin red, it was called 'purpuric acid' after the ancient purple. From this acid, Proust prepared the ammonium derivative which he called 'mureside' in 1818. In 1834

Instructions and dye samples for yellow etching on Turkey red textiles show how Runge combined theoretical chemistry with industrial textile production (Sandberg)

Friedlieb Runge[3] produced rosolic acid by oxidizing crude phenol, which was a step in the synthesis of fuchsin dye (below).

These products dissolved easily in water and were highly suitable for dyeing animal fibres. They rapidly became staple dyestuffs. Mureside was fabricated on a large scale by extracting uric acid from guano and picric acid was prepared from tar after Laurent's discovery in 1855. Not surprisingly, progress was empirical. Thanks to the methods of analytical chemistry perfected by Justus von Leibig (1803-73), in 1828 Friedrich Wohler succeeded in synthesising urea and extrapolated that there was a molecular architecture of organic compounds.[4]

As early as 1825 Faraday had separated benzene from tar. The reaction was rediscovered by Leigh in 1842, but neither immediately understood its significance. That was the achievement of Wilhelm von Hofmann (1818-92), who was then and now considered to be the father of synthetic dyestuffs. The

Leibig's chemical laboratory at Giessen, with Hofmann leaning on the right (CIBA Review, 1956)

former assistant to Leibig in his native Giessen came to teach at the Royal College of Chemistry in London in 1845. He and his enthusiastic researchers used the foul residue of lighting gas. There was plenty available as the gas industry had recently spread in England.

Hofmann knew that Runge had isolated aniline (then called 'kyanol') from wood tars in 1834 and that Zinin had reproduced it differently by breaking down nitrobenzene eight years later. Hofmann reasoned that this was the starting-point for the preparation of other derivatives. He therefore set about discovering the best industrial method for chemical reduction of nitrobenzine to produce aniline.

One of Hofmann's students, William Henry Perkin (1838-1907) was eighteen when he started at the Royal College in 1853. In his modest private laboratory Perkin began to study substances similar to aniline. He ambitiously decided to prepare quinine and started with its analogue allyltoluidin: "In the fireplace I had constructed an oven. There was neither running water or gas. Normally I worked with an old Berzelius alcohol lamp and I did the burnings with charcoal in a shed. And in this laboratory I worked nights and in the vacations." (His family recently gave the contents of his later laboratory to the Science Museum in London.)

During his Easter vacation in 1856, he was using a mixture of sulphuric acid and potassium bichromate as oxidiser on the allyltoluidin, when an unexpected reaction occurred. An uninteresting brownish substance was produced. Not put off easily, Perkin repeated the experiment with aniline instead of allyltoluidin and this time he obtained an ugly dark slush. Instead of throwing it away, he treated it with hot water and noted that it partially dissolved into a solution of a fine purple colour, from which he separated violet crystals. Perkin left off studying quinine and attempted to dye silk with his beautiful purple. It worked and the purple was quite fast and very bright. He had discovered the first artificial dyestuff, which he called 'lilac or purple colour' and which was later called 'mauveine' or 'mauve', after the colour of the mallow plant.

Wilhelm von Hofmann, aged 28, portrait by unknown artist, 1846 (CIBA Review, 1956)

Encouraged by friends, Perkin sent off a sample of dyed silk to Pullar's dye-works in Perth. Their reply was flattering, and he applied for a patent on August 26th, 1856. With the help of his father's capital he started a factory in Greenford near Harrow in 1857. He needed large quantities of aniline and used a mixture of sulphuric acid and sodium nitrate to convert benzene from the Miller & Co tar factory in Glasgow. His next step was to profit from Bechamp's method of reducing nitrobenzene with acetic acid and iron, discovered in 1845.

In spite of the beauty that the tint could give to silk — Queen Victoria herself used it for her Jubilee dress — it was not that enthusiastically received by dyers. His discovery appeared to be losing its appeal. Fortuitously, Perkin's patent was not drawn up correctly for France. The French immediately set up making mauveine without payment of royalties. The dye was a great success in France and boosted Perkin's trade in England so that by the age of 36 he was able to retire from business and devote himself to research.[5]

The flood-gates open

Perkin's discovery had massive consequences. At once chemists in several countries realised that coal tar could be the source of new discoveries and in London Hofmann concentrated his energies on it. The chronology of the

William Henry Perkin in 1860, aged 22: the discoverer of the first synthetic dye 'mauveine', portrait by unknown artist (CIBA Review, 1956)

synthesis of the range of colours produced by madder gives a flavour of the race for the old leviathan's market from 1856 until 1880:[6]

1856	Mauveine by Perkin
1858-9	Fuchsin, lilac by Verguin with acknowledgement to Hofmann
1859	Coralline by Persoz
1861	Methyl violet by Lauth
1862	Bismarck brown by Martius
1863	Aniline black by Lightfoot
1864	Aniline brown by Martius
1867	Rose magdala by Schiendt
1867	Nigrosine by Coupier
1869	Alizarin by Graebe and Liebermann
1875	Phloxine, Rose bengal by Nolting
1876	Alizarin orange by Strobel and Caro
1877	Anthracene brown by Seuberlich
1877-8	Oranges by Roussin and Poirrier
1878	Biebrich scarlet by Nietzki
1879	Cloth reds by Ohler
1880	Ponceau S by Pfaff and Nietzki

Brunello thought that the synthetic dye revolution was best understood as three advancing waves. The first was from 1856 to 1876 — the era of triphenylmethane, crowned with the synthesis of alizarin by Graebe and Liebermann in 1868; the second from 1876 to 1893 — the era of azo dyes, crowned with the synthesis of indigo blue by Adolf Baeyer in 1880; and the third from 1893 to 1902 — the era of sulphur dyes. The complete details can be found in Brunello and elsewhere, which leaves this story to concentrate on the displacement of madder.

Meanwhile, the race towards the synthesis of alizarin reached Lyons in 1858 at the dye-works of Frères Renard et Franc, where the chemist François-Emmanuel Verguin was at work. He had observed that aniline when heated to a high temperature in the presence of mercury chloride or tin chloride with various other reducible compounds, produced a dyestuff of a marvellous red colour. Because of its resemblance to the colour of fuschia blossoms the new dye was given the name 'fuchsin' and it was patented on April 8th, 1859. Hofmann is associated with this discovery because he had previously discovered the process without thinking of its industrial application.

Fuchsin was even more brilliant than mauveine and easier to use, even if its price was extremely high. In 1860 the La Fuchsine company had just been established when another chemist Louis Durand discovered that it could also be made by heating aniline with nitrate of mercury. This was patented by his employer Gerber who put it on the market under the name 'azaleine'. It cost a good third less than fuchsin.

The action moved-on to Basle in Switzerland. In France the patent law of 1844 protected products but not processes. Durand and Gerber's patent was cancelled and they transferred their business over the border to Basle. There, soon after Verguin made his discovery, another dyer Allesandre Clavel bought the license to manufacture fuchsin from Frères Renard for 100,000 francs and started operations. Next, J. J. Muller-Pack obtained the first fine basic dyestuffs for Geigy, also of Basle. In fast pursuit, Jean Gaspard Dollfus, an industrialist from Mulhouse who had moved to Basle upon the grant of a franchise from the city to produce illuminating gas and coal tar, began an even better business as a manufacturer of dyestuffs in 1862. His firm became the house of Durand and Huguenin. The three founder chemical companies evolved through take-overs. In 1873, Clavel's silk dyeing firm was acquired by Bindschedler and Busch and in 1884, the company was incorporated as the Societé pour l'Industrie Chimique à Bâle — the future CIBA. Muller's factory was acquired by Geigy in 1864. In 1886 Alfred Kern, then chief chemist at Bindschelder and Busch, made a partnership with Edward Sandoz, a sales representative at Durand and Huguenin, to form Sandoz SA. The Swiss and German chemical industries were at a point of explosive growth. Also in 1860, on the same day, January 26th, Nicolson in England and De Laire in France patented the classic arsenic process for the preparation of fuchsin, conceived by C Medlock. This became the standard method and was only substituted many years later by Coupier's less hazardous nitrobenzene process.

In London, Hofmann began studying fuchsin in 1861. In addition to violet, he obtained blue and green derivatives by a series of simple chemical operations such as heating fuchsin in the presence of aniline, ethyl iodide or methyl chloride. He also succeeded in demonstrating that fuchsin is the salt of a colourless base, which he called 'rosaniline'. Up until 1864, the name 'aniline' was applied to a product of aniline and toluidine. Coupier soon succeeded in isolating the two compounds, but saw that toluidine itself, when subjected to oxidization, gave a red colour which he called 'rosotoluidine'.

This seemed to contradict Hofmann's findings until Rosensthiel found that Coupier's tolouidine was a mixture of two isomers.[7] This demonstrated that Coupier's red was different from La Fuchsine's. The patent agents were kept busy. While the composition of the two reds remained unknown, Rosensthiel's work opened a new line of research for Hofmann, Kekule, Graebe, Caro, Dale, Schorlemmer and later E. and O. Fischer. In 1861 Lauth prepared 'methyl violet' or 'Paris violet', one of several dyes derived from the various fuchsins by putting together the amine groups with methyl, ethyl and benzene radicals . . . But this is not a book about organic chemistry and my present purpose is merely to show how dye research was ballooning.

Public reaction to the new dyes was initially enthusiastic, but soon cooled. They had discovered that energetic washing or prolonged exposure to sunlight decreased fastness. Dissatisfaction spread, doubtless fuelled by those with an interest in madder plantations, imported logwood or indigo. The expression 'fleeting as an aniline dye' entered the language. The fight-back began immediately. The English chemists Calvert, Cliff and Lower produced fast green and black by oxidation of aniline in contact with cotton. The method was perfected by Lightfoot and Charles Lauth whose dyeing process for aniline black largely survived in modern use.

In 1865 Hofmann, who was, after all, a German, gave in to entreaties from the Prussian government and left London to take up the chair of chemistry at the University of Berlin. A brain-drain ensued. His most promising students gave up important positions in England's best dyestuffs factories to follow him. England may have been the cradle of the new dyestuffs industry, but Perkin shortly had to admit that "Germany is today the headquarters of dyestuffs manufacturing." Far-sighted Bismarck had understood the national importance of a chemical industry. By the Treaty of Frankfurt (an appropriate location for a textile coup), Germany cunningly enabled France to buy German intermediate dyestuff products, which undercut their home manufacturers. This lanced the economic pressure for the French to develop their own industry and factories duly grew up along the Rhine that dominated the trade.

The formative histories of some of the German firms which were to become leaders of world industry illustrate the point. Friedrich Englehorn, an enterprising young jeweller from Mannheim, had travelled widely in search of innovation and had heard of Perkin's mauveine. At 30 he had already built his city's gas works and a few years later he sought to utilise the bulky cold tar waste product. By 1861 he had founded the Chemische Fabrik Dyckerhoff Clemm and Company to make intermediate colours and dyestuffs. This business prospered and on April 6th, 1865 the Badische Aniline und Soda Fabrik was created, which soon outgrew Mannheim and moved over the Rhine to Ludwigshaven. BASF attracted great German chemists and was responsible for the two major syntheses of madder and indigo.

At the same time, Friedrich Bayer a dealer in natural dyestuffs in Wuppertal, foresaw the increase in competition from synthetic dyestuffs. He proposed to his friend Friedrich Weskott, a skilled dyer, that they found a firm to manufacture magenta and aniline blue. On August 1st, 1863 they founded Friedrich Bayer and Company with just one employee at Wuppertal-Barmen. By the end of the first year there were 12 workers, a salesman and an apprentice. Within two years Bayer started a joint-venture aniline dyestuff factory in Albany, New York and rapidly opened sales offices throughout Europe. After the deaths of Weskott in 1876 and Bayer in 1880, the company was incorporated as Farbenfabrik Bayer and moved to Leverkusen, another of Germany's great chemical centres.

During this period other future world-class firms were growing too. They all started as synthetic dye manufacturers: Farbwerke Meister Lucius and Brunning in Hochst, Cassella in Frankfurt, Kalle in Biebrich and Elektron in Griesheim. Advances in manufacturing were complemented by discoveries in pure science.

In 1858 Kekule worked out the famous hexagonal structure of benzene, which was immediately taken up by the Swiss and Germans, but ignored by the English and French. Guided by Kekule's theory, in 1868 Carl Graebe and Carl Liebermann, who worked in Bayer's laboratory, established the structure of alizarin, the chief red colourant in madder red. In the same year they were able to reproduce chemically what nature alone had been capable of creating. They began with coal tar, from which they distilled anthracene. From anthracene they obtained dibromo-anthraquinone. From this compound, they succeeded in preparing the precious alizarin, by alkaline fusion. The men, who were engaged in pure

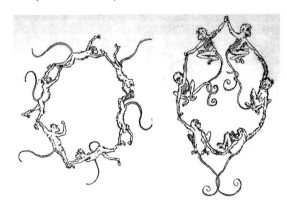

Whimsical illustration of the benzene ring where the monkeys' tails form molecular bonds (Berichte der Durstigen Chemischen Gesellschaft, Berlin, 1886; CIBA Review, 1956)

research, had made an agreement to give their work an industrial application with Heinrich Caro, an able technician who had been a success at BASF. This outmanoeuvred the ever-active Perkin in London, who had been following their progress and was also developing alizarin. After a close race which lasted over a year, Perkin was narrowly beaten by the Germans. Yet his process was simpler than that of the Germans. It was based on the sulphonation of the anthraquinone and its subsequent alkaline fusion. Perkin speedily came to an amicable agreement and soon alizarin was produced both in his factory at Greenford Green and in 1873 by Clavel in Basle. Similar methods were followed at Meister Lucius and Brunning and Farbenfabrik Bayer.

Synthetic alizarin was the first artificial dyestuff to be fast to light and washing. It contained none of the dulling and discolouring impurities of natural alizarin from madder roots and cost considerably less to produce. Within a few years the price was reduced to a tenth of its 1868 debut. As we have seen, France had overtaken Holland to become the main madder-grower in the world. To repeat, madder was a substantial trade with annual sales of £3,500,000 of which £1,000,000 was imported by Britain. The crash was devastating. A *quintal* of powdered madder cost 200 francs in 1865 and 25 francs in 1875.[8] By 1870 anyone travelling to Avignon and asking to see a madder plantation would be disappointed with the answer: "*Ah! Monsieur, voyez-vous, à présent ça se fait tout avec des machines!*" Madder had been replaced by grapevines.

After-effects

The new dyes were not single colours, but as a result of their chemistry, came in groups of colours. The first so-called 'alizarin' dyes were 'alizarin orange', synthesised by Graebe and Liebermann in 1874; 'alizarin red S' by Rosensthiel in 1874; 'alizarin brown S' by Brunet in 1881; and 'alizarin blue-black' by L. Schmidt in 1884. This family of dyes not only substituted natural mordant dyestuffs, but permitted the creation of new shades and fastnesses. In 1872 Wurth discovered sulphonated oils which were to be useful in the mordanting process for cottons and Durand and Huguenin specialised in printing cottons mordanted with chromium.

In search of ever-cheaper dyestuffs, Griess, a former student of Hofmann, had worked out the preliminary pure chemistry for 'azo' dyes in 1858, based on Kekule's theories. In 1862 his colleague Carl Alexander obtained the first soluble azo dye (meta-phenylen-diamine acted on by nitric acid). He later founded Aktiengesellschaft für Anilinfabrikation, better known as Agfa, in Berlin. 'Bismarck brown' the first azo dye, was created and launched on the market by the Manchester firm Roberts-Dale three years later. There was a pause until 1876 before other members of the new azo family were discovered. Caro and Witt developed the chrysoidines and Roussin obtained two azo derivatives from naphtalene, 'orange II' and 'roccelline'.

Even the new synthetic alizarin was soon displaced. 'Para red' had very brilliant tones and was faster and cheaper to produce than synthetic alizarin. It was created by 1889 when H. Koechlin and the Meister Lucius and Brunning chemists von Gallois and Ulrich succeeded in dyeing with insoluble dyes by impregnation of cotton with a phenol derivative followed by treatment with a diazo solution of an amine salt. With betanaphtol and paranitraniline, they perfected the production of para red.

Another unexpected effect of synthetics was to boost the Turkish dyeing industry. Turkish labour was cheaper than European and the simplicity of dyeing with synthetics meant that spinners and weavers could dye themselves and undercut the old monopolies of the guild dyers.[9] At the same time synthetics damaged the reputation of carpets made in western Anatolia, which had been enjoying an export boom from 1840 to 1870. Avaricious foreign merchants had taken control of rug-making. All rug producers were obliged to have their wool dyed by central dye-houses by their agents, who were of course the largest buyers. The same agents had links with the dye-houses. This separated the vitally connected activities of spinning, dyeing and weaving with sad results. By the 1880s European dye-masters had arrived in Ushak, famous for centuries as a carpet centre. In 1908 a group of Izmir-based European rug merchant houses formed a British trust called Oriental Carpet Manufacturers (OCM) and cornered the market. The ancient art of rug-weaving was reduced to a sorry mass-production industry which employed 50,000 knotters in 1913.[10]

Objects of perpetual desire

There is a technical reason why madder red from roots is a better colour to the eye than the synthetic dye. Madder-red dyes textiles a vibrant colour while the chemical colour is flat. While the main dye components of madder are alizarin and purpurin, madder red is made of more than 25 colouring agents (see Glossary) which appear and combine randomly to dye different parts of the fibre in different strengths. As Grossgeim put it, "the final dye effect depends on an entire and complicated process, including some sort of combination of the dye components, which are not only the colour pigments, but also a transitional solution of tannic substances." This produced a microscopic variation of mixtures and colours, with alizarin and purpurin dominant.

The process is similar to a Pointillist painting where the rainbow dots of colour merge into pulsating colour when viewed from a distance. The knot-grid of a carpet is further enriched by the variation of red in the strands of a single knotted tuft. When I look at madder red, my eyes are excited before I know what I am seeing.

16

William Morris:
the sumptuous resurrection

Early revivals & survivals

THE CHEMICAL revolution which led to the synthesis of alizarin and the replacement of madder took place in several countries in Europe. It is ironic that Westerners, as the cultured descendants of former colonial masters, were also often responsible for initiating the revival of natural dyes in Oriental lands. Exciting revivals blossomed, but popular public taste had turned towards the cheaper products of mass-production. The use of madder did survive in a few instances but the industry had almost disappeared.

There was one large-scale survival of natural dyes in the carpet industry. During the mid-19th century, the Ziegler Company of Manchester had a lucrative business bartering Persian silk in exchange for British Empire imports. In 1871 the 'pebrine' pestilence wiped out the silkworms, so Ziegler needed another commodity to exchange for the popular British goods. Imports of cheap cotton prints from British India had caused a slump in the Persian textile home market. As a result, in certain regions of Persia there was cheap skilled labour available to satisfy the expanding European middle-class demand for hand-woven carpets. Annette Ittig discovered the notebooks of Emil Alpiger (1841-1905), the Swiss manager of Ziegler's enterprises in Sultanabad, who had arrived in Persia in 1859. He wrote instructions that aniline dyes must be avoided at all costs, because they would fade.

Successful growth encouraged Ziegler to acquire a 40,000 sq yd compound in 1876. It was known as *kala* — 'the fortress' — on which were built warehouses and a dye-works that employed 80 dyers. Their solid investment was some £6000. All the wool was dyed and supplied to the local carpet-makers. There were more than 2000 local looms and a further 4000 looms in weavers' homes in the district. The 'made-for-export' designs were also supplied from Manchester, drawn on squared-paper cartoons. Ziegler recruited good managers. In 1886 Franz Theodore Strauss came to Sultanabad to manage the dye works with an interest in local plants and flora. Dr Mark Whiting, the specialist in carpet dyes, found that Alpiger was true to his word and that aniline dyes appeared only rarely during the 1890s. As late as 1902, according to their own records, Ziegler were still using natural dyes, unlike their rivals in Kirman or OCM in Turkey who had used synthetic dyes since the 1870s.[1]

As late as 1903 the Persian government passed a law forbidding the importation of chemical dyes. All chemically dyed fabrics were meant to be seized and destroyed. G. G. Lewis, an investigative American rug expert, added that "a dyer found guilty of using them would have his right hand cut off. The government has never been very strict in enforcing this law, else there would be at the present time — 1920 — many one-handed men in Persia."[2]

The Emir of Bukhara had banned the early coal-tar dyes since the 1870s with equal lack of success. By 1900 fuchsin, green, Congo red and benzopurpurine were commonly found in Central Asian bazaars.[3] Few traditional societies carried on using madder. Sedentary weavers were already in the hands of merchants. The new synthetics reached the nomadic trading posts quickly too. One almost ritual survival, the complicated and lengthy dye process from Bali and other islands in South and South-East Asia is described in chapter 13. Another was in francophone northern Africa, where the colonial power was trying to re-establish natural dyes among the Berbers in the 1950s.

Printing chintzes at Merton Abbey, The Morris Movement, 1911 (Fairclough & Leary)

The North African Berbers continued to use less and less madder and other natural dyes until at least 1956. An excellent report written by French dye experts described similar declines in Morocco, Algeria and Tunisia.[4] Independently, the White Sisters of Ghardaia, Mzab and Laghouat in Saharan Algeria had restarted natural dye workshops, to save money for the hard-pressed local people who had been buying imported synthetics for some 70 years.[5] One researcher, Lacroix reported that in the region of Ouarzazate there were about 400 dyer-weavers, 100 near Glaoua-sud and near Ait Ounila, 200 about Ait Ouaouzguite, and 100 in Sektana and Zenaga. Grossin wrote of Morroco leather which was dyed rose in Marrakesh and Tafilalet, and additionally dyed red in the Draa,[6] Coustillac found a battle going on in southern Tunisia between the apostles of progressive chemical dyes and the traditional women dyers of Sfax, the Isle of Djerba and Oudref. Although their numbers had diminished since Fleury wrote in 1896, the domestic dyers were not in the least worried about the convenience or price of chemical dyes. They mainly used wild madder *Rubia peregrina* roots although some gardens in Methouia cultivated *Rubia tinctorum*. The Djerba dye-house had been modernised for the production of vegetable dyes at the state's expense.[7]

Apart from these serendipitous survivals, natural madder was virtually knocked out. Only in England, William Morris continued to use it with patchy results in his textile workshops in Merton Abbey.[8] Morris and John Ruskin, whose *The Stones of Venice*, published in 1853, heralded the Pre-Raphaelite movement, may be considered with hindsight as Luddite reactionaries, a sentiment with which Clive Wainwright forcefully agreed.[9] At the most exciting time of discovery of new materials in history, they were arguably responsible that British material culture turned aside and looked to past times. An ambience was created for future poor industrial design which in following generations ignored rather than exploited industrial progress. Why in the late twentieth century did successful young people in Britain generally buy antiques — dead art, while their American or European counterparts bought live art?

The British Reform Bill of 1832 stimulated Free Trade and industrial development. From 1835 there was concern in Parliament about the dire state of British design. The first London School of Design at Somerset House, progenitor of the Victoria and Albert Museum, was founded by 1837. These events fuelled Henry Cole's ubiquitous righteous energy to promote the Great Exhibition in 1851. Its unexpectedly great financial surplus was partly used to found The South Kensington Museum opened amidst the fields of Kensington in 1857, only six years after the Queen had given the Museum a permanent home at Marlborough House. Among others, William Morris steered the aim of the museum to provide historical precedents for modern design in all materials. Prince Albert was another early enthusiast for the whole project and the museum's status was enshrined when the widow Queen laid the new foundation stone and renamed it the Victoria and Albert Museum in 1899.

The importance of the British textile industry ensured that the study of historical textiles was taken seriously from the start. Large collections of Oriental and European textiles were assembled. It started modestly with contemporary Indian textiles bought from the Great Exhibition and a small 'Chamber of Horrors' on display at the Museum of Practical Art from 1851. Collections that included European textiles were acquired from 1857. Augustus Pugin the high-minded architect and designer was on the judging committee of the Exhibition and — as Charles Dickens thought — ridiculously considered that excessive naturalism should be avoided.[10] Persian, Indian, Middle Eastern and Far Eastern textiles had aroused great admiration at the exhibition. From 1873 to 1885 Major Murdoch-Smith who was supervising the construction of the telegraph line linking Europe with India paused to amass the museum's great collections of Oriental textiles in Persia.

The Victoria and Albert Museum has been an inspiration for academics, textile designers and the public for over a century. The museum's textiles have kept alive an awareness of the beauty of natural dyes.[11] By coincidence, another dimension of colour-consciousness was encouraged by the British Museum. The sprawling Ancient Egyptian galleries, filled with brightly coloured objects in contrast with the muddy remains from other ancient cultures became an enduring popular and fashionable success.

Textiles were one of a variety of materials made or marketed by Morris, Marshall, Faulkner & Co., which was a somewhat amateurish undertaking founded in 1861. It had run out of funds by 1865, when Morris became the dominant partner. By 1870 Morris, Edward Burne-Jones, the artist and Philip Webb, the architect had become the active members.

In the early 1870s Morris began designing carpets for outside production. He also made his first design for printed cotton and returned to wallpapers. After various arguments between the partners the firm was reregistered as Morris & Co. in 1875. By 1880 Morris's chintzes and woven fabrics made a handsome profit which subsidised the more expensive handmade tapestries and carpets. In his essay 'Of dyeing as an Art' in the 1889 *Arts and Crafts Exhibition Catalogue*, Morris pronounced that, "there is an absolute divorce between the commercial process and the art of dyeing. Anyone wanting to produce dyed textiles with any artistic quality in them must entirely forego the modern and commercial methods in favour of those which are at least as old as Pliny, who speaks of them as being old in his time." He then described the sources of his own dyes as madder, kermes, lac and cochineal for reds.

From the early 1870s Morris was also dyeing silks experimentally but still had to use synthetics for blue, green, yellow and brown. By 1877 he was dyeing "blue silks in cochineal and madder to get purples." But as Mr Guy his assistant complained, "it is hard to get the colour on." Morris's essay continued with a statement on the importance of vegetable dyes:

They all make in their simplest forms beautiful colours: they need no muddling into artistic usefulness, when you need your colours bright (as I hope you usually do), and they can be modified and toned without dirtying, as the foul blotches of the capitalist dyer cannot be. Like all dyes, they are not eternal, the sun in lighting them and beautifying them, consumes them . . . These colours in fading remain beautiful, and never, even after long wear, pass into nothingness, through that stage of livid ugliness which distinguishes the commercial dyes as nuisances, even more than their short and no means merry life.[12]

In fact, he was a bit of a humbug. As well as using synthetics during his early 'experimental' period and in 'Daffodil', his last design for a chintz, in 1891 he also used aniline for printing the yellows of the flowers. He set up workshops at

Merton Abbey in 1881 where he dyed cloths and yarns. He was against all popular roller printing, choosing block printing instead. While his palette of colours was influenced by Persian textiles, the designs were in turn naturalistic, then animal-bird-plant combinations, then derived from medieval Italian silks, then from fifteenth-century Italian cut-velvets and finally from Ottoman-naturalistic designs.

He loved his printed textiles about which he wrote in a letter in 1875, "they look so beautiful (really) that I feel inclined to sit and stare at them all day . . . I don't suppose that we shall get many people to buy them however which will be a pity as we shall be obliged in that case to give up the manufacture." Weaving started in earnest after his move in 1881. Even though the colours are often muddy and the designs derivative, there is a certain unique charm to these textiles and their designs are still murdered today.

After Morris' death in 1896, there was a gradual decline in popular interest in natural dyes. It reappeared as a minority rustic activity, perhaps influenced — in the steps of Gertrude Jekyll — by the British passion for gardens and

Russian printed cotton Caucasian 'electric' and 'dragon' design with a deep and undimmed purp. and red, c. 1900 (Author's photo)

vegetable allotments, and on the literary side by D. H. Lawrence's ideas of a return to a socialist pastoralism and the post-Emily Pankhurst new role for feisty women, where upper-class patronage joined with manual labour. This was also reflected in the survival of hunting in traditional costume. The famous so-called 'pink', that is red hunting jackets were and are dyed with madder. To complete the confusion, 'pink' originally meant brown.[13]

The austerity and self-help attitude engendered by the economic ruin and social upheaval after the Second World War, gave rise to a range of new eccentricities in Britain. Romantic wind-swept (usually) women natural dyers with their tactile love of exotic wool from rare-breed sheep mingled with nouveau poverty held a charmed place. Violetta Thurstan's classic booklet first published in 1930[14] had run to a fifteenth edition by 1986. Dorothy Luke even dyed the yarn spun from the hair of her Samoyed dogs with madder.[15] Jill Goodwin doyen of home dyers and weavers put it with simple clarity. 'But colour was immensely important to us as children, as it must also have been to primitive man, and the brighter and clearer the colours the better we liked them."[16]

In another curious quirk of history, women got the vote in Azerbaijan in 1921 before they did in Britain. In Azerbaijan in the southern Caucasus where the world's first oil boom and consequent industrialisation had happened from the 1870s, they never gave up the dream of the return of natural dyes. In 1908 A. K. Rollov collected 224 varieties of dye plants there.

The aftermath of the Russian Revolution provided a short-lived platform for Socialist textiles. The hopelessly idealistic artists produced fantastic printed textiles from the late 1920s until the repressions of the early thirties. Designers came to the front with a startling range from traditional cotton prints to Constructivist designs. The high quality fabrics never went into their dreamed-of mass production and several of the rare prototypes look as if they used natural dyes, including Turkey red.[17]

Grossgeim continued: "The Caucasus is extraordinarily rich in the diversity of its dye plants. In recent times, the revival of the art of making carpets has increased interest in plant dyes ... In spite of the widespread growth of chemically coloured goods and the cheaper price of synthetic dyes, plant dyes have not lost their significance. This was confirmed at the two all-Soviet conferences on carpet production — in Moscow in December 1936 and in Baku in January 1939. The market for synthetic dyed carpets has almost stopped and the demand and price of old natural-dyed carpets has risen strongly. The revival of carpet production — that once famed handicraft

Russian print with Caucasian rug designs in steps which are reminiscent of carpet cartoons, mainly red with black and white, c. 1900 (Author's photo)

of the Caucasus — must go hand in hand with the return of plant dyes."

He then listed 65 yellows, 25 reds, 25 blue and violets, 24 blacks, 13 browns, 24 greens and 2 khakis, in total 178 plants. For reference, his reds are listed in chapter 2 and the other colours in appendix 1.1 (page 306).[18] The natural dye revival was to wait until 1999, after the end of Socialism, with the appearance of Magomekhan's *soumakh* weft-brocaded rugs.

The DOBAG Project

The lurid colours which governed the quality of twentieth-century carpets from all countries seemed to be in hopeless decline until rug production became linked to a growing interest and study of beautiful historic examples. In 1981 a German chemistry teacher Harald Böhmer and his wife and partner Renate extended their 20 years of visits and work projects in Turkey to found DOBAG (Doğal Boya Araştırma ve Geliştirme Projesi), the Natural Dye Research and

Development Project, under the aegis of Marmara University in Istanbul. Their interest in old carpets, natural dyes and the survival of Turkish village life was combined with their revulsion at the poor quality modern products, a dislike universally shared with other rug lovers. They were consistently helped by an American anthropologist, Josephine Powell, who had been studying and photographing the last Yörük nomads in Turkey. In 1982 she rediscovered the old method for producing a treasured deep-violet from madder without adding indigo blue. DOBAG has revolutionised modern rug production and encouraged thousands of other weavers to use natural dyes. There are many similar commercial ventures in Turkey and other countries which have followed DOBAG's lead to reintroduce natural dyes.

Sariahmetli mosque, 1995
(photo Anderson)

DOBAG use the designs found in old rugs in local mosques.[19] This historicism has always been a subject for debate, when compared with the products of — say — the American George Jevremovic's 'Woven Legends'. They employ 20,000 weavers from China to Moldova to Turkey and often provide their own vernacular designs like Ziegler once did. In contrast, Clive Rogers, then living in Brighton, was first to provide rugs with Western Art designs made with natural dyes in Turkey, like the bold 'Mondrian' carpet. He was indirectly followed by Christopher Farr in London who commissions British designer rugs made with natural colours in Turkey as well as glowing copies of 16th-century rug designs.

Although the Böhmers had studied old Turkish rugs for many years, the impetus for DOBAG only came in 1976. Dr Helmut

The author giving the DOBAG project back one of their rugs,
bought in London, with a design not found in the mosque, 1985
(photo Charlotte Vesey-May)

Selling DOBAG rugs in the sun, Yuntdağ village, 1985 (Author's photo)

Schweppe's new Thin-layer Chromatography (TLC) technique, which he had developed for paint pigments, enabled them to analyse the natural dyes in wool from small samples such as loose knots (see chapter 10). Böhmer then knew exactly what natural dyes to recreate. He analysed more than 200 carpets in Turkish museums and carried out botanical research to find locally available dye-plants to match those which he had analysed. Böhmer next convinced the German Development Service a government agency to support his hiring by (what became in 1982) the Faculty of Fine Arts at Marmara University.

His idea was for local people to create self-financing village co-operatives and more remarkably (in the Yuntdağ project described below) for women to be paid directly by the knot. Böhmer was approached by the prescient Head of Forestry in Ayvacık village. High on the Aegean Peninsula near Çanakkale, the inhabitants are Yörük settled nomads, with an ancient weaving tradition documented by numbers of old rugs in their mosque. Centred on Ayvacık, 220 households from 25 of the 79 surrounding hamlets have joined the co-operative, and now produce 1,000 carpets a year. The Ayvacık co-operative received a Turkish government start-up loan of $100,000 which was repaid within six years.

In 1982 the DOBAG project expanded southwards to the Yuntdağ region near Manissa. Yörük shepherds live there, scattered over 50 hamlets. Their traditional transhumance movements had been broken when they were settled. As a result, their restricted pastures were overgrazed which led to a decline of both pasturage and flocks. Because of their isolation, traditional folk arts such as carpet-weaving had survived. Their co-operative received a another German development grant to start up. By 1998, 130 women weavers held membership. They had greater freedom of choice of design and colours than the weavers of Ayvacık. Both areas are uphill from the west coast of Asia

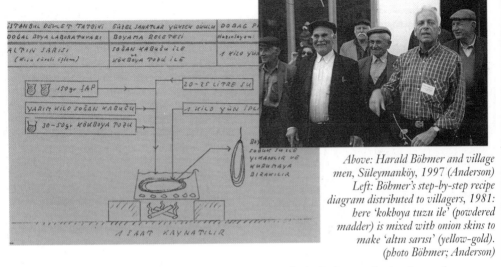

*Above: Harald Böhmer and village
men, Süleymanköy, 1997 (Anderson)
Left: Böhmer's step-by-step recipe
diagram distributed to villagers, 1981:
here 'kokboya tuzu ile' (powdered
madder) is mixed with onion skins to
make 'altın sarısı' (yellow-gold).
(photo Böhmer; Anderson)*

Minor, more than a day's drive from Istanbul. Böhmer devised vat-dye methods and taught them to the villagers. Intriguingly, Josephine Powell's madder violet remains a DOBAG secret.[20] The success of DOBAG is twofold. The co-operatives are prospering with waiting lists for membership. Secondly, an estimated 5,000 to 10,000 weavers throughout Turkey now imitate the DOBAG project's use of natural dyes.[21]

Near misses

Madder or alizarin almost found a new role in linoleum. Nairns of Kircaldy in Scotland started manufacturing impregnated cloths in 1847, and hard-wearing linoleum was patented by Fred Walton in Lancashire in 1863. In 1878 Forbo Nairn was permitted to produce linoleum and still makes it of cork shavings, wood flour, chalk and pigment compressed together with linseed oil onto a woven jute ground. The company considered the use of alizarin pigment but found that the light fastness did not last its standard 20 years so 'scarlet chrome' was used instead.

From 1994 to 1997 the European Union gave a grant of some £300,000 to the Institute of Arable Crops Research at the Long Ashton Research Station near Bristol to study the feasibility of growing madder and other dye plants. Their report praised the possibilities of madder. But they could neither find nor devise a mechanical extraction method, which made cultivation too labour intensive and expensive. The British government Ministry of Agriculture and Food subsequently gave a further similar research grant for woad cultivation.[22]

Left: Böhmer still demonstrating in Süleymanköy, 1997 (photo Böhmer; Anderson).
Above: Renate Böhmer explaining to a Yuntdağ villager in 1981 that the dried madder root which the man is holding was more than a weed in his cotton fields (photo Böhmer; Anderson).
Below: The Sezgin family of Süleymanköy near Ayvacık display their carpet commissioned by the British Museum in 1989 (photo Böhmer; Anderson)

Madder Red

Bottom left & right: Ayvacık women dyeing woollen yarn red with madder in tinned copper pots over a wood fire. They found that the tin combined with the mordant to brighten the red to orange, so aluminium pots were substituted, which did not change the red, 1982. Stirring the skin of wool (bottom left) and lifting it (right) to help the dye penetrate.
(photos Böhmer, Chenciner, 1984)

Bottom right: The traditional laborious hand-grinding of crushed roots. The top stone weighs 10 to 15kgs and it takes over an hour's work to grind a kilo of powder. 1kg of powder dyes enough red wool for a 1½sq metre red ground rug.
(photo Böhmer; Anderson)

17

The dyer's grail: alchemical philosophies & folklore

A tickling curiosity

"A MAN WAS building a canoe, and chewed some of the chips. He spat and saw that the saliva was black. In this way the people obtained that colour. Later they boiled everything to find out what colours various things would produce, and so obtained all their dyes." This charming Micmac Amero-Indian folktale emerged from their remarkable specialisation. As mentioned earlier, in the 17th century, the Micmacs were noted dyers of porcupine quills with only black, natural white and madder red, which was much admired by the French. So might this story give an explanation of the discovery of Turkey red?[1]

The Micmac made his original discovery in a void. Dyers were also involved in the rediscovery of lost methods and directional discovery of a desired result. Dyers repeatedly had to reinvent their techniques because of the disruption of wars and enforced population movements which regularly affected their small numbers. The dyer was a tranquil worker and there was no need for action until such accidents occurred. The dyer had access to few texts of this truly international craft, often described in unknown languages or ciphers. The defensive secrecy of the dyers' recipes and methods meant that, over the centuries, the hermetic art was repeatedly lost. How a non-chemist dyer could devise a 30-step process is a tantalising question. In general, discovery is stimulated by surreal leaps of thought which connect disparate ideas. Most original ideas occur at the meeting point of two different theoretical or practical disciplines which touch on the problem.

Imagine a dyer endlessly staring into his vat. He must have been obsessed with his craft. Before the advent or understanding of modern chemistry, his mind must have been filled with the magic of red. Different ways of understanding colour through different intellectual disciplines might unexpectedly have provided the inspiration. But what were his 'intellectual disciplines'? On the one hand, there were theories of the nature of colour which originated from Classical philosophers and had been preserved through Arabic writings from Baghdad and Cordova. Their theories endured over the millennium and were only overturned in Cambridge in 1704, where Isaac Newton's (1642-1727) studies on the refraction of light laid the basis for the modern understanding of colour.

The apparent contradictions of philosophical logic left the door ajar to a mystical approach. The influence of what became Romantic symbolism is best understood through authors like Field who coupled God and colour. The momentum of his ideas was delightfully expressed in his frontispiece for the translation from the French of Frederic Portal's at times perplexing monograph, 'Symbolic Colours'. The coloured engraving consisted of two or three biblical circular-rainbows, changed in different editions.[2] Such symbolic elitism contrasted strikingly with the massive folklore on red. It therefore would seem that the different disciplines were in place. Would philosophy, symbolism and folklore have provided sufficient stimuli to inspire invention?

There was one extra universal ingredient, the catalyst of professional pride. This arose from the dyer's ambivalent social position fenced in by the snobbery of society. As relatively well-educated common people, dyers were both respected and suspected by the community which they served. Their experiments with noxious substances in a conservative and super-stitious world set them

John Kyan, who in the mid-1830s became Field's mystic disciple after a successful career in fighting wood rot, explained that the top represented the Newtonian spectrum, the middle the Aureola produced by the Lenticular Prism and that the lower referred to Genesis 1:1-10 and 9:13. There are two versions, one without the prism.
(George Field; Portal)

apart from the illiterate majority and made them an unwitting threat to their rulers.

Some idea of the position of the dyer before the scientific revolution can be gained from a perceptive Francis Bacon in his seminal contribution to the two-cultures debate.[3] Bacon was the first — in 1605 — to condemn the attitude of "men of learning" as "vain and supercilious arrogancy . . . For it is esteemed a kind of dishonour unto learning to descend to inquiry or meditation upon matters mechanical, except they be such as may be thought secrets, rarities and special subtleties."[4] His views gained followers and after a first gathering in Royalist Oxford in 1645 at the outset of Cromwell's grim Protectorate, the Royal Society was eventually granted its charter in a more enlightened London in 1662. But the snobbery towards science continued both in high society and in the old universities.

But dyers were practical people and rarely wrote about their inspiration. George Field the leading colourman of the 1800s did. His mass of carefully recorded experiments and observations are the sole complete surviving example of the detailed private workings of an enquiring dyer's mind. There were 3,000 to 6,000 notes, depending on how they are counted, that spanned the years 1804 to 1825. What drove him to go on? His progress does not appear random. It seems that instead of chemical methodology, a different rhythm possessed his thoughts.[5] In 1808, when

Technological reality: automaton writing doll, made by Pierre Jaquet-Droz, Neuchatel c. 1770 — the demotion of technology from industrial potential to a toy. (Giedion)

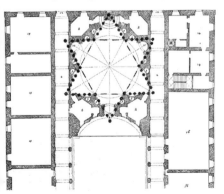

Architects had long used six-pointed stars, Francesco Borromini's Sant' Ivo Rome, 1642-62, and Field was not alone in thinking in terms of an architecture of colours (Giedion)

Romantic fantasy: John Smeaton, Eddystone Lighthouse 1774, the first concrete structure since the Roman period, locked in Romantic combat with an anthropomorphic wave (Giedion)

Field was at the height of his experimental powers, he drew a series of six-pointed chromatic stars and then wrote down his incantation. 'To this principle of Union, (which) pervades and holds all nature together is to be attributed not only physical and sensible but Moral Harmony."[6] He was a contemporary of Wordsworth and Field's mystical belief can be understood as a manifestation of the Romantic movement. But it is also the statement of a dyer, and from this text it is evident that all traditional dyers were obsessed by their art, especially those of the *grand teint* custodians of the valuable secrets of red, traditionally passed from father to son.[7]

Above: There was snobbery against Trade — Attic of a North of England cotton spinning factory c. 1835. The new self-acting mule spinning frames' space requirement was only met by a cast-iron roof framework. The roof invention was credited to J. B. Papworth, the designer of 'garden cities' in 1821. (Giedion)
Below: Another symbolic arch — F. W. Olmstead's early overpass in Central Park, New York City, built in 1858 was ignored. The overpass was only adopted in the late 20th century to deal with traffic confusion. (Giedion)

Neo-Platonists & Aristotelians

The philosophy of colour can conveniently be approached through the Arabs who translated and preserved the Ancient Greek philosophers' ideas for the West. The following theories were the philosophical armoury of alchemists, apothecaries and, by association, dyers. They are both diverse and complicated with much room for misinterpretation. It is understandable that they would have been thought of as 'The Mysteries' and not only by outsiders. In the light of later knowledge, it is tempting to be dismissive of the pioneering ideas which remained important, though hardly constructive, influences until and — surprisingly — after Newton's *Optics*.[8]

The simplified ground rules of colour are as follows. The colour of an object is observed with its three sensory variants of 'tonality' — colour in its strict sense, 'luminosity' — the extent to which the object transmits light, and 'saturation' — the intensity of the colour. White and black are achromatic colours with zero saturation. The complementary colours are those which neutralise each other and combine to form white, i.e. red and blue-green. Finally, of the seven colours of the spectrum, only three — blue, yellow and red — are fundamental.

One distinction of the Arabic language is the great richness of its chromatic vocabulary. In Arabic the word for 'red' may have originally signified 'more red than . . .', an example of the particularly narrow line separating names of colours and intensive themes in Semitic languages. To express the concept of colour Arabic uses one word, *lawn*, which also denotes 'shade', 'aspect', 'type', 'dish' (of food) and so on. The rainbow is the magical natural occurrence of the spectrum and is a good starting-point to understand the Arabic perception of colour. The Ancient Greeks and Romans attributed three colours to the rainbow. Aristotle lists red-brown (*algourgon*), green and purple, in which he saw a progressive weakening of light.[9] Plato in the *Timaeus* showed that it is possible to constitute all shades with four fundamental colours: black, blue, red and the colour of light. Classical Arabic dictionaries almost unanimously agree that 'the rainbow consists of strips in a circular

Above: Medieval dyers at work, Bruges, Flanders, Boock of Proprieties of Things, end 15th century (ack. British Library; Goodwin; Brunello)
Below: An alchemist in his laboratory, 15th century, from Thomas Norton's MS Ordinall. 'Coloris' is mentioned in the lower right-hand scroll (ack. British Museum; Forbes; CIBA Review)

arc, coloured yellow, red and green'. The philosophers were only able to agree on red.

Red evokes notions of blood, flesh, fruits and life. Before Islam, Frazer noted several creation myths where God makes the first man out of red clay pressed by the divine fingers (from Tahiti; the Melbourne Aboriginal People; Mota a Melanesian island; the Korkus, an Aboriginal tribe of central India, where a Shiva-like deity used red earth from an anthill; and the writer of Genesis who omitted to mention the colour of the clay from which Adam was made, but the soil of Palestine is a dark reddish-brown). Sometimes the clay is kneaded with the creator's own blood into his likeness (from the Maoris of New Zealand). Frazer also remarks that this theory is not universal and that many simple people's creation myth is based on a theory of evolution from totemic animals or plants.[10]

The two opposed and complementary colours — green and red — are also the colours of all vegetable and animal life. Red has always occupied a position of particular significance, in almost every sector of humanity and enjoyed a commensurate status in vocabulary. All its shades are represented in virtually all languages. Black, red and white form the trilogy of colours that are best recognised and accordingly the richest in terminology and symbolism. The most usual Arabic word for red, *ahmar*, derives from a word-root with the sense of ardour, violence and intensity. In addition to *adam* which is already encountered as the word for white, and perhaps the term for red in ancient Semitic, there are 51 other words for red in Arabic, with a further extensive vocabulary of mixtures and blends . . .

The three components of colour described above were not evenly perceived. Tonality was not of fundamental importance to Arab writers when describing the colour of, say, a landscape or a garment or other everyday object. They preferred indistinct touches to confer a general impression. In contrast, they were more impressed by luminosity and far more by saturation, ideas of which are intermingled in the innumerable adjectives which enrich Arabic literary expression. In earlier writing the adjectives applied to any colour.

The Arab philosophers were influenced by Ancient Greek theories of colour.[11] The Greek philosophers were struck by the indissoluble link between light and colour on the one hand and transparency on the other, which led to three distinct theories. Man's transparent eyes were the meeting point between external light and its internal equivalent, which favoured the theory of emanations. The theory, developed by Empedocles and revised by Plato[12] who explained that we see by means of 'rays of the nature of fire', that issue from the eye to meet the emanation from the seen object.

Aristotle rejected the theory of emanations, saying that what is visible is colour, and colour is that which is on the surface of what is visible by itself. The basis of all colour phenomena is the transparent, especially represented by air and water — the carriers, but only visible with the help of light. The transparent can immediately transmit qualitatively the colour of the visual object to the eye, independent of time and space. While Aristotle and the Arab philosophers insisted on the aqueous and non-igneous nature of the eye, the Master rejected the idea, propounded by Democritus, Leucippus and Epicurus, that vision is only the mirror reflection of an object. Instead, every object contains varying proportions of transparent air and water which make it susceptible to being coloured. The colour of a solid body is the limit not of the body itself, but the transparency which the body contains. The essence of colour is the act of determining a qualitative change in the light — itself active transparency. Colours are accordingly defined transparencies, which more or less approximate to white or black (not darkness which is the absence of actualisation of the transparent). The separate colours depend on their content of fire (luminosity or 'active' transparency) or earth (the absolute opacity) and result from a total, effective blending.

The application of this theory gave pause for thought to eminent Arab authors and translators such as Ali ibn Raban al-Tabari (d. 855), who worked out that colours resulted from varying quantities of dryness, humidity and heat. Red resulted from the synthesis of heat with dryness and humidity. Yellow was the more humid intermediary between red and black, and green the less humid intermediary between red and white. Al-Tabari's contemporary, Hunayn ibn Ishaq (d. 873) insisted that light was neither a form of fire nor a rarefied body, but a contingency borne by a body. Colour was the perfection of limpid and diaphanous bodies — such as water and air — which received the colour of an adjacent object. Water and air had potential colour, transformed into actual colour by the agency of light.

Members of the theologico-political school of the Mu'tazilis took divergent views. Al-Nazzam (d. 845) started with the postulate that accidents (movement, colour and taste) cannot be visible, and classed colours among the corruptible substances. Bishr b. al-Mu'tamir (d. 835) and the majority of the school considered colours as accidents due to the action of men alone, or produced by the nature of the things that they affect. Thus they were not subject to divine creation, but God remained the determinant cause of the accidental determination of substances. God created substances capable of producing by their own nature, well-determined accidents such as colour. Bishr's contemporary Mu'ammar declared that every accident required the existence of an infinite chain of determining entities, of which the initial cause was the Creator. Therefore Hisham al-Fuwati (fl. c. 900) flagrantly upped the stakes when he declared that colour did not constitute proof of the existence of God. Abu Hashim al-Djubba (d. 933) classed coloration among the real things that do not exist and that any substance endowed with colour was incapable of losing it. In contrast, Abu 'l-Kasim al-Balkhi (d. c. 931) declared that substance has always been endowed with colour. Both however agreed that substance depended on divine action while colour was engendered by the substance that bore it.

Arab Neo-Platonic theories developed ideas such as: the colours which we think that we perceive in fire are in fact the colours of terrestrial particles mixed with the fire, which like air and water was totally colourless. That explained why we have the illusion that the sky is blue, but not the stars which have their own colours. Al-Farabi (d. 950) thought that the primary bodies and elements such as fire and earth had no colour, while fire brought a tendency towards white and earth — black, with intermediary colours which resulted from different mixes of fire and earth.

During the second half of the tenth century, the Ikhwan al-Safa authors of an encyclopaedia returned to considering the pupil of the eye as essential. The visual faculty received the colours and then transmitted them to the imaginative faculty. Light and darkness were spiritual colours, transformed into white and black — corporeal colours — on contact with bodies. Red was one of the seven simple colours, derived from 'putrefactive' causes through excess of humidity and 'liquifactive' causes through excess of heat. The rainbow consisted of four colours: red, yellow, green and blue, corresponding to the four primary qualities: heat, dryness, humidity and cold and the four elements: fire, air, earth and water. The authors declared that the theory of emanations could only be supported by people 'having no experienceof things of the spirit and of nature'. Ibn Sina (d. 1037) largely agreed with Aristotle, but rejected the part of the theory that only whiteness was a colour and blackness — darkness. Black was illuminated and white could turn into black by three ways: through darkening grey; through red darkening to brown; and through green and indigo. It sounded like top-dyeing.

Ibn Bajija (d. 1139) in his *Treatise on the Soul* written under the Master's influence, postulated that the primary sensory element of vision was colour, through the seeing soul which exists in the eye, localised in the 'glacial' vitreous humour. Colour can only be perceived through an intermediary such as air and when a coloured object is placed directly before the eye, it cannot be perceived. The sheen of objects and animals were determined not by colour, but by impressions that affected the eye. Just as colour cannot be perceived without light, light cannot be perceived without colour. Ibn Rushd (called Averroes, d. 1198) added that colours, the result of a blending of fire with diaphanous body, found in light not the cause of their transmission through the visual organ, but a genuine essence and existence. Averroes veered away from mysticism in maintaining that light gives to the transparent the manner of being which enables it to be influenced by colour and, contrary to Ibn Badjidja, colour as such did not contain light. Happily, there was no official Arab-Muslim doctrine of colour.

Muslim mysticism

Such a diverse set of philosophical contortions opened the way for a later Muslim mystical vision of colour. Taking up Goethe's favourite theory of 'psychological colours'[13] the mid-19th-century Iranian theosophist al-Kirmani (d. 1870) was the first to belatedly challenge the theses of Newton. He stressed the difference between the existence and the manifestation of colour, which was entirely different from the Arab philosophers' concept of potential and actual existence. The eye participated in the perception of things and produced its own colour. Al-Kirmani drew support from certain verses of the Qur'an, such as 13:16 and 35:20 which forcefully state: "Are the blind man and he who sees equal; are darkness and light equal . . . ?" He then deduced that colours perceived by our eyes are bodies, not those of rays of light: "Light is the spirituality of colour; and colour is the corporality of light." The spiritual colour of the world of nature was red.

The point of the symbolism of colours is that colours are capable of acting on the human being, independently of the optical system. In addition, the sensation of colour is in essence an individual rather than a collective experience. Among the Arabs, one of the most striking manifestations of the symbolic connotations of colours is the phenomenon of opposites. In humanity's ancient collective unconscious, it does not seem that our ancestors felt the need to establish a tight partition between colours, which were regarded as being close if they offered similar attributes of luminosity and intensity, like yellow and red.

English & French Romantic mysticism

Romantic imagery such as Shelley's 'wrath's red fire', 'the red plague' and 'Satan's nose' and Tennyson's later ruins of 'Nature, red in tooth and claw' must have bathed George Field's imagination.[14]

George Field had a system of mystical tenets which started with the idea of Union and Moral Harmony mentioned above. Field was more a technologist than a research chemist, and he got his chemical theory at second hand. His standard chemical text-book Thomas Thomson's *System of Chemistry* (1802), would have introduced him to vitalistic notions of attraction and repulsion, that extended from material bodies to immaterial light. Field became preoccupied with the active polarity of colour at the light end of the scale, and passive at the dark. As he wrote later, "Black with White is the principle of all colours — i.e. chromatically or sensibly 'Dark & Light' and physically 'Carbon' which is fixed 'Hydrogen' with colourless 'Oxygen' affords the element of all 'Material Colours or Pigments' varied in Bases, of which 'Black' is fundamental or final . . ."[15] He would have been at home with the Arab philosophers whose melange of ideas he seemed to have adopted eclectically. On the other hand, he did produce excellent pigments and, unlike the Greeks and their school, he was interested in practical experiment.

Following in Goethe's steps he developed his 'Lenticular Prism' or 'chromascope', which allowed him to study the coloured fringes produced at dark edges by unequally refracted light — a woolly investigation into the relationship of colours to light and darkness (see page 280). His thought was based in essence on a notion of universal analogy. In his last work[16] he wrote of his 'Physeter' — a pressurised filter (see page 159) which he had developed decades earlier and which won him the gold Isis medal at the Society of Arts in 1817. He explained that it functioned in "a manner analogous to the operation of nature in springs, and in the animal economy, in which respiration, vascular filtration, and that circulation which immortalised the name of Harvey, are carried on." If he looked down at his own writing hand, he also must have noticed that his blue veins produced red blood — a remarkable continuous dye change.

His next most important analogical structure was the triad, which as Gage points out, he was introduced to through music by the founder of the Bath Harmonic Society, Dr Henry Harington. At the same time as Harington's son was a close friend of the painter Thomas Barker, Dr Harington *père* had published in 1806 a paper entitled 'Symbolon Trisagon, or the Geometrical analogy of the catholic doctrine of triunity . . . demonstrated by the triunity of certain simultaneous sounds'. Harington received an admiring letter from a Rev William Jones in Suffolk, who enthused about "the wonderful Trinitarian coincidence in optics as in sounds." Jones continued to describe pure light refracted by a prism into the three primary colours, "that is light: but when they are joined, the same that were three are now one without distinction, the glory equal, the majesty co-eternal." Numerism has always been attractive to certain echelons of mysticism.

This heady doctrine was to illuminate Field's life's work where he produced colours, which joined the earthly palette with the superior embodiment of these God-given primary truths. His brilliant practical work on standardisation and measurement of colours — his 'Chromometer' or 'Metrochrome' which he began to develop in 1810[17] — was based on his expanded hieratic ideas:

> That Nature, even in Chemical Compounds affects Harmonic Proportions, that we have used them habitually in our Experimental researches, and found them conducive to our own ends . . . especially in Explosive Mixtures, [citing Newton who] in his experiments as Master of the Mint found that the most fusible of all metallic alloys was afforded by Three of Tin, Five of Lead, and Eight of Bismuth . . . The like analogy holds in the Third, Fifth and Octave of the Chord constituting the Musical Triad, and the same proportions hold in the Yellow, Red and Blue neutrality of colours, on which their Harmonys depend.[18]

Field was not swayed by theories on optics contained in Francesco Algarotti's popular *Sir Isaac Newton's Philosophy Explain'd for the Use of Ladies*.[19] He contested Newton's view that white was not a colour *per se* but an assemblage of colours. Algarotti also emphasised the Platonic regularities that underlay natural forms and contested the view attributed to Poussin that colours are in painting what rhythm is in poetry.[20] Field's *Chromatic Equivalents*, which rested on a set of 'primaries', had come to be recognised as quite arbitrary by the end of his life, 1854, in the light of serious physics theory from James Clerk Maxwell and Hermann von Helmholtz. They clearly distinguished between the subtractive primaries as understood by painters and the additive primaries which constitute light and which they showed might be red, blue and green.

Field was above all an idealist whose programme of research was animated by a sense of the universal significance of pigment: "There is the ideal in colouring as well as in forms, which belongs to the perfection of beauty and sentiment, which are the chief objects of attainment to the painter, and that to which the philosophic minds of the Greeks aspired."[21] It should not be overlooked that Field was considered to have developed the best standard coloured madder lakes in the world. Field also provided an illustration for Portal's extraordinary writings.

Portal's theosophical ideas were drawn from all the Ancients. He clearly explained his 'grammatical rules of the language' of the symbolism of colours, and differentiated between the seven colours of natural philosophy and the five primitives of painting. The system recognised three degrees: of 'existence', 'manifestation' and 'the resulting act'. He explained that "the symbol of yellow emanates from the symbol of red" and not the colours themselves. He completed his syntax with "the Rule of Combinations, where purple — which is of a red azure — signifies the love of truth . . . and the Rule of Oppositions, where red signifies love, egotism and hatred and, united with black, infernal love and all the passions of degraded man."[22] He drew on extensive sources of red symbolism to form an eclectic synthesis. The 'western' tradition was represented by a collection of Ancient Egyptian, Old and New Testament and Apochrypha biblical and classical and pseudo-alchemical sources. An exotic brew of all the remaining ancient civilisations was contributed by the religions of Avesta, Bhuddism, Hindooism and Mithraism, and the cultures of the Chinese, Indians and Incas. Swedenborg and St Croix's Mysteres du Paganism rubbed shoulders with Xenophon and Electricity. The ouija boards must have been jumping.[23]

The folklore of red

A cursory glance at the massive collections of folklore of several languages reveals that in every culture only a fraction of the stories contain reference to colours. Of the colours, black, white and red are by far the most frequently mentioned and, in English, in about equal numbers. From a Folklore Society survey of 722 'colour folk-tales', there were 219 mentions of white, 176 of black and 161 of red and 241 all other colours together.[24] Obviously a separate book could be written about the folklore of red alone, so it was necessary to be selective.

There seem to be no folk tales which mention madder red as opposed to other reds. Indeed it is rarely specified what sort of red dye was referred to. There is but one allusion made by Culpeper who described madder as "an herb of Mars."[25] Another story referred to cochineal, in an obscure interpretation of a Hasidic homily on public and private sin: "Though your sins be like scarlet thread, they shall whiten like snow; if they redden like the worm that emits crimson dye, they shall become like wool."[26] It is the significance of the coloured object rather than its dye source which features in the lore. As both the best Turkey red dye as well as carpets and textiles came from the Orient, it seemed worthwhile to look at Arabic folklore which for present purposes also contains Turkish, Persian and Caucasian material. On the Western side, as the largest consumer of madder in the 19th century was Britain, which took over 30 per cent of world trade during the 1860s, it was welcome to find that the Folklore Society at University College London had devoted a conference in 1991 to the (mostly British) folklore of colour. Combined with other material from their library, the wide-ranging references to red present a picture of the folklore of red which is probably echoed in other European cultures. Red Easter eggs provide but one example of such a geographical spread (see appendix 17.1, page 350).

Arabic folklore

For the Arabs, 'Death is livid and white in contrast to the redness of life. Red is the colour of fire and of blood, of passion, of impulse and of danger. It is fundamentally linked to the vital force and to the warlike qualities. It is a gushing colour, hot and male, unlike blue and green. The name of the first man Adam, signifies 'red' in Hebrew. As with yellow its symbolism is ambivalent, both divine and infernal. The Burning Bush has its equivalent in the Fiery Furnace. The red sulphur of Islamic esotericism denotes Universal Man, the product of the action of hermetic red. It is said that at the battles of Badr and Hunayn, the angels who assisted the faithful against the infidels wore red turbans and belts. But, on the other hand, when the Eternal decreed the destruction of Saba' and of its dam, He sent red rats to undermine the edifice. 'Red' death was caused by emission of blood. In the streets, an unlucky year was called 'a red year'. In Syria, the expression 'his eye is red' applied to a cruel person; and 'his wool is red' meant that he is accursed.

The Arabian Nights has but one barely fictional tale of 'Abu Kir the Dyer and Abu Sir the Barber'. The two wily Arab townsfolk leave Alexandria and set sail from Egypt to find their fortune. After various twists and turns of the plot, Abu Kir, who has made and lost a fortune by introducing different coloured dyes to his adopted infidel city, at last finds favour with the king by building a hammam or public bath.[27]

English-language folklore

John Hutchings of the Folklore Society used the results of his recent extensive surveys to formulate the basis of the folklore of colour. The colour triad of black, white and red predominates, which mirrors its importance in anthropology and language. These colours are found in all body decoration. In addition, studies of 'primitive' languages have established that these are always the first three colour names to be included in a vocabulary.

Red is one colour that was used for cures and protection over the ages. The Old Testament's scarlet thread and sacrificial bird blood formed part of purification rites.[28] But by c. AD 390 St John Chrysostom railed in vain against red thread amulets. Local pagan competition, represented by the Druids, thought that "red-berried roan and red thread put witches to their speed." A red coral necklace is worn to protect children from disease. Red wool or cloth keeps rheumatism, smallpox (John of Gaddesden, 1318) or a sore throat at bay. Animals were similarly protected. In the 19th century in County Tyrone a red rag was tied around the leg of a cow to keep away the evil eye. Buildings too benefited from red as a 'good' colour to keep off demons, adorning door and window stone surrounds — like our own old farmhouse in the Bewcastle Wastes of Cumbria. In contemporary culture, the Red Cross (of crusader shields), red hospital blankets, red letter boxes, VIP's red carpets, red double-decker buses and the red rose of the New Labour Party all symbolise institutions that protect the structures of society.[29]

The triad of colours is transferred to human hair as dark, fair and red. Red-headed people are unlucky on land and water, have a bad temper, are mad, or are bad for milk and butter and weakness in cattle. Milk from a red (-haired) cow has healing properties. In the hospital and at home the presence of red and white flowers in the same vase is a matter of ill omen. This colour combination was apparently linked with the Crucifixion. Colour symbolism in narrative is dualistic, giving comfort and planting fear. There are examples of comfort in the 'Bible of the Folk', such as the robin who received his red breast as he tried to comfort Jesus on the Cross. Alternatively, the robin was scorched by flames as he tried to take water to the souls in hell.[30] The more frightening stories usually contain black, rather than white or red. Rare instances of red are fairies, predominantly dressed in red caps and capes, and the middle-world Red Riding Hood.

The function of colour in amulets and cures is to act as a visible and tangible declaration of belief, which no doubt acts as a psychological reinforcement of purpose. For omens or indications, the function seems to be merely an adjective such as 'red hat — no drawers' or 'pink for a girl — blue for a boy'. Its use in narrative may be similar and certainly colour is used to heighten atmosphere. In custom or belief the mechanism of colour is to set apart an individual on an occasion (as a bride) or to make distinct the occasion (as Christmas decorations) or the site (as a laying-out area).[31]

Red was rarely used in connection with death. Yet a sumptuous red velvet covered Princess Charlotte's coffin. Within more common coffins, red was sometimes used as a trimming for white burial stockings. The royal red velvet may have inspired the fashionable Victorian widow to replace red for black mourning attire at society weddings.[32] Red is rarer still in marriage. 'Married in red, you'd better be dead', though probably taken from an etiquette book, may indicate a tradition of deep red as a colour of mourning. Strikingly, in the mid-fifteenth century one Sir William's bride, Joan, was clad in red, and during the American Revolution patriotic brides wore red.[33]

Rowe described surviving calendar customs, where colour was used either as a symbol or as a decoration. The use of colour in markings, artefacts or costume may simply define a character, status, separate group or clan. It can also contain significant but sometimes hermetic allusions to historical events. He gives two examples. The Boggins mummers at Haxey Hood in their red costumes portrayed Father Christmas, King George or the Black Prince (or some other villain) and Old 'Obby 'Oss' of Padstow's May Day wore party dress, with ribbons and scarves of red. Long ago the Padstow women donned red cloaks and marched with their 'Oss over to Stepper Point, to convince Napoleonic would-be invaders that there was an English encampment there. More recently, the Chief Boggin would seek out any local lad whose 'face fitted' — a good 'sway man' or indeed if he was simply wearing red, to be a Field Boggin. He was elevated to a kind of referee of the enthusiastic game of mayhem for that Hood Day, by the authority of a red caddice (worsted) ribbon tied around his arm. That January 6th, the now complete procession of 13 Boggins boasted the Chief Boggin, Lord and Fool, followed by ten Field Boggins wearing old red sweaters.[34] In the Welsh Mabinogion tales, a compilation of Celtic myths and Arthurian legends, otherworldliness is distinguished in a pack of white hounds by their reddish ears, by a troop of 'red-clad' horsemen and by Arthur's red-haired servant riding a wild red horse.[35]

As a more formal way of identification, heraldry arose in the twelfth century in north-west Europe. The Royal College of Heralds in London, founded in the fifteenth century, is the oldest continuing such institution in the world. Originally six colours were permitted for coats-of-arms: Argent, Or, Gules, Azure, Sable and Vert. Brocklebank has counted that after silver and gold, red (gules) was most common, occuring in 55 per cent of arms — ahead of black (sable) at 36 per cent.[36] In far earlier proto-heraldry, the Old Irish body of warrior-heroes about Conchobar mac Nessa, king of Ulster in the first century AD, were called the Red Branch.

Wilfred Owen's hieratic "Red lips are not so red as the stained stones kissed by the English dead" beautifully united the symbols of patriotism, love, death and stones with red dye.[37] A scientific connection has recently been demonstrated with Culpeper's youthful 'herb of Mars' alluding to red's aggressive aspect, (probably from Shakespeare's 'red as Mars his heart' and again from Life of Alisaunder 'Mars was swythe red ferliche' and Chaucer in the Knightes Tale 'The rede statue of Mars, with spere and targe').[38] Sadly, shortwave red perception diminishes with ageing and consequent degeneration of the macula receptors in the eye. Young people really see the world with a reddish tinge and old people watch it turn brown. The 'rose-tinted' spectacles of (ever) youthful optimists are real.[39] The sexual connotations of pink rather than red are elegantly adduced in the quip 'What's pink and hard in the mornings? — *The Financial Times* crossword', which illustrates Roland Barthes' limp explanation in *Elements of Semiology* that the joke involves both performer and audience connecting "two systems of signification which are imbricated but are out of joint with each other." That is of course an analogue of the process of discovery.[40]

To return from the poetic to the prosaic, there are 64 references to red folk-literature in the exhaustive *Stith-Thompson Index of World Folklore*, many of which are not mentioned in the above selection. Red has naturally passed into common usage: 'a red rag to a bull'; 'the pink' for hunting costume, red-tape, red-handed, red shirt, red flag, redcoat, but 'red lattice' for tavern has disappeared. The folklore of red was deep and wide in all cultures.

In violent contrast, it was no coincidence that Ted Hughes chose 'Red' as his last poem in last volume *Birthday Letters*, published in 1998 as he was dying. The master chose his symbols of red to fashion a final dual image of his and his beloved Sylvia Plath's deaths. "Red was your colour . . . ," he began. A history of passion: blood-red, red-ochre for warming the dead, haematite bones, their red room, judgement chamber, casket for gems. He wrapped his vision in textiles: the carpet of blood, ruby curtains, cushions, window seat, burgundy velvet skirt. He moved closer to the intimate, fragile cloth: Aztec sacrifice; as skin on blood, poppies, salvias, doomed roses. "Your lips a dipped deep crimson/You revelled in red." The open vein of a stiffening wound, "dripping weeping roses", "in the pit of red."

The dyer's grail

The most elusive natural dye method of all was rediscovered in 1998. The ancient secret of dyeing Tyrian purple from molluscs had been lost since the fall of Constantinople in 1453, when the Pope himself had to change his imperial (temporal) purple to 'Cardinal's red'. An Englishman, John Edmonds' recent rediscovery of murex purple must rank alongside cracking the Oriental secret of

Turkey red in Europe in the 1750s. John Edmonds explained — in retrospect — the psychological process which led him to imitate the Ancients. He followed a similar route — without the Romantic overtones — as George Field's 'method of analogues' (c. 1808) when he paraphrased his own method for dyeing with woad when dyeing with molluscs. As an engineer whose first enthusiasms were history and archaeology and farming, he was aware of the principle 'that science follows discovery' and opted for the practical life. About 20 years ago he began working as a volunteer at the new Chiltern Open Air museum. He set up a 3.5 acre model of a medieval open field, with various traditional rotational crops, where he cultivated woad to the couched stage, in the old manner.

After 1580, the technique of dyeing with woad alone had been replaced by dyeing with imported tropical indigo added to the woad vat. The role of the woad was purely as a fermenting medium for the indigo. By then they were also adding slaked lime to the vat to maintain the required alkalinity. The dyer's technique was purely empirical, honed by long experience, but relied on the changing smell and feel of the liquor. The medieval concept of 'rightness' seemed important. There are dyers regulations for madder from 1330s to 1480s from Flanders and Artois which give one mysterious indicator of rightness when they refer to the *'waranchure'* as a good or bad *'mestre'*. *Mestre* seems to have been a combination of concentration of dyestuff, additives and temperature.[41] Edmonds had also noted why medieval beer assayers wore leather trousers. They spilt the test beer on a wooden table, sat on it and when they just stuck to the table, the beer was 'right'.[42]

All crafts in the Middle Ages, including dyeing, were closely guarded commercial secrets, particularly the woad vat for which, in any case, there was at the time no rational explanation. Edmonds read widely and found that William Partridge's way of doing things in 1823 seemed best. As late as 1811, Eliyah Bemiss described his own folk memory, that a better blue could be obtained from pure woad, that led to his experiments with a pure woad vat. Though there is much information about the pure woad vat, the process was obsolete before the invention in 1909 of the pH scale for the measurement of acidity, neutrality and alkalinity (see Glossary). In other words the scientific explanation of indigo dyeing by fermentation was only discovered after the process was obsolete. It was a complex process and there was even no explanation of three principle steps. Firstly, why the raw material — woad leaves — if treated in the correct manner, generated an insoluble indigo pigment? Secondly, why fermenting woad — at an appropriate temperature and alkalinity — reduced its indigo to a soluble dye which could be transferred to textiles immersed in the vats? And thirdly, when the cloth, wool or yarn was exposed to the air, why did it turn a permanent blue?

Edmonds calculated that double the amount of woad was needed to replace the imported indigo in the 18th-century vat. This gave good results with modern controls of temperature and alkalinity, though success was apparent when a telltale scum appeared on the surface and the liquor beneath turned a greenish colour. In 1995, shortly before he attended a woad conference in Toulouse, he was given a 1418 Florentine recipe written for the secret training of apprentices in the Arte della Lana guild of dyers, which had been discovered by Dominique Cardon, an authority on the history of dyes. He followed the old method and was able to give the conference a demonstration. He used finely filtered woad ash to control the alkalinity and spotted the telltale though the subtle signs of the 'mature or comforting smell' when the vat is in order. Here was a fifteenth-century dyer come back to explain today how to set and maintain the woad vat at a pH of 9, which — like beer — dropped during fermentation.

After his success, he was encouraged to research the biotechnology which took place in woad fermentation. He duly identified the bacteria involved and confirmed the old woad dyers' optimal empirical conditions. He was next approached by an Israeli chemist who was dyeing with imperial purple extracted from murex but using a modern chemical to dissolve the purple pigment. Since Tyrian purple had a similar chemical structure to indigo, it seemed to the chemist that a like method could be used to recreate biblical purple, so he sent some murex to Edmonds. There were virtually no recipes in classical literature except for an incomplete account by Pliny the Elder. Edmonds worked out that murex, like woad, should dissolve in an alkaline fermenting vat, so he tried a sample of the woad liquor, which worked. But the residual indigo masked any purple.

Edmonds next applied Occam's razor. In his local supermarket, he found an ingredient which was freely available in biblical times — a jar of common European cockles, related to murex molluscs, handily preserved in vinegar. The only other additional available material needed was wood ash from the vat fire. The shellfish meat in water would provide the fermenting agent and finely sieved wood-ash would control the alkalinity. Faced with the health risk of putrefying shellfish, he again referred to Pliny who insisted that purple dyers always added about 10 per cent of sea salt to their vats. This reminded him that the recognised amount of salt which turns pork into ham, to suppress bacterial action, is 13 per cent, so he added that proportion of salt to the purple vat. At an acidity of pH 9 and 50°C, the purple pigment required about 10 days to dissolve to the same greeny colour change which was the marker for indigo. When wool was immersed in the vat for several hours and then lifted out and exposed to the air, it first appeared to be a green colour and then turned deep purple. Eschewing the mysteries, John Edmonds — along with, I suspect, the Micmac whittler and George Field — concluded that, to paraphrase Pascal, "as in all things, serendipity favours the mind prepared."

The discoveries of dyeing compare closely in personal, economic and social terms with other technological advances which have opened up commercial expansion. To repeat, the process involved literate craftsmen and artisans, traditionally from the lower middle classes. The dyers by their merit posed a threat to the establishment which while wanting the dyers' abilities made their lives difficult. Unlike some other innovations, the madder story has no sudden solutions and therefore no individual heroes.

In contrast with more measurable successes of technological discoveries, Europe's retrieval of the method to dye Turkey red which had been lost between 1492 and 1750 had a less obvious result. Although much of the textile trade had passed to Asia, much of Asia, especially India had come under European domination through military or economic means. It is possible that the economic need to rediscover and improve the method of Turkey red dyeing had some mutual effect on the progress of the industrial revolution. If Turkey red added to what is now called the service economy, it is paradoxical that red dyed printed fabrics were at the forefront of mass production. Madder cultivation changed the economies of Holland, France and Turkey. Turkey red dyeing added significantly to the economies of Great Britain, India, France and Russia.

The discovery of Turkey red acted as an example to future generations that impossible innovation could be made real. There was a dramatic development of industrial potential as the synthetic dye industry developed from the 1870s — especially the synthesis of alizarin from coal-tar residue of gas used for town-lighting. As a result, a number of the early participants laid the foundations of the modern organic chemical industry.

There were far-reaching social implications too. Throughout history, fashion and dress have played a central unifying part in peace and war. For survival, societies seem to require a mystical-spiritual dimension in addition to material success. Red always held a central role in the vocabulary of symbols — madder red in military uniforms might provide a cockerel target, just one example of how it effectively responded as one of the more important tangible signs of status. The red dress of rulers – nobles, clergy, judges and academics provided further evidence. The glory of red made people feel good – both the wearers and those it was supposed to impress, in addition to being a constituent of visual beauty and quality. Such powerful language reinforced the cohesion needed by many levels of society.

The general effects of the innovation of madder dyeing might have been of interest to Emperor Charles V, the British East India Company, Colbert, Napoleon or Bismarck. Possibly these far-reaching implications might have seemed a little distant to the innovators themselves. What the cultivators, dyers, pigment makers, painters and weavers all shared was an obsession to get it right and to spread the rewards of the gifted eye.

*Mordant preparation —
scraping cream of tartare
from the inside of a
barrel, c. 1497, woodcut
(Hortus Sanitatis,
Strasbourg; Brunello)*

Glossary

Currencies, weights & measures

CURRENCIES

Akce is an Ottoman silver coin, in 1510 = one gold piece, or ducat = 54 *akces*, in 1580, 60. (Inalcik, 1973, pp 46, 115; 1326-1914 rates, Inalcik, 1994, p973).

Dutch currencies were as complicated as the political powers involved. Priester has sorted out the conversions, with the aid of J. de Kantner's *Handboekje* of 1812: £1 Flemish = 20 schillings; 1 schilling = 12 grotes or pennies; 1 mijten = 1/24 grote; 6 gulden = £1 Flemish; 1 gulden, also written as fl = £1 Dutch. 1 gulden = 2.03 French francs. (Priester, 1998, p423) 1 stiver = 2 grotes (Flemish) (Priester, 625). In fine silver in 1586 1 gulden = 11.42 grams, in 1839 devaluing by 17% to 9.45 gms. (Priester, 423) In silver in 1600 1 schilling = 5.75gm. (Steensgaard, 417) 1 ducat or rijksdaalder = 51 stuivers in 1672 which increased to 53 in 1762 and eased to 52 in 1806.(Priester, 424)

In 1848 4 French francs = 1 silver rouble; 40 francs a kg (40 roubles per 16kg?) c. 1859

In 1820s 3.5 assignat roubles = 1 silver rouble

WEIGHTS

1 kantar = 56.449 kg (Inalcik, 1973, 222)

In Italy around 1858 1 kantar = 5.5 poods = 88kg, which is different (Schaefer, 1403)

1 pood = 16 kg

1 kapan a Caucasian weight = 4 takkhams = 100 pounds, funt (Karpov) = 23 1/8 / 30 chetverts (Dal')

1 kapan of seeds covers 1/3 hectare and weighs 2 poods, 10 pounds in Russian units, or that is about 32kg + 10 lbs = 75lbs, not 100lbs (Karpov)

1 funt = 1 pound = 32 lota (½ oz lead plumb) or 96 zolotnikov (Dal') (4.26gm Smirnitskii)

1 ton per acre = 140 poods per hectare

1 quintal = 1 cwt, but

1 Marseilles quintal = 38.8kg (Steensgaard, 1973, 165, 415), but

1 metric quintal = 100kg (SOED)

Caucasian madder was usually delivered in large hemp sacks called kharals and sold by weight. Depending on its place of origin a 'kharal' contained slightly differing weights:

Persia	7 Russian poods
Khiva	8
Baku	6
Petrovsk	7
Kouba	7.5
Derbent	7.5

10,000 'weight' of madder each x 200lb, or 2 million lbs in total. (Miller)

While a loaded horse could carry fifty to sixty batmans or 3 to 3½ cwt, a camel could manage half as much again and a mule 300 to 400lbs. Ittig quoted larger Persian 'mule-loads' called khaira of 100 batmans or 650lbs. Depending on its definition, a 'bale' weighed between 213 and 276 lbs. The strongest human porters in Port Petrovsk (Makhachkala) the northern Caspian port of Daghestan were the Persian stevedores who could carry seven 20 kg boxes of fruit at a time on a Turkish-style back-saddle.

Measures

1 arshin = 71cm in the Caucasus and, according to Ittig, a longer 41in in Persia
1 gemet = '300 sq rods of 12 ft' = 4,800 sq yds = approx 4,100 sq m (Miller)
The gemet measure of area also varied from 0.392 hectare in Blooi to 0.446 hectare in Gent. The
   Schouwen gemet was actually 0.4168 hectare. (Priester, 425)
1 sazhen = 2.13m; 1 desiatin= 3200 square sazhen; 1 desiatin = 2.7 acres (Smirnitskii A I, 1985,
   Russko-Angliiskii Slovar', Moscow)
1 sabu = 1/12 desiatin (Khashaev)
1 vershka = 4cm
'Two spits and two shovelings or 2 spades deep' (Miller)
24-26° Reamur = 30-32.5°C

Technical terms

Colouring or **coloration** refers to applying a colour-producing material onto a fabric by physical
   means, such as by painting, rubbing or pressing it into the fibre. The coating process yielded
   colours onto fabrics that were in general not very fast (i. e. stable) to washing.
Dyeing a textile refers to the fixing of a colouring substance into the textile by chemical means so
   that a chemical bond is produced between the dye and the fibre.
A **colorant** can be classified as a dye, pigment or lake, though the latter two may also be
   considered as dyes if the resulting colour is not fugitive.
The **true dyes** were generally of an organic origin with a chemical affinity for the fibre. One of
   the simplest colouring techniques was to press natural products into the body of the fabric
   with albumen or clotted blood. These items included leaves, flowers, fruits, sticks, wood,
   shells, feathers, hair, fur, berries, nuts etc. For example, Easter Eggs in Cumbria are still dyed
   by wrapping and tying flowers around the egg with a greasy rag strip. Another early colouring
   technique included physically applying inorganic matter to the textile. (Koren, 18)
The simpler **natural dye** is called a **direct dye** or **substantive dye** (Ryder, 1983, 755), where, as
   Elisabeth Barber graphically but contradictingly says 'what you see is pretty much what you
   get. If you chop and simmer the root of the madder plant which still grows wild on Crete, you
   get a dark red soup which will dye wool an orangy red.' (Barber, 1994, 113)
Several of the dyes used by the ancients belong to the class of more complex **vat-dyes** or
   adjective dyes (Ryder, ibid.). The crude dye stuff is usually insoluble and the colouring matter
   has to be reduced to a so-called leuco-solution in which the fibre can then be dyed. The fibre
   can then be exposed to the air or oxidised in the solution itself and the dye precipitated on to
   the fibre. Vat-dyes complicate the dyeing process as four stages are involved: 1. Washing and
   cleaning the wool; 2. Treating the wool with a mordant;. 3. Fermenting and dissolving the
   dye; and 4. The actual dyeing process during which the leuco-dye has to be oxidised to the
   coloured dye. The process was even more complicated by top-dyeing of for example indigo
   with madder to make purple. For these reasons the ancient dye-shop, which contained a large
   number of vats, did not always dye in many colours. (Forbes, 1956, 134)
Mordant means 'biting-in'. For most dyes, mordants treat the fibres first to make them more
   receptive to the dye. The mordant is a separate chemical which combines with the dye in such
   a way as to attach the colouring matter to the fibre with a light and wash-fast chemical bond.
   Acid mordants are used to bond basic dyes and basic mordants to bond acid dyes. Acid
   mordants have generally been derived from tannin, readily available from oak galls or bark, or
   occasionally from vegetable oils. Basic mordants come from salts of various metals,
   particularly aluminium, chromium, iron, copper, zinc or tin. (Rice J W, 1963, 'The
   conservation of historical textile colorants', *Textile Museum Journal*, 1.2, Washington, 55-61:
   59; Barber, 1991, 236)
'Basic dyes' may be accepted by the protein fibre after it has been dyed by an **'acid dye'**. This is
   known as **topping**.

Glossary

Developers are chemicals which are applied after the fibre is removed from the dye-bath and that react in such a way as to alter or enhance the colour and then fix the dye again. For example, wool dyed in madder with an alum mordant turns a richer deeper red when treated with ammonia-water developer. (Rice, 1963, 59; Barber,1991, 236)

A **pigment** is a dry colour and, alone or in a binder, may be coated onto the fibres; it may also be transferred into the fibres by immersing them in a water mixture containing this pigment. For example, in 19th-century rural England the reddleman smeared red ochre pigment onto the chest of a ram — reddled his brisket — which if he was a 'good worker' would rub off and so identify the ewes which the ram had covered (Hilary Rose, pers comm; Thomas Hardy, *Return of the Native*, ch. 9).

A **lake** is a water-insoluble coloured substance made by precipitating an organic material by means of a salt onto or into the fibres.

The **colour of madder lakes** varies greatly depending on the organic colorants and the inorganic substrates. Many madder lakes tend toward rose-red, but pink hues containing mostly purpurin or pseudopurpurin are known. Partial precipitation of an alum extract of garancine (see chapter 7) with soda or potash gives a deep-red madder lake, while complete precipitation yields a light red; the same is true for chalk precipitates. If a small amount of a tin compound is added at the end of precipitation, the colour of the resultant madder lake is more intense. (Gentele J G, 1909, *Gentele's Lehrbuch der Farbenfabrikation*, 3, Braunschweig, 27-37) When iron sulphate is added, black violet or madder violet results and chromium alum gives a red-brown colour. For the finest of red nuances, iron-free alum must be used: brown-tinged madder lakes usually result from iron salts present in the laking agent. (Cremer F G, 1895, Studien zur Geschichte . . ., Dusseldorf, 125-33) Lakes of pure alizarin on alumina are generally somewhat bluer than natural madder lakes. According to Mayer (Mayer C, 1911, 'Krapplacke . . .', *Chemiker-Zeitung*, 35, 1353-4), obtaining alizarin lakes with a brilliant hue requires precipitation with alum together with calcium and sodium phosphates.' (Schweppe, 112.)

Madder lake is listed as CI Pigment Red 83, no. 58000:1 and CI Natural Red 9, nos. 75330, 75420 in The Colour Index, (1971, vols 3-5, 3rd ed, 1971, Bradford).

Stannous madder lakes are scarlet. Carmine-containing madder lakes are carmine red, called 'madder carmine'. Madder lakes with a high content of pseudopurpurine and/ or purpurineare pink, called 'pink madder' or 'rose madder'. Alizarin lakes are red with a bluish tint.

The **alum lake** made with 'Alizarin Red W' (CI no. 58005) can also substitute for madder lake as can a number of 'azo' (later synthetic) dyestuffs in the form of calcium, barium, strontium or manganese lakes used alone or with other pigments. Examples are Permanent Red 6B (CI no 15610), Lake Red C (CI no 15585), Lithol Red RS (CI no 15630), Lithol Rubine brands (CI nos 15825, 15850, 15856), and Litholbordotoner TR. The alum lake of Helio Fast Rubine RL (CI no 58210) is a good substitute for pink madder lakes (Wagner, 1939).

Chemical terms

By 1997, Schweppe had identified 25 colorants found in madder called '**naturally occurring hydroxyanthraquinones**' and two other constituent colorants. As the authoritative G. W. Taylor, comments on Schweppe's hydroanthraquinones, 'the principle colorants are alizarin and purpurin'. (Taylor G W, 1990, 'On the Nature of dyeing with madder and related dyestuffs', DHA 9, York, 23)

Anthraquinones are merely descriptions of the basic organic chemical structure — triple linked hydrocarbon hexagons $C_{14} H_8 O_2$, obtainable from coal tar — of a group of molecules which provide a variety of colour substances in madder. Different species and varieties of madder plants can be identified by the presence and proportions of these prevalent anthraquinones. The chemistry is complex and requires at least a first degree in the subject, so those who are further interested are referred to Schweppe, H. & Winter, J., 1997, in *A Handbook of Artists' Pigments*, vol. 3, pp 113-121. The chemicals have developed in the plants to ensure their survival and not to provide dyes, so it may seem obvious that the colorants are neither accessible nor simple to identify. A list of the names of the principle colour components of madder and their origin are sufficient to consolidate their mention in the text:

Alizarin is the main colouring matter in *Rubia tinctorum*, but is also found in related plants. (Ruberythric acid is the form in which alizarin occurs in fresh madder roots).

Purpurin is after alizarin the most significant colouring material of madder.

Pseudopurpurin is needed to produce purpurin. It appears in *Relbunium*.

Rubiadin occurs as the glucoside of madder.

Munjistin can be synthesized from pseudopurpurin.

Morindone is a glycoside of *Morinda citrifolia* and other *M.* species and from *Coprosma* species.

Xanthopurpurin was isolated from impure purpurin from pure madder; found as Xantho purpurin-1-methyl ether and Xanthopurpurin-3-methyl ether.

Rubiadin-1-methyl ether is also a secondary component of *Coprosma* species.

Hystazarin-3-methyl ether.

Anthragallol

Anthragallol-2-methyl ether,

Anthragallol-1, 3-dimethyl ether and

Anthragallol-1, 2-dimethyl ether were found in *Coprosma* species.

Soranjidiol was also found in *Coprosma* species.

6-Methylxanthopurpurin

Lucidin can be derived from xanthopurpurin and occurs in *Rubia iberica*, as does **Ibericin**

Alizarin-1-methyl ether

2-Benzylxanthopurpurin

6-Methylquinizarin

Damnacanthol

Damnacanthal

Nordamnacanthal

Physcion

and the additional 'constituents' from Schweppe, 120:

Galiosin occurs in some *Galium* species and *Rubia peregrina* and *R. cordifolia*.

Rubiadin-3-beta-primeveroside derives from *Galium verum* and *G. mollugo*.

Cardon in 1990 used F Mayer's previously standard list published in 1943, which included two with different nomenclature '**christophin**' and '**quinizarin**' which must be duplicates. (Cardon, 1990, n386; Mayer F, 1943, 'The Chemistry of Natural Colouring Matters', American Chem Soc, New York)

Glucoside, one of a class of vegetable substances which being treated with dilute acids or alkalis, or subjected to the action of ferments, turn into glucose and some other substance. First used in 1866 (SOED, 861).

Popular names for chemicals

(Adrosko, 118, 119; from Turner F M, ed, 1930, *The Condensed Chemical Dictionary*, 2nd ed, New York)

Alum	Potassium aluminium sulphate	$KAl(SO_4)_{2.12} H_2O$
Barilla water	Barilla Salsola soda is a maritime plant growing largely in Spain, Sicily and the Canary Islands, b. is an impure alkali produced by burning dried plants of this and allied species or from kelp used in making soda and soap. (SOED, 1978, Oxford, 158)	
Bleaching powder	Calcium hypochlorite	$CaOCl_2$
Blue vitriol	Hydrated copper sulphate	$CuSO_{4.5} H_2O$

Glossary

Borax	Hydrated sodium tetraborate	$Na_2B4O_{7.10}H_2O$
Caustic potash	Potassium hydroxide	KOH
Caustic soda	Sodium hydroxide	NaOH
Chalk	Calcium carbonate	$CaCO_3$
Chrome mordant	Potassium dichromate	$K2Cr_2O_7$
Copperas	Hydrated ferrous sulphate	$FeSO_{4.7}H_2O$
Cream of tartare	Potassium acid tartrate	$KHC_4H_4O_6$
Fuller's earth	Hydrated magnesium and aluminium silicate	
Green vitriol	Copperas	
Lime water	Water solution of calcium hydroxide	$Ca(OH)_2.H_2O$
Lye	Caustic soda	
Milk of lime	Hydrated calcium hydroxide	$Ca(OH)_2$
Muriatic acid	Hydrochloric acid	HCl
Natron	Native sesquicarbonate of soda occurring in solid or solution forms, SOED)	
Nitre	Potassium nitrate	KNO_3
Peroxide	Hydrogen peroxide	H_2O_2
Potash	Potassium carbonate	K_2CO_3
Sal soda	Hydrated sodium carbonate	$Na_2CO_{3.10}H_2O$
Slaked lime	Milk of lime	
Soda ash	Sodium carbonate	Na_2CO_3
Tannic acid (tannin)	Gallotannic acid	$C_{14}H_{10}O_9$
Vitriol	A sulphate, usually of iron or copper	
Washing soda	Sal soda, see Barilla water	
Wine stone	Cream of tartare	

The **pH level** is the first and enduring measurement of acidity and was discovered in 1909. The scale is from 0 to 14. From 6 to 0 the acidity increases, 7 is neutral and from 8 to 14 the alkalinity increases. It is commonly used and the table shows the pH levels of most of the dyeing chemicals above. (Coustillac L, 1959, 'Note sur la Teinture Vegetale dans le Sud-Tunisien', *Cahiers des Arts et Techniques d'Afrique du Nord*, No 5, 136).

```
0    1    2    3    4    5    6    7    8    9    10    11    12    13    14
acidité forte          acidité faible      : neutre : alcalinité forte        alcalinité faible
```

```
 * acide chlorhydrique - esprit de sel (1,0)
    * acide sulfureux (1,4)
      * acide oxalique (1,6)
         * acide tartrique (2,2)
         * acide tannique (2,2)
         * acide citrique (2,2)
         * jus de citron (2,3)
          * oseille (2,4)
            * acide acétique (2,8)
            * acides gras (2,9 à 3,3)
                 * lie de vin - crème de tartre (3,2)
               * vinaigre (3,2)
                   * tannin ou matières tannantes à l'état naturel (3,5)
                 * alun et ses dérivés (3,5)
               * vases, boues acides (3,5)
                   * couperose ou vitriol (sulfates de zinc-cuivre-fer) (4,5)
                      * urine (6,7 à 8,5)
                       * chlorure de sodium (6,8)
                      * suint (lanoline) (7,0)
                          * eaux calcaires (7,5 à 9)
                          * eaux alcalines (7,5 à 8,5)
                          * argile - limons (7,5)
                         * craie (9)
                               * acétates de cuivre (verde!) (9,5)
                             * carbonate de soude (11,6)
                              * chaux vive éteinte et lait de chaux (12,4)
                               * soude caustique (13)
```

Table of acidities of the above chemicals (H. T. Braun, Revue par l'Institut Solvay de Bruxelles, Cahiers, No 5, 136)

Political Mathematician's Shaking the Broad bottom'd Hemispheres. James Gillray, 9 January, 1807.
An elaborate 'hieroglyphic' fantasy in the earlier emblematic tradition: the Radicals Cobbett, Burdett and
Horne Tooke attempt to dislodge the 'Ministry of all the Talents' from power. The ministers encased in Charley
(Fox's) Old Breeches gorging on the perquisites of office, oblivious of the nation's peril or their own instability.
(Draper Hill)

The Phlogiston theory was published in 1733. It described a hypothetical substance or principle supposed to exist in combination in all combustible bodies and to be disengaged in the process of combustion. In this way, it defined the matter of fire, conceived as fixed in inflammable substances. (SOED,1571)

Suphuric acid was traditionally prepared by burning sulphur with saltpetre. The earliest mention of this method was by Albertus Magnus (1193-1280), and subsequently by Basilio Valentino in 1450. In the fourteenth century Pseudo-Geber prepared it by distilling alum with iron sulphate. In 1613 Angelo Sala from Vincenza obtained it by burning sulphur in moist air. His method was modified by La Fevre and Lemery in 1666. The first industrial plant was built as late as 1740 outside London by Ward and Richmond, where sulphur and saltpetre were burned in an iron capsule and the steam was condensed in glass balls — this became a metaphor for political ridicule in the hands of the satirist James Gillray, coloured by watercolour madder lake. Larger scale production in lead chambers began in Birmingham in 1746.

Other red dyestuffs

Though clearly outside the scope of this book, other reds are often mentioned as 'rivals' of madder. (Adrosko, 1971, 25-30; Goodwin, 1982, 52-8, 62; Donkin) The following are the most well known, in alphabetical order:

Annatto (*Bixa orellana*). Seed husks of the tropical shrub produce pink reddish and orange hues on cotton and silk and yellow-orange colours on butter and cheese. Not wash-fast.

Archil or **Orchil** (*Rocella tinctoria*) is a purple lichen dye growing on the rocks on the Mediterranean coastline and from the 18th century on the Canary Islands, Cape Verde Islands, India and Ceylon. It was not light-fast and often used to top other colours, giving a peculiar softness.

Brazilwood (*Caesalpina echinata*, *C. sappan*), from India, Malaya and Ceylon and later from the time of its discovery by Europeans, Brazil and from the 1850s, Nicaragua, Columbia and Venezuela. The red dyestuff was extracted from wood-chips. It was cheaper but more fugitive than madder.

Cochineal (*Dactylopius coccus*) from the New World, first recorded in Antwerp in 1540. English merchants made it available in Baku in 1580 and it was known in China from 1700. (FitzGibbon and Hale, 1997, 348) The bluish red dyestuff is obtained from dried insect shells. The original habitat is the prickly *Opuntia* cactus. Depending on market conditions, this varied between equally to more expensive than madder. As well as a textile dye it is a widespread food colorant.

Cudbear (a compound of *Ochrolechia tartarea*, *Urceolaria calcarea* and *Cladonia pyxidata*) is closely related to orchil, but this purple is even more fugitive.

Gum-Lac (*Laccifer lacca*) from Tibet and China and also Burma, Siam and India, from the dried bodies of insects (*Lakshadia chinensis*, *L. communis*) similar to Cochineal and sold on the sticky twigs of their habitat — *Ficus* trees and others. The carmine and scarlet dyestuff was more expensive than madder and not used in Europe except in artists' pigments. It was only seriously exported to England from 1796 as a half-price substitute for cochineal. Though the colour was less brilliant, the dye was durable.

Henna, from the dried leaves of Egyptian privet (*Lawsonia inermis*) grown in Egypt, India, Persia and Palestine. Since antiquity it has been used as a beauty aid for hair and fingernails. It can also dye wool or silk.

Kermes, from southern Europe and the Middle East. The ancient scarlet dyestuff is obtained from dried shells of the female shield louse (*Coccus ilicis*) whose habitat is the kermes oak and the holm oak. This was the next most expensive dyestuff and the dearest red, a dye for wool, silk and leather. Also called **Venetian Scarlet** (see page 56).

Logwood (*Haematoxylon campecianum*) from the red core of the crooked tree, was banned in England as a fugitive substitute dye for a century after its discovery in the bays of Campeachy and Honduras. When a fixative was found, the fast growing tree was planted in Jamaica and supplied black, purple, violet and blue dyes, which were equivalent to other dye woods.

Murex bandaris, from the Mediterranean, is the famous Tyrian purple dye of antiquity, extracted from mollusc shells. This was the most expensive dye.

Red Ochre, a soil pigment, containing iron oxide, was the earliest colour and widespread throughout the world.

Safflower (*Carthamus tinctorius*), a thistle-like plant from Egypt and some parts of the Indian subcontinent. A pinkish-red for cottons and silks — original 'red tape' is obtained from the flower-head. Not light-fast.

Appendices

Note

All appendices are by Shtorkh unless credited to others.
Abbreviations: kr = 000s of silver roubles; kp = 000s of poods; madder prices in roubles per pood.

Appendix 1.1

Caucasian non-red dye plants from A. A. Grossgeim (*Rastitel'nye Resursy Kavkaza*, 1946), with comments by Harald Böhmer (1992): "No comment to a plant on this list means: I do not know about this plant."

'The dye components of plants other than madder are no less complicated. It is effectively this complexity which causes plant dyes to create the beautiful aesthetic effect which chemical dyes lack. Details of the chemical classification of dye plants of Karabagh are thoroughly recorded by V A Petrov, following the basic classification of Fritz Meyer.' Illustration numbers refer to Grossgeim.

'For example, from the isocyclic chemical group, in Karabagh we come across naftochinon-type pigments (*Juglans regia*, *Anchusa italica* and *Echium rubrum*), anthracene-type pigments, pigments of *Rubia tinctorum* as enumerated above, chrizofan acids from *Rumex pulchra*, elodin from the fruit of *Rhamnus* and others. Further, from the heterocyclic group, we come across pigments of the flavin and isoflavin groups (*Glycyrrhiza glabra*, *Origanum vulgare*, *Genista tinctoria*, *G. transcaucasia*, *Reseda lutea*, the fruit of *Rhamnus*, *Cerasus avium* and *Cephalaria gigantea*), then a piridine derivative (*Berberis vulgaris*). In addition, there are dye pigments of uncertain composition (*Euphorbia*, *Cornus mas.*, *C. australis*, *Colutea cilicica*, *Paliurus* and others).'

Plants giving yellow colours

The largest diffusion of plant pigments are the pigments giving a yellow dye colour; but further, not all plants giving a yellow dye have widespread and generally known usage, in particular, a rather small group of plants are employed for carpet production.

General Comment: Many many plants give a yellow dye, but most of those yellow colours are not light-fast (Böhmer).

1. *Acer platanoides — Aceracae*. Maple. *Klën (r)*, *tkhki (ar)*. Use the leaves for dyeing.
2. *Adonis vernalis — Ranunculaceae*. Lychnis. *Goritsvet (r)*, *khoruz gyulyu (az)*. Use the roots for dyeing.
3. *Aethusa cynapium — Umbelliferae*. *Kokorysh (r)*, *dzaglis kindzi (g)*. Use the leaves for dyeing wool.
4. *Alchimilla — Rosacea*. [?Cufflets]. *Manjetka (r)*, *shekhduran (az)*, *gailatat (ar)*, *marmuchi (g)*. The leaves and stems dye wool with an alum mordant.
5. *Anthemis tinctoria — Compositae*. Dyer's camomile. *Pupavka krasil'naia (r)*, *choban iastygy (az)*, *igabokh (ar)*, *iraga (g)*. The flowers are used for dyeing wool and silk; but the quality of the colour is poor. — Good, not poor (Böhmer)
6. *Anthriscus silvestris — Umbelliferae*. [?Posy]. *Buten' (r)*, *khidaterev (ar)*, *chkimi (g)*. The leaves and stems, with an alum mordant, dye wool with a distinctive yellow.
7. *Anthyllis Boissieri — Leguminosae*. [?Ulcerous]. *Iasvennik (r)*, *ner-knar (ar)*. The leaves are used for dyeing wool.
8. *Barbarea vulgaris — Cruciferae*. Winter-cress. *Surepka (r)*, *ktsmntsuk (ar)*. The flowers are used

for dyeing silk, and the roots for wool.

9. *Berberis vulgaris* — *Berberidaceae*. Barberry. *Barbaris (r), zirindj (az), ktsorukh (ar), kotsakhuri (g)*. The plant gives a yellow and golden-yellow tone. [Leather dye — Brunello] — Only the roots contain the yellow dye ingredient Berberin, which gives a good dye and has been used in Turkey. (Böhmer)

10. *Betula verrucosa* — *Betulaceae*. Birch. *Berëza (r), toz agadjy (az), kechi (ar), arki (g)*. For dyeing wool use the bark. A richer tone is obtained from the leaves.

11. *Bidens tripartita, B. cernua* — *Compositae*. Bur-marigold. *Chereda (r), barmag (az), katvilezu (ar), orkbila (g)*. The stems and leaves give a bright yellow colour for wool.

12. *Carpinus caucasica* — *Betulaceae*. Hornbeam. *Grab (r), veles (az), bokhi (ar), rtskhila (g)*. The inner layer of the bark is used for dyeing wool.

13. *Cephalaria gigantea et al.* — *Dipsacaceae*. *Tsefaliariia (r), kosot terepuk (ar), makhobeli (g)*. The plant is widely distributed in the higher and sub-alpine zones throughout the Caucasus. From its inflorescence *[sotsvetii (r)]* is obtained a very rich fiery-yellow colour for woollen yarn. It is widely used in carpet production.

14. *Circaea lutetiana* — *Onagraceae*. [?Double-rose-petal]. *Dvulepestnik (r), ovazadzet (ar)*. Use the roots for dyeing.

15. *Cotinus coggygria* — *Anacardiaceae*. Skumpiia (r), saragan (az), narindjapiat (ar), trimli (g). The wood is used for dyeing wool, silk and leather yellow with an orange tone. — Used in Turkey too (Böhmer).

16. *Datisca cannabina* — *Datiscaceae*. *Datiska (r), deli chetene (az), vairi kanep (ar), datvis kanapi (g)*. The leaves, roots and shoots give an individual beautiful bright yellow fast colour for wool and silk. It is known that formerly these plants were specially cultivated as dye plants, but then the culture was entirely abandoned. It was used in carpet production. — Used in Turkey too (Böhmer)

17. *Euphorbia Boissierana, E. Seguierana* — *Euphorbiaceae*. Spurge. *Molochai (r), syuddien (az), ishaknuk (ar), rdziana (g)*. For dyeing use the highest shoots and the inflorescence. This dye is occasionally used in carpet production.

18. *Evonymus europaea, E. verrucosa, E. velutina* — *Celastraceae*. Prickwood, spindletree. *Beresklet (r), iarmoshov (az), ileni (ar), chanchkata (g)*. The fruit with an alum mordant gives a straw-yellow colour.

19. *Foeniculum vulgare* — *Umbelliferae*. *Fenkhel' (r), raziana (az), khorom-samit (ar), tseretso (g)*. The leaves and stems give a dark yellow colour.

20. *Galium mollugo* — *Rubiaceae*. *Podmarennik = ?sub-madder (r), etketiren (az), makardakhot (ar), khovera (g)*. The leaves and stems with an alum mordant are used for dyeing. — The roots give a red dye, used in Europe (Böhmer).

21. *Genista tinctoria, G. transcaucasica* — *Leguminosae*. Genista, dyers' broom. *Drok (r), naz (az), dekhnatsakhik (ar)*. Especially important is *G. transcaucasica*; in Karabagh this appears to be the basic source for yellow dye for carpet production. It gives a darkish-yellow dye of great fastness. It is also used to dye silk. — Correct (Böhmer).

22. *Glycyrrhiza glabra* — *Leguminosae*. Liquorice. *Solodka (r), biian (az), matutik (ar), dzirtkbila (g)*. The extract from the over-ground part of the plant gives silk a yellow and straw-yellow dye. An extract from the roots [with lime, *izvesti (r)*] may be added to give a yellow ochre or [golden] crown colour (A. Abdullaev).

23. *Helichrysum arenarium* — *Compositae*. Immortelle. *Bessmertnik (r), guruchichek (az), antaram (ar), nego (g)*. For dyes use the flowers, leaves and stems. — Used in Turkey too. (Böhmer)

24. *Heracleum sp. div.* — *Umbelliferae*. Borshchevik (r), baldyrgan (az), bokh (ar), dutsi (g). Used with an alum mordant *[osnove (r)]* for dyeing wool and silk.

25. *Hieracium umbellatum et al.* — *Compositae*. Hawkweed. *Iastrebinka (r), gurageni (az), kharnuka (g)*. Used for dyeing wool and silk.

26. *Hypericum perforatum* — *Guttiferae*. St Johns Wort. *Zveroboi (r), dazy (az), arevkurik (ar), krazana (g)*. The stems and leaves used for dyeing woollen, silk and cotton fabrics. With a pre-added decoction of sorrel (oxalic acid) a pale yellow colour is obtained; with a pre-added decoction of mint, an orange-red.

27. *Impatiens noli tangere* — *Balsaminaceae*. [Touch-me-not]. *Nedotroga (r), dzernakhoris (ar), ukadrisa (g)*. Use the leaves and flowers for dyeing wool.

28. *Iris pseudacorus* — *Iridaceae*. Yellow iris, [?darling/swallow]. *Kasatik (r), susen (az), girik (ar), zambakhi (g)*. The dye is obtained from a preliminary infusion in vinegar of the roots and blossoms. The dye is very fast.

29. *Leucanthemum vulgare* — *Compositae*. *Nivianik (r), antem (ar), anagvirla (g)*. The dye is obtained from the flowers.

30. *Ligustrum vulgare* — *Oleaceae*. Privet. *Biryuchina (r), birgez (az), vairisring (ar), kvido (g)*. A decoction of wood and bark dyes silk, wool and canvas [for the war effort] with an ochre colour.

31. *Lycopodium selago* — *Lycopodiaceae*. Club-moss. *Plaun (r), kibrit otu (az), getnamushk (ar)*. The plant gives a fast yellow colour.

32. *Lysimachia nummularia* — *Primulaceae*. [?Verbena/pussy-willow]. *Verbeinik (r), voski ekhegn (ar)*. The leaves are used for dyeing.

33. *Lysimachia vulgaris*. Loosestrife. *Verbeinik (r)*. The stems and leaves give a yellow colour.

34. *Morus alba* — *Moraceae*. Mulberry. *Sholkovitsa (r), tut (az), tteni (ar), tuta (g)*. The wood and leaves give a yellow dye. — Correct (Böhmer).

35. *Ononis arvensis* — *Leguminosae*. [?Steel]. *Stalnik (r), eznagrel (ar)*. The stems and leaves with an alum mordant give a grey-yellow colour.

36. *Orchis triphylla* — *Orchidaceae*. *Iatryshnik (r), sakhleb (az), borkis (ar), gulgulis-kaba (g)*. With an alum mordant the plant gives a yellow colour with a distinct tint, which is used for dyeing yarns.

37. *Ostrya carpinifolia* — *Betulaceae*. [?Drunken hornbeam]. *Khmelegrab (r), ukhravi (g)*. For dyeing use the inner layers of the bark.

38. *Paris quadrifolia, P. incompleta* — *Liliaceae*. [?Ravens' eyes]. *Voronii glaz (r), lokhari (ar)*. For dyeing use the spring leaves.

39. *Physalis alkekengi* — *Solanaceae*. [?Senna cherry]. *Vishnia puzyrnaia (r), erkilasy (az), bochoch (ar), dudgubo (g)*. The fruit is used for dyeing silk with a yellow and orange tone.

40. *Plumbago europaea* — *Plumbaginaceae*. *Svinchatka (r), baga iarpagy (az)*. Use the leaves and shoots for dyeing.

41. *Populus nigra* — *Salicaceae*. Black poplar. *Osokor' (r), govak (az), kakhamakhi (ar), verkhvi (g)*. For dyeing use the bark.

42. *Potentilla anserina* — *Rosaceae*. Palmate. *Lapchatka (r), giitarna (az), akhpat (ar), martskva-balakhi (g)*. Use the stems and leaves for dyeing.

43. *Reseda lutea, R. luteola* — *Resedaceae*. Yellow mignonette, weld. *Rezeda (r), naz (ar)*. A widely known plant dye, the upper leaves and stems of which give a yellow of distinct tinge for dyeing silk. The dye is very fast in reaction to the action of light and atmosphere, but fades after washing. It is not found in carpet production. — This plant must have been used in carpet production. It contains the light-fast and wash-fast dye ingredient luteolin. (Böhmer)

44. *Rhamnus cathartica* — *Rhamnaceae*. Purging buckthorn. *Krushina (r), murdarcha (az), gakri (ar), kheshavi (g)*. Use the fresh bark for dyeing. — The unripe berries have been used in Europe and Turkey for dyeing. The bark has not been used in Turkey. (Böhmer)

45. *Rhamnus frangula* (ill. 63). Black alder tree. *Krushina (r), khechreli (ar)*. Use the inside of the roots for dyeing. — The bark can be used. It contains the dye ingredient Emodin. (Böhmer)

46. *Rhus coriaria* — *Anacardiaceae*. Sumac. *Sumakh (r), sumakh (az), drakhtatsar (ar), tutubo (g)*. Use the root stems for dyeing. — The leaves and stems can be used for dyeing but Böhmer doubts that the roots give a yellow dye. (Böhmer)

47. *Rumex acetosa* — *Polygonaceae*. Common sorrel. *Shchabel' (r), avelik (az), aveluk (ar), golo (g)*. With St John's Wort added before dyeing, it gives a pale-yellow colour. — Correct. (Böhmer)

48. *Rumex acetoselloides*. *Shchabel' (r)*. The dye is obtained from the roots. — Correct. (Böhmer)

49. *Scabiosa columbaria* — *Dipsacaceae*. [?Widow]. *Vdovushki (r), kosksuk (ar)*. Use the stems and leaves for dyeing.

50. *Serratula coronata* — *Compositae*. [?Sickle]. *Serpukha (r), melis-dzvala (g)*. The plant is used for dyeing wool. — *S. Tinctoria* is a well-known dye-plant from Europe. (Böhmer)

51. *Sisymbrium officinale* — *Cruciferae*. [?Idler]. *Guliavnik (r), khozakn (ar), gongola (g)*. Use the leaves for dyeing.

52. *Solidago virgaurea* — *Compositae*. [?Gold/whiskey-punch]. *Zolotarnik (r), voskepunch (g)*. Use the stems, leaves and flowers for dyeing.

Appendices

53. *Statice Meyeri* — *Plumbaginaceae. Kermek (r), avil (ar), mlashe chochkhi (g).* Use the roots for dyeing.
54. *Statice spicata. Kermek (r).* Use the roots for dyeing.
55. *Succisa pratensis* — *Dipsacaceae.* [?Grey?vodka]. *Sivets (r), tsvtsvuk (ar).* For dyeing use the seeds.
56. *Thalictrum flavum* — *Ranunculaceae.* Common yellow meadow rue. *Vasilistnik (r), kara kaitarma (az), gndzmndzuk (ar).* Use the leaves for dyeing.
57. *Trifolium canescens* — *Leguminosae.* Clover. *Klever (r), chemen iondjasy (az), ereknuik (ar), samkura (g).* With an alum mordant, the dye from the flowers is used for wool.
58. *Trifolium strepens. Klever (r).* The dye is extracted from the flowers.
59. *Ulmus foliacea, U. suberosa* — *Ulmaceae.* Elm. *Il'm (r), gara agach (az), tekhi (ar), tela (g).* For dyeing use the bark.
60. *Urtica dioica, U. urens* — *Urticaceae (ill. 32).* Stinging nettle. *Krapiva (r), gichitken (az),ekhindj (ar), chinchari (g).* A yellow colour comes from the roots.
61. *Viburnum lantana* — *Caprifoliaceae.* [?Proud]. *Gordovina (r), bashyn agadjy (az), gerimastin (ar), uzani (g).* The leaves with an alum mordant give a straw-yellow colour.
62. *Vicia variabilis et al.* — *Leguminosae.* Sweetpea. *Goroshek (r), lerge (az), vik (ar), tsertsvela (g).* Use a decoction of the stems for dyeing.
63. *Xanthium strumarium* — *Compositae.* Lesser burdock. *Durnishnik (r), syupyurge (az), tsetskhlekala (g).* The dye is obtained from the leaves and roots.

For not a pure yellow colour, but a mixture with other colours:

64. *Galium verum* — *Rubiaceae. Podmarennik (r).* The dye gives a green-yellow colour. — Doubtful. The roots contain red dye ingredients. (Böhmer)
65. *Lathyrus silvester* — *Leguminosae.* Plane tree. *China[r] lesnaia (r).* With the addition of Dagestani kermek (r), Statice Owerini, a distinctive yellow-brown dye is produced.

Plants giving a blue and violet colour

The colour blue plays an important role in carpet ornament. To obtain this colour it has for long been necessary to import it from India. Attempts to cultivate *Indigofera* have shown that is not suited to the Caucasus. Also in the Kirovabad (Ganje) region they tried to grow another plant, as a source for a beautiful blue colour — *Polygonum tinctorum*, but that attempt too was halted, as the plant was unsuitable. More recently in the Kirovabad region it was possible to gather *P. tinctorum* established in the wild. From local plants, the most interesting source of blue seems to be woad, *vaida* (r), *Isatis tinctoria*, growing in Northern Caucasus; other varieties for this purpose have not been researched, but among them it must doubtless be possible to find a plant which can give a blue dye. The colour violet does not play a large role in the design of carpets and is usually obtained from double-dying with indigo and madder.
General comment: Most of the plants in this list contain in the flowers blue or violet Anthocyans which are not suitable for dyeing textiles. See comment on red in chapter 2.

1. *Alkanna orientalis* — *Borraginaceae. Alkanna (r).* A violet colour is extracted from the roots. — The violet dye ingredient has been used to dye food, but is not suitable to dye wool. (Böhmer)
2. *Anthyllis Boissieri. Iazvennik (r).* A blue colour is obtained from the flowers.
3. *Atriplex hortensis* — *Chenopodiaceae.* Garden orach, [?Goose-foot]. *Lebeda (r), sirken (az), mokhrateluk (ar), tutubo (g).* A blue colour is obtained from the stems.
4. *Atropa caucasica (ill. 57).* Deadly nightshade. *Krasavka, belladonna (r).* The plant gives a blue colour.
5. *Chrozophora tinctoria* — *Euphorbiaceae. Khrozofora (r).* The juice from the fruit and the leaves are used to tint many different materials, such as Dutch cheese, wine and blue sugar paper[?]; the dye is also used for blueprints when washing white linen [perhaps an early form of resist copying?]. — Correct. (Böhmer)
6. *Consolida orientalis* — *Ranunculaceae. Sokirki (r), vochlakhot (ar), sosani (g).* The flowers are used for dyeing silk blue, without boiling, and violet, with boiling the dye.
7. *Eupatorium cannabinium* — *Compositae.* [?Hemp]. *Poskonnik (r), apuzanuk (ar), vardkanapa (g).* A blue colour is extracted from the stems and leaves.

8. *Fraxinus excelsior* — *Oleaceae*. Common ash. *Iasen' (r), ven (az), khatseni (ar), ipapi (g)*. The bark gives a blue colour.
9. *Gentiana pneumonanthe* — *Gentianaceae*, and other types. [?Bitter]. *Gorechavka (r), khadjotu (az), bog (ar)*. These plants are used for dyeing wool with a light-blue colour.
10. *Geranium silvaticum* — *Geraniaceae*. Geranium. *Geran' (r), etirshakh (az), khordeni (ar), nemsitsvera (g)*. The blue colour comes from the flowers.
11. *Inula helenium* — *Compositae*. Horseheel. *Deviasil (r), andyz (az), kkhmukh (ar), mziura (g)*. The blue colour is obtained from the dried roots. The dye is sufficiently fast.
12. *Iris violacea*. Iris, [?Darling]. *Kasatik (r)*. A light-blue dye for silk is obtained from the flowers.
13. *Isatis tinctoria* — *Cruciferae*. Woad. *Vaida (r), lrdjun (ar)*. The blue colour is derived from the leaves. — Correct. The dye ingredient is Indigo! (Böhmer)
14. *Knautia arvensis* — *Dipsacaceae*. [?Scab]. *Korostavnik (r), ishakand (ar)*. A blue colour is extracted from the leaves.
15. *Ligustrum vulgare*. *Biryuchina (r)*. The berries with [?]soda, *sodoi (r)*, give a light-blue colour.
16. *Lycopodium annotinum, L. clavatum*. [?Clubmoss.] *Plaun (r)*. A blue colour is obtained from the stems and leaves.
17. *Mercurialis perennis* — *Euphorbiaceae*. [?Glade]. *Prolesnik (r), kmshtruk (ar)*. The stems and leaves give a blue colour.
18. *Neslia paniculata* — *Cruciferae*. *Nesliia (r)*. It is possible to obtain a blue colour from the leaves.
19. *Orobus niger* — *Leguminosae*. *Sochevichnik (r), kholer-vairi (ar)*. A blue colour is obtained from the flowers.
20. *Polygonum aviculare* — *Polygonaceae*. [?Ergot]. *Sporysh (r), gyrbugum (az), mandik (ar), matitela (g)*. A blue dye comes from the roots.
21. *Rhamnus frangula* (ill. 63). Buckthorn. *Krushina (r)*. A violet colour is obtained from the fruit.
22. *Scabiosa columbaria*. *Vdovushki (r)*. A blue colour is obtained from the flowers.
23. *Stellaria media* — *Caryophyllaceae*. [?Wood-louse]. *Mokritsa (r), djin djilim (az), astkhik (ar), junjruki (g)*. With alum and blue sandalwood the plant is used for dyeing wool with a blue colour.
24. *Succias pratensis*. *Sivets (r)*. A blue colour is extracted from the roots.
25. *Vaccinium myrtillus* (ill. 14). Bilberry, Myrtle whortleberry. *Chernika (r)*. The berries with alum give a violet colour for wool and cotton wares.

Plants giving a black colour

Black is important for outlines in carpets, and is obtained by two means: either by repeated layers of blue dye on wool until it is saturated with the colour, and is nearly black, or the method of combining tanning substances with darkening iron salts, e.g. the use of iron vitriol as a mordant, instead of alum.

The following plants can give a colour close to black.

General comment: I guess that most of the plants in this list contain tannins which produce, with iron salts, black colours. But in many cases the iron mordant is not mentioned. It is doubtful that these plants give a black colour without an iron mordant.

1. *Acer platanoides*. Maple. *Klen (r)*. The dye from the leaves with iron vitriol gives an almost black colour.
2. *Actaea spicata*. *Voronets* (r). To dye wool black, use a decoction of ripe berries and roots with alum.
3. *Armeniaca vulgaris* — *Rosaceae*. Apricot. *Abrikos (r), erik (az), tsiran (ar), cherami, gargari (g)*. A black colour is obtained by carbonising the stones. — Strange! (Böhmer)
4. *Castanea sativa* — *Fagaceae* (ill. 1). Spanish edible chestnut. *Kashtan (r), shabalyt (az), shaganak (ar), tsabli (g)*. Use the leaves, young branches and chestnut husks to give a brown or black-brown colour.
5. *Cornus australis* — *Cornaceae*. *Svidina (r), gara murdarcha (az), khoneni arevelian (ar), shindantsla (g)*. With an iron mordant the plant dyes wool with a black-brown colour.
6. *Euphorbia aleppica, E. amygdaloides et al . . .* [?Cypress]. *Molochai (r)*. These plants give a black colour.
7. *Fraxinus excelsior*. Common ash. *Iasen' (r)*. The black colour comes from the bark.

Appendices

8. *Geranium ibericum.* Geranium. *Geran' (r).* The black dye is extracted from the roots and the leaves.
9. *Lathyrus silvester.* Plane tree. *China(r) (r).* With an iron mordant a black colour is obtained.
10. *Ligustrum vulgare.* Privet. *Biryuchina (r).* The berries, with acid, give a black colour.
11. *Lycopus europaeus — Labiatae.* European bugle-weed. *Zyuznik (r).* Juice from the stems and leaves gives a black or black-brown colour.
12. *Lysimachia vulgaris.* Common loosestrife. *Verbeinik (r).* All parts of the plant give a black colour.
13. *Myricaria alopecuroides — Tamaricaceae. Mirikariia (r), chaiiovshany (az), momaber-murt (ar).* The bark and other parts of the plant give a black colour.
14. *Nymphaea alba — Nymphaeaceae.* White water lily. *Kuvshinka belaya (r), su zambagy (az), getezri shushan (ar), dumpara (g).* Use the old roots for dyeing.
15. *Origanum vulgare — Labiatae.* Common marjoram. *Dushitsa (r), gara ot (az), zvirak (ar), tavshava (g).* The stems, leaves and flowers, with iron vitriol, give a black colour.
16. *Rhamnus cathartica.* Purging buckthorn. *Krushina (r).* A decoction of the bark with iron vitriol gives a black colour.
17. *Rhamnus frangula (ill. 63).* Black alder. *Krushina (r).* The bark with pomegranate rind gives a black colour.
18. *Rhus coriaria.* Sumac. *Sumakh (r).* The black dye is taken from the leaves. — Iron must be added. Böhmer has obtained black in this way. (Böhmer)
19. *Rumex acetosa.* Common sorrel. *Shchavel' (r).* Together with blue sandalwood, the plant gives a fast black dye.
20. *Sorbus graeca — Rosaceae.* Mountain-ash. *Riabina (r), gush armudu (az), tstikhndzor (ar), chnavi (g).* A brown-black colour is obtained from the leaves.
21. *Statice Meyeri, S. spicata. Kermek (r).* The black colour comes from the roots. A grey colour, rarely occurring in local dyes, is produced by a few plants.
22. *Alkanna orientalis. Alkanna (r).* Use the roots for dyeing.
23. *Pterocarya fraxinifolia — Juglandaceae. Lapina (r), ialan goz (az), lapani (g).* The leaves and bark are used for dyeing silk grey.
24. *Sanguisorba officinalis — Rosaceae.* Great burnet. *Krovokhlebka (r), aryunkam (ar), tavsiskhla (g).* A decoction of the flowers with tin gives a grey colour.

General comment: Grey is seldom used in carpets and other textiles. Many plants produce a grey colour. (Böhmer)

Plants giving a brown colour

The colour brown does not play a large role in carpet decoration, but it is encountered often enough. The basic source for brown colour for carpets is the walnut (*Juglans regia*) and wild pomegranate (*Punica granatum*). The following plants give a brown colour.

General comment: There are many plants which produce a brown or brownish colour. *Juglans regia* is the best. (Böhmer)

1. *Cotinus coggygria. Skumpiia (r).* The wood, with a chrome mordant, gives a brown dye for wool, silk and leather.
2. *Fraxinus excelsior. Iasen' (r).* The bark produces a brown colour.
3. *Galium mollugo. Podmarennik (r).* The stems and leaves, with an alum mordant, give a brown colour. — Doubtful. (Böhmer)
4. *Glycyrrhiza glabra (ill. 37). Solodka (r).* The extract from the above-ground part of the plant gives a brown colour for silk.
5. *Juglans regia — Juglandaceae.* Walnuts. *Gretskii orekh (r), roz (az), ynkuiz (ar), kakali (g).* The dye source is the peel of the walnut; the dye is fast, of deep brown colour, and is widely used in carpet production. The leaves and bark give a brown dye especially used for dyeing silk. — Correct, but walnut brown has not been often used in Caucasian carpets. (Böhmer)
6. *Lagonychium farctum — Leguminosae.* Mimosa. *Mimozka (r), pishik khaiasy (az), kharpup (ar).* A walnut-brown colour for silk is obtained from the blossoms with a soda and ammonium hydrate mordant.
7. *Ligustrum vulgare. Biryuchina (r).* The berries, with vitriol, give a brown colour.

8. *Nymphaea alba. Kuvshinka bela (r).* The old roots give a brown colour.
9. *Peganum harmala — Zygophyllaceae (ill. 39).* [?Tombstone]. *Mogil'nik (r), yuzerlik (az), spand (ar), mariam-sakmela (g).* The extract from the seeds has a bright crimson colour; experience of dyeing gives a yellow-brown and rose colour. In Central Asia the plant is used for dyeing skullcaps [worn by most men — however today these are usually black].
10. *Punica granatum (ill. 9).* Pomegranate. *Granat (r).* For dyeing wool brown for carpets, use the rind of the fruit of the wild pomegranate. To obtain a brighter brown colour, dye repeatedly. — Böhmer's own experiments show mainly the same results. (Böhmer)
11. *Rhamnus cathartica.* Purging buckthorn. *Krushina (r).* The dried bark gives a brown dye.
12. *Rhamnus frangula (ill. 63).* Black alder. *Krushina (r).* The inside bark dyes with a red-yellow colour, which turns brown with the action of an alkaline solution. — Böhmer's own experiments show mainly the same results. (Böhmer)
13. *Rhus coriaria.* Sumac. *Sumakh (r).* A brown colour is obtained from the bark of the roots.

Plants giving a green colour

The colour green plays a large role in decorating carpets. It is usual that green is obtained by double-dyeing, starting with a yellow dye and then with blue, usually indigo. In this way it is possible to obtain the whole range of green tones from very dark to the brightest. But it is noteworthy that some plants give a green colour by themselves; indeed, their application in the production of local dyeing was most naturalistic.

General comment: The above introduction is correct. Böhmer thinks that there was always double-dyeing. It is not possible to dye a lasting green with chlorophyll from green plants. With an iron mordant some yellow dye ingredients give an olive green which also does not last very long. Nos. 3, 4, 5, 6, 7, 10, 11, 16, 18, 21, 22 contain only chlorophyll! (Böhmer)

1. *Anchusa officinalis. Volovik (r).* The flowers produce a green colour.
2. *Artemisia Sosnowskyi — Compositae. Polyn' (r), iovshan (az), oshindr (ar), avshani (g).* A. K. Rollov noted that this plant was the only one in existence which was used directly to dye wool with a green colour.
3. *Asperula rivalis. Iasmennik (r).* The leaves give a green colour.
4. *Betula verrucosa.* Birch. *Berëza (r).* The leaves give a green colour.
5. *Capparis spinosa (ill. 33). Kapersy (r).* A dye for silk is obtained from the roots with a chrome mordant and with potassium alum, giving a dark-green colour.
6. *Genista tinctoria. Drok (r).* Although this plant is generally used for its yellow dye (v.s.), it is also possible to obtain green dye from the leaves and young shoots.
7. *Glycyrrhiza glabra (ill. 37). Solodka (r).* An extract from the aboveground parts of the plant give a green dye for silk.
8. *Isatis tinctoria.* Woad. *Vaida (r).* It is possible that a green dye can be extracted from the leaves. — Contains indigo! (Böhmer)
9. *Lagonychium farctum — Leguminosae.* Mimosa. *Mimozka (r).* The flowers, with a chrome alum mordant, give a yellow-green dye for silk.
10. *Ligustrum vulgare. Biryuchina (r).* The berries, with a potash mordant, give a green dye.
11. *Menyanthes trifoliata — Gentianaceae.* Bog bean. *Vakhta (r), erekterevuk (ar), tsklis-samkura (g).* The leaves give a green colour.
12. *Ononis arvensis — Leguminosae. Stal'nik (r).* [?Steel]. The plant, with an iron vitriol mordant, gives a green colour.
13. *Paeonia tenuifolia — Ranunculaceae. Pion (r).* The leaves and stems give a green colour.
14. *Paris incompleta — Liliaceae.* [?Ravens' eyes]. *Voronii glaz (r).* A green dye is obtainable from the unripe fruit.
15. *Rhamnus frangula (ill. 63).* Black alder tree. *Krushina (r).* A green dye is obtainable from a decoction of the ripe fruit.
16. *Senecio vulgaris — Compositae. Krestovnik (r), garnanaber (ar), tavkvitela (g).* A green dye is obtainable from the leaves, stems and flowers.
17. *Serratula coronata — Compositae.* [?Sickle]. *Serpukha (r).* The plant gives a green dye for wool.
18. *Stachys silvatica — Labiatae.* Wild hedge nettle. *Chistets (r), porug (az), abekhakhot (ar), deda-putkara (g).* The plant gives a green colour.

19. *Statice spicata. Kermek (r)*. The green colour comes from the roots.
20. *Succisa pratensis — Dipsacaceae*. [?Grey?vodka]. *Sivets (r)*. The green dye comes from the roots.
21. *Urtica dioica, U. urens — Urticaceae (ill. 32)*. Stinging nettle. *Krapiva (r)*. The green dye comes from the leaves.

Different mixtures with green tones are obtained from the following plants:

22. *Betula Litwinowi*. Birch. *Berëza (r)*. The leaves give a grey-green or green-blue colour.
23. *Capparis spinosa (ill. 33)*. *Kapersy (r)*. The plant gives a brown-green colour.
24. *Sambucus nigra — Caprifoliaceae (ill. 12)*. Black fruited elder tree. *Buzina (r), gendalash (az), tantrevni (ar), didgula (g)*. The berries give a beautiful olive-green colour for silk.

Plants giving a khaki colour

The standard colour for khaki has varied rather a lot in recent times. Today the colour khaki is obtained from mineral dyes, but plant dyes could give an almost identical colour.

General comment: This seems to be a colour for military uniforms! There is research of different Academies of Sciences on this topic. (Böhmer)

1. *Punica granatum (ill. 9)*. Pomegranate. *Granat (r)*. One method, devised by the Academy of Sciences of Azerbaijan SSR, prepares a mixture of dyes from available mineral substances with dyes from pomegranate rind. An almost standard khaki dye has been produced.
2. *Euphorbia Maleevi, E. Seguierana, E. iberica, E. macroclada, E. Boissierana — Euphorbiaceae*. Spurge. *Molochai (r)*. Another method, devised by the Botanical Institute of the Academy of Sciences of the Armenian SSR, obtains the khaki dye from the above types of spurge. The best results come from the most widely used species — *E. Seguierana*.

Appendix 2.1:
Madder in ancient and modern languages

From the Ancient Oriental languages, in Khotan Saka 'madder, red dye stuff' is *rrūnai*, the root is **raud-* 'red' and is widespread in Indo-iranian and is naturally found in most of the words for 'madder'. BS *manjisthā*, Nepali *majhito'*,[1] *menesch*,[2] related to the Indian *mnitsch*.[3] Tib *bchod*; Sid *rūnai*; compound, *rrūnā-ttīm* 'madder seed'. From **raudana-* N Pers *rōdan, rōnās*, Pashto *lwaren*; Waxii *urudan*, Sarikoli *araden*. From **raudana-* 'reddening stuff' to IE Pok *reudh-* 'be red'. Av *raodita-*, O Ind *rohit-, rohi-, rohita-, loha, rodhra-, lodhra-* 'tree from whose bark red powder comes', *rudhira-*; Greek and Latin above, Celt O Ir *rūad*, Welsh *rhudd*; old Slav *rudū* 'red', Tokhara B *ratre*, A *rtar*.[4]

From Biblical lands, Sumerian *ulal* (?), Akkadian *hūrratu*[5] Egyptian hieroglyphs *'jp3'* (I.68.13) rather than *'ns.tjw'* (III.324.3), a red dye made from a plant of the same name. It may be identical with the heraldic plant of Upper Egypt which in Edfu inscriptions is said to have been used to dye unguents red;[6] also *sophobi* in the Roman period. Etruscan *lappa minor*.[7] In Hebrew *pu'ah*.[8]

In modern Oriental languages: *ronās* in Persian, *royan* in Dari Afghan Persian[9] *ruyan* in Kokand;[10] *kokboya/chiocboya*[11] or *chionbozza* or *eckme* in Turkish, or *hazala* in (Ottoman) Cyprus; *rujan* among the Turkmen;[12] in 17th century Indian Morinda species (below) were known as *āl* or *al, saranguy* and *chiranjee*;[13] in the Caucasus *boiag otu* in Azeri, *toron* in Armenian, *enro* in Georgian, in 30 Daghestan languages only *sono* in Avar, *ruhunar* in Lezgin, *kokboya* in Kumykh, *khuna* in Dargin;[14] among the Arabs *foyoy* or *fouoy* or *fuwwah* and particularly *lizari* or *alizari* which was the general term used in the Levant,[15] from *'usara*, meaning 'juice'[16] and *rizari*, meaning 'little root', in Crete.[17]

Berber languages have Latin words: in Mozabite *trubia*, but in bastard M. *izoran el fuwa*, means 'roots of madder', in Chaouia *rubia* and in Kabyle *tarubia*.[18] The Chinese name for

Tibetan madder is *zang* (Tibetan), *qian cao* (Pinyin), or *tsang chi'en ts'ao* (Wade-Giles).

In Europe, in French madder is known as *la garance, garance commune, garance tinctorale*,[19] derived from Frankish *wratja*[20] and *warentia* (Charlemagne), *warencia* probably derived from Low Latin *barantia*;[21] *madhra* in place names in Old Norse and *madra* in Swedish and *modra, maure* in Norwegian;[22] *matara* in Old High German[23] *roete* in Old German, *rezza, retzel, retzwurz, krap, grapp, meerkrapp, meergrapp*,[24] *rothe, farber rothe, farberwurzel* in German; related to West Freisland *miede,* in Middle Lower German and Middle Dutch *meede*;[25] *krappe, meede, meekrappe, mee*[26] in Dutch; *garanza, roza, rozza*,[27] *rubea, rubia, robia* or *robbia* (the family of artists, the della Robbia were said to be descended from a dyer), *roza di Fiandra, sandis, gorma*,[28] *alosso* (c. 1400),[29] *granzuolli* or *ciocchi*[30] in Italian; *rubia, granza, roja*,[31] *ruvial* in Spanish; *marena* or *krap*[32] and *marennik* in the Ural region[33] in Russian; *chervets* in Ukrainian;[34] *morena barvirska* in Czech; *buzer* in Hungarian; *mædere* in Old English,[35] *mather* in 17th-century Scotland[36] and 'dyer's madder' in English.[37]

Artist's 'madder lake' is known as *krapplack* in German, *laque de garance* in French, *laca de rubia* in Spanish, *laca de ruiva* in Portuguese, *lacca di robbia* in Italian, *festobuzer* in Hungarian, *krapplak* in Russian, *qian cao* (Pinyin) or *chi'en ts'ao* (Wade-Giles) in Chinese and *seiyoo akane* ('western' *akane*) in Japanese. The words for 'lake' should be distinguished from those for the red dye 'lac'. Artist's 'alizarin' is known as *alizarin* in German, *alizarine* in French, *alizarina* in Spanish, *alizarina* in Portuguese, *alizarina* in Italian, *alizarin* Russian, *qian su* (Pinyin) or *chi'en su* (Wade-Giles) in Chinese and *arizarin* in Japanese.

Appendix 2.2
Botanical names of madder plants used in dyeing

There was of course no ready-made exhaustive botanical list of all the madder-like dye-bearing plants. This reflects the empirical nature of botanical studies. It seemed best to start with the longest list — Shtorkh's extracts from De Candolle's *Prodomous* of c. 1800 — which covered such groups of species as *Rubia, Morinda, Galium* and *Apserula*, but not *Relbunium* or *Coprosma*. Several other authors offered different specialised lists, which both identified 'new' plants and also provided variants of botanical and poluar names and locations for the same plant. Their additions and modifications have been credited so as to provide a comprehensive collection of existing knowledge.

A. *Exinvolucratae* — all madder species with flowers without capsules

a   *Rubiae cordifoliae* — with heart-shaped leaves.

a1   *Rubia cordifolia* L. — with mid-sized leaves; from eastern Siberia, Dauria and east of lake Baikal, Jaroslavl;[38] Schaefer adds China and Japan; Brunello adds the mountains of Central and Eastern Asia and India where Taylor writes it is called *munjeet* and is reduced to Rubia munjista Roxb., below in Hooker's *Flora of British India*; Targain adds Nepal.

a2   *Rubia mungista* Roxb. — from the mountains of Nepal and north Bengal; valued in India and exported to England and France (= *Rubia cordifolia*).

a3   *Rubia Cruciata* Baill . . . — from Crimea and east of Lake Baikal (= *Galium Cruciatum*).

a4   *Rubia javanna* DC Prod. — from the mountains of Java (= *Rubia cordifolia*).

b   *Rubiae tinctoriae* L. — all species contain dyestuffs.

b1   *Rubia angustifolia* L. — from Madeira, the Balearic islands, Gibraltar and Portugal.

b2   *Rubia longifolia* — long leaves; grows in Corsica and Madagascar (= *Rubia angustifolia*).

b3   *Rubia tinctorum* L. — by far the commonest, from Asia Minor and Greece,[39] the East, north Africa, south Europe and wild in Russia in Riazan, Saratov, Simbirsk, Orenburg, Crimea, the Caucasus and the Caspian Steppes, and probably in Turkmenia[40] Cardon[41] added Persia, and naturalised in Lyons and Alsac. Schaefer added that it was cultivated in Holland, Silesia, Hungary, Provence and Alsace.

b3a   *R. t. pubescens* — from Derbent and the Caucasus. Not found in Hooker and Jackson or Grossgeim (abbreviated below to 'Not found').

Appendices

b3b *R. t. iberica* L. — from Spain; finest quality dyestuff (= *Rubia tinctorum*).
b4 *Rubia peregrina* L. — south and central Europe, Russia from Nizhny-Novgorod down to the Caspian sea; Schaefer adds that it originated in Persia and was brought to Spain by the Arabs and from there it found its way to Minorca and to Piedmont; Karpov added Africa, France and southern England, the Burren and the Aran Islands of Ireland.[42] 'Peregrina' means 'the lady voyager'[43] called 'Levant madder'.[44]
b5 *Rubia lucida* L. — wild from south and central Europe; called 'lucent' madder (= *Rubia peregrina*).
b5a *Rubia lucida angustifolia* — from south France and Sicily. Not found, perhaps the same as *Rubia angustofolia*.
b6 *Rubia Bocconi* Petagn. — from the lime soils of Naples and Sicily; called 'Bocconi's' madder.(= *Rubia peregrina*).
b7 *Rubia splendens* Hoffmgg. & Link — from Lisbon; called 'splendid' madder (= *Rubia peregrina*).
b8 *Rubia Olivierii* — from Khios (= *Rubia lucida*; = *Rubia tenuifolia*).
b9 *Rubia Thunbergii* DC Prod. — from the Cape of Good Hope.

B. *Involucratae* — all madder species with flowers covered with capsules

a *Rubia chilensis* Willd. — from Chile; with smooth seeds and leaf divided by a rib (= *Relbunium hypocarpium*).
b with fluffy seeds and leaf divided by a rib:
b1 *Rubia hypocarpia* DC Prod. — from Jamaica and cultivated in India (= *Relbunium hypocarpium*).
b2 *Rubia Relbum* L. — from Chile, Brazil and Caracas; used in Chile (= *Relbunium hypocarpium*).

Additional *Rubia* plants from other authors:

Miller (1758) mentioned that Sir Hans Sloane had wild madder from Scanderoon (the port midway between Tarsus and Aleppo) and Aleppo; that wild madder grew in England at St Vincent's Rock near Bristol and on rocks near Biddeford in Devon, and that:
Rubia sylvestris aspera L. — rough wild madder, was tried in Holland and found to have little heart and inferior colour (*Rubia Sylvestris* Brot = *Rubia peregrina*; *Rubia sylvestris* Miller = *Rubia tinctorum*).
Karpov made a list of 14 varieties including the following not apparently noted above, some of which did not appear in Hooker and Jackson:
Rubia fruticosa Ait. — growing in the Canary Islands.
Rubia atropurporaea and *Rubia asperrima* — growing in Kamelezia (approximate area between Moscow and Kazan and Central Asia). Neither found, perhaps they should be *Rubia purporaea* Decne (= *Rubia cordifolia*) and *Rubia aspera* Pohl (= *Relbunii sp.*) respectively.
Rubia vallichiana — growing in Siberia, Dauria (eastern Siberia) and Jaroslavl (= *Rubia cordifolia*, non-botanical source Karpov). Not found, perhaps it should be *Rubia vaillantia* DC.[45]
Rubia alata — growing in eastern India. Not found.
Rubia clematifolia Reinw. — growing on the island of Java (= *Rubia cordifolia*).
Brunello added:
Rubia sikkimensis Kurz — growing in India, very similar to *R. cordifolia* L.[46]
Schweppe & Winter from Hayashi[47] added:
Rubia akane Nakai — growing in Japan
Buchanan noted that:
It is impossible to identify the species cultivated in a particular area, where local names were used. In 1842 on the island of Schouwen in Zeeland there were three species grown: 'darmstats', 'glazemakers' and 'arabian', of which the last was preferred. Nearby, in Aksel and Gulst 'arabian', 'swiss', 'gaspar' and 'old-French' were grown, of which 'old-French' was the worst because it gave a blackish-red when milled into krap.[48]

Shtorkh mentioned several species of *Morinda* from Southeast Asia:

Taylor contributed:
Morinda citrifolia L. — known as *soranjee*, and *bengado* by Thunberg[49] known as 'Indian mulberry'
Morinda tinctoria Roxb., also known as *soranjee*, both from India, often considered as the wild form of *M. citrifolia* L.[50]
Schweppe & Martin added:
Morinda umbellata L. — known as *mang kouda*, *oungkoudou* or *jong-koutong* in Malasiya and Java

Barrowcliff & Tutin[51] and Paris & Abiusso[52] added:
> *Morinda longiflora* G. Don — growing in tropical locales in West Africa including the Ivory Coast

Other 'madder' plants:

Oldenlandia umbellata L.[53] was known as Indian madder or *chay*,[54] growing on the sandy plains of India, Sri Lanka and Myanmar/Burma[55]
Sandberg[56] added:
> *Terminalia Chebula* Retz., known as *birda* in the Indian subcontinent (*Terminalia Chebula* Willd. = *Terminalia Bellerica*)

Galium and *Asperula* are related to madder and produce a limited quantity of dyestuff. But cultivation was not profitable because the roots were too small.

Galium is known as *le gaillet* or *caille-lait* in French because of its use in cheese preparation; *lobkraut* or *meyerkraut* in German and 'cheese-rennet', 'bedstraws' or 'gallium' in English. There are 45 varieties of *Galium* of which the following produce red, but less plentifully or conveniently than true madders:

1. *Galium boreale* L. — 'Northern bedstraw' native to North America,[57] from north Russia; called 'White bedstraw' by Sandberg who says that it was known in Viking times and called *mattara* in East Bothnia in Finland; pale-red dyestuff.
2. *Galium coriaceum* Bunge — for tanning leather from Altaic Siberia.[58]
3. *Galium glaucum* L. — wild along rivers and lake shores in Russia; red from roots; called 'grey' type. (= *Asperula galioides*)
4. *Galium Mollugo* L. — called 'Wild madder',[59] 'Great Ladies' Bedstraw', from the Steppes; bright red; called 'Astrakhan' or 'white-flower' type.
5. *Galium palustre* L. — from marshy locations; pale-brown; called 'marsh' type.
6. *Galium spurium* L. — from east Russia; used by Tatars to dye cloth red.
7. *Galium verum* L. — 'Yellow Lady's bedstraw'[60] or 'Our Lady's bedstraw', from the pretty legend that it served as the Infant Jesus' cradle, from across Europe and Siberia; good red; called the 'true' type (= *Rubia vera* Baill).
8. *Galium tinctorum* L. — 'Dyer's bedstraw',[61] North American Amero-Indian dye for porcupine quills, known as *tissaouhianne* or *tyssa-voyana*, cultivated and used by the Micmac Indians[62] (= *Galium trifidum*; *Galium tinctorum* Scop. = *Asperula tinctoria*).
9. *Galium sylvaticum* — recommended by Arduino 1766, from Venetian region (added by Cardon)[63]
10. *Galium Aparine* L. — from the Latin, *aperio* 'I take' — called 'Cleavers' or 'Goose-Grass', (= *Rubia Aparine*; *Galium Aparine* Wall = *Galium Mollugo*)
11. *Galium rubiodes* L.
12. *Galium Cruciata* L. Scop. (= *Cruciata laevipes* Opiz)
13. *Galium saxatile* L.

Asperula is known as *asperure* or *hépatique* in French; *labkraut* or *guldenklee* in German; and 'hepatica' or 'liver-wort' in English. Fifteen varieties can be found in Russia of which one produces red:
Asperula tinctoria L. — bright red dye for wool; *asperule de bois* and *asperule des teinturiers* in French; *farbermeister* in German; called 'Dyer's Woodruff' and the 'dyeing' type in English; also used in Oland and Gotland.[64]
Asperula odorata L. Scop. (recommended by Arduino 1766) (= *Galium odoratum* L.), called 'Sweet Woodruff' in English; *asperule odorante* in French; *waldmeister* in German.

Leuchs thought that *Galium boreale* with malt gave the best colour. Cardon preferred the unknown outsider *Galium saxatile*.[65]

Fester added from the Peruvian Paracas culture, c. 700 BC, (1000 BC-200 BC) *Relbunium hypocarpium* Hemsl. — relbun roots known as *chapichapi* (= *Rubia relbun* L.); and with Saltzmann and others noted the following which were used later. There are some 25 local varieties several of which contain red dyestuff:[66]

Relbunium ciliatum
Relbunium bigeminium
Relbunium tetragonum
Relbunium hirsutum
Relbunium richardianum

The *Rubiaceae* family of the genus *Coprosma* are found in Australia and New Zealand (Greek *kopra* = dung; *osme* = odour).[67]
Coprosma lucida Forst. — called 'orange leaf'.
Coprosma grandifolia Hook. (possibly = *grandiflora*)
Coprosma areolata Cheesm. — called *karamu* by the Maori.[68]

Dioscorides[69] wrongly listed
Calamus Draco Willd. — dragon's blood, actually resin of *Pterocarpus Draco* L. or rattan palm, *cinnabaris*; realgar, a soft red compound of arsenic, known to Pliny as *sandaraca*.[70]

Appendix 2.3
Burnett and Thompson's 'Table of dyestuff contents of Galium to aid plant identification in dye analysis'[71]

ANTHRAQUINONES	A	B	C	D	E
Hydroxy-2 anthraquinone	−	+	+	+	+
Méthoxy-2 anthraquinone	+	+	+	+	−
Hydroxy-1 methyl-2 anthraquinone	+	+	−	−	+
Méthoxy-1 methyl-2 anthraquinone	+	+	−	−	+
Alizarine	+	+	−	+	+
Méthyl-1 éther d'alizarine	+	−	−	+	+
Méthyl-2 éther d'alizarine	+	+	−	+	+
Purpuroxanthine	+	+	+	+	−
Diméthyl éther de purpuroxanthine	+	+	−	+	+
Rubiadine	+	+	−	−	+
Lucidine	+	+	+	+	+
Purpurine	+	+	+	+	+
Pseudopurpurine	+	+	+	+	+

A = *Galium aparine* L.		**D** = *Galium mollugo* L.
B = *Galium saxatile* L.		**E** = *Galium odoratum* (L.) Scop.
C = *Galium verum* L.		= (*Asperula odorata* L.)

Appendix 2.4
Caucasian plants giving red dyes

Grossgeim's list of plants giving a red colour with Harald Böhmer's written comments (1992). To repeat, C. Böhmer is the founder of the Turkish DOBAG Natural Dye Rug project which has started a renaissance in natural dyed rugs (see chapter 16).

The colour red, with its typical shade of claret, is very important in carpet production, as it is the main colour found in carpets. The fundamental plant, which gives a red dye for carpets, is

Rubia tinctorum. This is known as madder, *krapp* or *marena* (Russian), *boiag otu* (Azeri), *toron* (Armenian), *enro* (Georgian). This plant undoubtedly grows wild in the Caucasus, but now much of it is found locally as a result of the plantations being left to run wild. While in earlier times cultivated madder was widespread, nowadays it has entirely disappeared. There once were vast plantations of madder in south Karabagh and the Kubinski region of Azerbaijan.

Other sources of red dye can be provided by the following plants. Böhmer writes: "No comment to a plant in this list means: I do not know about this plant."

Böhmer's general comment: Plants which contain light-fast red dye ingredients are well known (*Rubia, Asperula, Galium* and a few others.) In the list are plants which contain red dyes which belong mainly to the so-called Anthocanes. These are not suitable for dyeing wool, silk or cotton. They change or bleach out or wash out in a short time. The red dye in *Hypericum* is Hypericin. It can only be extracted with oil and does not make a red colour on wool, silk or cotton.

1. *Actaea spicata* — *Ranunculaceae*. [?Raven]. *Voronets (r), agravakn (ar)*. The young leaves and branches with an alum mordant dye wool with a red colour.
2. *Aeluropus repens* — *Gramineae*. [?By the stream]. *Pribrejnitsa (r), tulku guirugu (az)*. A. K. Rollov shows that in naturally occurring hollows in the Ararat region, the roots of this plant attract a special insect, having some characteristics similar to Meadow Cochineal. From this plant a red colour is prepared, which can dye different materials, including paints [?inks] for miniatures in old church books. — On the root of this plant lives the Ararat kermes (*Porphyrophora hameli*) as a parasite. Dyeing red with this root means dyeing with Ararat Kermes, a dye insect! (Böhmer pers comm)
3. *Anchusa officinalis* and *A. italica*. [?Ox-blood]. *Volovnik (r), syumyurgen (az), gavajinak (ar)*. In the roots are found a special alkaline dyeing substance, giving a beautiful red colour. Certainly, in earlier times these dyes, particularly the second, were used in carpet production, but the dye was later superceded by madder.
4. *Arnebia cornuta* — *Borraginaceae*. *Arnebiia (r)*. The roots give a red colour because of the presence of alkaline.
5. *Asperula arvensis, A. odorata, A. aparine. Iasmennik (r), chetiriarpag (az), getni astkhuk (ar), chitistvala (g)*. The roots of all three types give a red colour. — Correct (Böhmer)
6. *Atropa caucasica* — *Solanaceae Belladonna. Krasavka belladonna (r), khanym otu (az), maatsu morm (ar), shmaga (g)*. The plant gives a low quality red colour.
7. *Betula Litwinowi*. Birch. *Berëza (r)*. The bark dyes wool with a red-yellow colour.
8. *Bryonia dioica* — *Cucurbitaceae. Perestupen' (r), kustusham (az), losh (ar), leshura (g)*. Use the berries for dyeing.
9. *Chenopodium foliosum* — *Chenopodiaceae. Mar' (r), tere (az), teluk (ar), natsarkatama (g)*. Use the leaves and stems for dyeing wool.
10. *Comarum palustre* — *Rosaceae*. Marsh cinque-foil. [Sabre]. *Sabel'nik (r), lutsadekh (ar)*. Use the leaves and stems for dyeing wool.
11. *Crataegus kyrtostyla* — *Rosaceae*. Hawthorn, [?knout]. *Boiaryshnik (r), emishan (az), tsrptkin (ar), kuneli (g)*. A decoction of the bark, leaves and shoots serves for dyeing wool.
12. *Echium rubrum* — *Borraginaceae*. Bugloss, [?bruise, rouge]. *Siniak, rumianka (r), ijakhot (ar), dzirtsitela (g)*. Use the bark; it give a beautiful carmine-red (pink-red) colour for wool. For double strength, begin with the infloration of *Cephelaria gigantea*, and then add the roots of E. rubrum to obtain a very bright fiery-red colour.
13. *Echium vulgari. Siniak (r)*. Use the flowers to obtain a red colour.
14. *Empetrum nigrum* — *Empetraceae*. Black-berried crow berry. *Ernik (r), aknatsar (ar), ketsera (g)*. The fruit with an alum mordant gives a cherry-red colour.
15. *Gallium boreale, G. molugo, G. verum*. Northern bedstraw, [?Sub-madder]. *Podmarennik (r)*. The roots with an alum mordant give a red colour for wool. — Correct (Böhmer)
16. *Geum rivale* — *Rosaceae. Gravilat (r), chyngyl otu (az), shaokram (ar), nigvzis-dzira (g)*. The roots give a red-brown colour.
17. *Hypericum perforatum*. St Johns Wort. *Zveroboi (r)*. The stems, leaves and inflorescence give a red colour for wool, silk and cotton cloths. — See above (Böhmer)
18. *Ligustrum vulgare*. Privet. *Biryuchina (r)*. Berries with Glauber's salts (Sodium sulphate) give a purple colour, with urine — red.

19. *Onosma echiodes — Borraginaceae. Onosma (r), ishakotot (ar), (g).* The roots give a red colour for cloth. — May be right (Böhmer)
20. *Paeonia kavachensis — Ranunculaceae. Pion (r), kadj vart (ar), iordasalami (g).* The flowers give a red colour for dyeing wool and cotton, and a pale-red colour for linen and silk.
21. *Rhamnus cathartica. Krushina (r).* Use the dried bark wetted with alum for dyeing. — Wrong. (Böhmer)
22. *Rhus coriaria. Sumakh (r).* Red colour is obtained from the fruit. — Wrong (Böhmer)
23. *Rhumex tuberosis, R. pulcher, R. alpinus, R. obtusifolius. Shchavel' (r).* The roots are used without mordant to obtain a red dye with brown or dark-brown tinges.
24. *Scherardia arvensis — Rubiaceae. Jerardiia (r).* Use the roots for dyeing.
25. *Vaccinium myrtillus — Ericaceae.* Bilberry, whortleberry. *Chernika (r), gara gile (az), mrtenakan gapalasin (ar), motsvi (g).* Use the berries with [?] *iar'yu (r),* lime and ammonium chloride.

The berries of *Berberis vulgaris et al.* give a rose colour. When the berries are mixed with *Mentha aquatica,* called mint, *miaty (r), iarpyz (az), katvaket (ar), pitna (g),* and St John's Wort they give an orange-red colour.

Note the abundance of plants which give red from the *Rubiaecae* family, and those of a similar nature to the madder family, such as the *Borraginaceae* family, resulting from the wide distribution of alkalines in their roots.

Appendix 4.1
Russian imports of cotton and cotton thread in thousands of poods

Year	Cotton	White cotton thread	Dyed cotton thread	Total
1822 to 1826	70	241	20	330
1827 to 1831	103	418	25	546
1832 to 1836	180	514	16	709
1837 to 1841	330	532	4	866
1842 to 1846	610	548	3	1,161
1847	862	411	3	1,276
1848	1,231	386	3	1,621
1849	1,355	279	4	1,639
1850	1,201	169	3	1,373
1854	1,454	66	4	1,524
1857	519	78	3	599
1858	2,448	261	13	2,722
1859	2,794	127	17	2,938
1860	2,611	116	15	2,741
1861	2,491	103	16	2,610
Subtotal:	12,697	1,996	81	19,044

Appendix 4.2
Derbent madder prices

1815	20r
1817	15r
1822	12r
1832	7r
1833-45	6r

Post 1845 production and sales of madder roots in the Derbent area, from 'police' figures:

1845	80,520 poods	@ 5r per pood	402,600 silver roubles
1846	64,746p	@ 4r 50k	221,438r
1847	41,397p	@ 5r	206,985r
1848	44,791p	@ 4r 75k	212,757r
1849	66,254p	@ 4r	265,016r
1850	72,632p	@ 4r 50k	326,844r
1851	79,305p	@ 4r	317,220r
1852	141,138p	@ 4r 25k	599,836r
1853	131,307p	@ 3r 80k	498,966r
1854	130,396p	@ 4r 50k	586,782r
1855	123,881p	@ 3r 50k	433,583r
1856	154,183p	@ 5r 50k	848,006r
1857	157,042p	@ 6r rising to 12r	1,411,818r

Appendix 4.3
Derbent madder exported from the Pricaspiskii region in 1862

from Baku	930 poods
from the lower wharf	8,380 poods
from Derbent	197,430 poods
from Petrovsk (Makhachkala)	6,460 poods
Total:	213,200 poods
	@7 roubles a pood is 1.5 million silver roubles

Appendix 5.1
Rotational crops

Four different crop cycles for Schouwen-Duiveland c. 1817-1819, in guldens/ hectare:[72]

Year	Crop cycle			
	I	II	III	IV
1	rest	rest	rye	rest
2	rapeseed	winterbarley	paardebonen	wheat
3	wheat	madder	rest	summerbarley
4	peas	madder	wheat	madder
5	wheat	flax	oats	madder
6	oats	rye	madder	paardebonen
7	paardebonen	potatoes	madder	rye
Expenses	942 gl/ha	1149	1380	1280
Income	945	1572	1424	1410
Surplus	3	423	44	130

For III 20 loads of manure were used, compared to double for I, II and IV, which was worthwhile when madder was a rotational crop. Expenses are as complete as possible. *Paardebonen* are large beans, perhaps field beans, as in the song 'Oats and beans and barley grow . . .'

Appendices

Appendix 6.1
Shtorkh's expenditure figures for four-year seed crop, Derbent 1833

For a 2,000 sq *sazhen* (9,080 sq m; 1s = 2.13m) plantation with 1 *kapan* (48kg) seeds
Expenses:

1.	Seeds	1 *kapan* best seeds	40.00r
2.	First year	60 labourers @ 60k/day no food	
		@ 40k/day with food	36.00r
3.	Second year	10 labourers	6.00r
4.	Third year	12 labourers	7.20r
5.	Summer watering	@ 3r/watering	9.00r

Total: — 98r
Total per hectare: — 102r

Appendix 6.2
Karpov's Caucasian figures, 1850s for four-year yield from seed

Karpov's accounts are for production from one *kapan* of seeds. (A *kapan* of seeds covers 1/3 hectare and weighs 2 poods, 10 pounds in Russian units, or that is about 32kg + 10 lbs = 75lbs, not 100lbs: there must be differing units here.) While labour is the largest cost, the Derbent price for seeds would vary from 5-20 roubles per *kapan* depending on the quantity of the local harvest.

Seed expenditure:

1.	purchase of 1 *kapan* of seeds		15 roubles
2.	rent of land		8r
3.	digging up the soil		
	1 day x 30 labourers or 5 days x 6 labourers		
	@ 35 kopeks per labourer per day		10r 50 kopeks
4.	sowing done by farmer/owner		nil
5.	harrowing the seeds into the soil		
	1 day x 5 labourers, rate as above		1r 75k
6.	first year adding layer of soil		
	1 day x 15 labourers, rate as above		5r 25k
7.	second year adding thicker layer of soil		
	1 day x 20 labourers, rate as above		7r
8.	third year adding thicker layer of soil		
	1 day x 25 labourers, rate as above		8r 75k
Total expenditure:			56r 25k

Seed income:

	second year	3 *kapans*	45r
	third year	5 *kapans*	75r
	fourth year	5 *kapans*	75r
Total income:		13 *kapans* sold for 15 r/*kapan*	195r

Root expenditure:

1.	watering for three years, price of water 50 kopeks per watering 6 x 50 kopeks	3r
2.	2 days x 1 labourer, at above rate, per watering over three years, 12 labourer days	4r 20k
Subtotal watering:		7r 20k
3.	weeding	
	first year 15 labourers x 1 day, rate as above	5r 25k
	second year 12 labourers x 1 day, rate as above	4r 20k
	third year 10 labourers x 1 day, rate as above	3r 50k
Subtotal weeding:		12r 95k
4.	digging up the roots	
	digging 35 labourers x 1 day, rate as above	
	gathering 70 boys x 1 day, @25k per day	
	subtotal digging	29r 75k
5.	steaming 4 labourers x 2 days, @40k per day 3r 20k	
	fuel for initial heating 1 cart-load of timber	1r
	fuel per kapan of roots 3 cart-loads of timber	3r
Subtotal steaming:		7r 20k
6.	drying and packing 2 labourers x 4 days @ 40k per day 3r 20k	
7.	contingencies	20r
Total expenditure for roots:		80r 30k
Total expenditure:		136r 55k

Root income:

An average fifth-year crop from 1 *kapan* of seeds is 60 poods of roots sold for 6r/ pood	360r
Total income roots and seeds:	555r
Total surplus:	418r 45k (equivalent to 307% profit)

Appendix 6.3
'Ministry' Caucasian 1850s five-year yield from seed
& two-year yield from shoots

The following accounts list the average farmer's expenses per hectare on the five-year method:

First year of a madder plantation

Clearing the field of trees, bushes etc.	23r
Ploughing	14r
Buying seeds (3 kapans for one hectare — Karpov)	26r
Sowing	0.9r
Harrowing	4.25r
Watering	6r
Weeding	12r
Ridging up	7r
Buying tools etc.	8r
Total expenditure for first year	101.15r

Appendices

Second year

Watering	6r
Weeding	6r
Ridging up	7r
Buying tools etc.	8r
Total expenditure for second year	27r

Third year

Watering	6r
Weeding	6r
Collecting seeds	12r
Ridging up	7r
Buying tools etc.	8r
Total expenditure for third year	39r

Fourth year

Watering	6r
Weeding	6r
Collecting seeds	12r
Buying tools etc.	8r
Total expenditure for fourth year	32r

Fifth year

Extraction of madder roots	170r
Steaming, drying and packing roots	9r
Buying hemp sacks	22r
Total expenditure for fifth year	201r
Total expenditure for five years	400r
Income year 3: 8 kapan of seeds	32r
year 4: 8 kapan of seeds	32r
year 5: 100 poods of roots (@ 6r/pood)	600r
Total income	664r
Net Profit	264r
Net profit per annum (from date of sowing in year 1 to date of extraction in year 5)	60r
equivalent to 75% average annual profit	

An average farmer's expenses per hectare using the kaliam method:

First year

Watering in August	3r
Ridging up	7r
Buying tools etc.	8r
Total expenditure for first year	18r

Second year

Watering	6r
Weeding	6r

Ridging up		7r
Collecting seeds		12r
Buying tools etc.		8r
Subtotal 39 roubles		
Extraction of madder roots		170r
'Rent'		16r
Subtotal		186r
Total expenses		243r

Income year 2: 8 *kapan* of seeds — (Cheap seeds, Karpov)		32r
year 2: 80 poods of madder roots		480r
Total income		512r
Net profit		269r
Net profit per annum		134r

equivalent to 111% average annual profit

Appendix 6.4
Dutch expenditure and income for madder cultivation in 1690, 1817 and 1843[73]

	Zeeland 1690	Schouwen 1817	Schouwen 1843
Expenses in gl/ hectare			
First year			
Buying shoots	60	72	-
Moving shoots	-	-	3
Gathering shoots and planting	48	43	30
Banking-up earth	-	-	3
First-year weeding	38	43	25
Covering stalks with earth	29	7	6
Smoothing	-	5	4
Second year			
Harrowing in the spring	-	2	3
Second-year weeding	19	43	20
Extraction	120	144	150
Moving roots to the stove	24	18	13
Rental and purchase of casks*	101	132	137
Transport and sales commission	14	10	-
Total+	453	519	394
Ground madder kg/ hectare	1,200-1,400	1,400	1,500
Price guldens/ 50 kg	f12	f30	f25
Return guldens/ hectare	f288-f336	f840	f750
Surplus guldens/ hectare	f165-f117	f321	f356

* Rental includes drying and pounding roots
+ Total excludes outgoings for manure, horse-work before planting the shoots, tenths (tithes), tax, land rent and interest.

Appendix 8.1
Composition of madder analysed by burnings

	A: Alsace/ Koechlin	B: Alsace/ Koechlin	C: Dutch/ May
Potassium	20.30%	18.07%	2.73%
Natron	11.04%	7.19%	20.57%
Lime	24.00%	19.84%	13.01%
Magnesium	2.60%	2.50%	2.53%
Iron Oxide	0.82%	2.28%	2.13%
Phosphoric acid	3.62%	3.13%	13.44%
Sulphuric acid	2.56%	1.45%	2.28%
Potassium and Ferric chloride	3.27%	8.98%	10.04%
Silica	1.16%	3.63%	13.10%
Coal acid	25.83%	21.35%	11.00%
Coal	4.13%	11.48%	5.93%
Total	99.43%	100.62%	99.36%

From the above, the following amounts of alkaline salts were calculated to be present:

Potash	29.00%	27.00%	3.30%
Soda	15.79%	11.66%	30.85%
Lime	34.24%	29.60%	15.77%
Total	79.09%	68.26%	49.92%
Phosphoric acid	5.17%	4.67%	16.29%
Silica	1.77%	5.42%	15.88%

Appendix 10.1
List of paintings tested for madder

Abbreviations of tests used in list of paintings below:

chem	= micro-chemical
ESA	= emission spectroscopy
FTIR	= Fourier transform infrared — more powerful modern technique for smaller samples
FS	= fluorescence spectroscopy
GLC	= gas-liquid chromatography
HPLC	= high-performance liquid chromatography — more powerful modern technique permitting quantitative identification of the constituents of colorants
IR	= infrared spectroscopy
micr	= light microscopy
MS	= micro-spectrophotometry
spec	= spectrophotometry
TLC	= thin-layer chromatography
UVF	= ultraviolet fluorescence
UVS	= ultraviolet-visible absorption spectroscopy
XRD	= X-ray diffraction
XRF	= X-ray fluorescence

Date, Country	Artist, Title	Analyst and method or School
Egyptian, AD160-180	Funerary portrait Woman 63394 tempera on wood, ? er-Rubayat	Merryweather A, et al, 1997 pers comm UVF
Russian, 6-7thc	Icon, encaustic on wood The Martyrs, Mus Eastern and Western Art. Kiev	Birstein et al, 1978 IR
Tibet, 15-19thc	Thang-ka paintings on cotton pr coll, Netherlands	Mehra, 1970 micr, TLC
Italian, 1456	MS illumination in a Missale Romanum (location not given)	Wallert, 1986 spec
Italian, 15thc	Leonardo da Vinci, Last Supper, Santa Maria delle Grazie, Milan (St Simon's mantle and to right of figure)	Kuhn, 1985 micr, chem madder in: dark rose (bordeaux); two red-brown; and bright rose — all glazes
Italian, 1520	Altobello Melone, Christ Carrying the Cross, Nat Gall London, NG6546	Kirby, 1994 and 1996 micr
Early Netherlands, c. 1440	Rogier van der Weyden and workshop The Exhumation of St Hubert, NG783 (red robe of extreme left figure)	Kirby and White, 1996 HPLC, probably madder
Early Netherlands, pr 1460s	Dieric Bouts, The Virgin and Child with Saints Peter and Paul, NG774 (reddish-purple of St Paul's robe)	Kirby and White, 1996 HPLC, madder
Early Netherlands, pr 1475-1500	Dieric Bouts, workshop, Christ crowned with Thorns, NG712 (red of Christ's robe)	Kirby and White, 1996 HPLC, madder
Early Netherlands, c. 1500	Master of St Giles, Saint Giles and the Hind, NG1419 (red of left edge of courtier's robe)	Kirby, 1996 HPLC, madder and kermes
Early Netherlands, c. 1500	Master of St Giles, The Mass of Saint Giles, NG4681, companion to NG1419 (red paint of the carpet)	Bomford and Kirby, 1977; Kirby and White, 1996 MS, TLC, in 1977, madder
Early Netherlands, pr c. 1500-1550	after Quinten Massys, Christ, NG295.1 (wine-red of Christ's sleeve)	Kirby and White, 1996 HPLC, madder
Early Netherlands, early 16thc	attrib Jan Provoost, The Virgin and Child in a Landscape, NG713 (pink of Virgin's cloak)	Kirby and White, 1996 HPLC, brazilwood and madder
German, 1466	Herlin altarpiece, Church of St James, Rothenberg	Brocelman-Bokstijn et al, 1970 GLC, micr, IR, TLC

Appendices

German, c. 1485	Studio of The Master of the Life of of the Virgin, The Mass of St Hubert Nat Gall London, NG253	Kirby, 1977 spec, TLC
German, pr 1470-80	Master of Liesborn, Saints Cosmas and Damian and the Virgin, NG261 (red glaze on bottom edge of St Damian's cloak)	Kirby and White, 1996 HPLC, probably madder
German, c 1465-90	attr Master of Liesborn, The Crucifixion with Saints, NG262 (red glaze of drapery, second figure from left)	Kirby and White, 1996 HPLC, probably madder
German, 1497	attr Albrecht Dürer, The Painter's Father, NG1938 (pink background, left hand edge, after extraction of paint medium)	Kirby and White, 1996 HPLC, madder
German, pr 1505-10	Master of the Saint Bartholomew Altarpiece Saints Peter and Dorothy NG707. Reverse Saint John the Evangelist and the Virgin and Child (red glaze of shadow on St John's left sleeve)	Kirby and White, 1996 HPLC, probably madder
Swiss, early 16thc	Niklaus Manuel, panel paintings Kunstmus Bern, Kunstmus Basel Kunsth Zurich, pr coll Bern	Kühn, 1977 micr
French, c. 1500	Master of Moulins (Jean Hey), Charlemagne and the Meetings of Saints Joachim & Anne at the Golden Gate, NG4092 (glaze of St Joachim's red hat; Charlemagne's pink cloak)	Kirby and White, 1996 HPLC, madder; probably madder
English, 1610-19	William Larkin, Portrait of Susan Villiers, Countess of Denbigh, pr coll (some of the red areas)	Chorley C, published by Kirby and White, 1996 method not given mixture of madder and cochineal
Flemish, 1629-30	Peter Paul Rubens, Minerva protects Pax from Mars ('Peace and War'), NG46 (glaze on Pax's red drapery)	Kirby and White, 1996 HPLC, probably cochineal and madder
Dutch c. 1654	Jan Vermeer, Christ in the House of Mary and Martha, Nat Gall Scotland, Edinburgh	Kühn, 1968 IR
French, 19thc	Henri Fantin-Latour, Chrysanthemums John G Johnson coll, Philadelphia, cat no 990	Tucker M, pers comm to Schweppe, 1984 micr, UVF
Dutch, 19thc	Hafkenscheid Collection of Pigments Technical Univ Delft	Pey, 1989 HPLC

Appendix 11.1
Dominique Cardon's ground rules for dyeing wool with madder[74]

In the Mediterranean basin and western Europe, dyers favoured the following quantities: a classic alum mordant of 25% by weight of alum to wool, cream of tartare 6%, and tin, etain 0.5%. The warm dye-bath contains 35 to 40% by weight of powdered madder to wool.

The dye-bath was warmed slowly to 85°C which was not exceeded but maintained for 2 hours, while the wool was continually moved about. If the temperature dropped, part of the dye risked precipitation with resulting loss of intensity. Whereas if the dye-bath was overheated, the dye went brown. If the madder was acidic, hard-water was used and if that was unavailable, chalk was added. There had to be an excess of lime solution which combined with the metallic salts of the mordant to form a very durable integrated colour with the wool fibre. A warm soap bath after dyeing eliminated the yellow tinge which was caused by some of the colourants in madder such as purpuroxanthin.

Appendix 11.2
Modern craft recipes & light-fastness and wash-fastness

The following modern craft dye methods may be of specialist interest to the practitioner, but their diversity also demonstrates that there is still no best method and that an empirical approach is still followed. As John Edmonds, the woad and murex dyer[75] has stressed, dye recipes can only give half the story. Even when no secrecy was intended, it is impossible to note down all the fine adjustments carried out almost subconsciously as the result of long experience. The same natural dyeing process carried out by the same dyer is always slightly different, partly because of the variations in the fibre, the ingredients, the water, the uniformity of and exact temperature in the dye bath and even the weather. The methods also confirm that it is easier to dye wool than cotton or silk (see illustration, page 204).

Buchanan's modern American craft dyeing method is redolent of pioneering days:

> Different roots vary in strength, but usually dried madder dyes double its weight of fibres. Old recipes call for a dye-bath of hard-water, but adding lime or chalk dust, or a tablespoon of baking soda per gallon of water gives the same effect. This makes the water alkaline which improves the dissolving of the pigment alizarin.
>
> Soak the ground roots in water for 12 hours. Then heat the dye bath very slowly to between 140° and 160°F, measuring the temperature with a thermometer. If overheating occurs, browns result instead of reds. Strain out the roots which can be used again for paler shades. Add wet, pre-mordanted wool or silk to the dye-bath and simmer at 140° to 160°F for an hour, then let the fibres cool in the dye-bath. Rinse in soapy water and then in clear water. On wool and silk madder gives several different shades of red with different mordants and additives.
>
> Multiple immersions are needed to dye pre-mordanted cotton, flax or other plant fibres with madder. Simmer the fibres for an hour at 120° to 160° F, cool, rinse and dry. Re-wet the fibres and simmer them again in a fresh pot of dye, repeating as needed until the colour is rich and dark.
>
> The dye-bath can be reused for coral, pink or beige. Use madder tops for dyeing as you use the roots, allowing double the weight of dried tops to fibre, that is a quarter the strength of the roots.[76]

Appendices

More detailed modern American craft dyeing methods[77] different recipes for Lacquer-Red wool, Dark Lacquer-Red wool, Bright Orange wool, Garnet-Red wool and Dark Red cotton and their respective mordants:

Lacquer-Red wool of 'good' colour fastness (see below) requires 8oz (dried) madder for 1lb of wool. Use alum mordant described below. Soak the madder in a small quantity of water overnight. The following morning heat it to boiling and pour the hot liquid into 4 gallons of cool water. Before immersing the mordanted wool in the dye-bath, thoroughly rinse it and squeeze out excess moisture. Immerse the wool, heat the bath to boiling and continue to boil it for 45 minutes, rinse and dry.

Dark Lacquer-Red wool of 'good' colour fastness requires 1lb of madder for 1lb of wool. Use alum mordant. Soak the madder in a small quantity of water overnight. The following morning add enough water to make a 4 to 4½ gallon dye-bath. Before immersing mordanted wool in the dye-bath, thoroughly rinse it and squeeze out excess moisture. Heat the bath gradually until it reaches 140° to 160°F. Maintain this temperature while stirring constantly for two hours. Allow the bath to cool, then remove the wool, rinse and dry.

Bright Orange wool of 'fair to light, good to washing' colour fastness requires for 1lb of wool: ½oz cream of tartare, 1oz stannous chloride, ½oz quercitron extract and 1½oz dried madder. Dissolve the cream of tartar and ¼ of the stannous chloride in 4 to 4½ gallons of water. Thoroughly wet the wool, which does not require mordanting, squeeze out excess moisture, and immerse it in the stannous chloride solution. Heat to boiling, and boil for 45 minutes. Remove the wool. Add the quercitron, madder and remainder of the stannous chloride to the dye-bath, stirring well until dissolved. Return the wool to this dye-bath, stir and continue to boil for 30 minutes longer. Rinse and dye.

Garnet-Red wool of 'good' colour fastness requires 8oz dried madder for 1lb of wool. Use chrome mordant described below and then follow the previous directions for dyeing Lacquer-Red wool.

Dark Red cotton of 'good to light, fair to washing' colour fastness requires 8oz of dried madder for 1lb of cotton. Use alum-tannin-alum mordant described below. First dye-bath: prepare a 4 to 4½ gallon dye-bath using 2oz of madder which has been soaked in water overnight. Before immersing the cotton, thoroughly rinse it and squeeze out excess moisture. After immersion heat to lukewarm — 95°F while stirring the bath and maintain this temperature for an hour. Allow the dye-bath containing the cotton to cool overnight. At the same time prepare a fresh madder infusion, similarly soaking 3oz of madder overnight for the second dye-bath. The process is repeated in the second dye-bath and the last 3oz of madder are soaked overnight for the third dye-bath. The following day the same process is repeated for the third dye-bath. Rinse well, wash the materials in soapsuds, rinse again and dry.

For mordanting wool, alum mordant requires 4oz potash alum (see glossary) and 1oz cream of tartare for 1lb of dry wool. Dissolve the alum and cream of tartare in 4 to 4½ gallons of cold soft-water. Immerse the wool after first wetting it and squeezing out the excess moisture. Gradually heat the mordant bath to boiling, and boil it gently for an hour. The wool should be turned and stirred in the bath to ensure penetration. As the liquid boils away it should be topped up with water. Allow the wool to stand overnight in the mordant. Next morning squeeze out excess moisture, roll the wool in a dry towel and store in a cool place. Rinse the mordanted material well just before dyeing.

For mordanting wool, chrome mordant requires ½oz potassium dichromate for 1lb of dry wool. Dissolve the potassium dichromate in 4 to 4½ gallons of cold soft water and follow the preceding directions for mordanting wool with alum.

For mordanting cotton, alum-tannin-alum mordant requires 8oz potash alum, 2oz sodium carbonate and 10oz powdered oak galls, or 1oz tannic acid or extract from 4 to 6oz dried sumach leaves for 1lb dry cotton. Dissolve 4oz of alum and 1oz of sodium carbonate in 4 to 4½ gallons of cold soft water. Immerse the cotton after wetting it thoroughly and squeezing out the excess water. Stir while gradually heating to boiling and boil for an hour.

Allow the material to remain in the bath overnight. **+** Next morning squeeze out excess moisture, rinse and put the cotton into a bath of oak galls (or alternatives) heated to 140° to 160°F. Work the cotton for an hour and leave it in the bath overnight. Next day, rinse it briefly. Then dissolve the remainder of the alum and sodium carbonate in the same amount of soft water and repeat the mordanting process above, up to **+**. Next morning squeeze the excess moisture out of the cotton and rinse thoroughly before dyeing. To prepare the extract of sumach leaves, soak the dry leaves in water for ½ an hour and boil for ½ an hour, strain the liquid and allow the bath to cool to 140° to 160°F.

Further colours can be obtained by top-dyeing wool with madder. There are two methods of top-dyeing used for different colour shades.

For Method 1, 4oz of dry madder are required for 1lb of dry wool. Soak madder in water overnight. Next morning add water to the dye extract to make a dye-bath of 4 to 4½ gallons. Thoroughly wet the wool and squeeze out excess moisture. Immerse in the dye-bath. Heat the dye-bath to 140° to 160°F. Stir while maintaining the temperature for ½ hour; rinse and dry.

For Method 2, 8oz of madder are required for 1lb of wool. In the same way as above make the double strength dye-bath. Follow the same method but maintain the temperature for half the time, ½ hour.

The following eleven shades of colour can be obtained in wool by top-dyeing with madder:[78]

Shade	Mordant	First dye	Method	Top-dyeing
Light terra cotta	alum	broomsedge	brass wool	Method 1
Burnt-orange	chrome	broomsedge	brass wool	Method 1
Lacquer Red	alum	broomsedge	brass wool	Method 2
Dark henna	chrome	broomsedge	brass wool	Method 2
Dull orange	chrome	fustic	gold wool	Method 1
Rose-brown	chrome	fustic	gold wool	Method 1 plus boiling the wool in the dye-bath
Burnt-orange	alum	fustic	gold wool	Method 1
Terra cotta	alum	goldenrod	brass wool	Method 1
Rose-brown	chrome	goldenrod	brass wool	Method 1
Terra cotta	chrome	quercitron or black oak	gold wool	Method 1 'Bark Method 1'
Dark coral pink	alum	quercitron or black oak	gold wool	Method 1 'Bark Method 1'

Another American craft dye method with even more variations from Palmy Weigle produces a rich range of four colours at a time:[79]

To dye 2oz of wool, prepare 4 skeins of wool. Pre-mordant two skeins with alum and two with chrome. Place ½oz of pulverised madder in a muslin bag and soak in ½ gallon of water overnight. Next day use medium heat to bring the dye-bath to the boil and let it boil vigorously for 10 minutes. Remove the madder from the dye-bath and divide the dye evenly into two dye-pots. (The root may be used for a second weaker dye-bath later.)

Place the alum mordanted skeins into one dye-pot and the chrome mordanted skeins into the other. Simmer the yarn in the pots for ½ hour. Add a pinch of tin to the first bath and swap one of the alum mordanted skeins. Add a pinch of iron to the other bath. Simmer both baths for 10 minutes. Rinse all the skeins thoroughly. Alum gives red; alum and tin, red-orange; chrome, garnet; and chrome and iron, deep dark red.

Violetta Thurstan confirmed the following variant effects of mordants on wool: Alum and cream of tartare gives brownish red; tin and cream of tartare, bright red; chrome, reddish brown; and iron, purplish brown.[80]

This contrasts with Jill Goodwin's results:

Alum and cream of tartare give red; stannous chloride (tin) and cream of tartare, bright orange; bichromate of potash, red, orange; and bichromate of potash with ½ teaspoonful of ferrous sulphate added for the last fifteen minutes of simmering, deep dark red.

Her dyeing method is also different:

Allow 3oz of fresh dried madder or ½oz of commercial madder to each gallon of hard-water, soak overnight with 2 teaspoonfuls — a tenth of an ounce — of powdered chalk added. Next day raise the temperature of the dye-bath from cold to 158oF within an hour, never allowing the liquid to boil. The best colours are obtained at 140°F, above which browning of reds occurs. Strain off the roots. Re-simmer the roots with more hard-water and use for paler shades. Immerse clean, wet, mordanted wool — no weight given — and continue simmering for 30 to 40 minutes. Allow the wool to cool in the dye-bath, then rinse thoroughly, wash in warm soapy water, rinse again and dry in the open air.[81]

Su Grierson provided more scientific methods and defined the colours using the Methuen dye code. *The Methuen Handbook of Colour* contains over 1,200 colour samples. A typical code is '1 A 8'; The first number '1' refers to the 30 pages of colour plates, each one devoted to a different colour hue — '1' means 'page 1' — greenish yellow. The squares of colour on each page are arranged in gradations of tone and intensity. The tone or amount of blackness in the colour is the letter of the code from 'A' — clear and bright — to 'F'- very dark. The third part of the code is a number from '1' to '8' which identifies the intensity or depth of colour present — '8' being a very intense or strong colour. With reproducible accuracy, Grierson gave three reds, top-dyes and mordants:[82]

'Paprika red' — 8 B 8 — and 'tomato red' — 8 C 8 — were obtained from dried home-grown madder roots, extracted in their third summer, used whole and chopped, but not powdered. Roots were heated slowly and kept just below boiling for 4 hours. Alum mordanted yarn was then immersed with the roots, and kept hot for a further 12 hours before being rinsed and dried. This colour 'paprika' was a clear yellowy-red. For the stronger 'tomato-red' colour, the yarn was then removed and the roots were boiled vigorously for a further 2 hours. After cooling the liquid the yarn was re-immersed and heated below boiling for a further 6 hours. The final colour is strong and clear, but still has a bricky red tone.
'Lobster/lake red' — 9 B/C 8 — was obtained from imported powdered madder of unknown origin. The powder was heated slowly in water, and boiled for about one hour before being strained through a cloth. The alum mordanted yarn was immersed into the cooled dye-bath and heated, but not boiled, for 6 hours. This sample has more redness to its colour without the brickiness of the above root dye colour.
Top-dyes on madder: woad gives 'Madeira' — 8 E 5; indigo gives 'blackish blue' — 20 F 8; Lichen purple gives 'garnet red'- 11 E 8; and clover gives 'reddish orange'- 7 B 6/7.
Mordants with madder: alum gives 'flame red' — 7 A 8 and 'lobster/ lake red' — 9 B/C 8; tin gives 'poppy red' — 8 A 8 and 'lake/ blood red' — 9/10 C 8; copper gives 'Cuba' — 9 E 8; iron gives 'maroon' — 1 F 8++.

In an even more scientific manner, Gill Dalby described the modern measurement of fastness and gave three wash-fastness indices to each of her five dyeing recipes. The earliest tests for fastness guaranteed the reputation of a city's dyes. By 1515 the Venetians had developed a test for the fastness of dark woollen cloth, the first of many. The cloth was boiled for ½ an hour in a fixed concentration of three parts alum and one part cream of tartare. Centuries later, to keep up standards of dyed wool in Gobelins tapestry, the Frenchman Du Fay de Cisternay extended these tests to include action of air and sun. He specified different additives for boiling different groups of colours and different orderings of the tests.[83] He chose as a standard a colour which faded rapidly over 12 summer days and measured other colours against this. Later that century Bancroft studied mordants to discover the amount required to give maximum light fastness. Chevreul in the 1800s looked at the effects of humidity and moisture on light fastness.[84] As fastness has been a concern of dyers throughout history, it is worth describing these standards in detail.

At the end of the 19th century, the British Association for the Advancement of Science commissioned a comprehensive series of tests on fastness using standards. The length of exposure to a constant source of light needed to fade the standard to a predetermined colour was called the Standard Fading Period (SFP). Dyes were placed in five classes between fast and fugitive. Class I dyes faded rapidly after only one SFP; class II after 2 SFPs; class III after 3 SFPs; class IV after 7 SFPs; and class V, the fast dyes which survived 11 SFPs. Even this improved method of testing was too vague. Ironically the best tests have come in after the demise of natural dyes:

Fastness depends on five factors: 1. The type of fibre, i.e. wool, silk, cotton, linen and so on; 2. The mordanting technique and the amount and type of mordant used; 3. Dyeing technique and the time that the fibre is in the dye-bath and the temperature of the dye-bath; 4. The depth of the finished colour which depends on the quality of the dyestuff, the quantity of dyestuff used and (again) the length of time that the fibre is in the dye-bath; and 5. Environmental changes, such as climate and humidity. For example, with wool, a reduction in moisture content may actually slow down the fading process.

The tests for light fastness or LF for wool are based on British Standard No 1006. Samples of a specified size and uniform surface are exposed to daylight along with eight graded dyed wool standards. Choose the standard with the same fading as the exposed sample, LF '1' has low light fastness, LF '8' is very fast. Temperature and humidity changes can give different results and therefore need be recorded and controlled. Daylight must be at a specified time of year, with the sample facing north (south in Australia) and at a specific angle, avoiding any shadow, car exhaust fumes, winds and so on. Strong artificial light allows tighter environmental control and gives quicker results. For ad hoc home testing, divide the sample in two, keeping one — the control sample — in the dark, which is regularly compared with the exposed sample to find out when fading occurs. A simplified method is to use logwood dyed wool as a standard with LF '2-3', which is good enough. The thread is wound onto a piece of off-white card similarly to the test sample. Part of the test sample is also covered with card to provide a dark control sample.

The tests for wash fastness for wool, based on the I.S.O. wash fastness test No 2, which is equivalent to the British Standard CO_2 test, vary from a mild hand wash to a severe hot alkaline wash. Three indices of '1' to '5' are obtained showing the change in shade, the staining effect on wool and the staining effect on cotton. '1' will wash out or stain other fibres and '5' is very fast. The small sample is a dyed cloth or a knitted yarn, 10cm x 4cm, sandwiched between an undyed piece of wool and an undyed piece of cotton. The sandwich is then washed in a weak ½% soap solution at 50°C for 45 minutes. The sample is then assessed for loss of colour and staining of wool and cotton by comparing it with a grey scale, with each step bearing a fastness number between '1' — large contrast — and '5' — no contrast. The fastness is assessed by the same number on the grey scale which corresponds to the washed and unwashed sample. Staining is assessed in the same way.

Choice of dyestuff obviously depends on fastness. It is as important when mixing colours. Often in old rugs, greens have changed to blue as the yellow has faded away. Staining is also a factor when the textile will be washed frequently. It is not easy to define a minimum wash fastness value as gentle washing with a small amount of acetic acid in the water can avoid running. Always test a small sample or corner first.

Dalby's following recipes use the Methuen colour codes and fastness numbers:[85]

Recipe 45: Dyestuff 100% madder root; mordant 8% alum, 7% tartare. Method: Put the root into a dye pan with enough water to cover the wool and leave to soak overnight. Next day immerse the pre-mordanted wool and slowly bring the temperature of the dye-bath up to 1400F /600C over 1 to 1½ hours. Keep at this temperature for an hour. Allow the dye-bath to cool, preferably overnight, then remove the wool and rinse it well. Wash the wool in hand-hot barely soapy water, then rinse to remove soap.
Colour 9C8; light fastness 4-5; wash fastness 4, 3, 4-5
    Recipe 46: Dyestuff 100% madder root; mordant 1% chrome, 2% formic acid.

Method: as recipe 45.

Colour 10E8; light fastness 5; wash fastness 4, 3, 3-4

Recipe 47: Dyestuff 100% madder root; mordant 2% copper, 2% acetic acid. Method: Put the root into a dye pan with enough water to cover the wool and leave to soak overnight. Next day immerse the premordanted wool and slowly bring the temperature of the dye-bath up to simmering over 1 hour. Keep at this temperature for 45 minutes. Leave the wool in the dye-bath until it is cool enough to handle and then remove it and rinse. Wash the wool in hand-hot barely soapy water, then rinse to remove soap.

Colour 8D6; light fastness 3-4; wash fastness 2-3, 4, 4-5

Recipe 48: Dyestuff 100% madder root; sadden (dull the colour) with 5% iron. Method: as recipe 47, but remove wool 30 minutes before the end of dyeing and add the dissolved iron. Replace the wool.

Colour 8F5; light fastness 3-4; wash fastness 4, 2-3, 3-4

Recipe 49: Dyestuff 100% madder root; 8% oxalic acid, 7% tin. Method: as recipe 47.

Colour 9A9; light fastness 4-5; wash fastness 4-5, 3, 3-4.

Sandberg & Sisefsky reported the following partially measured dye tests with madder in 1982.[86] The main recipe was for dyeing wool red with madder in three strengths:

Ingredients	strength:	a	b	c
Wool yarn		100gm	100gm	100gm
Madder		25gm	50gm	100gm
Alum		20gm	25gm	30gm
(Wine stone, cremor tartari)		5gm	5gm	5gm
Soft water		5l	5l	5l

The yarn is mordanted in alum and possibly wine stone for 60 to 90 minutes at 90°C and kept in the mordant bath until it cools down or overnight. Before dyeing the mordanted yarn is rinsed. The remaining wine stone makes the red more yellow.

Soak the finely ground madder in water the day before dyeing. Pure soft-water is slightly warmed and the soaked madder is added to the bath which is then heated to 60°C to 70°C.

Further temperature increase must be avoided and the bath must not be filtered. The yarn is wetted in hand-warm water, squeezed out, and immersed in the dye-bath for two hours. For the first 10 minutes the yarn is drawn out and replaced using wooden rods, making sure that the dye penetrates the ties holding the skeins of yarn. For the clearest possible red colour, the dye-bath must be kept at constant temperature between 60°C and 70°C — not the usual 90°C. After dyeing the yarn is washed rinsed and dried.

If dyeing has taken place at less than 70°C, the bath may still contain a lot of dyestuff. Even the weakest, strength 'a', can be after-treated — apparently dyed again with optional potash or ammonium hydrate — as long as serviceable dye remains, though the weaker red can become somewhat yellow with after-treatment.

Light-fastness for full strength madder dyes is 4-5, more powerful deep reds can reach 6, as can all darker madder dyes, such as browns. With rose dyes light-fastness drops below 4, but is higher than corresponding cochineal dyes. Madder dyes do not lose clarity with bleaching, unlike many red coloured dye woods.

Appendix 13.1
Comparative prices of roots, krap & garancine
(Shtorkh and Ministry)

Year	Garancine(S) Average	Moscow price of Dutch krap		?Turkish roots (S) Average	Derbent price of roots Average
		Low	High		
1846	19.12r				
1847	24.75r	6.00r	11.50r		4.75r
1848	-	6.00r	10.00r		5.65r
1849	22.52r	6.00r	10.00r		4.10r
1850	22.83r	4.00r	10.00r		4.50r
1851	-			6.42r	
1852	-			4.36r	
1853	16.73r			3.47r	
1854	-	5.00r	9.00	2.45r	4.50r
1855	-			3.13r	
1856	-			4.17r	
1857	7.00r	10.00r			8.00r
1858	6.00r	9.00r			7.00r
1859	6.00r	10.00r			9.00r
1860	5.50r	10.00r			9.00r
1861	5.50r	9.50r			7.00r

Russian imports were nearly all ground powder; only Turkey exported roots:
Roots represented 0.31% of all krap (by value) in 1854
Roots represented 7.41% of all krap (by value) in 1855
Roots represented 3.98% of all krap (by value) in 1856 (S)

Appendix 13.2
Percentages of all Russian madder imports
sold at Nizhegorodsky Fair

1844	1.4%
1845	0.9%
1846	0.6%
1847	0.9%
1848	2.4%
1849	8.5%
1850	10.2%
1851	18.2%
1852	20.9%
1853	28.9%
1854	na
1855	na
1856	27.9%

Appendices

Appendix 13.3
Price of krap at the port of delivery

Years	1844	1845	1846	1847	1848	1849	1850
Baltic ports	5.98r	9.75r	8.27r	7.36r	6.81r	5.80r	6.13r
Black Sea & Azov	9.00r	10.00r	9.00r	7.90r	5.10r	4.00r	3.52r
By land via west	2.50r	6.44r	6.15r	5.60r	8.48r	7.03r	6.50r
Average	5.97r	8.73r	7.81r	6.95r	6.79r	5.61r	5.38r

Years	1851	1852	1853	1854	1855	1856	Average 1844-1856
Baltic ports	6.06r	6.00r	5.54r	6.02r	-	7.00r	6.15r
Black Sea & Azov	-	4.78r	4.68r	2.45r	-	-	5.49r
By land via west	3.74r	3.57r	3.43r	2.54r	3.26r	5.40r	4.98r
Average	4.90r	4.78r	4.55r	3.67r	3.26r	6.20r	5.74r

Appendix 13.4
Price of krap at the port of delivery

1844	low	average	high
St Petersburg	7.78r	8.05r	9.90r
Moscow	7.50r	9.83r	12.16r
Riga	7.50r	9.83r	12.16r
Odessa	5.39r	5.76r	6.13r
Astrakhan	6.00r	7.44r	9.00r
Average	6.47r	7.77r	9.29r

1845	low	average	high
St Petersburg	9.62r	10.60r	11.57r
Moscow	8.50r	10.87r	11.22r
Riga	4.70r	6.25r	7.80r
Odessa	6.29r	6.63r	6.93r
Astrakhan	5.00r	5.65r	7.15r
Average	6.82r	8.00r	8.93r

1846	low	average	high
St Petersburg	7.35r	8.96r	10.68r
Moscow	7.75r	9.81r	11.04r
Riga	4.70r	6.25r	7.80r
Odessa	6.00r	6.32r	6.64r
Astrakhan	5.00r	5.52r	6.28r
Average	6.16r	7.37r	8.49r

1847	low	average	high
St Petersburg	6.50r	8.04r	9.58r
Moscow	6.33r	8.69r	11.80r
Riga	4.70r	6.30r	7.91r
Odessa	5.57r	5.73r	5.88r
Astrakhan	4.00r	5.76r	7.15r
Average	5.42r	6.97r	8.44r

1848	low	average	high
St Petersburg	5.84r	7.55r	9.29r
Moscow	6.12r	8.02r	9.88r
Riga	4.70r	6.35r	8.00r
Odessa	5.00r	5.28r	5.57r
Astrakhan	4.25r	7.05r	7.15r
Average	5.18r	6.85r	7.98r

1849	low	average	high
St Petersburg	5.50r	6.93r	9.50r
Moscow	6.00r	7.66r	10.00r
Riga	4.70r	6.36r	8.00r
Odessa	3.78r	4.03r	4.28r
Astrakhan	3.00r	5.66r	6.00r
Average	4.59r	6.13r	7.55r

1850	low	average	high
St Petersburg	5.50r	6.50r	7.50r
Moscow	4.00r	7.71r	10.00r
Riga	4.70r	6.35r	8.00r
Odessa	3.78r	3.82r	3.86r
Astrakhan	3.00r	4.46r	6.00r
Average	4.19r	5.77r	7.07r

1851	low	average	high
St Petersburg	5.00r	7.25r	7.50r
Moscow	5.50r	7.26r	9.00r
Riga	5.00r	6.50r	8.00r
Odessa	3.78r	4.57r	5.50r
Astrakhan	3.00r	4.84r	5.50r
Average	4.45r	6.08r	7.10r

1852	low	average	high
St Petersburg	5.00r	6.25r	7.50r
Moscow	5.50r	7.00r	9.00r
Riga	5.00r	6.50r	8.00r
Odessa	-	-	-
Astrakhan	3.50r	4.37r	5.50r
Average	4.07r	6.03r	7.05r

1853	low	average	high
St Petersburg	5.33r	6.40r	7.20r
Moscow	5.46r	6.02r	8.04r
Riga	6.33r	7.92r	9.50r
Odessa	-	-	-
Astrakhan	2.36r	3.84r	5.36r
Average	4.87r	6.07r	7.52r

1854	low	average	high
St Petersburg	6.04r	6.93r	7.81r
Moscow	4.33r	7.16r	8.46r
Riga	7.00r	8.08r	9.16r
Odessa	-	-	-
Astrakhan	2.91r	4.23r	5.54r
Average	5.07r	6.60r	7.74r

1855	low	average	high
St Petersburg	7.00r	7.61r	8.23r
Moscow	6.00r	7.83r	9.66r
Riga	7.16r	8.09r	9.00r
Odessa	-	-	-
Astrakhan	2.50r	3.68r	4.61r
Average	5.66r	6.80r	7.87r

1856	low	average	high
St Petersburg	7.25r	7.72r	8.25r
Moscow	7.16r	8.12r	9.92r
Riga	8.00r	10.00r	12.00r
Odessa	-	-	-
Astrakhan	3.68r	4.41r	5.50r
Average	6.52r	7.56r	8.92r

Appendix 13.5
Price of Dutch & Breslau krap
at Nizhegorodsky Fair

1845	starting at 7 to 13r per pood,	average 9r
1846	8 to 15r,	average 9r 41k
1847	6 to 10r,	average 8r
1848	8 to 20r,	average 9r
1849	6r 60k to 7r 15k,	average 6r 87k
1850	8 to 9r,	average 8r 50k
1851	6r 85k to 8r,	average 7r 42k
1852	8 to 8r 50k,	average 8r 25k
1853	7r 50k to 8r,	average 7r 75k
1854 & 1855	no krap was brought to the Fair	
1856	8r 50k to 9r,	average 8r 75k

Appendix 13.6
Average Russian market prices of madder krap
imported from Europe

	1844		1845
Prussia	6.48r	Prussia	9.21r
German *landern*	6.33r	German *landern*	6.39r
Holland	6.00r	Holland	9.80r
France	8.00r	France	9.76r
Belgium	6.00r	Belgium	9.80r
Italy	6.00r	Italy	9.44r
Austria	9.00r	Austria	10.00r
Turkey	5.00r	Turkey	6.45r
Average	6.62r	Average	8.85r

	1846		*1847*
Prussia	7.97r	Prussia	6.62r
German *landern*	7.96r	German *landern*	7.00r
Holland	8.19r	Holland	7.29r
France	8.34r	France	7.24r
Belgium	8.19r	Italy	7.27r
Italy	6.13r	Austria	7.89r
Austria	8.91r	Turkey	5.47r
Turkey	6.15r	Average	6.97r
Average	7.73r		

	1848		*1849*
Prussia	6.27r	Prussia	6.16r
German *landern*	6.75r	German *landern*	5.50r
Holland	6.74r	Holland	5.50r
France	6.89r	France	6.14r
Italy	6.74r	Great Britain	4.78r
Austria	10.62r	Austria	6.38r
Turkey	5.10r	Turkey	4.00r
Average	7.01r	Average	5.49r

	1850		*1851*
Prussia	6.20r	Prussia	3.90r
German *landern*	5.96r	German *landern*	6.00r
Holland	6.00r	Holland	6.00r
France	6.34r	France	6.13r
Belgium	6.00r	Belgium	6.00r
Austria	6.35r	Great Britain	5.88r
Average	6.14r	Austria	2.90r
		Average	5.26r

	1852		*1853*
Prussia	3.62r	Prussia	3.57r
German *landern*	6.00r	German *landern*	5.65r
Holland	6.00r	Holland	5.50r
France	5.98r	France	5.60r
Belgium	6.00r	Great Britain	5.95r
Great Britain	6.00r	Austria	3.65r
Austria	3.45r	Turkey	4.68r
Turkey	6.00r	Average	4.94r
Average	5.38r		

	1854		*1855*
Prussia	2.44r	Prussia	3.19r
Holland	6.00r	Austria	4.77r
France	6.00r	Average	3.98r
Belgium	6.00r		
Austria	4.30r		*1856*
Turkey	2.45r	Prussia	4.74r
Portugal	7.31r	German *landern*	9.00r
Average	4.93r	Holland	7.00r
		France	7.00r
		Great Britain	5.82r
		Austria	5.44r
		Turkey	2.68r
		Others	7.00r
		Average	6.09r

Appendix 14.1
Kasaba's Ottoman exports of madder & the British trade[87]

Year	Ottoman exports value £000	Percentage of total exports to Britain	Izmir price s.d./cwt	Izmir quantity exported 000 cwt = x 3½ poods
1840	562	45.0		
1841	516	42.0		
1842	465	39.8		
1843	546	43.9		
1844	479	37.0		
1845	654	44.6	45.8	67
1846	510	47.5	36.5	53
1847	511	29.3	33.1	59
1848	725	48.2	27.1	77
1849	842	40.0	29.8	100
1850	923	41.0	38.8	109
1851			34.3	118
1852	1096	48.6	37.1	120
1853	1013	33.2	41.4	120
1854			38.1	27
1855	246	10.7	40.3	94
1856	1303	54.6		101
1857	403	17.1		134
1858	401	15.3		154
1859	430	15.7	42.2	171
1860	421	13.2		166
1861	395	25.8		175
1862	326	18.1		145
1863	312	12.6	48.4	127
1864	258	9.0	39.0	106
1865	189	8.3	40.0	97
1866	290	15.0	35.0	143
1867	183	12.8	40.8	
1868	398	19.7	45.0	148
1869	224	10.5	70.0	60
1870	154	8.2	64.0	63
1871	153	6.8	52.0	54
1872	99	3.8	50.0	68
1873	42	1.6	50.0	37
1874	105	4.6	15.0	72
1875	41	1.5	18.0	21
1876	18	0.6	16.0	15

NB Overall figures for 1840-53 represent official values, for 1854-71 real values and for 1872-76 declared values. (?)

Appendix 14.2
Russian tariffs per pood

European trade	1819	1831	1841	1850	1857
Dried roots	30k	50k	80k	80k	10k
Powdered krap	50k	80k	1r	1r	50k
Garancine by sea	-	-	2.50r	1.60r	1.60r
Garancine by land	-	-	2r	1.20r	1.20r

Black sea ports & Caucasus points of entry					
Dried roots	-	-	-	30k	10k
Asian madder	-	-	-	50k	50k
Depending on price levels	-	-	5%	5%	

All Russian wholesale imports; Russian-European krap imports; Russian-Asian madder imports			
1844	0.51%	0.11%	0.12%
1849	1.07%	0.23%	0.82%
1853	0.66%	0.15%	0.76%
1856	0.22%	0.22%	0.27%

Russian treasury tax receipts on:

	European roots	Euro krap	Euro Total	Asian roots
1851	8.2kr	68.8kr	77.0kr	na
1852	0.5	78.4	78.9	na
1853	0.9	54.4	55.3	na
1854	0.0	31.9	31.9	7.5
1855	0.4	8.0	8.4	7.3
1856	0.6	28.7	29.4	4.5
Total	10.8	270.2	281.0	19.2
Average	1.8	45.0	46.8	6.4

Appendix 14.3
European imports to Russia by place of entry

Average	Weight	%	Value	%
Baltic	71kp	93.1%	492kr	94.6%
Continental	4kp	4.9%	19kr	4.0%
Black Sea & Azov	2kp	2.0%	8kr	1.4%
Total	77kp	100%	519kr	100%

The ledgers of the three principal customs houses at St Petersburg, Moscow and Riga record the following average annual trade between 1844 and 1856:

	Average Weight	%	Average Value	%
St Petersburg	61kp	84.7%	417kr	84.3%
Moscow	10kp	14.5%	72kr	15.0%
Riga	0kp	0.4%	2kr	0.4%
Total	71kp	100%	493kr	100%

Appendices

Appendix 14.4
Krap imports to Russia[88]

Under the 1797 tariffs:	1800	14.4 kp
	1801	26.1
	1802	54.7
	1803	49.7
	1804	28.5
	1805	14.7
	1806	47.1
	1807	27.7
	1808	10.5
	1809	4.0
	1810	16.9
Under the 1811 tariffs:	1811	38.3
	1812	13.4
	1813	24.2
	1814	28.1
	1815	39.6
Under the 1816 tariffs:	1816	20.3
	1817	37.7
	1818	72.4
	1819	49.3
Under the 1819 tariffs:	1820	46.7
	1821	14.2
Under the 1822 tariffs:	1822	37.9
	1823	42.5
	1824	43.6
	1825	45.5
	1826	59.3
	1827	73.3
	1828	74.2
	1829	73.2
	1830	66.3
Under the 1831 tariffs:	1831	66.0
	1832	67.6
	1833	46.6
	1834	79.4
	1835	120.2
	1836	82.7
	1837	90.7
	1838	154.8
	1839	154.8 (*?misprint*)
	1840	166.4
Under the 1841 tariffs:	1841	99.0
	1842	121.5
	1843	104.6
	1844	63.3
	1845	110.7
	1846	106.4
	1847	107.4
	1848	74.0
	1849	111.8
	1850	87.9

Under the 1850 tariffs:	1854	32.3 *(Apologies that the missing years were absent from the library in Tblisi)*
	1857	76.2
Under the 1857 tariffs:	1858	55.6
	1859	66.6
	1860	73.7
	1861	50.2

Appendix 14.5
Krap imports from Europe, garancine mix

representing % of all madder excluding garancine

1851	69kp		400kr	84%
1852	78kp		461kr	98%
1853	54kp		298kr	98%
1854		small		
1855	1kp		2kr	0%
1856	1kp		5kr	0%

Garancine imports from Europe % of non garancine					Madder imports from Europe incl garancine	
1844	-		-		73kp	377kr
1845	-		-		124kp	947kr
1846	3kp	2%	48kr	5%	134kp	862kr
1847	7kp	6%	174kr	22%	161kp	951kr
1848	-		-		94kp	501kr
1849	12kp	11%	290kr	45%	187kp	937kr
1850	14kp	16%	326kr	60%	161kp	865kr
1851	14kp	18%	300kr	64%	152kp	767kr
1852	14kp	18%	300kr	64%	156kp	767kr
1853	13kp	22%	220kr	72%	120kp	522kr
1854	not available					
1855	not available					
1856	not available					

Appendix 14.6
European imports of krap to Russia by country

Year	1844		1845		1846		1847		1848	
Prussia	1kp	4kr	1kp	10kr	1kp	5kr	1kp	8kr	1kp	7kr
German *landern*	small		2kp	11kr	0kp	2kr	1kp	4kr	0kp	1kr
Holland	42kp	255kr	56kp	544kr	59kp	484kr	60kp	436kr	37kp	246kr
France	13kp	108kr	34kp	331kr	38kp	341kr	43kp	312kr	33kp	229kr
Great Britain	-	-	4kp	39kr	-	-	-	-	-	-
Belgium	1kp	5kr	-	-	small		-	-	-	-
Italy	0kp	1kr	0kp	3kr	small		0kp	1kr	0kp	1kr
Austria	1kp	5kr	1kp	5kr	1kp	5kr	1kp	6kr	0kp	3kr
Turkey	small	1kr	4kr	0kp	3kr	2kp	9kr	3kp	13kr	
Total	58kp	377kr	98kp	947kr	99kp	814kr	107kp	777kr	74kp	501kr

Year	1849		1850		1851		1852		1853	
Prussia	2kp	10kr	2kp	12kr	5kp	20kr	4kp	14kr	3kp	11kr
German *landern*	1kp	8kr	2kp	10kr	1kp	4kr	1kp	5kr	small	
Holland	53kp	292kr	50kp	299kr	31kp	184kr	34kp	202kr	24kp	129kr
France	53kp	324kr	33kp	210kr	37kp	226kr	40kp	238kr	28kp	157kr
Great Britain	0kp	2kr	-		3kp	17kr	0kp	2kr	0kp	2kr
Belgium		-	1kp	7kr	2kp	14kr	1kp	6kr	-	
Italy	small		-	-		-		-		
Austria	1kp	5kr	0kp	2kr	1kp	2kr	0kp	1kr	0kp	1kr
Turkey	1kp	4kr	-	-	small	0kr	2kr			
Total 112kp	647kr	88kp	539kr	79kp	467kr	80kp	467kr	56kp	303kr	

Year	1854		1855		1856		Average		% value
Prussia	3kp	9kr	8kp	27kr	3kp	15kr	3kp	11.6kr	2.3%
German *landern*	-		-		0kp	1kr	1kp	4.1kr	0.8%
Holland		5kp	29kr	-	25kp	175kr	40kp	256kr	50.0%
France	23kp	140kr	-		1kp	4kr	31kp	216kr	42.2%
Great Britain	-	-			0kp	1kr	1kp	10.3kr	2.1%
Belgium		0kp	1kr		-	-	1kp	5.4kr	1.1%
Italy		-		-		-	0kp	0.6kr	0.1%
Austria	0kp	2kr	0kp	2kr	small		0kp	3.2kr	0.6%
Turkey	small		-		small		1kp	3.1kr	0.6%
Portugal	-		-		0kp	1kr	on entry		0.1%
Total	32kp	181kr	9kp	28kr	30kp	202kr	77kp	512kr	100%

To cross-check Shtorkh, the Ministry tables showed:

Russian imports of krap by country of origin from 1847 to 1861:

Year	Prussia	Hanseatic Cities	Holland	France	Sardinia & Sicily	Austria	Turkey	Other	Total
1847	1.3p/8.4r	0.6/4.4	60/436	43/312	0.2/1.4	0.8/6.1	1.6/9.2	nil	107/777
1848	1.2/7.5	0.2/1.1	37/246	33/229	0.1/0.7	0.3/3.4	2.6/13	nil	74/501
1849	1.7/10	1.4/7.8	53/292	53/324	small	0.8/5.2	1.1/4.3	0.5/2.2	112/647
1850	1.9/12	1.7/9.9	50/299	33/210	nil	0.4/2.5	nil	1.1/6.6	88/549
1854	3.5/8.5	nil	4.8/29	23/140	nil	0.4/1.7	0.1/0.3	0.3/1.9	32/181
1857	3.4/18	15/102	34/242	22/157	nil	0.2/1.2	0.1/0.5	1.8/14	76/533
1858	3.0/14	0.2/1.8	14/105	32/239	nil	0.2/1.6	nil	6.2/47	56/408
1859	3.6/16	0.4/3.2	26/184	35/243	small	0.1/0.3	0.1/3.3	0.1/5.7	67/456
1860	4.1/16	0.1/0.4	33/258	36/284	nil	0.4/1.2	nil	0.3/2.1	74/562
1861	3.5/12	0.4/3.4	5.0/40	39/314	0.3/2.3	0.4/2.6	nil	1.4/11	70/384

Appendix 14.7

Size of deliveries of Derbent madder 1849-1854:

5 deliveries	< 100 poods
80	100-500
45	500-1000
15	1000-1500
17	1500-2000
3	2000-2500
2	2500-3000
4	> 4000

Madder Red

Kharal sizes :

Persia	7 Russian poods
Khiva	8
Baku	6
Petrovsk	7
Kouba	7.5
Derbent	7.5

Delivery costs per pood:

Derbent–Astrakhan	by sea	20-30 kopeks
Astrakhan–Nizhegorodsky		25-35
Nizhegorodsky–Moscow	by road	37
	by waterway	15-20
Nizhegorodsky–Ivanovo	by road	25-30
	by waterway	12

Appendix 14.8a
Sales at Nizhegorodsky Fair

(% by weight. Holland & Breslau from Schaefer;[89] Bukhara & Derbent from Shtorkh)

	H & B	del'd	sold	unsold	Bukhara			Derbent			Total del'd	
1848	3.7kp	59.0kr	10.2kr	nil kr							1kp	10kr
1849	1.5 6%	12.6	10.1	2.5	7.0kp	29%	24.7kr	16.0kp	65%	110kr	25	147
1850	1.1 4%	9.3	8.1	1.2	10.0	37%	34.3	16.0	59%	114	27	158
1851	1.1 2%	8.3	7.3	1.0	7.0	15%	21.0	40.0	83%	223	48	252
1852	1.0 1%	8.3	7.5	0.8	13.0	18%	41.0	60.0	81%	330	74	380
1853	0.7 1%	5.4	4.6	0.9	15.0	19%	52.0	70.0	82%	410	87	467
1854	nil				4.0		14.0	not available			n/a	n/a
1855	nil				9.0	10%	30.6	85.0	90%	474	94	505
1856	2.5 4%	21.9	12.9	9.0	not available			60.0		314	n/a	n/a

Appendix 14.8b
Madder imports by port from Europe

(Weight in 000 poods, price in 000 roubles, all figures rounded up, i.e. 4500r to 5kr)

Year	1844		1845		1846		1847		1848	
Baltic	48kp	286kr	95kp	928kr	96kp	796kr	98kp	722kr	71kp	480kr
Continental	10kp	91kr	1kp	10kr	1kp	9kr	1kp	11kr	1kp	7kr
Black Sea & Azov	small		1kp	9kr	1kp	9kr	8kp	44kr	3kp	13kr
Total	58kp	377kr	98kp	947kr	99kp	814kr	107kp	777kr	74kp	501kr

Year	1849		1850		1851		1852		1853	
Baltic	108kp	629kr	87kp	532kr	73kp	445kr	75kp	448kr	52kp	290kr
Continental	1kp	9kr	1kp	7kr	6kp	21kr	4kp	14kr	3kp	11kr
Black Sea & Azov	2kp	9kr	small		small		1kp	4kr	0kp	2kr
Total	112kp	647kr	88kp	539kr	99kp	814kr	80kp	467kr	56kp	303kr

Year	1854		1855		1856		Avg:	Weight %	Value %	
Baltic	28kp	171kr	-		26kp	181kr	71kp	93.1%	492kr	94.6%
Continental	4kp	9kr	9kp	28kr	4kp	20kr	4kp	4.9%	19kr	4.0%
Black Sea & Azov	small		-		0kp	1kr	2kp	2.0%	8kr	1.4%
Total	32kp	180kr	9kp	28kr	30kp	202kr	77kp	100%	519kr	100%

Ministry five-yearly averages of Russian imports of European krap:

1822 to 1827	46.8kp p.a.
1827 to 1831	57.4
1832 to 1836	79.7
1837 to 1841	133.6
1842 to 1846	101.5

Customs ledger trade in madder:
Weight in 000 poods; price in 000 roubles, all figures rounded up, that is 4500r to 5kr.

Year	1844		1845		1846		1847		1848	
St Petersburg	47kp	282kr	85kp	830kr	87kp	712kr	83kp	608kr	58kp	390kr
Moscow	-		9kp	87kr	9kp	82kr	14kp	107kr	12kp	86kr
Riga	1kp	4kr	1kp	6kr	small		1kp	3kr	0kp	1kr
Others	small		1kp	6kr	0kp	1kr	1kp	4kr	1kp	4kr
Total	48kp	286kr	95kp	928kr	96kp	796kr	98kp	722kr	71kp	480kr

Year	1849		1850		1851		1852		1853	
St Petersburg	86kp	471kr	64kp	382kr	63kp	377kr	59kp	357kr	45kp	249kr
Moscow	22kp	155kr	23kp	148kr	10kp	66kr	15kp	91kr	7kp	39kr
Riga	small	0kp	2kr	0kp	2kr	0kp	1kr	0kp	2kr	
Others	1kp	4kr	-		-		-		-	
Total	108kp	629kr	87kp	532kr	73kp	445kr	107kp	777kr	52kp	290kr

Year	1854		1855		1856		Avg:	Weight %	Value %	
St Petersburg	27kp	163kr			25kp	178kr	61kp	84.7%	417kr	84.3%
Moscow	1kp	7kr	none		0kp	2kr	10kp	14.5%	72kr	15.0%
Riga	0kp	1kr	bought		0kp	1kr	0kp	0.4%	2kr	0.4%
Others	-				-		0kp	0.4%	2kr	0.3%
Total	28kp	171kr			26kp	181kr	71kp	100%	493kr	100%

Appendix 14.9
The price of different contracts of Caucasian madder from 1846 to 1856

	price/pood	weight in poods		price/pood	weight in poods
1846	5.00r	1.3kp	1847	6.00r	0.3kp
	4.50r	0.4kp		5.00r	31.6kp
	3.65r	56.5kp		4.50r	0.7kp
	3.55r	1.3kp		4.00r	6.2kp
				3.84r	0.7kp
				3.75r	0.1kp
				3.00r	1.8kp

	price/pood	weight in poods		price/pood	weight in poods
1848	6.00r	37.0kp	1849	16.42r	small
	5.55r	0.5kp		8.00r	small
	5.33r	0.6kp		7.80r	small
	4.66r	0.5kp		5.00r	61.1kp
	4.00r	6.1kp		4.00r	6.1kp
	2.50r	0.1kp		3.50r	0.3kp
1851	7.00r	0.7kp	1852	5.00r	0.1kp
	5.00r	1.3kp		4.66r	0.2kp
	4.26r	0.4kp		4.00r	143.4kp
	4.00r	61.1kp		3.60r	1.5kp
	3.62r	1.7kp		2.00r	0.6kp
	3.50r	10.4kp			
	3.45r	0.6kp			
1856	6.00r	2.6kp			
	5.80r	7.0kp			
	5.50r	36.9kp			
	5.40r	5.8kp			
	5.25r	70.1kp			
	5.15r	3.9kp			
	5.00r	3.8kp			
	4.50r	1.9kp			

Local prices for Baku region madder:

1845	3.22r
1846	3.10r
1847	3.62r
1848	3.50r
1849	3.70r
Average	3.43r

Nizhegorodsky Fair prices for Asian madder:

	Derbent	*Bukhara*
1849	6.60-7.15r; average 6.97r	3.40-3.70r; average 3.55r
1850	7.15-7.30r; average 7.22r	3.43r
1851	5.43-5.72r; average 5.53r	3.00r
1852	5.00-5.90r; average 5.45r	3.15r
1853	5.40-7.00r; average 6.20r	3.44r
1854	prices not available	

	Derbent, Kouba & Kizliar	*Bukhara & Khiva*
1855	5.25-6.00r; average 5.62r	-
1856	8.25-8.70r; average 8.48r	-
1857	10.75-13.50; average 12.12	6.50r
Average	7.20r	3.85r

Appendices

Appendix 14.10

Prices of Asian and Caucasian madder imported to Russia via Astrakhan, according to the Derbent customs ledgers were:

1844	5.00r
1845	5.00r
1846	4.23r
1847	4.73r
1848	5.64r
1849	4.02r
1850	4.93r
1851	3.96r
1852	3.50r
1853	4.00r
1854	5.00r
1855	3.92r
1856	5.52r
Average	4.75r

according to Baku customs ledgers:

1853	2.96r
1854	3.29r
1855	3.18r
1856	2.49r
Average	2.98r

according to Petrovsk (Makhachkala) customs ledgers:

1853	3.76r
1854	4.16r
1855	3.12r
1856	5.00r
Average	4.01r

according to Nizovsk customs ledgers:

1853	3.00r
1854	3.96r
1855	2.30r
1856	4.48r
Average	3.43r

Appendix 14.11

Prices of Asian madder at ports of entry:

	Astrakhan	via Orenburg and Siberia
1844	5.49r	2.11r
1845	3.92r	2.11r
1846	3.00r	2.47r
1847	2.53r	2.85r
1848	-	3.82r
1849	1.55r	3.12r

1850	-	2.88r
1851	2.55r	2.86r
1852	2.00r	2.93r
1853	5.23r	2.86r
1854	2.00r	2.93r
1855	2.23r	2.75r
1856	-	2.38r
Average	3.28r	2.78r

Average prices of madder from Asia:

	Various regions	Persia	Khiva	Tashkent	Bukhara
1848	3.82r	-	-	-	-
1849	3.13r	1.55r	-	-	-
1850	2.90r	-	-	-	-
1851	2.86r	2.55r	-	-	-
1852	3.00r	2.00r	2.00r	1.60r	-
1853	-	2.11r	2.83r	1.58r	2.00r
1854-6	-	2.04r	2.41r	1.59r	2.00r
Overall average	2.01r				

Appendix 14.12:
Asian imports by customs entry points to Russia

Year	1844		1845		1846		1847		1848	
Astrakhan	1kp	6kr	1kp	4kr	0kp	1kr	1kp	2kr		
Orenburg & Siberia	4kp	9kr	12kp	25kr	7kp	18kr	21kp	59kr	13kp	49kr
Caucasus	-			0kp	1kr	-		-		
Total	5kp	15kr	13kp	30kr	8kp	19kr	21kp	61kr	13kp	49kr

Year	1849		1850		1851		1852		1853	
Astrakhan	4kp	6kr	-		6kp	16kr	12kp	24kr	10kp	20kr
Orenburg & Siberia	22kp	68kr	28kp	81kr	20kp	56kr	20kp	58kr	24kp	70kr
Caucasus	-	-	-	-	0kp	2kr				
Total	26kp	74kr	28kp	81kr	26kp	72kr	32kp	82kr	34kp	92kr

Year	1854		1855		1856		Average total	
Astrakhan	4kp	17kr	1kp	11kr	-			
Orenburg & Siberia	22kp	64kr	24kp	65kr	15kp	34kr	21kp	59kr
Caucasus	-		-		1kp	2kr	*Total*	
Total	25kp	81kr	25kp	76kr	16kp	36kr	272kp	766kr

Appendix 14.13
Asian madder imports by place of origin

Year	Khiva	Persia	Tashkent	Bukhara	Asia Minor
1844	4kp	1kp	*details were only provided after 1852;*		
1845	10kp	3kp	*before then, the above were included in*		
1846	6kp	2kp	*'Persia & other countries'*		
1847	16kp	5kp			
1848	10kp	3kp			
1849	19kp	6kp			
1850	21kp	7kp			
1851	19kp	6kp			
1852	22kp 62kr	8kp 16kr	2kp 3kr	-	-
1853	26kp 73kr	6kp 13kr	2kp 4kr	small	2kr
	74%	18%	7%		

1854 ⎫
1855 ⎬ *only total figures available*
1856 ⎭

The above table is confirmed by 'Ministry' figures for Asian competition with the Derbent industry.

Central Asian exports to Russia in

1847	21.4kp	worth 60.8kr
1848	12.8	49.0
1849	25.9	74.3
1850	27.9	80.7

From the Central Asian entrepots of Khiva, Bukhara and Tashkent madder was exported through Orenburg and Siberia. Smaller low value amounts came through Astrakhan from Persia:

1847	0.8kp	worth 0.9kr
1849	4.2	6.5 (i.e. 1.5r a pood)

Appendix 14.14
'Various dyes' imported to Russia from Asia by origin
(meaning madder-based dyeing agents) (Ministry)

Year	Anatolia	Persia	Kirghiz steppe	Khiva	Bukhara	Tashkent	Total
1847	5.8 kr	29.5	nil	56.6	nil	2.7	94.7
1848	4.8	43.8	nil	49.1	nil	nil	97.7
1849	15.3	32.3	3.1	21.0	46.9	nil	128.6
1850	1.6	31.0	1.1	61.5	7.6	11.3	114.1
1854	5.0	81.5	nil	61.6	4.4	3.9	156.4
1857	6.8	76.4	nil	47.9	1.2	23.0	155.3
1858	4.3	94.0	0.5	25.2	3.7	11.1	138.8
1859	56.2	51.2	nil	nil	0.7	11.6	119.7
1860	21.0	89.2	1.1	0.9	37.4	23.4	167.2
1861	45.9	75.6	nil	0.9	4.8	30.0	157.3
Totals:	169.6	604.6	5.9	324.7	100.9	117.1	1,319.8

Appendix 17.1
The red Easter egg

Red Easter eggs provide one example to illustrate how folklore symbols are international. Red is by far the most popular colour for Easter eggs. Easter eggs are traditionally red in Czech lands, in Hungary and even Cumbria, where they are direct-dyed by wrapping in plants. "Oh when will Easter come," says a Macedonian children's rhyme, "bringing red eggs?" The dye for red eggs was rarely specified. However, madder has been traditionally used to dye Easter eggs red in Greece, Russia and Cyprus.[90]

Like blue in Muslim lands, red is apotropaic in Europe. One example of individual protection comes from Alsace, as long ago as 1553, Nicholas Kirchmeyer — Naogeorgus — referred to parents presenting their children with a red egg on Easter morning to give them rosy cheeks and a consequent long life. Defence on a larger scale is invoked in Scandinavian and Transylvanian legends where red Easter eggs divert the Antichrist from causing the end of the world.

Red is connected to divine love in pagan and Christian lore. In Roman times a hen laid a red egg when Alexander Severus was born, which was a sign presaging his rise to divine emperor. The idea was adapted by the Christian church. In parts of Austria, they say that while the Easter Hare produces many colours of eggs on Easter Sunday, it only lays red ones on Maundy Thursday in token of the Passion of Christ.

For revivalist Christians it is an article of faith that one can only be reborn into eternal life through the cleansing blood of the Saviour and legends from many countries represent the Blood with red eggs. In Former Yugoslavia, the Virgin Mary brings eggs, stained by the blood of Christ at the foot of the Cross, while in Russia St Mary Magdelene holds an egg which turned red as proof of the Resurrection, when an Estonian sect believed that all the stones in the world would turn red. Both the Greek Patriarch and the Russian Patriarch presented red and gold eggs representing the human and divine dual identities of Christ. Anthony Jenkinson in 1558 noted that the Russian people carried red eggs at Easter, while the upper classes had theirs gilded.

Earthly love too is signified by red Easter eggs, which inevitably leads to fertility, as evidenced by the High German: *"Himmel ist blau, die Eier sind rot, Ich will Dich leben, bis in den Tod!"* — "The Heavens are blue, The eggs they are red, And I will love thee, Until I am dead!" Romanian Easter eggs are simply called 'red eggs' with 'red' meaning 'beautiful',[91] while Tyrolean girls traditionally secured a man's love with a present of red eggs. Red eggs are also known as love apples, aphrodisiacs, leading to marriage and a family. The fertility aspect may correlate with the current ancient Persian New Year agrarian fertility festival of *Novrows* custom of staining eggs known as the 'Festival of the Red Eggs'.[92]

Notes

Foreword: The gifted eye

1. Vol 11, No. 2, 1999 edition of Oxford University Press's *Journal of the history of collections* was devoted to the importance of the overlooked C. D. E. Fortnum. Fortnum was belatedly credited to have the gifted eye behind the primary acquisitions of the Victoria and Albert Museum rather than the better-known Henry Cole and Sir Charles Robinson.
2. 'Editorial: Art and money: post-Saatchi painting', *Modern Painters*, 1989, which also referred to his earlier article in *Art Monthly*. During his unfairly short life, Peter Fuller astonishingly yet magnificently swung from Marxism through Freud to Conservatism. His most enduring voice was the journal *Modern Painters* which survives him.
3. Grossgeim, A. A., *Flora Kavkaza*, 2nd edn; *Opredelitel' rastenii Kavkaza*, 1st edn; & *Rastitel'nye resursy Kavkaza*. Grossgeim is the russification of 'Grossheim'. Back in London (on May 29th, 1992, according to my library request-slips) I found that seven volumes of his *Flora of the Caucasus* were also available in the British Library scientific branch. His shorter 661-page single volume *Plant resources of the Caucasus* was also there. It was written as part of the Soviet war effort, with an intriguing chapter on plant dyes, including khaki for military uniforms (see chapter 2 for his reds and appendix 1.1, page 306, for his other colours).
4. Archipov, I. O., *O krasiashikh veshestvakh derbentskoi mareny*.
5. Karpov, Lt, *Marena/o vozdelyvanii eia v' Derbente/v' primenenii k' Orenburgskomu krayu.*, 37pp — 'Madder, its cultivation in Derbent as applied to cultivation in the Orenburg region', (abbr 'K'); Shtorkh', P. A., *Marena, v' sel'sko-khoziaistvennom', torgovom' i krasil'nom' otnosheniiakh'*, 270pp — 'Madder, in agriculture, trade and in connection with dyestuffs', (abbr 'S').
6. Various authors, names not given, *O Prikaspiskoi maren'*, 63pp — 'The cultivation of madder in the Prikaspian or near-Caspian region', extracts from *Kavkaz' Gazet*, Nos 11, 12, 13, 14, 15, 17 &18, (abbr 'The Ministry' or 'M').
7. Kasumov M. A. O., *aftoreferat* to Azerbaijan Academy of Sciences, Botanical Institute im. V. L. Komarova, *Krasl'nye rasteniia azerbaidzhana i ikh ispol'zovanie v kovrovom proizvodstve*.
8. Petrov, V. A., *Rastitel'nye krasiteli Azerbaidzhana*.
9. Marggraf, O. V., *Ocherk kustarnykh promyslov Severnogo Kavkaza*.
10. Khashaev Kh-M, *Zaniatiia naseleniia dagestana v XIX veke*.
11. Schlumberger is a famous name in the later oil industry. Incidentally, the oil industry began in Baku in Azerbaijan in the 1870s as well as in Pennsylvania.

1. Russian dreams of the bearded root

1. Ministry.
2. Khashaev, 73.

2. The word & the plant

1. SOED, s.v. 'madder'.
2. Johnson H, World Atlas of Wine.
3. Discorides, Materia Medica 3.160.
4. 'Phenix' — Jehan le Begue in Merrifield, vi; 'phoinix' — Andrew Dalby (pers comm), see chapter 3.
5. Dioscorides idem.
6. Schaefer G, 'The Cultivation of Madder', CIBA Review 39, 1398-1406.
7. Tarrant A W S, Hutchings J, Wood J, eds, 'Colours and the names we give them', *Colour and Appearance in Folklore*, 1-6:5.
8. Diderot et D'Alembert, Encyclopedie, t.7, 478; Le Piieur d'Apligny, L'Art de la Teinture, 12.
9. Huxley A, Griffiths M R, eds, The New Royal Horticultural Society Dictionary of Gardening, v4, 140.
10. S.
11. K.
12. B, 384.
13. Rhind W, The Vegetable Kingdom, 508-11, s.v. 'madder'.
14. Buchanan R, A Weaver's Garden, 90.
15. Decaisne J, Memoires couronnes par L'Academie . . .Bruxelles, 12, 'Recherches anatomiques et physiologiques sur la garance'.
16. Cardon, 41-3; Coeurdoux R P, Memoires geographiques . . .; Roxburgh W, Plants of the Coromandel Coast.
17. Cardon, 40-1.
18. Paul Bygrave, Chelsea Physick Garden (pers comm).
19. Hooker J D, Jackson B D, Index Kewensis Plantarum Phanerogamarum.

20. Hippocrates, De morb. mul i.
21. Pliny, Natural History 26.89; 34.11, as a diuretic; Cardon, 36.
22. Dioscorides, 3.143.
23. Theophrastus, History of Plants 6.1.4, 7.9.3, 9.13.4, 9.13.6; Andrew Dalby (pers comm).
24. Gerard J, Woodward M, ann, Gerard's Herball, 1636 Th Johnson ed, 256-7; there are at least ten editions and the original covered the period 1596 to 1599.
25. Culpeper, N., Culpeper's Complete Herbal, 109, 225.
26. Hilton, A C, 'Madder, an ancient source of dye', East Anglian Magazine, 381.
27. Flachat J C, Observation sur le commerce et sur les arts . . .,t. II, 349.
28. Cardon, 38.
29. Robertson, W, 'Dye Plants in a Scottish Garden', Dye Plants and Dyeing — A Handbook, 89.
30. Davidson, A, The Oxford Companion to Food, 1999, s.v. 'colour'.
31. Perry, C, Medieval Arab Cuisine, forthcoming.
32. Cardon.
33. Schaefer, 1400.
34. S.

3. The 5,000-year-old plant

1. Koren (Kornblum) Z C, 'The Colors and Dyes on Ancient Textiles in Israel', eds Sorek C, Ayalon E, Colors from Nature / Natural Colors in Ancient Times, 15-23.
2. Brunello (abbr 'B'), 67.
3. Barber, 1991, 111.
4. Forbes, v4, 1956, 99, n142.
5. Ryder M, Sheep and Man, 97ff.
6. Walton Rogers P, Archaeology of York 17/3, 663 (abbr 'AY'); AY 17/11, 1770.
7. Betts A, Journal of Archaeological Science, 21, 489-99.
8. Mellaart J, Catal Huyuk, A Neolithic Town in Anatolia, 219.
9. Huyghe R, ed, Larousse Encyclopedia of Prehistoric and Ancient Art, London, though dated, gives a background to the various cultures.
10. B, 67.
11. Marshall J, Mohenjo-daro and the Indus Civilisation, dating v1, 102-12; textiles v1, 33, 194; v2, 585; Koren, 15; Forbes 1956, v4, 106-7.
12. Germer R, Die Textil Farberei und die vervundung gefarbte texteilen im Alte Egypte.
13. Loret V, 1930, in Kemi, 'Revue de Philologie et d'Archeologie Egyptiennes et Coptes 3, 2ff; Germer, n159.
14. Germer, 7, 9; Wouters J, Studies in Conservation 30, London, 119ff; Wouters J, Maes L, Germer R, 'The Identification of Hematite as a Red Colorant on an Egyptian Textile from the Second Millennium BC' Studies in Conservation 35, 89-92.
15. McDowell R S, Archaeological Textiles Newsletter 3, 9; Flinders Petrie W M, Kahun, Gurob and Hawara, 28.
16. Germer, 15, 18, 19.
17. Sheffer A, Rothenberg B, ed, The Egyptian Mining Temple at Timna, 224ff.
18. Germer, 18, 68-70; Eastwood G M, 'Egyptian Dyes and Colours', DHA 3, 9-15.
19. Vogelsang-Eastwood G, Pharaonic Egyptian Clothing, 138; Pfister R, 'Les Textiles du Tombeau de Toutankhamon', Revue des Arts Asiatiques XI, 207-18; 209.
20. Forbes R J, Man the Maker, 54.
21. Germer, 80; Wouters, Maes & Germer, 89-92.
22. Koren, 15.
23. Forbes, 1956, v4, 128, n146.
24. Dr Stephanie Dalley (pers comm).
25. Gelb, 247.
26. Dalley S, 'Ancient Assyrian Textiles and the Origins of Carpet Design', Iran No 29, 124, 117-35; von Soden, s.v. '*hurratu*'; Stol M, ed Ebeling E, Meissner B, Reallexikon der Assyriologie, s.v. 'kleidung'; s.v. 'leder industrie', 527-43.
27. Koren, 16.
28. Ezekiel 27:24; Koren, 15.
29. Genesis 46:13; I Chronicles 7:1; & Judges 10:1.
30. J. F., Roth C. et al, eds, Encyclopaedia Judaica, 329 (abbr 'Enc Jud').
31. Exodus 1:15.
32. Mishna, Shab. 896 and Yer.'Er. 26c; The Jewish Encyclopaedia, IX, 265.
33. Sheffer A, Tidhar A, 'Textiles and Basketry at Kuntillat 'Arjud', 'Atiqot 20, 1-26.
34. Leviticus 19:19, Deuteronomy 22:10.
35. Exodus 28:2ff, 39:2ff.
36. Genesis 37:3.
37. Sheffer, A, 'Ancient Textiles Decorated with Color from the Land of Israel', eds Sorek C, Ayalon E, Colors from Nature / Natural Colors in Ancient Times, 32,33.
38. Barber, 1994, 114.
39. Herodotus, Histories,4, 189.
40. Theophrastus, History of Plants, 6.1.4, 7.9.3, 9.13.4, 9.13.6.
41. Homer, Iliad, 4.142.
42. Homer, Odyssey, 23.201; Andrew Dalby, (pers comm), independently suggested by Barber, 1991, 232.
43. Sappho, fragment 20 Edmonds, 19 Bergk.
44. Aristophanes, Peace, 1174 with scholia.
45. Aeschylus, Agamemnon, 910, 946, 957, 959.
46. Der kleine Pauly.
47. Alciphron, Letters 3.10.4.; Dalby (pers comm).
48. B, 91.
49. Plutarch, Alexander 36; Dalby (pers comm).
50. B, 93.
51. Forbes, v4, 1956, 140.
52. Howard P, The Times 9 April, 1999.
53. B, 97-100.
54. Aristotle, school of, De Coloribus; Hett W S, ed and tr, Aristotle, Minor Works, 19; Donkin R A, Anthropos, v72, 'The Insect Dyes of Western and West-Central Asia', 847ff.
55. Dalby (pers comm); B, 385.

Notes

56. Pliny, Natural History, 26.89.
57. Midgelow G W, 'Report on the Dyes', 80; Whiting M C, Sugiura T, 'Additional Study of the Dyes'; both in Crowfoot E, 'Textiles', Lapp P W, Lapp N L, Discoveries in the Wadi ed-Daliyeh (AASOR 41), 60-77; Koren, 28.
58. Crowfoot G M, 'The Linen Textiles'; Bartelemy D, Milik J, Qumran Cave I. Discoveries in the Judean Desert I, no 3, 18-38.
59. Mishna, Kila'im 28:4.
60. Sheffer, 33; Masschelein-Kleiner, L et al, 'Analysis of Dyestuffs on textiles from 'En-Boqeq'; Sheffer A, Tidhar A, 'The textiles from the 'En-Boqeq Excavation in Israel'. Textile History 22 (1).
61. Schaefer, 1399.
62. Mishna, Shev 5:4; Enc Jud, 329.
63. Forbes, 1956, v4, 106-7, n143; Strabo XII, 8.16 cap.578.
64. Pliny, Natural History 19.47 on dyeing; tr Andrew Dalby (pers comm) correcting Schaefer, 937, 1400.
65. Ryder, 2211.
66. Andrew Dalby (pers comm).
67. B, 385; Forbes, v4, 1956, 106-7, n143; Pliny, Natural History, 7. 196.
68. Shtorkh', trying to interest 19th-century Russians in cultivation.
69. B, 102.
70. B, 95.
71. Forbes, 1958, 97.
72. B, 107.
73. Vospicus, Vita Aureliani.
74. B, 107.
75. B, 102.
76. B, 111.
77. Wild J P, Textile Manufacture in the Northern Roman Provinces, 81.
78. Gansser A, 'The Colouring of Leather', CIBA Review 81, 2954. Mommsen T, ed, Edictum Diocletiani de Pretiis Rerum Venalium.
79. Strabo XIII, 4. 14 cap.630.
80. B, 41.
81. Petrov, 37-42; the great carpet felt applique with animal combat scenes, to which Petrov presumably referred, appeared to Bunker to be from an earlier date, derived from the Pazyryk style of the fourth century BC; Bunker E, Chatwin B, Farkas A, 'Animal Style' Art, 61ff, 108.
82. Saltzman, 28.
83. B, 80.
84. Saltzman, 32.
85. Sandberg, 76-7.
86. Whitehead, 1, 2, 5, 66, 70.
87. Koren, 28; Masschelein-Kleiner, 40-41.
88. Minorsky V, A History of Sharvaan and Darband in the 10th-11th centuries, 127, 184.
89. Leix A, 'Early Islamic Textiles', CIBA Review 43, 1573-80: 1575.
90. Hamarneh, 1973.
91. Cardon, 36; Ibn Hawqal, Wiet G, tr, from 'Book of routes of the provinces', Les textiles dans le monde musulman, 340-1, 378.
92. Abu-Mansur-bin-Ali-Harawi, Achundov V tr, 'On plants'. Achundov is of course a Caucasian name, probably from Daghestan..
93. Pertz, pt2, 140-1, no23; Walton P, 'Textiles, Cordage and Raw Fibre from 16-22 Coppergate', The Archaeology of York The Small Finds.
94. Cardon, 36; Roussel P, La Garance . . ., unpubl thesis.
95. Merrifield, 175.
96. Loyn and Percival, tr, Capitulare de Villis vel Curtis Imperialibus, No 70, 3.
97. B,126.
98. Schaefer, 1400.
99. Walton Rogers P, c. 1987, AY 17/5, Table 25, 1256, 1283; 1997, AY 17/11, 1769-70.
100. Pritchard, 1983; Hall et al, 1984; Walton, 1984.
101. 'Gerefa', c. 1100, Corpus Christi College Cambridge MS 383 in Swanton M, 26, 1975; Walton, AY, 400 ('Gerefa' means 'steward' in Old English and was M R James's abbreviation for Be gesceadwisan gerefan, a description of how a competent Anglo-Saxon reeve should run his estate, Page R I, 'Gerefa some — problems of meaning', Bammesberger A, ed, Problems of Old English Lexicography, 211, Regensburg,1985; Bosworth and Toller, An Anglo-Saxon Dictionary, s.v. 'Gerefa', Oxford, 1964; James M R, A descriptive catalogue . . . in the library of Corpus Christi . . ., 231, where Liebermann dates it 1125-30; ack Gill Cannell (pers comm).
102. Walton 1984, 30.
103. Carus-Wilson, 1954, 218; Book of Brother Stephen of St Augustine's Canterbury, c. 1300, Corpus Christi College Cambridge MS 301, f.75v; ack Gill Cannell (pers comm)..
104. Not 'BC' as Brunello misread it; B, 14.
105. Scammell, G V, 1981, The world encompassed . . .c. 800-1650, Map, 2ff.
106. Forbes, 1958, 97.
107. Scammell, 1981; 1995, 'European seamanship in the great age of discovery', Ships, oceans and empire . . . 1400-1750, IV, 357-76.
108. Wescher H, 'Indian Cotton Prints in the Middle Ages', CIBA Review 64, 2359-60.
109. Wouters J, 'Dye Analysis of Chinese and Indian Textiles', DHA 12, 12-22:12-13.
110. Goitein S D, A Mediterranean Society, v1, 344 — his monumental translation of the manuscripts of the Cairo Geniza, 'a room for discarded writings', where Jews deposited now-fascinating ephemera, from the tenth to thirteenth centuries, in the belief that writings on which the name of God might be found should be 'buried' and not thrown away.
111. Cardon, 43; Pfister R, 'Materiaux pour servir a l'etude des textiles egyptiens posterieurs a la conquete arabe', Revue des Arts asiatiques, X.
112. Wescher, 2359.
113. Cardon, 36; Varthema L, Schefer C, ed, Le viateur en la plus grande partie de l'Orient.
114. Inalcik H., with Quataert D, 1994, An Economic and Social History of the Ottoman Empire, 1300-1914, 38.

115. Inalcik, 1973, The Ottoman Empire, 125.
116. Forbes, 1958, 112, 115.
117. B, 189.
118. Amram, D, The Makers of Hebrew Books in Italy, 38; Heller M J, Printing the Talmud.
119. Schetky, 6; Mazzino E et al, Il Centro Storico di Genova, 21.
120. B, 165.
121. Schaefer.
122. Thirsk J, Alternative Agriculture, A History from the Black Death to the Present Day, 104, n1.
123. De Poerck G, La Draperie Medievale en Flandre et en Artois, 174-9; ack. Penelope Walton Rogers; de Nie W L J, De ontwikkeling der noord nederlandsche textiel ververij . . .14th-18thc, 128-37; Espinas G, La draperie dans la Flandre francaise au moyen age, Paris; Espinas G, 'Documents rel. draperies de Valenciennes en moyen age', Soc d'Hist du droit des pays Flammands, Picards et Wallons, Docs et Trav no.1.
124. Miller Philip, The Method of Cultivating Madder, As it is now practised by the Dutch in Zealand: (Where the best Madder is produced), vi.
125. B,140; cf Persian regulations c. 1900 chapter 16.
126. Wescher H, 'Development of the Fairs of Champagne', CIBA Review 65, 2368-78: 2375, 2384.
127. Schetky, 7.
128. B, 152.
129. Lerner F, 'Textiles and Dyestuffs at the Frankfurt Fairs — The Dyestuffs Trade', CIBA Review 103, 3713-5: 3715.
130. B, 172.
131. Entwisle E A, The Book of Wallpaper, 30.
132. Schaefer, 1400-1.
133. Hilton, 379-81; Wells H, The Maddermarket Theatre, Norwich; Thirsk, 104; Slicher van Bath B H, The Agrarian History of Western Europe, 272; Campbell B M S, 'Agricultural progress in medieval England: Some evidence from eastern Norfolk', EcHR 2nd ser. 31/1, 26-46: 41.
134. Inalcik, 1994, 365.
136. Thirsk, 104-5; Brewer J S ed, Letters and Papers . . . Henry VIII, iv.1.125; Tawney R H, Power E eds, Tudor Economic Documents, i.329; Hulme E W, 'The history of the patent system . . .', Law Quarterly Review, 46: 141-54, 61: 44-56, 45; Allen D E, 'A probable 16th-century record of Rubia tinctorun', Watsonia 14, 178.
137. Inalcik, 1994, 370.
138. Inalcik, 1973, 138.
139. Gerard J, 1633 ed, The Herball, London; Schaefer.
140. Assisa de Tolloneis, Acts Parl. Scot. Vol 1.
141. Willan 1976, 15; Walton, 401.

4. The venturer's legacy

1. Inalcik, 1994, 351.
2. Inalcik, 1973, 137.
3. Cardon, 36.
4. Flachat, tII, 351.
5. Flachat, tII, 353.
6. Juvet-Michel, 1091.
7. Brunello, 203-204.
8. Brunello, 222.
9. Brunello, 230.
10. Cardon, 37.
11. Schaefer, 1401-2.
12. Duhamel du Monceau H L, Elements d'Agriculture.
13. Thirsk, 116; Anon,under Miller's influence, Impartial Considerations on the Cultivation of Madder in England, pamphlet bound in a volume of Acts of Parliament in 1865, BL 213.i.4(100).
14. Shaefer, 1412ff.
15. 'Frauzen' according to Cardon, 36.
16. Schaefer, 1402.
17. Juvet-Michel A, 'Oberkampf', CIBA Review 31, 1103-5; Elliott D, Ryan J, eds, Art into Production, 50, 52.
18. Brunello, 261-2.
19. Thirsk, 105; Rymer T, ed Holmes G, Foedera . . ., vol xvii 410-15; ack Jervoise of Herriard Collection, Sherfield MSS, 44M69, L33, 24; PRO SP 16, 44, no 1.
20. Thirsk, 108; Sherfield, 15; 111, CSPD 1625-49: Addenda, 442.
21. Thirsk, 111; Sherfield, 25, 26, 32.
22. Thirsk, 112; Harley, 140-1; PRO C.66/2338/20 on patent rights, SP.16/315/141 and SP.16/321/19 on the Dutchman's offer, SP.16/323/54 on land for madder, C.66/2749/2 on indenture.
23. Walton Rogers P, A Textile Lining in a Civil War Helmet, unpubl.
24. Thirsk, 112-3.
25. Brunello, 273.
26. Thirsk, 113; Woodcroft B, Alphabetical Index of Patentees of Inventions, 1617-1852, 526; PRO E134 idem.
27. Steensgaard N, Carracks, Caravans and Companies, 186-7.
28. Thirsk, 106, 114; VCH, Glos., viii.204; Miller, 1758, 21; Houghton J, ed Bradley R, A Collection of Letters for the Improvement of Husbandry and Trade, vol ii.372.
29. Thirsk, 114; Anon, 1765, 30; van der Poel J M G, Ceres en Clio, 165, thanks to Joan Thirsk.
30. Hudson D, Luckhurst K W, The Royal Society of Arts, 1754-1954, 89-90.
31. Miller, 1758, vi-ix.
32. c. 800BC in Barber E W, 1994, Women's Work: The First 20,000 years, 19; and 1200 to 400BC in Barber E W, 1999, The Mummies of Urumchi, Figs 21 & 22, 144-5.
33. Henshall A S, 'Early Textiles found in Scotland', Proc of Soc Scottish Antiquaries, vol lxxxvi, 1-29:8.

35. Errera, I., *Collection d'Anciennes Etoffes Egyptiennes*, 192-3, Nos 447-51, 10th-12th century Egyptian; Rogers, C. (ed), *Early Islamic textiles*, Granger-Taylor, H., 38-9, pl VIII, blue cotton; idem, Eastwood, G., 40-1, Fig 27, 'Quseir al-Qadim', 14th-15th century, possibly imported.
36. David Caldwell (pers comm); Eaves I, 'On the remains of a Jack . . .', Journal of The Arms and Armour Society, vol xiii, no 2, 81-154: 135-6, 151, pl cxxiii; Gabra-Sanders T, 'A piece of a Jack . . .', Journal of The Arms and Armour Society, vol xiv, no 3, 147-152.
37. Wedderburn D, 'Wedderburn's Compt Book 1587-1630' and 'Shipping Lists of Dundee 1580-1618', Publ Scot Hist Soc v XXVIII.
38. Grierson, 6-7.
39. Francis Shaw,1980.
40. Grierson, 22.
41. idem, 8, 14.
42. idem, 18, 19, 76.
43. Cardon, 41.
44. O'Brien C, The British Manufacturers Companion and Calico Printers Assistant.
45. Brunello, 252.
46. McNair A, 'Perspective', The Herald, December 21, 1998, 13.
47. Irwin J, The Kashmir Shawl.
48. Schaefer, 1415ff.
49. Rankin K, The Identification of Colouring Matters in Paisley Shawls, Paisley College of Technology, unpubl thesis; Grierson, 15-17.
50. Walton Rogers P, Taylor G, Orientations, April 1997, 83.
51. Schaefer,1401.
52. Brunello, 247.
53. Schaefer, 1416; Sandberg, 143-62.
54. Brunello, 245.
55. Schaefer, 1403.
56. idem, 1401.
57. Ellis Asa Jr, The Country Dyer's Assistant; Adrosko R J, Natural Dyes and Home Dyeing, 8.
58. Adrosko, 21; Betts E M, ann, Thomas Jefferson's Garden Book 1766-1824, 433, 447, 450-2.
59. Lynde, 8 in Adrosko, 8.
60. Bishop, vol 2, 241, 1866, in Adrosko,23.
61. Brunello, 264.
62. Brunello, 270.
63. M.
64. Schaefer, 1411.
65. M.
66. M.
67. Chenciner R. B., *Kaitag Textile Art of Daghestan*.
68. Sherfield, 19.
69. Thirsk, 116; Jacob E., *The History of the Town and Port of Faversham in . . . Kent*, pp 97-100, 1774.
70. Khashaev, 77; from Nakhshunov I R, dissertation, 1954.
71. Kasaba R, The Ottoman Empire and The World Economy, The 19th century, 67, 84, 88, 90, 125, 149.

72. Inalcik, 1994, 908.
73. Kasaba, 84.
74. idem, 88.
75. Fairlie, 497, 1964; Urquart, 176, 1833; Lilley, 243, 1978; referred to in Kasaba, 90.
76. Kieffer L, Saisons d'Alsace, 51, 8-30 on the Alsace madder industry.
77. Schaefer, 1403.
78. Nicholson H, King George the Fifth, His Life and Reign, 51.
79. Brunello, 269.
80. Schaefer, 1403.
81. 1.6 million francs = about 108,000 poods for 0.4 million silver roubles; 12.1mF = about 757,000 poods for 3.0 million silver roubles.
82. Wiskerke C, 'De geschiedenis van het meekrapbedrijf in Nederland', Economisch-historisch Jaarboek XXV, 29-30, thanks to Joan Thirsk.
83. 25,000 kantars; 1 kantar = 5.5 poods; at 69 to 85 francs a kantar.
84. Peel R, 'Turkey red dyeing in Scotland: its heyday and decline', *JDSC*, vol 68, No 12.
85. Grierson, pp 32-3.
86. Schaefer, pp 1403-4.

5. *The care of madder from seed to sack*

1. De Poerck, pp 176-7; Bezemer, De Blecourt, 'Rechtsbronnen van Zierikzee . . .', Verken der vereeniging . . . vaderlandsche recht, reeks 2. no 9, p369.
2. Priester P, A. A. G. 37, Geschiedenis van de Zeeuwse Landbouw circa 1600-1910, madder 323-77, weights and measures 423-9, appendix 625-32.
3. Anon, 1765.
4. Ministry (abbr 'M').
5. Shtorkh' (abbr 'S').
6. M.
7. Schaefer, pp 1398-9.
8. Flachat, tII, p341.
9. Schaefer, p1400.
10. ibid., p1403.
11. S.
12. Karpov (abbr 'K').
13. Thirsk, p113.
14. M.
15. K.
16. M.
17. S.
18. Schaefer, p1403.
19. S.
20. Miller, 1758, p36.
21. M.
22. S.
23. Miller, p34; Schaefer, p1400.
24. idem, p6.
25. Thirsk, p110.
26. Sherfield, p19.

27. Anon, 1765.
28. Priester, 342.
29. M.
30. Buchanan, 88-92.
31. M.
32. S.
33. Miller, 4.
34. M.
35. K.
36. Schaefer, 1402.
37. ibid., 1400; Miller, 5.
38. Thirsk, 107.
39. Lidbeck G, MS at the Vetenskap Akademie; Sandberg, 80.
40. Hilton, 381.
41. 1 arshin = 71cm.
42. M.
43. K.
44. S.
45. M.
46. Hilton, 381.
47. M.
48. Miller, 6.
49. K.
50. M.
51. M.
52. M.
53. K.
54. Schaefer, 1399.
55. Miller, 28.
56. S.
57. K.
58. M.
59. S.
60. Harald Böhmer (pers comm).
61. Thirsk, 110; Sherfield, 19.
62. Burnett and Thomson, 2437-41; Cardon, 34.
63. Flachat, tII, 339.
64. K.
65. confirmed by Cardon.
66. Wulff, 190.
67. Schaefer, 1404.
68. Schaefer, 1399.
69. Hilton, 381.
70. S.
71. Miller, 8, 29.
72. Rhind, 509.
73. M.
74. 1000-3000 lbs or 31 — 93 poods per gemet = '300 sq rods of 12 ft' = 4,800 sq yds = approx 4,100 sq m and 500-1000 lbs from light soil; Miller, 4.
75. Hilton, 381.
76. Thirsk, 115-6.
77. 1 arpent = 48,000 sqft = approximately ½ hectare produced a top 8,000 lbs = 248poods.
78. Schaefer, 1402.
79. S.
80. Schaefer, 1399.
81. S.
82. Schaefer, 1402.
83. K.

6. *The farmer's rewards, banks & bankruptcy*

1. Thirsk, 253.
2. Joan Thirsk (pers comm).
3. Schaefer, 1401.
4. Thirsk, 107; Sherfield, 10.
5. Thirsk, 113; PRO E134, 31 & 32 Chas. II, Hil. 6.
6. Dan Harman (pers comm).
7. Thirsk, 106.

7. *The purer the colour: ground krap & garancine*

1. Schaefer, 1399.
2. Miller, 9.
3. K.
4. M.
5. S.
6. Thirsk, 109.
7. De Kanter J, De meerkrapteler; Priester, 350, A 5.7.
8. Flachat, tII, 341.
9. Boerendonck J, Historische Studie over de Zeeuwschen Landbouw, 103; Bezemer and De Blecourt, 316; De Poerck, 177.
10. De Poerck, 177.
11. Thirsk, 116; Chassagne S, Oberkampf, un Entrepreneur capitaliste au Siecle des Lumieres, 119-120.
12. Miller, 31-33.
13. Flachat, tII, 352.
14. Schaefer, 1402, 1406; Bancroft E, Experimental Researches concerning the Philosophy of permenant Colours.
15. Grunskaya-Petrova I P, 'Rubinovyi tsvet narodnymi metodami', AzFAN No4.
16. De Poerck, 177-8.
17. ibid., 178.
18. Flachat, tII, 345, 348-9.
19. Rhind, 510-1; Cardon, 37; Dambourney L A, Recueil de procedes et d'experiences . . ..
20. Schaefer, 1405.
21. Wulff, 190.
22. S.
23. Schaefer, 1406.
24. Robiquet, Colin, 'Memoire de Ms Robiquet et Colin sur la question 'Separer la matière colorante de garance'', *Bulletin de la Société industrielle de Mulhouse*, 126-45.
25. Schweppe, 121.
26. Priester, 632.
27. Schlumberger H, 'Uber die Krappblumen . . .', *Dingler's Polytechnisches Journal*, 126, 206-10.
28. Schweppe, 122; Schaffer, G., 'Krappextrakt Pernod', *Bulletin de la Société industriele de Mulhouse*, 33, 307; Schultz G, Farbstofftabellen, 7th edn, 1:498-500, 510-12, 638-9, 2:7.

8. Inside the vat

1. Schaefer, 1399.
2. Belcher J, 'Of the bones of Animals Changed to a Red Colour by Aliment only'; 'K', CIBA Review, 947.
3. Hummel J J, Knecht E, Encl Brit, v XVII, 280, s.v. 'madder'.
4. 'W N', CIBA Review, 1315.
5. Schaefer, 1398.
6. Grierson, 194-5.
7. Schaefer, 1406.
8. S.
9. Schweppe, 121-2.

9. Almond husks, brick dust & 'super-fine-fine'

1. S.
2. De Poerck, 178-9.
3. Thirsk, 111.
4. De Poerck, 182, 186.
5. Pubetz A, 'Krap und Krapplack', Praktisches Handbuch . . ., 298-321; Schweppe, 123-4; Adrosko, 23.
6. Gage J, George Field and his Circle . . ., 28.
7. Anon, A Compendium of Colours, 221.
8. Browne Sir T, Hydriotaphia, Urn Burial, 141; Robert Irwin (pers comm).
9. Gillian Vogelsang-Eastwood (pers comm).
10. Sanderson J ed Foster W, The Travels of John Sanderson in the Levant 1584-1602, Hakluyt Society, 44-49; ack Harley, 152-3 on 'mummy'.
11. Dal' V, Tolkovyi Slovar', t2, 938.
12. Schaefer, 1404.
13. De Poerck, 179.
14. Harley's term, Harley, 140.
15. Miller, 10.
16. Kirby J, White R, 'The Identification of Red Lake Pigment Dyestuffs', National Gallery Technical Bulletin, v 17, 65 (abbr 'Kirby').
17. Miller.
18. Shtorkh; Schaefer, 1405.
19. Grierson, 194.
20. Priester, 340.
21. Schaefer, 1406.
22. Cardon, 34.
23. idem.
24. Schaefer, 1406.
25. Hilton, 380.

10. Leonardo's choice madder lakes

1. Fairbairn L et al, Paint and Painting, 78.
2. Foster G V, Moran P J, 'Plants, Paints, and Pottery: Identification of madder pigment on Cypriot ceramicware', Archaeometry, Proceedings of the 25th International Symposium.
3. Higgins R A, 'The Polychrome Decoration of Greek Terracottas', Studies in Conservation, 15 (1970), 272-7.
4. Vitruvius 7, XIV, 1 and 2.
5. Wallert A, 'Unusual pigments on a Greek marble basin', Studies in Conservation, 40, 3 (1995), 177-88.
6. Farnsworth M, 'Second-century BC rose madder from Corinth and Athens', American Journal of Archaeaology, 55, 236-239.
7. Schweppe H, Winter J, West-Fitzhugh E ed, A Handbook of Artists' Pigments, 109-135 (abbr 'Schweppe').
8. Russell W T, 'Egyptian Colours', in Flinders Petrie W M, Medum, 44-48.
9. Walker S, Bierbrier M, Ancient Faces, 97; Andrew Middleton, (pers comm).
10. Davy H, 'Some Experiments and Observations on the Colours Used in Paintings by the Ancients', Philosophical Transactions 105, 97-124; Schweppe, 111.
11. Gotting H, Kuhn H, 'Die sogenante . . .Theophanu', Archivalische Zeitschrift 64, 19-22; Roosen-Runge H, 'Artikel:Farbe . . .', Reallexikon zur deutschen Kunst, 6, 1463-92; Schweppe, 111.
12. SOED, s.v. 'rubric'.
13. Radosavijevic V, 'The Technique of Old Writing and Miniatures', Conservation and Restoration of Pictorial Art, 202-6; Schweppe, 112.
14. Yu Feian, tr Silbergeld J, McNair A, Chinese Painting Colors . . .; Feller R L, Curran M, Bailie C, 'Identification of Traditional Organic Colorants Employed in Japanese Prints . . .', Keyes R S, Japanese Woodblock Prints . . ., 253-66.
15. Phillips T, 'Mappae Clavicula — A treatise on the Preparation of Pigments . . .', Archaeologia 32, 183-244; Smith C S, Hawthorne J G, 'Mappae Clavicula . . .', Transactions of the American Philosophical Society, NS 64, pt 4; Schweppe, 109-135.
16. Merrifield, 34.
17. Merrifield, 248.
18. Vitruvius, lib vii, cap xiv; Merrifield, 250; Cardon, 36.
19. Roosen-Runge H, Farbgebung . . . Studien . . . Mappae Clavicula und Heraclius.
20. Brannt W T, Varnishes, Lacquers, Printing Inks, and Sealing waxes . . ., 268.
21. Schweppe, 111-2.
22. Birch W D G, British Catalogue of Seals; Alan Alston (pers comm).
23. Plictho; Merrifield, cxxxii.
24. Merrifield, cxxxvi.
25. Kirby, 56.
26. ibid., 66.
27. ibid., 67.
28. Merrifield, v II, 432-5, 456-7.
29. Kirby, 67; The Nurnberger Kunstbuch, Nurn Statsb, MS cent VI, 89; Ploss E E, Ein buch von alten Farben . . ., 113-4; Braekman W L, ed, Middelnederlandse verfrecepten.; SCRIPTA Medieval and Renaissance Texts

and Studies, Vol 18: text I, MS 517, Wellcome Hist Med Libr, no 45, 46-7; text II, T' Bouck van Wondre, no 9, 66 (on dyeing vlocken); Instruction generale pour la teinture des laines, 24-5, 31, 73; de La Hyre P, Memoires de l'Academie Royal des Sciences depuis 1666-1669, IX, 637-730: 670.

30. Kirby, 64.
31. Merrifield; Eraclius, 249, 251.
32. ibid., 34.
33. Merret C, The Art of Glass, tr and addition to Neri Antonio, L'Arte Vetraria, lib v11, cap 118.
34. Stowe MS 680, f135v; Harley, Artists' Pigments 1600-1835, 4, 2nd ed, 1982.
35. Sloane MS 5250, ff80v, 81; Harley, 1982, 9, opp 130.
36. de Massoul C, A treatise on the Art of Painting, 208; Harley, 1982, 141.
37. Hoofnail J, New Practical Improvements . . . (upon) Robert Boyle, . . . Tinctures and Pigments; Harley, 1982, 141.
38. Kitab al-Ifada wa'Itbar fi'l-Umur al-Mashad; Robert Irwin (pers comm).
39. Chenciner R, 'The millennium dome and other satirical tubbies from two centuries ago', unpubl Proceedings Oxford Food Symposium.
40. Field G, MSS, 1804-1854, 11 notebooks, called 'Practical Journals'; photocopy Courtauld Institute of Art, London, originals Winsor & Newton archive, Harrow; Practical Journal 5, 549.
41. The Gentleman's Magazine, new series xlii, 524-5; Harley, 1982, 143.
42. Gage, 7-8.
43. Field, Practical Journal 3, experiment 107, ack Courtauld Institute.
44. Gage, 8.
45. Kirby, 69.
46. Townsend J H, 'The Materials of J M W Turner: pigments', Studies in Conservation 38, 231-54.
47. Fairbairn, 28-30; Harley, 1970, 128 .
48. From 1804 Transactions of the Society of Arts; Annals of the Fine Arts, vol II, Art VIII, 199-200.
49. Wagner H, Die Korperfarben, 2nd ed, 340, 408.
50. Pubetz; Tauber E, 'Uber Krapplack und Alizarinlacke', Chemiker-Zeitung 33, 1345.
51. Cohn G, 'Farbestoffe, naturliche', Ullmanns Encyl . . .Chemie 5, 2nd ed, 135-7.
52. Wagner, idem.
53. Murometsov A K, Ivanova M, 'Preparation of Pink Alizarin Lakes', Chemical Abstracts 35, 2344.
54. Kuhn H, 'Naturwissenschaftliche Unter-suchung von Leonardos 'Abendmahl . . .', Maltechnik/ Restauro 4, 24-51:25, 40-1, 44-5.
55. Schweppe; Kirby, 56-80.
56. Kirby, 57, 67.
57. Pers comm Peter Beech; Letter from Perkins Bacon to the Brazilian government, dated July 5th, 1844, which followed a letter to specify the ingredients to the ink-makers from Perkins Bacon; De Worms, P., *Perkins Bacon Records*, vol 2, London, 1953, 573; pers comm Harry Dagnall.

11. The secret recipes of Turkey red

1. Cardon, 36.
2. Su Grierson (pers comm).
3. Adrosko, 4.
4. Taylor G W, 'Reds and purples: from the classical world to pre-Conquest Britain' in Walton P, Wild J P, Textiles in Northern Archaeology.
5. Faber, 289.
6. Wulff H E, The Traditional Crafts of Persia, 190.
7. Taylor G W, 1991.
8. Rogerson and Dallas, 167, 1984.
9. Walton Rogers P, unpubl.
10. idem.
11. Walton Rogers P, 1997, 1769-70.
12. Sylvester D, Mills J, King D, The Eastern Carpet in the Western World, 12.
13. Raby J, 'Court and Export: Market Demands in Ottoman Carpets 1450-1550', Oriental Carpet and Textile Studies, 2, 29-38.
14. Merrifield, cxv.
15. De Poerck, 174-86.
16. ibid., 174.
17. Brunello, 179.
18. Driessen, 1740.
19. Reininger, 963.
20. Brunello, 189.
21. Burani G, Giornale Solario; Venetian State Archives, Registro Leona, f22; Brunello, 165.
22. Brunello, 189.
23. St Clare Byrne M, ed, The Lisle Letters.
24. Haklyut R, Taylor E R G, ed, 1935/I, 137-9, The Original Writings and Correspondence of the Two Richard Hakluyts (Hakluyt Society, 2nd Series, 76,77), in Donkin; also in The Principal Navigations, Voyages and Discourses of the English Nation, 202, in Wulff, 193.
25. Ramsay G D, The English Woollen Industry, 1500-1750, 62.
26. Anderson S, An English Consul in Turkey, 153.
27. In Victoria & Albert Museum stores, approx., 6in x 4in; North Papers, Bodley; National Register of Archives 242 -1198.
28. Stoianovich, 1974, 82; Grenville H, Observations sur l'etat actuelle de l'Empire Ottoman, 62; ANAE, BIII, MS, Rapport de Mantaran sur le Commerce du Levant, 10; Leix A, 'Trade Routes of the Middle Ages', CIBA Review 10, 316.
29. Davis R, Aleppo and Devonshire Square, 100-2.
30. Yule H, Burnell A C, Hobson-Jobson, The Anglo-Indian Dictionary, s.v. 'chintz', 201-2 (abbr 'Hobson-Jobson').

31. Gittinger, 31ff; Fig 21,40.
32. Sandberg, 129, who omitted to mention that it was first called 'callaca' in 1578 in Draper's Dictionary, 42, and 'calecut' by Francis Drake in 1579, World Encompassed, Hakluyt Soc, 139, who confused it with the chief port of Malabar — Hobson-Jobson, s.v. 'calico', 147-8.
33. Irwin J and Brett K B, Origins of Chintz; Taylor G W, 1993, 'Red Dyes on Indian Painted and Printed Cotton Textiles', DHA 12.
34. Skelton R, The Indian Heritage. Court Life and Arts under Mughal Rule.
35. Penelope Walton Rogers (pers comm).
36. Naqvi H K, 'Dyeing of cotton goods in the Mughal Hindustan (1556-1803)', Journal of Indian Textile History VII, 47; Gittinger, 20.
37. Sandberg, 123-8: 129.
38. Baker G P, Calico Painting and Printing . . ., 33; Gittinger, 180.
39. ack Sandberg, 135.
40. ibid., 138.
41. ibid., 138 no sources given, but likely to be true.
42. Hobson-Jobson, s.v. 'piece-goods', 705-9.
43. Brunello, 243.
44. Driessen L A, 'Calico Printing and Cotton Industry in Holland', CIBA Review 48, 1748-54: 1749.
45. Juvet-Michel A, 'The Controversy over Indian Prints', CIBA Review 31, 1091.
46. Sandberg, 102.
47. Cardon, 35.
48. Le Pileur d'Apligny, 'Memoire Contenant le procede de la teinture du coton rouge-incarnat d'Adrianople sur le coton file',Treatise.
49. Le Pileur d'Apligny, 1776, 48.
50. ibid., 57.
51. ibid., 12, 20-22ff, 44, 144.
52. Diderot et D'Alembert, Encyclopedie, 1757, s.v. 'Garance', t. 7, 478-9; 1765, s.v. 'Teinture', t. 16, 8-33: 21; 1772, Planches, t.10, engravings of Gobelins wool and silk dyeing processes, ack Alain Chenciner (pers comm).
53. Schaefer, 1412ff.
54. Flachat, tII, 357.
55. ibid., 405-45; 338-352; 437-440.
56. Pallas S P, St Petersburgisches Journal 1777, vol 1, 18-29, ack Petrov; Sandberg, 105 referred to 'a written document published in Goteburg in 1781'.
57. Brunello, 247.
58. Juvet-Michel, 1113.
59. Lavoisier et al,Journ de Phis, XI, 526; Brunello, 232; Flachat, tII, 405-15.
60. Cardon, 36.
61. idem.
62. Sandberg, 108; Packer Th, trn, Handbok for Fargare.
63. Juvet-Michel, 1113.
64. Grierson, 196.
65. Luetkens C, 'Manchester — Cotton's Rise', CIBA Review 1962/2, 25-33: 31.
66. Schaefer, 1412ff.
67. Home F, Experiments of Bleaching.
68. Higgins S H, A History of Bleaching; Black J, Experiments upon Magnesium, etc.
69. Berthollet C L, 'Description du Blanchement des toiles et des fils avec l'acide muriatique oxigene', Annales de Chimie; Brunello, 258-9.
70. Forbes, 1958, 213.
71. Flachat, t II, 437-440.
72. Cardon, 35.
73. Grierson, 32.
74. Schaefer, 1416.
75. Sandberg, 105.
76. Driessen L A, 'How to Print Batik Imitations', CIBA Review 58, 2125-6.
77. Rauch J, [Recipe Letters], 34.
78. Adrosko, 23.
79. Rogerson B, A Traveller's History of North Africa, 256-83.
80. Bibl Nat, MSS, FF 6429, Paris, 'Memoire sur Tunis, avec corrections et notes' fol 33-61; Stoianovich, 100.
81. Barnaby Rogerson (pers comm).
82. Schweppe, 121.
83. Fairclough and Leary, 34.
84. Latour A, 'Glove Manufacture', CIBA Review 61, 2227-35: 2234.
85. Haller, 1420.
86. Crum W, 'On the Manner in which Cotton unites with Colouring Matter', Journal of the Chemical Society of London.
87. Barber, 1994, 113.

12. An Oriental tradition

1. Forbes, 1958, 54.
2. Warren P, 'A Textile Town — 4500 Years Ago', Illustrated London News 252, 25-7; Warren P, Myrtos: An Early Bronze Age Settlement in Crete, 262-3; Barber, 1991, 239.
3. Horn P, 'Textiles in biblical times — Dyeing', CIBA Review 1968/2, 17-23: 21, Fig 16.
4. Barber, 1991, 238.
5. Albright-Kelso, AASOR 21-22, 53a; Negev A, ed, Archaeological Enc of the Holy Land.
6. Robinson S, A History of Dyed Textiles; The Jewish Enc, I, 23,24.
7. Mishna Yer. B. K. 10:7c.
8. The Jewish Enc, I, 24.
9. Gelb ed, s.v. 'birmu'.
10. Stephanie Dalley (pers comm).
11. Barber, 1999, 28 Cherchen man; 62 carbon dating.
12. Schaefer G, 'Die fruhesten Zeugdruke', CIBA Review 24, 854-61; Carter T F, The Invention of Printing in China, 2nd ed, 193-7; Forbes, v4, 137.
13. Barber, 1991, 207; Gertsiger, pl 24, [1972] 1975.
14. Pliny, Natural History, 24.94.
15. Dioscorides, 3.143.
16. Cardon, 36.
17. Flinders Petrie W, Anthribis, 11; Forbes, v4, 130, n146.

18. Egyptian Gazette, April 23, 1935; Forbes, v4, 136, n147.
19. Forbes, v4, 141, n148.
20. Virgil, Eclogues, 4.42-5.
21. Faber G A, CIBA Review 9, 311.
22. Ryder, 164; Pliny, Natural History, 8.197; Forbes, v4, 133, n146.
23. Forbes, v4, 138.
24. Sandberg, 83.
25. Cardon, 37; Schweppe H, 'Identification of Dyes on Old Textiles', J.A.I.C., 19, 17.
26. Berlin pap 8316; Erman A, Krebs F, Aus den Papyri der Kgl Mus Berlin, 255; Forbes, v4, 133.
27. Berlin pap 'S.B.' 8013; Forbes, v4, 139, n147.
28. Reinking K, 'Ueber die alteste Beschreibung der Kupenfarberei im Papyrus Graecus Holmiensis', Mell Textilber No 5, 349-51; 'Ueber die Farberei mit Krapp in Altertum', Mell Textilber No 20, 445-8; Forbes, v4, 136, n147.
29. Dr Esra Kahn (pers comm).
30. Baron S W, A Social and Religious History of the Jews, II, 249, 261.
31. Xenophon, Cyropaedia, 245; Forbes, v4, 139, n147.
32. Talmud, Men. 42b.
33. Talmud, Kelim 16:6.
34. Talmud, Tosef. Shab. 9 (10):19.
35. Mishna, Yer. Shab 3b.
36. The Jewish Enc, 24.
37. Enc Jud, 327.
38. Schaefer G, 'The History of Turkey red Dyeing', CIBA Review 39; Leix, 321.
39. Wulff, 193-4.
40. Drake S, Coleing L, Allgrove J, The Qashqaa'i of Iran, 54.
41. Wulff, 190.
42. Harris in Hawley W A, Oriental Rugs, Antique and Modern, 40-41; Wulff, 192.
43. Enc Jud, 330.
44. Enc Jud, 328.
45. Rubens A, A History of Jewish Costume, 23-4; Baron, IV, 167.
46. Goitein, v1, 92.
47. Baron, IV, 166.
48. Goitein, 50.
49. Wischnitzer M, A History of Jewish Crafts and Guilds, 65.
50. Goitein, 107.
51. Baron, IV, 168.
52. Baron, IV, 163, 168.
53. Baron, IV, 113.
54. Goitein, 106.
55. Talbot Rice D, Islamic Art, 158.
56. Various authors, Cahiers des Arts et Techniques d'Afrique du Nord, no 5, 112 (abbr 'Cahiers').
57. Galotti J, 'Weaving and Dyeing in North Africa', CIBA Review 21, 738-60:740, 756.
58. Cahiers, 113.
59. ibid., 114.
60. ibid., 118-9.
61. ibid. 121-5.
62. ibid., 129-132. Barnaby Rogerson (pers comm).
63. The Jewish Enc, 24; Enc Jud, 328.
64. Al-Jahiz, Al-Tabassur fi'l-Tigara; quoted by Serjeant in Islamic Textiles XV-XVI, 35,70; quoted by Goitein, 416.
65. Baron, IV, 166.
66. Wischnitzer, 63, 79, 86, 96.
67. Bennett I, ed, Rugs and Carpets of the World, 17, 265.
68. Schaefer, 1401ff; Faroqhi S, Towns and townsmen of Ottoman Anatolia, Trade, crafts and food production in an urban setting, 1520-1650, dyes, 145-153: 152.
69. Godfrey Goodwin (pers comm).
70. Curuk C, Cicekciler E, Ornekleriyle Turk Cadirlari; cover, Topkapi Sarayi Museum Library, A3593; Atil E, thesis, SOAS Library London; Tim Stanley (pers comm).
71. Inalcik, 1994, 57.
72. Inalcik, 1994, 352.
73. Enc Jud, 330.
74. Chenciner R B, Kaitag — Textile Art from Daghestan, 20, 128-142; Salmanov E, Chenciner R B, Architecture of Baku, 24-5; Mamed-Zade K M, Stroitel'noe iskusstvo Azerbaidzhana, 229.
75. Dal' V, v2, 938.
76. Chenciner R B, 'Textiles & Architecture in Dagestan', Mimar 34, 70-7: 75.
77. Magomedkhan Magomedkhanov (pers comm).
78. Chenciner, 1997, 18, 175.
79. Marggraf, Ch 5,127-132, XXI-XXV.
80. Magomedkhan Magomedkhanov (pers comm).
81. Krauze I, 'Zametki o krasil'nom iskusstve tuzemtsev; Oglobin V A, 'Dyeing Crafts in the Central Asian Protectorates', giving traditional dye recipes in Appendix I; Wouters J, 1997, 'Appendix II — Dye analysis of 19th-century *ikats* from Central Asia', in FitzGibbon and Hale, 361; analysis table, 350.
82. Chenciner R B, Magomedkhanov M, 'Persian exports to Russia . . .', Iran XXX, 123-131.
83. Errera L, The Russian Jews, 177.
84. Enc Jud, 328.
85. The Jewish Enc, 24; Wolff Dr, Narrative of the Mission of Dr Wolff to Bukhara, v.ii, 3; von Schwarz F, Turkestan, die Wiege der Indogermanische Volker, 441.
86. K.
87. S.
88. Nichols J, 'Linguistic Diversity and the First Settlement of the New World', Language vol 66, no 3, (1990), 475-521.
89. Fester G A, 'Los colorantes del Antigua Peru', Archeion 22, 229-41, Archeion 23, 195-6; Saltzman, 39; Brunello, 80.
90. Buhler A, 'Turkey Dyeing in South and South East Asia', CIBA Review 39, 1423-6.
91. Hofenk-de Graaff J H, 'L'Analyse des materieres colorantes dans les textiles anciens', Bulletin de Liason du CIETA 35, 12-21: 12.
92. Museum no TL. 2869.1; Barber, 1991, 149.
93. Pfister, 1937, 210-1; Carter H, Mace A C, The Tomb of Tut-ankh-Amen I.

94. Verkovskaia A S, 'Tekstil'nye Izediia iz Raskopok Karmir-Blura', in Piotrovskii B B, Karmir-Blur III, 67-71: 67-8.
95. Campbell Thompson R, 'An Assyrian Chemist's Vade-mecum', Journal of the Royal Asiatic Society 1934, 771-85: 776-8; Stol, 537 s.v. 'gabu'; Gelb, 247, s.v. 'huuratu', also referred to 'gabu'.
96. Lucas A, Harris J R, Ancient Egyptian Materials and Industries, 4th ed, 154, 257-9.
97. Oppenheim A L, 'Essay on Overland Trade in the First Millenium BC', Journal of Cuneiform Studies 21, 236-54: 237, 243.
98. Pliny, Natural History, 35.52.183-4; ack Barber, 1991, 237.
99. Leix, 320.
100. Inalcik, 1994, 341.
101. Wescher H, 'Dyestuffs and Chemicals' (Alum), CIBA Review 62, 2287.
102. De Poerck, 174, n5.
103. Leix, 314-20.

13. Fashionable prices

1. Joan Thirsk (pers comm).
2. Gittinger, 59-61.
3. Schaefer, 1406, with additions.
4. Thirsk, 109.
5. Mubahat S Kutukoglu, ed, Osmanlilarda narh muessesesi ve 1640 tarikhli narh defteri, Istanbul; On two occasions, the Ottoman government issued lists of state-imposed prices to attempt to bring order to the markets. These prices included sugar, wax and spices. The madder prices were adjacent to prices for red and white alum. The prices were aimed at controlling the atars in the great bazaar of Constantinople and lower than export prices; Tim Stanley (pers comm). The quote for pounded madder implies that Turkey did not only export roots..
6. Thirsk, 113, PRO E134, 31 and 32 Chas. II, Hil.6.
7. Thirsk, 114; Anon, 1765, idem.
8. Table H.8, Posthumus N W, Nederlandsche prijsgeschiedenis, I, 412-5; Priester, 361, G 5.7.
9. Fitzpatrick A L, The Great Russian Fair, Nizhnii Novgorod, 1840-90, 14-33.
10. Wieczynski J L, ed, The Modern Encyclopaedia of Russian and Soviet History, v20, 245; v25, 26; Prokhorov A M, ed, Bolshaia Sovetskaia Enseklopedeia, s.v. 'yamarki', 1045; s.v. 'Gor'kii', 405-8; s.v. 'Makar'evskaia yamarka', 681-2.
11. His descendant, Prince Michael Gruzinski, my undergraduate contemporary, and I suppose, friend, mysteriously fell to his untimely death onto the spiked railings in front of his run-down rooming-house in Earl's Court in London, in full diplomatic morning dress holding his briefcase. Showing his ancestral form, Michael once accosted the bemused then Mayor of Paris Jacques Chirac on the grand staircase in Lancaster House with his usual demands of "And . . . what — ah! do you do?" and after a pause "And . . . where — ah! do you come from?"
12. Chenciner and Magomedkhanov, 123-130; Fekhner, M. V., Torgovlia russkogo gosudarstva so stranami vostoka v XVI veke, 22ff.

14. The 19th-century madder boom

1. Schaefer, 1403-4.
2. This was partly confirmed by a report in 1896 — well after the introduction of synthetics — that Tunisians still bought madder from Djerib and Tripoli as well as Asia Minor; Fleury V, 'Les Industries Indigenes de la Regence', Revue Tunisienne 1896, 180.
3. Schaefer, 1403.
4. Cardon, 35.
5. ibid., 36.
6. Kasaba, 122, 125.
7. Rhind, 511.
8. Cardon, 41-2.
9. Hilton, 380.
10. Stoinanovich T, 'Pour un modele du Commerce du Levant', Bulletin, Assoc Int d'Etudes du Sud-Est Europeen, 61-120: 96; republ, Between East and West, v1, 39-89: 64.
11. Gr. Nebol'sin', Statistscheskiia zametki o vneshnei torgovle Rossia, 1835; Statisticheskoe obozrenie vneshnei torgovli Rossia, 1850.
12. Markovin V I, Dorogami i tropami Dagestana.
13. Ukaz soch 2, 454-7; Khashaev, 93.
14. Berezin I, Ukaz, soch, 1, 65; Khashaev, 101.
15. Evetskii O, Ukaz, soch, 57; Khashaev, 101.
16. Khashaev, 105-6.
17. Khashaev, idem.
18. Barbaro, 'Travels of Venetians in Persia', 147; Wulff, 190.

15. Coal tar reds
& the death of madder

1. Brunello, 275-301.
2. ibid., fig 149.
3. Runge Ferdinand (?), Technische Chemi, del 1&2; Sandberg, 146.
4. Jenny W, Bradley W, Schroeter J, Voegelin W, 'Sir William Henry Perkin', CIBA Review 115, 2-49, 19.
5. Brunello, 275-80.
6. ibid., 301.
7. One a liquid pseudotoluidine and the other a solid paratoluidine.
8. Cardon, 35.
9. Inalcik, 1994, 913.
10. Inalcik, 1994, 917-20.

16. William Morris:
the sumptuous resurrection

1. Ittig A L, A Technical and Historical Study of the Qajar Carpet Industry: The Cases of Garrus, Sultanabad and Kirman, unpubl thesis Oxford, 143, 175-7, 244; Whiting M, 'Progress in the Analysis of Dyes of Old Oriental Carpets', Hali Vol II, No 1, Spring 1979.
2. Lewis G G, The Practical Book of Oriental Carpets, 23; Anderson J, Return To Tradition, 5.
3. FitzGibbon & Hale, 344.
4. Cahiers des Arts et Techniques d'Afrique du Nord, no 5, 111-136.
5. Cahiers, 127-8.
6. ibid., 115, 113.
7. ibid., 129, 135.
8. Fairclough O, Leary E, Textiles by William Morris and Morris & Co. 1861-1940, 35.
9. Ruskin J, The Ruskin Reader being passages from Modern Painters, The Seven Lamps of Architecture and The Stones of Venice, Orpington; Clive Wainwright (pers comm).
10. Morley H, 'False Principles', Household Words.
11. Somers Cocks A, The Victoria and Albert Museum, 2-15, 94-111.
12. Fairclough, 33-4.
13. Goodwin J, A Dyer's Manual.
14. Thurstan V, The Use of Vegetable Dyes.
15. Luke, Schekty, 59.
16. Goodwin, 9.
17. Elliott and Ryan, 46-96.
18. Grossgeim, 1946, ch XI, 355-371; tr by the author, 1992.
19. Anderson, 30, pl 49.
20. Chenciner R B, 'The DOBAG Project', Arts and The Islamic World, 25-8; Anderson, 3, 6, 8, 13, 19.
21. Harald Böhmer, (pers comm, 1981-1999).
22. Joan Thirsk (pers comm); David Cook (pers comm); Report ref: EU AIR — CT 94 — 0981 (DG12 SSMA), Thuringer Landesanstalt fur Landwirtschaft, a group from Iena and Levos Pflanzenchemie Forschungs-u-entwittelungsgesellschaft mbH & Co KG, from Wieren near Luneberg Heath, University of Bristol, Cultivation and extraction of natural dyes for industrial use in natural textile production.

17. The dyer's Grail: alchemical
philosophies & folklore

1. Whitehead, p66.
2. Portal F., Inman W. S.,tr, 'Symbolic Colours', 3 sections, Weale's Quarterly Papers in Architecture, II, sect 1, 10-12, III, sect 2, 1-17, sect 3, 11-15.
3. Kearney H, ed, Origins of the Scientific Revolution, 121; Harley, 1982, 33.
4. Bacon F., The Advancement of Learning.
5. Forbes R. J., 'Modern Chemistry and Alchemy', CIBA Review 1961/5, 2-16; Forbes R J, 'Alchemy, Dye and Colour', CIBA Review 1961/5, 17-22; Forbes R J, 'The Pots of Geber's Cooks', CIBA Review 1961/5, 23-32.
6. Field, Practical Notebook 5, 543.
7. Penelope Walton Rogers (pers comm).
8. Morabia A, Bosworth C E et al ed, The Encyclopaedia of Islam, v.5, s.v. 'lawn', 698-707; Edmund Bosworth (pers comm).
9. Aristotle, Meteora, iii, 4, 373.
10. Daghestani myths, Chenciner R B, Daghestan Tradition and Survival, 191-200; Frazer Sir J G, Folklore in the Old Testament, pt 1, ch 1, 8, 9, 12, 18, 19, 29.
11. EspeciallyAristotle De anima, ii, 418a-419a and De sensu et sensib., 437b-440b.
12. Plato Timaeus, 458ff.
13. Goethe J W, Farbenlehre.
14. Shelley, Laon,ix,x,7; Char.,Ist, I, 9; Devil,vii,I; Tennyson, Guine,426; in Mem., lvi, 14-5.
15. Field, Practical Journal 11, s.v. 'B'.
16. Field G, The Analogy of Logic, 289.
17. Field, Practical Journal 8.
18. Field, Practical Journal 11, s.v. 'H'.
19. Algarotti F, Sir Isaac Newton's Philosophy Explain'd for the Use of Ladies 20; Algarotti F, An Essay on Painting written in Italian by Count Algarotti, FRS, FSA, 39, 48; Gage, 29-31.
21. Field, Practical Journal 11, 138; Gage, 60.
22. Portal, Weale II, 'First Section', 10-12.
23. Portal, Weale III, 'Second Section' on 'red', 1-17; 'Third Section' on 'rose', 11-14.
24. Hutchings, J., 'A survey of the use of colour in folklore — a status report', Colour and Appearance in Folklore, 56-6. Different titles in the contents and article, see 31.
25. Culpeper, 109.
26. Newman L. I., 'Public versus Private Sins', The Hasidic Anthology, 166.2, 444.
27. Irwin, R., The Arabian Nights: a companion, 121.
28. Numbers 19:2-9; Leviticus 14:4-7.
29. Tatem M, 'Purple — a tale of Blue Blood and Scarlet Raiment', Colour and appearance in folklore, 46-50.
30. Bowman M, 'The Colour Red in the Bible of the Folk', Colour and appearance in folklore, 22-5.
31. Hutchings J, 'Status of the Colour in Folklore Survey', Colour and appearance in folklore, 56-60.
32. Richardson R, 'Colour in Death', Colour and appearance in folklore, 31-5.
33. Monger G, 'Colour in Marriage', Colour and appearance in folklore, 26-30.
34. Rowe Doc, 'Well, the colour is because . . . that's the colour it is', Colour and Appearance in Folklore, 6-10.
35. Wood J, 'Colour in Mabinogion Tales', Colour and Appearance in Folklore, 16-21.

Notes

36. Brocklebank R, 'Colour in Heraldry', *Colour and Appearance in Folklore*, 11-15   .
37. Owen W, Macbeth G ed, 'Greater Love', The Penguin Book of Sick Verse, London, 223.
38. Shakespeare, T & C, v,2,164; L. of A., 297; C.T.A., 975.
39. Haegerstrom-Portnoy G, 'Short wavelength sensitive cone sensitivity loss with ageing', Jn Opt Soc Am, vol 5, no 12, 2160; Marshall J, ed, 'Susceptible Visual Apparatus', Vision and Visual Disfunction, no 16, 76 — the macula ageing and age related macula degeneration; 150 — light ageing and visual performance.
40. Boyes G., 'Not quite blue: colour in the mock-obscene riddle', *Colour and Appearance in Folklore*, pp 40-45; Heather P. J., 'Colour symbolism', *Folklore*, V, LIX, LX, Part I, 178, Shakespeare to Romantic English literature and common usage; Part IV, 316-22, pre-Shakespeare English literature; Opie, I. & Tatem, M. (eds), *A Dictionary of Superstitions*, Oxford, s.v. 'RED lucky to card players', 'RED unlucky to lovers', 'RED CARS lucky', 'RED FLOWERS unlucky', 'RED HAIR unlucky', 'RED THREAD cures', 'RED THREAD protects', pp 325-7; Leach, M. (ed.), *Funk & Wagnalls Standard Dictionary of Folklore, Mythology and Legend*, s.v. 'Red Branch', 'Red heads', 'red rag', pp 929-30; Stith-Thompson, *Motif-Index of Folk-Literature*, s.v. 'Red', pp 633-4.
41. De Poerck, p183.
42. John Edmonds, personal communication.

Appendices

1. Targain O, Schetky E, Dye Plants and Dyeing, Plants and Gardens, vol 20, No3, 47.
2. Master Peter, Theophilus, The Book of Master Peter of St Omer on Making Colours.
3. Merrifield M P, Original Treatises dating from the XIIth to the XVIIIth centuries on the Arts of Painting.
4. Bailey, H. W., *Dictionary of Khotan Saka*, s.v.'rrunai', 366; Ron Emmerick (pers comm).
5. Gelb I et al, eds, The Assyrian Dictionary, Vol 6, 'H', 247, s.v. 'huuratu'; von Soden W, Akkadisches Worterbuch, s.v. 'hurratu'.
6. Germer R, Die Textil Farberei und die vervundung gefarbte texteilen im Alte Egypte, 119, 120.
7. Forbes R J, 1956, Studies in Ancient Technology, v4, 106-7, n143.
8. Singer I, ed, The Jewish Encyclopaedia, IX, 265.
9. Schweppe H, 1993, Handbuch der Naturfarbstoffe; Schweppe H, Winter J, 1997, A Handbook of Artists' Pigments, Vol 3, 113-121, 116.
10. FitzGibbon K, Hale A, Ikat Silks from Central Asia, 344, 347.
11. John Wilson, 1757; B,233.
12. Leix A, 'Felt and Knotted Fabrics in Turkestan', CIBA Review 40, 1457-63: 1461.
13. Gittinger M, Master Dyers to the World . . ., 21; Schweppe and Winter, 111.
14. Magomedkhan Magomedkhanov (pers comm).
15. Schaefer,1404.
16. Cardon D, Chatenet G du, Guide des Teintures Naturelles, 34 (abbr 'Cardon').
17. Barber E J W, 1991, Prehistoric Textiles, 232.
18. Bonete Y, Cahiers des Arts et Techniques D'Afrique du Nord, No 5, 121; Golvin L, Les Arts populaires en Algerie, tI, 92,n36.
19. Brunello F, Hickey B, tr, The Art of Dyeing in the history of mankind, (abbr 'B'), 384.
20. Cardon, 33.
21. B, 131.
22. OED.
23. ibid.
24. B, 384.
25. OED.
26. ibid.
27. B, 131.
28. Sloane MS, 1754.
29. Codex Riccardiano, 2580; B, 164.
30. Rosetti Gioanventura, Plictho, [Binder], XX; Schweppe and Winter, 111.
31. B,384.
32. K.
33. ibid.
34. ibid.
35. OED.
36. Grierson S, The Colour Cauldron.
37. Shtorkh (abbr 'S').
38. K.
39. K.
40. Leix A, 'Costumes of the Settled Population of Turkestan', CIBA Review 40, 1441-9: 1449.
41. Cardon, 34.
42. Grierson, 193.
43. Cardon, 37.
44. Huxley and Griffiths, v.4, 140.
45. Grossgeim A A, Flora Kavkaza, 1st ed, v4, 20.
46. Perkin A G, Hummel J J, 'The Colouring principles of Rubia sikkimensis', Journal of the Chemical Society 63, 1157-60   .
47. Hayashi K, 'Chemical procedure for the determination of plant dyes in Ancient Japanese textiles, International Symposium on the Conservation of Cultural Property . . ., 39-50.
48. Buchanan, 88-92.
49. Thunberg C P, Resa uti Europa, Africa, Asia; ack Sandberg.
50. Cardon, 43.
51. Barrowcliff M, Tutin F, 'Chemical examination . . .' Journal of the Chemical Society 91.
52. Paris M R, Abiusso N, 'Sur les derives anthraquinoniques . . .', Annales pharmaceutiques francaises 16, 660-5.
53. B.
54. Buhler A, 'Turkish Red Dyeing in South and South East Asia', CIBA Review 39, 1423-6: 1424.

55. Schweppe and Winter, 116.
56. Sandberg G, The Red Dyes, 79.
57. Buchanan.
58. Hooker and Jackson.
59. Buchanan.
60. ibid.
61. ibid.
62. B, 26; Whitehead R H, Micmac Quillwork, Micmac Indian Techniques of Porcupine quill decoration, 1600-1950.
63. Cardon, 39-40.
64. Sandberg, 79.
65. Cardon, 40; Burnett A R, Thompson R H, 'Biogenesis of the Anthraquinones in Rubia tinctorum L.', J Chem Soc, 2437-41; Leuchs J C,Traite complet des proprietes . . . .
66. Yacovleff E, Herrera F L, 'El Mundo vegetal delos antiguos peruanos', Revista del Museo Nacional 3, 241-322; 4, 29-102; Towle M A, The Ethnobotany of Pre-Columbian Peru; Saltzman M, McLean C C, Connell P, eds, 'Analysis of Dyes in Museum Textiles or You Can't Tell a Dye by Its Color', Textile Conservation Symposium in Honor of Pat Reeves, 27-39 (abbr 'Saltzman').
67. Huxley and Griffiths, s.v. 'Coprosma', v.1, 712-4.
68. Mell, 1924; Briggs et al, 1948, 1949, 1952, 1955; Huxley and Griffiths.
69. Dioscorides, 3.160.
70. Pliny, Natural History 33.38-39.115-17, 34.54-5, 176-7; Barber, 1991, 231. Hooker and Jackson, s.v. 'Rubia', v.ii, 745; s.v. 'Galium', v.1, 991-6; s.v. 'Coprosma', v.i, 611; s.v. 'Relbunium', v.ii, 695; s.v. 'Terminalia', v.11, 1046; s.v. 'Calamus', v.i, 376; s.v. 'Pterocarpus', v.ii, 652. Linnaei C, Richter H ed, Codex Botanicus Linnaeanus.
71. Cardon, 40; Burnett and Thomson, 2437-41.

72. RAZ Provinciaal Bestuur 1813-1850, 2812; Priester, 342.
73. Priester, 341, T 5.3, combining RAZ Provincial Bestuur 1813-1850, 2812, 2827; RAZ Commissie van Landbouw, 26.
74. Cardon, 45.
75. John Edmonds (pers comm).
76. Buchanan, 91.
77. Adrosko, 68, 69, 95, 96, 107, 109.
78. The first dye methods do not involve madder and are outside the scope of this book. Those who persevere may find 'broomsedge brass wool' in Adrosko, 79; 'fustic gold wool' in Adrosko, 86; 'goldenrod brass wool' in Adrosko, 87; and 'bark method 1' in Adrosko, 72.
79. Weigle P, ed, 'Handbook on Natural Plant Dyeing', Plants & Gardens, 16; (special printing of Plants & Gardens, v29, no2, 72); Weigle P, Ancient Dyes for Modern Weavers.
80. Thurstan V, *The use of vegetable dyes*, 33.
81. Goodwin J, A Dyer's Manual, 66.
82. Anon, The Methuen Handbook of Colour; Grierson, 68, 195-6.
83. Du Fay de Cisternay, Instructions; Brunello, 224.
84. Dalby G, Natural Dyes, Fast or Fugitive, 6.
85. ibid, 6-11, 33-4.
86. Sandberg, 180-1.
87. Kasaba, 122, 125.
88. See note 11, chapter 14 (page 361).
89. Schaefer, 1401.
90. Foster & Moran, p186.
91. Leix, p2433.
92. Newall, V. J., 'Colour in traditional Easter egg decoration', *Colour and Appearance in Folklore*, 36-9.

Select bibliography

Abu-Mansur-bin-Ali-Harawi, Achundov V tr, 'On plants', 1893.
Assisa de Tolloneis, Acts Parl. Scot. Vol 1.
Adrosko R J, *Natural Dyes and Home Dyeing*, New York, [1986] 1971.
Aeschylus, *Agamemnon*.
Al-Jahiz, Al-Tabassur fi'l-Tigara; Serjeant R, *Islamic Textiles* XV-XVI.
Albright-Kelso, *AASOR* 21-22, 1943.
Alciphron, *Letters.*
Algarotti F, *Sir Isaac Newton's Philosophy Explain'd for the Use of Ladies*, [1739] 1765.
Algarotti F, *An Essay on Painting written in Italian by Count Algarotti, FRS, FSA*, 1764.
Allen D E, 'A probable 16th-century record of *Rubia tinctorum*', *Watsonia*, 14, 1982.
Amram, D, *The Makers of Hebrew Books in Italy*, London, 1963.
Anderson J, *Return To Tradition*, Seattle, 1998.
Anderson S, *An English Consul in Turkey*, Oxford, 1989.
Anon, Gerefa, Corpus Christi College Cambridge MS 383, c. 1100.
Anon, Codex Riccardiano, 2580, Florence; Gargiolli G, L'Arte della seta in Firenze . . ., 1868.
Anon, SCRIPTA Medieval and Renaissance Texts and Studies, vol 18, Brussels: text I, MS 517, Wellcome Hist Med Libr, London, no 45, 46-7, late 15thc.
Anon, *T' Bouck van Wondre* [The Book of Marvels], Brussels, 1513.
Anon, Stowe MS 680, f135v, BL.
Anon, Sloane MS 1754, BL.
Anon, Sloane MS 5250, ff80v, BL.
Anon, *Instruction generale pour la teinture des laines*, Paris, 1671.
Anon, under Miller's influence, 'Impartial Considerations on the Cultivation of Madder in England', pamphlet bound in a volume of *Acts of Parliament* in 1865 in BL, 213.i.4(100), 1765.
Anon, *A Compendium of Colours*, no date, probably 1797.
Anon, various authors, names not given, O Prikaspiskoi maren, extracts from *Kavkaz Gazet*, nos. 11, 12, 13, 14, 15, 17 & 18, 63pp, Tblisi, 1863 ['The cultivation of madder in the Prikaspian or near-Caspian region'], (abbr 'The Ministry' or 'M').
Anon, *The Colour Index*, vols 3-5, 3rd ed, Bradford, 1971.
Anon, *The Methuen Handbook of Colour*, no date, c. 1985.
Archipov I O, *O krasiashikh veshestvakh derbentskoi mareny*, 1869.
Aristophanes, *Peace.*
Aristotle, *Meteora.*
Aristotle, *De anima.*
Aristotle, *De sensu et sensib* . . .
Aristotle, school of, *De Coloribus*: Hett W S, ed and tr, Aristotle, Minor Works, London, 1963.

Bacon F, *The Advancement of Learning*, 1605.
Bailey, Sir H W, *Dictionary of Khotan Saka*, Cambridge, 1979.
Baker G P, *Calico Painting and Printing* . . ., London, 1921.
Bancroft E, *Experimental Researches concerning the Philosophy of permenant Colours*, London, 1794.
Barbaro, *Travels of Venetians in Persia*, 1471.
Barber E J W, *Prehistoric Textiles*, Princeton, 1991.
Barber E W, *Women's Work: The First 20,000 years*, New York & London, 1994.
Barber E W, *The Mummies of Urumchi*, London, 1999.
Baron S W, *A Social and Religious History of the Jews*, New York, 1952 — only the first 4 vv are indexed.
Barrowcliff M, Tutin F, 'Chemical examination . . .', *Journal of the Chemical Society*, 91, 1907-18, 1907.
Belcher J, *Of the bones of Animals Changed to a Red Colour by Aliment only*, c. 1736.
Bennett I (ed.), *Rugs and Carpets of the World*, London, 1977.
Berthollet C L, 'Description du Blanchement des toiles et des fils avec l'acide muriatique oxigene', *Annales de Chimie*, Paris, 1785.
Betts A, *Journal of Archaeological Science*, 21, 489-99, London, 1994.

Betts E M (ann.), *Thomas Jefferson's Garden Book 1766-1824*, Philadelphia, 1944.
Bezemer, De Blecourt, 'Rechtsbronnen van Zierikzee . . .', Verken der vereeniging . . . vaderlandsche recht, reeks 2. no 9, Gravenhage, 1908.
Birch W D G, *British Catalogue of Seals*, 1892.
Black J, *Experiments upon Magnesium, etc,* ?London, 1756.
Boerendonck J, *Historische Studie over de Zeeuwschen Landbouw*, Diss. Wagenigen, 1935.
Bonete Y, *Cahiers des Arts et Techniques D'Afrique du Nord*, No 5, 1959.
Bowman M, 'The Colour Red in the Bible of the Folk', *Colour and Appearance in Folklore*, 22-5, London, 1991.
Boyes G, 'Not quite blue: Colour in the mock-obscene riddle', *Colour and Appearance in Folklore*, 40-45, London, 1991.
Braekman W L (ed.), *Middelnederlandse verfrecepten* . . . , Brussels, 1986.
Brannt W T, *Varnishes, Lacquers, Printing Inks, and Sealing waxes* . . . , Philadelphia, 1893.
Braun H T, Revue par l'Institut Solvay de Bruxelles, Brussels, no date c. 1950; in *Cahiers*, No. 5, 136.
Brewer J S (ed), *Letters and Papers . . . Henry VIII*, iv.1.125, London, [1862-1910] 1870.
Brocklebank R, 'Colour in Heraldry', *Colour and Appearance in Folklore*, 11-15, London, 1991.
Browne Sir T, *Hydriotaphia: Urn Burial*, London, 1669.
Brunello F, Hickey B, tr, *The Art of Dyeing in the History of Mankind*, 2nd ed, Vicenza, 1973, (abbr 'B').
Buchanan R, *A Weaver's Garden*, Colorado, 1987.
Bunker E, Chatwin B, Farkas A, *'Animal Style' Art*, New York, 1970.
Buhler A, 'Turkish Red Dyeing in South and South East Asia', *CIBA Review*, 39, 1423-6, Basle, 1941.
Burnett, A R, & Thomson, R H, 'Biogenesis of the Anthraquinones in *Rubia tinctorum* L.', *J Chem Soc*, 2437-41, Cambridge, 1968.

Campbell B M S, 'Agricultural progress in medieval England: Some evidence from eastern Norfolk' *EcHR* 2nd ser. 31/1:26-46, 1983.
Campbell Thompson R, 'An Assyrian chemist's Vade-mecum', *Journal of the Royal Asiatic Society* 1934, 771-85, London, 1934.
de Candolle A P, *Prodromous*, c. 1800.
Cardon D, Chatenet G du, *Guide des Teintures Naturelles*, Paris-Lausanne, 1990 (abbr 'Cardon').
Carter H, Mace A C, *The Tomb of Tut-ankh-Amen I*, New York and London, 1923.
Carter T F, *The Invention of Printing in China*, 2nd ed, New York, 1955.
Chassagne S, *Oberkampf: un Entrepreneur capitaliste au Siecle des Lumieres*, Paris, 1980.
Chenciner R B, 'The Dobag Project', *Arts and The Islamic World*, 25-8, London, 1984.
Chenciner R B, 'Textiles & Architecture in Dagestan', *Mimar*, 34, 70-7, London, 1990.
Chenciner R B, & Magomedkhanov M, 'Persian exports to Russia . . .', *Iran* 30, 123-131, London, 1992.
Chenciner R B, *Kaitag: Textile Art from Daghestan*, London, 1993.
Chenciner R B, *Daghestan: Tradition and Survival*, London, 1997.
Coeurdoux R P, *Memoires geographiques* . . . , Paris, 1768.
Cohn G, 'Farbestoffe, naturliche', *Ullmanns Encyl . . . Chemie*, 5, 2nd ed, 135-7, 1930.
Cooper T, *A Practical Treatise of Dyeing and Callicoe Printing*, Philadelphia, 1815.
Coustillac L, 'Note sur la Teinture Vegetale dans le Sud-Tunisien', *Cahiers des Arts et Techniques D'Afrique du Nord*, No 5, 136, 1959.
Cremer F G, *Studien zur Geschichte* . . . , Dusseldorf, 1895.
Crowfoot G M, 'The Linen Textiles' in Bartelemy D, Milik J, *Qumran Cave I. Discoveries in the Judean Desert* I, no 3, Oxford, 1955.
Crum W, 'On the Manner in which Cotton unites with Colouring Matter', *Journal of the Chemical Society of London*, London, 1863.
Culpeper N, *Culpeper's Complete Herbal*, [1653] 1821.
Curuk C, Cicekciler E, *Ornekleriyle Turk Cadirlari*, Istanbul, 1983.

Dalby G, *Natural Dyes, Fast or Fugitive*, 1985.
Dalley S, 'Ancient Assyrian Textiles and the Origins of Carpet Design', *Iran* No 29, 117-35, London, 1991.
Dal', V., *Tolkovyi slovar'*, SPb and Moscow, [1881] 1903-9.
Dambourney L A, *Recueil de procedes et d'experiences* . . . , Paris, 1786.
Davis R, *Aleppo and Devonshire Square*, London, 1967.
Davy H, 'Some Experiments and Observations on the Colours Used in Paintings by the Ancients', *Philosophical Transactions* 105, 97-124, London, 1815.
Decaisne J, 'Recherches anatomiques et physiologiques sur la garance', *Memoires couronnes par L'Academie . . . Bruxelles* 12, Brussels, 1837.

Diderot et D'Alembert, *Encyclopédie*, Neufchastel, 1757-72.

Dioscorides, *Materia Medica*.

Donkin R A, 'The insect dyes of western and west-central Asia', *Anthropos*, 72, pp 847ff, Fribourg, 1977.

Drake F, *World Encompassed*, Hakluyt Society, 139, 1579.

Drake S, Coleing L, & Allgrove J, *The Qashqa'i of Iran*, Manchester, 1976.

Draper's Dictionary, 1578.

Driessen L A, 'Leyden, the City of Wool', *CIBA Review*, 48, 1739-47, Basle, 1944.

Driessen L A, 'Calico Printing and Cotton Industry in Holland', *CIBA Review*, 48, 1748-54, Basle, 1944.

Driessen L A, 'How to Print Batik Imitations', *CIBA Review*, 58, 2125-6, Basle, 1947.

Duhamel du Monceau H L, *Elements d'Agriculture*, Paris, 1762.

Eastwood G M, 'Egyptian Dyes and Colours', *DHA* 3, York, 1984 (see under Vogelsang-Eastwood).

Eastwood G, Rogers C ed, *Early Islamic Textiles*, 40-1, Chicago, 1983.

Eaves I, 'On the remains of a Jack . . .', *Journal of The Arms and Armour Society*, vol xiii, no 2, 81-154, London, 1989.

Elliott D, Ryan J, eds, *Art into Production*, Oxford, 1984.

Ellis Asa Jr, *The Country Dyer's Assistant*, Brookfield, Mass, 1798.

Entwisle, E A, *The Book of Wallpaper*, Bath, 1970.

Erman A, Krebs F, *Aus den Papyri der Kgl Mus Berlin, Berlin pap 8013, 8316*, Berlin, 1899.

Errera I, *Collection d'Anciennes Etoffes Egyptiennes*, Brussels, 1916.

Errera L, *The Russian Jews*, 1894.

Espinas G, *La draperie dans la Flandre francaise au moyen age*, Paris, 1923.

Espinas G, 'Documents rel. draperies de Valenciennes en moyen age', *Soc d'Hist du droit des pays Flammands, Picards et Wallons, Docs et Trav* no.1, Paris and Lille, 1931.

Faber G A, 'Dyeing in Greece', *CIBA Review*, 9, 284-90, Basle, 1938.

Faber G A, 'The Roman Dyers', *CIBA Review*, 9, 291-5, Basle, 1938.

Faber G A, *CIBA Review*, 9, Basle, 311, 1938.

Fairbairn L et al, *Paint and Painting*, Tate Gallery exhibition, London, 1982 (also Staples P).

Fairclough O, Leary E, *Textiles by William Morris and Morris & Co. 1861-1940*, London, 1981.

Farnsworth M, 'Second-century BC rose madder from Corinth and Athens', *American Journal of Archeaeology* 55, 236-239, 1951.

Faroqhi S, *Towns and townsmen of Ottoman Anatolia, Trade, crafts and food production in an urban setting, 1520-1650*, Cambridge, 1984.

Du Fay de Cisternay, *Instructions*, Paris, 1737.

Fekhner M V, *Torgovlia russkogo gosudarstva so stranami vostoka v XVI veke*, Moscow, 1956.

Feller R L, Curran M, & Bailie C, 'Identification of Traditional Organic Colorants Employed in Japanese Prints . . .' in Keyes R S, *Japanese Woodblock Prints . . .*, 253-66, Ohio, 1984.

Fester G A, 'Los colorantes del Antigua Peru', *Archeion* 22, 229-41, 1940.

Fester G A, *Archeion* 23, 195-6, 1943.

Field G, MSS, 11 notebooks, called 'Practical Journals', 1804-1854; photocopy Courtauld Institute of Art, London, originals Winsor & Newton archive, Harrow: 1. 'Rubia . . .', 1804; 2. 'A Journal . . .', 1806; 3. 'A Journal . . .', 1807; 4. 'A Journal . . .', 1808; 5. 'Chromatics', 1808; 6. 'Examples . . .', 1809; 7. 'Practical Journal', 1809; 8. 'Chromatics . . .', 1811; 9. 'Chromatopia . . .', 1819; 10. 'Ultramarine', 1818-1833; 11. 'Chromatopoia . . .', c. 1848-1854.

Field G, *The Analogy of Logic*, 1850.

FitzGibbon K, Hale A, *Ikat Silks from Central Asia*, London, 1997.

Fitzpatrick A L, *The Great Russian Fair, Nizhnii Novgorod, 1840-90*, Oxford, 1990.

Flachat J C, *Observation sur le commerce et sur les arts . . .*, Lyons, 1766.

Fleury V, 'Les Industries Indigenes de la Regence', *Revue Tunisienne* 1896, 1896.

Flinders Petrie, W M, *Kahun, Gurob and Hawara*, London, 1890.

Flinders Petrie, W, *Anthribis*, London, 1908.

Forbes, R J, *Studies in Ancient Technology*, v4, Leiden, 1956.

Forbes, R J, *Man the Maker*, London, 1958.

Forbes, R J, 'Modern Chemistry and Alchemy', *CIBA Review*, 1961/5, 2-16, Basle, 1961.

Forbes, R J, 'Alchemy, Dye and Colour', *CIBA Review*, 1961/5, 17-22, Basle, 1961.

Forbes, R J, 'The Pots of Geber's Cooks', *CIBA Review*, 1961/5, 23-32, Basle, 1961.

Foster, G V, Moran P J,'Plants, Paints, and Pottery: Identification of madder pigment on Cypriot ceramicware', *Archaeometry, Proceedings of the 25th International Symposium*, Amsterdam, 1989.

Frazer, Sir J G, *Folklore in the Old Testament*, London, 1918.

Gabra-Sanders T, 'A piece of a Jack . . .', *Journal of The Arms and Armour Society*, vol xiv, no 3, 147-152, London, 1993.

Gage J, *George Field and his Circle: from Romanticism to the Pre-Raphaelite Brotherhood*, Cambridge, 1989.

Galotti J, 'Weaving and Dyeing in North Africa', *CIBA Review*, 21, 738-60, Basle, 1939.

Gansser A, 'The Colouring of Leather', *CIBA Review*, 81, 2954, Basle, 1950.

Gelb I et al, eds, *The Assyrian Dictionary*, Vol 6, 'H', Chicago, 1956.

Gentele J G, *Gentele's Lehrbuch der Farbenfabrikation* 3, Braunschweig, 1909.

Gerard J, Woodward M (ann.), *Gerard's Herball*, [1927] 1971; Th Johnson ed, 1636; there are at least ten editions and the original text covered the period 1596 to 1599.

Germer R, *Die Textil Farberei und die vervundung gefarbte texteilen im Alte Egypte*, Weisbaden, 1992.

Gessler E A, Schneider H, 'Uniforms', *CIBA Review*, 93, 3334-56, Basle, 1952.

Giedion S, Space, *Time and Architecture*, Cambridge Mass, 1949.

Gittinger M, *Master Dyers to the World . . .*, Washington, 1982.

Goethe J W, *Farbenlehre*, 1808.

Goitein S D, *A Mediterranean Society*, Berkeley, 1967.

Golvin L, *Les Arts populaires en Algerie*, no date ?c. 1950.

Goodwin J, *A Dyer's Manual*, London, 1982.

Gotting H, Kühn H, 'Die sogenante . . .Theophanu', *Archivalische Zeitschrift* 64, 19-22, 1968.

Granger-Taylor H, & Rogers C (eds.), *Early Islamic Textiles*, Chicago, 38-9, 1983.

Grenville H, *Observations sur l'Etat actuelle de l'Empire Ottoman*, 1965.

Grierson S, *The Colour Cauldron*, Perth, 1986.

Grossgeim A A, *Flora Kavkaza*, Tbilisi, 1928-34.

Grossgeim A A, *Rastitel'nye Resursy Kavkaza*, Moscow, 1946.

Grossgeim A A, *Opredelitel' Rastenii Kavkaza*, 1st ed, Moscow, 1949.

Grossgeim A A, *Flora Kavkaza*, 2nd ed, Moscow, 1950-1967.

Grunskaya-Petrova I P, 'Rubinovyi tsvet narodnymi metodami', *AzFAN*, 4, Baku, 1939.

Haegerstrom-Portnoy G, 'Short wavelength sensitive cone sensitivity loss with ageing', *Jn Opt Soc Am*, vol 5, no 12, 2160, 1988.

Hakluyt R, Taylor E R G (ed.), *The Original Writings and Correspondence of the Two Richard Hakluyts*, Hakluyt Society, 2nd Series, 76, 77, London, 1935/I.

Hakluyt R, *The Principal Navigations, Voyages and Discourses of the English Nation*, London.

Haller R, 'The Technique of Early Cloth Printing', *CIBA Review*, 26, 933-7, Basle, 1939.

Haller R, 'The Chemistry and Technique of Turkey red Dyeing', *CIBA Review*, 39, 1417-21, Basle, 1941.

Harley R D, *Artists' Pigments 1600-1835*, London, 1970; 2nd ed, 1982 has more illustrations.

Hawley W A, *Oriental Rugs, Antique and Modern*, New York, 1913.

Hayashi K, 'Chemical procedure for the determination of plant dyes in Ancient Japanese textiles', *International Symposium on the Conservation of Cultural Property . . .*, Tokyo, 1979.

Heather P J, 'Colour Symbolism', *Folklore* V, LIX, LX, London, Part I, 178, Shakespeare to Romantic English literature and common usage; Part IV, 316-22, pre-Shakespeare English literature, 1948-9.

Heller M J, *Printing the Talmud*, New York, 1992.

Hellot J, *L'art de la teinture des laines et des etoffes de laine en grand et petit teint*, Paris, 1750.

Henshall A S, 'Early Textiles found in Scotland', *Proc of Soc Scottish Antiquaries*, vol lxxxvi, 1-29, 1951-2.

Heraclius, attr, *De coloribus et artibus Romanorum*, 10th c.

Herodotus, *Histories*, 4.

Higgins R A, 'The Polychrome Decoration of Greek Terracottas', *Studies in Conservation*, 15 (1970), 272-7, London, 1970.

Higgins S H, *A History of Bleaching*, London, 1924.

Home F, *Experiments of Bleaching*, Edinburgh, 1756.

Hilton A C, 'Madder, an ancient source of dye', *East Anglian Magazine*, 1949, 1949.

Hippocrates, *De morb. mul*, i.

Hofenk-deGraaff, J H, 'L'Analyse des materieres colorantes dans les textiles anciens', *Bulletin de Liason du CIETA*, 35, 12-21, Lyons, 1972.

Homer, *Iliad*.

Homer, *Odyssey*.

Hoofnail J, *New Practical Improvements . . . (upon) Robert Boyle, . . . Tinctures and Pigments*, London, 1738.

Hooker J D, Jackson B D, *Index Kewensis Plantarum Phanerogamarum*, 2 vols, Oxford, 1895.

Horn P, 'Textiles in biblical times: Dyeing', *CIBA Review*, 1968/2, 17-23, Basle, 1968.

Houghton J, ed Bradley R, *A Collection of Letters for the Improvement of Husbandry and Trade*, 4 vols, London, [1681] 1727-8.

Select bibliography

Howard P, *The Times*, 9 April, 1999.
Hudson D, Luckhurst K W, *The Royal Society of Arts, 1754-1954*, London, 1954.
Hulme E W, 'The history of the patent system . . .,' *Law Quarterly Review*, 46: 141-54, 61: 44-56, London, 1896-1900.
Hummel J J, Knecht E, *Encl Brit*, v XVII, 280, s.v. 'madder', 1911.
Hutchings J, 'Status of the Colour in Folklore Survey', *Colour and Appearance in Folklore*, 56-90, London, 1991.
Hutchings J, Wood J, eds, *Colour and Appearance in Folklore*, London, 1991.
Huxley A, & Griffiths M R (eds.), *The New Royal Horticultural Society Dictionary of Gardening*, London, 1992.
Huyghe R (ed.), *Larousse Encyclopedia of Prehistoric and Ancient Art*, London, 1966.

Ibn Hawqal, Wiet G, tr, from 'Book of routes of the provinces', *Les textiles dans le monde musulman*, Paris, 1978.
Inalcik H, *The Ottoman Empire*, ?Chicago, 1973.
Inalcik H, with Quataert D, *An Economic and Social History of the Ottoman Empire, 1300-1914*, Cambridge, 1994.
Irwin, J, Brett K B, *Origins of Chintz*, London, 1970.
Irwin, J, *The Kashmir Shawl*, London, 1973.
Irwin, R, *The Arabian Nights, A Companion*, London, 1994.
Ittig, A L, *A Technical and Historical Study of the Qajar Carpet Industry: The Cases of Garrus, Sultanabad and Kirman*, 2vv, unpubl thesis Oxford, 1983.

Jenny W, Bradley W, Schroeter J, Voegelin W, 'Sir William Henry Perkin', *CIBA Review*, 115, 2-49, Basle, 1956.
Johnson H, *World Atlas of Wine*, London, 1971.
Juvet-Michel A, 'The Controversy over Indian Prints', *CIBA Review*, 31, 1091, Basle, 1940.
Juvet-Michel A, 'Oberkampf', *CIBA Review*, 31, 1103-5, Basle, 1940.
Juvet-Michel A, 'The technique of French textile printing', *CIBA Review*, 31, 1109-16, Basle, 1940.

'K.', 'The Effect of Madder on Animal Bones', *CIBA Review*, 26, 947, Basle, 1939.
De Kanter J, *De meerkrapteler*, 1802.
De Kanter J, *Handboekje*, 1812.
Karpov, Lt, *Marena o vozdelyvanii eia v Derbente v primenenii k Orenburgskomu krayu*, 37pp, SPb, 1859 ['Madder, its cultivation in Derbent as applied to cultivation in the Orenburg region'] (abbr 'K').
Kasaba R, *The Ottoman Empire and The World Economy, The 19th century*, New York, 1954.
Kasumov M A O, *Kraslnye rasteniia azerbaidzhana i ikh ispolzovanie v kovrovom proizvodstve*, *aftoreferat* to Azerbaijan Academy of Sciences, Botanical Institute im. V L Komarova, Baku, 1973.
Kearney, H (ed.), *Origins of the Scientific Revolution*, 1964.
Khashaev, Kh-M, *Zaniatiia naseleniia dagestana v XIX veke*, Makhachkala, 1959.
Kieffer, L, *Saisons d'Alsace* 51, 8-30, 1974.
Kirby, J, White R, 'The Identification of Red Lake Pigment Dyestuffs', *National Gallery Technical Bulletin*, v 17, London, 1996 (abbr 'Kirby').
Koren (Kornblum) Z C, 'The Colors and Dyes on Ancient Textiles in Israel', eds Sorek C, Ayalon E, *Colors from Nature/Natural Colors in Ancient Times*, Tel Aviv, 1993.
Krauze I, *Zametki o krasil'nom iskusstve tuzemtsev*, Moscow, 1872.
Kühn H, 'Naturwissenschaftliche Untersuchung von Leonardos "Abendmahl . . ." ', *Maltechnik/Restauro*, 4, 24-51, Munich, 1985.

de La Hyre P, *Memoires de l'Academie Royal des Sciences depuis 1666-1669*, IX, 637-730, Paris, 1730.
Latour A, 'Glove Manufacture', *CIBA Review*, 61, 2227-35, Basle, 1947.
Lavoisier et al, *Journ de Phis*, XI, ?Paris,1778.
Leach M (ed.), *Funk & Wagnalls Standard Dictionary of Folklore, Mythology and Legend*, New York, 1950.
Leix A, 'Costumes of the Settled Population of Turkestan', *CIBA Review*, 40, 1441-9, Basle, 1941.
Leix A, 'Felt and Knotted Fabrics in Turkestan', *CIBA Review*, 40, 1457-63, Basle, 1941.
Leix A, 'Late Classical and Early Christian Textiles', *CIBA Review*, 43, 1551-8, Basle, 1942.
Leix A, 'Ancient Textiles of Eastern Asia', *CIBA Review*, 43, 1566-72, Basle, 1942.
Leix A, 'Early Islamic Textiles', *CIBA Review*, 43, 1573-80, Basle, 1942.
Leix A, 'Ingredients for Plant Dyes in use in Peasant Art', *CIBA Review*, 66, 2432-3, Basle, 1948.
Leix A, 'The Symbolic Meaning of Red in Peasant Art', *CIBA Review*, 66, 2433-4, Basle, 1948.
Lerner F, 'Textiles and Dyestuffs at the Frankfurt Fairs — The Dyestuffs Trade', *CIBA Review*, 103, 3713-5, Basle, 1954.

Leuchs J C, *Traité complet des proprietes . . .*, Paris, 1829.
Lewis G G, *The Practical Book of Oriental Carpets*, Philadelphia, 1920.
Linnaeus C, *Species Plantarum*, 1753.
Linnaei C, Richter H (ed.), *Codex Botanicus Linnaeanus*, Leipzig, 1840.
Loret V, 'Revue de Philologie et d'Archeologie Egyptiennes et Coptes' 3, *Kemi*, Paris, [1887, 1892, 1906] 1930.
Loyn & Percival (tr), *Capitulare de Villis vel Curtis Imperialibus*, 1975.
Lucas A, Harris J R, *Ancient Egyptian Materials and Industries*, 4th ed, London, 1962.
Luetkens C, 'Manchester — Cotton's Rise', *CIBA Review*, 1962/2, 25-33, Basle, 1962.

McDowell R S, *Archaeological Textiles Newsletter* 3, Leiden, 1986.
McNair A, 'Perspective', *The Herald*, December 21, 1998, 13, Glasgow.
Mamed-Zade K M, *Stroitelnoe iskusstvo Azerbaidzhana*, Baku, 1983.
Mantaran, ANAE, BIII, MS, 'Rapport de Mantaran sur le Commerce du Levant', 1753.
Marggraf O V, *Ocherk kustarnykh promyslov Severnogo Kavkaza*, Moscow, 1882.
Markovin V I, *Dorogami i tropami Dagestana*, Moscow, 1988.
Marshall J, *Mohenjo-daro and the Indus Civilisation*, Delhi, [1931] 1973.
Marshall J (ed.), 'Susceptible Visual Apparatus', *Vision and Visual Disfunction*, no 16, 1991.
Masschelein-Kleiner, L et al, 'Analysis of Dyestuffs on textiles from 'En-Boqeq' in Sheffer A, Tidhar A, 'The textiles from the 'En-Boqeq Excavation in Israel', *Textile History* 22 (1), 1991.
de Massoul C, *A treatise on the art of painting*, London, 1797.
Mayer C, 'Krapplacke . . .', *Chemiker-Zeitung* 35, 1911.
Mayer F, 'The Chemistry of Natural Colouring Matters', *American Chem Soc*, New York, 1943.
Mazzino E et al, *Il Centro Storico di Genova*, 3rd ed, Genoa, 1974.
Mellaart J, *Catal Huyuk, A Neolithic Town in Anatolia*, London and New York, 1967.
Merrifield M P, *Original Treatises dating from the XIIth to the XVIIIth centuries on the Arts of Painting*, New York and London, 1967 [London, 1849].
Merret C, *The Art of Glass*, 1662, tr and additions to Neri Antonio, *L'Arte Vetraria*, Florence, 1612.
Midgelow G W, 'Report on the Dyes'; Crowfoot E, 'Textiles', Lapp P W, Lapp N L, 'Discoveries in the Wadi ed-Daliyeh', *AASOR*, 41, 1974.
Miller Philip, *The Gardener's Dictionary*, ?London, 1733.
Miller Philip, *The Method of Cultivating Madder, As it is now practised by the Dutch in Zealand: (Where the best Madder is produced)*, ?London, 1758.
Minorsky V, *A History of Sharvaan and Darband in the 10th-11th centuries*, Cambridge, 1958.
Mommsen T (ed.), *Edictum Diocletiani de Pretiis Rerum Venalium*, Berlin, 1958.
Monger G, 'Colour in Marriage', *Colour and Appearance in Folklore*, 26-30, London, 1991.
Morabia A, Bosworth C E et al (eds), *The Encyclopaedia of Islam*, v.5, s.v. 'lawn', 698-707, 1986.
Morley H, 'False principles', *Household Words*, London, 1852.
Mubahat S Kutukoglu (ed.), *Osmanlılarda narh müessesesi ve 1640 tarikhli narh defteri*, Istanbul, n.d.
Murometsov A K, Ivanova M, 'Preparation of Pink Alizarin Lakes', *Chemical Abstracts*, 35, 2344, [1940] tr 1941.

Naqvi H K, 'Dyeing of cotton goods in the Mughal Hindustan (1556-1803),' *Journal of Indian Textile History*, VII, 45-56, 1967.
Gr Nebol'sin', *Statisticheskiia zametki o vneshnei torgovle Rossia*, SPb, 1835.
Gr Nebol'sin', *Statisticheskoe obozrenie vneshnei torgovli Rossia*, SPb, 1850.
Negev A ed, *Archaeological Encyclopaedia of the Holy Land*, Nashville, 1986.
Newall, V J, 'Colour in traditional Easter egg decoration', *Colour and Appearance in Folklore*, 36-9, London, 1991.
Newman L I, 'Public versus Private Sins', *The Hasidic Anthology*, New York, 1944.
Nichols J, 'Linguistic Diversity and the First Settlement of the New World', *Language*, Vol 66, no 3, (1990) 475-521, 1990.
Nicholson H, *King George the Fifth, His Life and Reign*, London, 1952.
de Nie W L J, *De ontwikkeling der noord nederlandsche textiel ververij . . .14th-18thc*, Leiden, 1937.

O'Brien C, *The British Manufacturers Companion and Calico Printers Assistant*, 1790.
Oglobin V A, 'Dyeing Crafts in the Central Asian Protectorates', ?Moscow, no date c. 1900.
Opie I, Tatem M eds, *A Dictionary of Superstitions*, Oxford, 1989.
Oppenheim A L, 'Essay on Overland Trade in the First Millenium BC', *Journal of Cuneiform Studies* 21, 236-54, 1967.
Owen W, Macbeth G (ed.), 'Greater Love', *The Penguin Book of Sick Verse*, 223, London, 1963.

Packer, Th, tr, *Handbok for Fargare*, Stockholm, 1840.
Pallas, S P, *St Petersburgisches Journal 1777*, v.1, SPb.

Select bibliography

Paris, M R, Abiusso N, 'Sur les derives anthraquinoniques . . .', *Annales pharmaceutiques françaises*, 16, Paris, 1958.

Pauly, A (ed.), *Der Kleine Pauly*, Stuttgart, 1964-75.

Peel, R, 'Turkey red dyeing in Scotland. Its Heyday and Decline', *JDSC*, 68:12, Bradford, 1952.

Perkin, A G, Hummel J J, 'The colouring principles of Rubia sikkimensis', *Journal of the Chemical Society*, 63, 1157-60, London, 1893.

Master Peter, Theophilus, *The Book of Master Peter of St Omer on Making Colours*, c. 1300.

Peters, R H, 'Early Dyeing Theories', *CIBA Review*, 1964/2, 2-12, Basle.

Petrov, V A, *Rastitelnye krasiteli Azerbaidzhana*, Baku, 1940.

Pfister, R, 'Materiaux pour servir a l'etude des textiles egyptiens posterieurs a la conquete arabe', *Revue des Arts Asiatiques* X, Paris, 1936.

Pfister, R, 'Les Textiles du Tombeau de Toutankhamon', *Revue des Arts Asiatiques* X1, 207-18, Paris, 1937.

Phillips, T, 'Mappae Clavicula: a treatise on the Preparation of Pigments . . .', *Archaeologia* 32, 183-244, London, 1847.

Le Pileur d'Apligny, *L'Art de la Teinture*, Paris, 1776.

Le Pileur d'Apligny, 'Memoire Contenant le procede de la teinture du coton rouge-incarnat d'Adrianople sur le coton file', *Treatise*, Paris, 1765.

Plato, *Timaeus*.

Pliny, *Natural History*.

Ploss, E E, *Ein buch von alten Farben . . .*, Heidelberg, 1962.

Plutarch, *Alexander*.

van der Poel, J M G, *Ceres en Clio*, Wageningen, 1964.

De Poerck, G, *La Draperie Medievale en Flandre et en Artois*, 3 vols, Bruges, 1951.

Portal, F, & Inman, W S, tr, 'Symbolic Colours', 3 sections, *Weale's Quarterly Papers in Architecture*: II, sect 1, 10-12, III, sect 2, 1-17, sect 3, 11-15, 1844-5.

Posthumus, N W, *Nederlandsche prijsgeschiedenis*, Leiden, 1943-64.

Priester P, A. A. G. 37, Geschiedenis van de Zeeuwse Landbouw circa 1600-1910, Wageningen, 1998.

Prokhorov, A M (ed.), *Bolshaia Sovetskaia Enseklopedeia*, 1974-7.

Pubetz, A, 'Krap und Krapplack', *Praktisches Handbuch . . .*, 298-321, Berlin, 1872.

Raby, J, 'Court and Export: Market Demands in Ottoman Carpets 1450-1550', *Oriental Carpet and Textile Studies*, 2, London, 1986.

Radosavijevic, V, 'The Technique of Old Writing and Miniatures', *Conservation and Restoration of Pictorial Art*, 202-6, London, 1976.

Ramsay, G D, *The English Woollen Industry, 1500-1750*, London, 1982.

Rankin, K, 'The Identification of Colouring Matters in Paiseley Shawls', upublished thesis, Paisley College of Technology, 1977.

Rauch, J, [Recipe Letters], New York, 1815.

Raynal l'abbé, Bibl Nat, MSS, FF 6429, 'Memoire sur Tunis, avec corrections et notes' fol 33-61, Paris, fl 1760.

Reininger, W, 'The Florentine Textile Industry of the Middle Ages', *CIBA Review*, 27, 957-66, Basle, 1939.

Reinking, K, 'Über die alteste Beschreibung der Kupenfarberei im Papyrus Graecus Holmiensis', *Mell Textilber*, No 5, 349-51, 1925.

Reinking, K, 'Ueber die Farberei mit Krapp in Altertum', *Mell Textilber*, No 20, 445-8, 1939.

Rhind, W, *The Vegetable Kingdom*, London, 1877.

Rice, J W, 'The Conservation of Historical Textile Colorants', *Textile Museum Journal*, 1.2, Washington, 1963.

Richardson, R, 'Colour in Death', *Colour and Appearance in Folklore*, 31-5, London, 1991.

Robinson, S, *A History of Dyed Textiles*, London, 1969.

Robertson, W, 'Dye Plants in a Scottish Garden', in *Dye Plants and Dyeing: A Handbook*, New York, 1964.

Rogerson, B, *A Traveller's History of North Africa*, London, 1998.

Roosen-Runge, H, *Farbgebung . . .Studien . . . Mappae Clavicula und Heraclius*, 2 vv, Munich, 1967.

Roosen-Runge, H, 'Artikel:Farbe . . .', *Reallexikon zur deutschen Kunst*, 6, 1463-92, Stuttgart, 1973.

Rosetti Gioanventura, *Plictho de larte de tentori* [Binder of the dyers' art], Venice, 1548 (abbr 'Plictho').

Roth C et al, eds, *Encyclopaedia Judaica*, Jerusalem, 1971 (abbr 'Enc Jud').

Roussel P, La Garance . . ., unpubl thesis for a D Pharm, June, 1984, Montpellier University, 1984.

Rowe Doc, 'Well, the colour is because . . . that's the colour it is', *Colour and Appearance in Folklore*, 6-10, London, 1991.

Roxburgh W, *Plants of the Coromandel Coast*, London, 1795.

Rubens A, *A History of Jewish Costume*, London, 1967.
Ruskin J, *The Ruskin Reader, being passages from Modern Painters, The Seven Lamps of Architecture and The Stones of Venice*, Orpington, 1895.
Russell W T, 'Egyptian Colours', in Flinders Petrie W M, *Medum*, 44-48, London, 1892.
Ryder M, *Sheep and Man*, London, 1983.

St Catherine's Convent, *Nurnberger Kunstbuch*, Nuremberg, c. 1460, Nurn Statsb, MS cent VI.
St Clare Byrne, M (ed.), *The Lisle Letters*, Chicago, 1981.
Salmanov, E, & Chenciner, R B, *Architecture of Baku*, London, 1985.
Saltzman M, McLean C C, Connell P, eds, 'Analysis of Dyes in Museum Textiles or You Can't Tell a Dye by Its Color', *Textile Conservation Symposium in Honor of Pat Reeves*, 27-39, Los Angeles, 1986 (abbr 'Saltzman').
Sandberg G, trn, *The Red Dyes*, Asheville NC, 1997.
Sanderson J, Foster W (ed.), *The Travels of John Sanderson in the Levant 1584-1602*, Hakluyt Society, London, 1931.
Sappho, fragment 20 Edmonds, 19 Bergk.
Scammell G V, *The world encompassed . . . c800-1650*, Aldershot, 1981.
Scammell G V, 'European seamanship in the great age of discovery', *Ships, oceans and empire . . . 1400-1750*, IV, London, 1995.
Schaefer G, 'Die fruhesten Zeugdruke', *CIBA Review*, 24, 854-61, 1938, Basle.
Schaefer G, 'The Cultivation of Madder', *CIBA Review*, 39, 1398-1406, Basle, 1941.
Schaefer G, 'The History of Turkey red Dyeing', *CIBA Review*, 39, 1407-16, Basle, 1941.
Schaefer G, 'Some Old-Fashioned Ways of Cleaning Textiles', *CIBA Review*, 56, 2034-8, Basle, 1947.
Schaffer G, 'Krappextrakt Pernod', *Bulletin de la Societe industriele de Mulhouse*, 33, 1887.
Schetky E, *Dye Plants and Dyeing*, reprinted from Plants and Gardens, vol 20, no3, Brooklyn NY, 1964.
Schlumberger H, 'Über die Krappblumen . . .', *Dingler's Polytechnisches Journal* 126, 206-10, 1852.
Schultz G, *Farbstofftabellen*, 7th ed, 1:498-500, 510-12, 638-9, 2:7, Leipzig, 1931.
von Schwarz F, *Turkestan: die Wiege der Indogermanische Volker*, no date c. 1900.
Schweppe H, 'Identification of Dyes on Old Textiles', *JAIC*, 1980.
Schweppe H, *Handbuch der Naturfarbstoffe*, 1993.
Schweppe H, Winter J, West-Fitzhugh E ed, *A Handbook of Artists' Pigments*, Washington, 1997.
Sheffer A, in Rothenberg B (ed.), *The Egyptian Mining Temple at Timna*, London, 1988.
Sheffer A, Tidhar A, 'Textiles and Basketry at Kuntillat 'Arjud', *'Atiqot*, 20, 1991.
Sheffer A, 'Ancient Textiles Decorated with Color from the Land of Israel', in C. Sorek & E. Ayalon (eds.), *Colors from Nature/Natural Colors in Ancient Times*, Tel Aviv, 1993.
Sherfield MSS, 44M69, Jervoise of Herriard Collection, Hants RO, 1620 sqq.
Shtorkh', P A, *Marena, v selsko-khoziaistvennom, torgovom i krasilnom otnosheniiakh*, 270pp, SPb, 1859, ['Madder, in agriculture, trade and in connection with dyestuffs'], (abbr 'S').
Singer I (ed.), *The Jewish Encyclopaedia*, IX, New York, 1905.
Skelton R, *The Indian Heritage: Court Life and Arts under Mughal Rule*, London, 1982.
Slicher van Bath B H, *The Agrarian History of Western Europe*, London, 1963.
Smirnitskii A I, *Russko-Angliiskii Slovar'*, Moscow, 1985.
Smith C S, & Hawthorne J G, 'Mappae Clavicula . . .', *Transactions of the American Philosophical Society*, NS 64, pt 4, Philadelphia, 1974.
Soden W von, *Akkadisches Worterbuch*, Wiesbaden, 1965-81.
Somers Cocks A, *The Victoria and Albert Museum*, Leicester, 1980.
Staples P, 'A guide to the History of Pigments' 10-23; 'The Manufacture of Artists' Colour', 31-4, *Paint and Painting*, London, 1982.
Steensgaard N, *Carracks, Caravans and Companies*, Lund, 1973.
Stith-Thompson, *Motif-Index of Folk-Literature*, 6vv, s.v. 'Red', 633-4, Bloomington, 1966.
Stoianovich T, 'Pour un modele du Commerce du Levant', *Bulletin, Assoc Int d'Etudes du Sud-Est Europeen*, 61-120, Bucharest, 1974: 96; reprinted in Between East and West, v1, 39-89, New York, 1992.
Stol M, ed Ebeling E, Meissner B, *Reallexikon der Assyriologie*, Berlin, 1983.
Strabo, XII, XIII.
Sylvester D, Mills J, King D, *The Eastern Carpet in the Western World*, London, 1983.

Talbot Rice D, *Islamic Art*, London, [1965] 1975.
Tarrant A W S, 'Colours and the names we give them', *Colour and Appearance in Folklore*, 1-5, London, 1991.
Tatem M, 'Purple — a tale of Blue Blood and Scarlet Raiment', *Colour and Appearance in Folklore*, 46-50, London, 1991.
Tauber, E, 'Uber Krapplack und Alizarinlacke', *Chemiker-Zeitung*, 33, 1345, 1909.

Select bibliography

Tawney, R H and Power E (eds), *Tudor Economic Documents*, London, 1924.
Taylor, G W, 'On the Nature of dyeing with madder and related dyestuffs', *DHA*, 9, York, 1990.
Taylor, G W, 'Reds and purples: from the classical world to pre-Conquest Britain' in Walton P, Wild J P, *Textiles in Northern Archaeology*, London, 1990.
Taylor, G W, 'Red Dyes on Indian Painted and Printed Cotton Textiles', *DHA*, 12, York, 1993.
Theophilus *see* Peter.
Theophrastus, *History of Plants*.
Thirsk, J, *Alternative Agriculture: A History from the Black Death to the Present Day*, Oxford, 1997.
Thunberg, C P, *Resa uti Europa, Africa, Asia*, Uppsala, 1778.
Thurstan, V, *The Use of Vegetable Dyes*, Leicester, 1930.
Towle, M A, *The Ethnobotany of Pre-Columbian Peru*, Chicago, 1961.
Townsend, J H, 'The Materials of J M W Turner: pigments', *Studies in Conservation*, 38, 231-54, London, 1993.
Turner, F M (ed.), *The condensed chemical dictionary*, 2nd ed, New York, 1930.
Turner, William, *New Herball*, 1568.

Various authors, *Cahiers des Arts et Techniques d'Afrique du Nord*, no 5, 111-136, Toulouse, 1959 (abbr 'Cahiers').
Varthema, L, & Schefer C (eds), *Le viateur en la plus grande partie de l'Orient*, Paris, 1895.
Vauquelin, *De la loi du contrast simultane des couleurs*, 1839.
Verkovskaia A S, 'Tekstilnye Izediia iz Raskopok Karmir-Blura', in Piotrovskii B B, *Karmir-Blur* III, Yerevan, 1955.
Virgil, *Eclogues*.
Vitruvius 7, XIV, 1 & 2.
Vogelsang-Eastwood, G, *Pharaonic Egyptian Clothing*, Leiden, 1993 (see Eastwood).
Vogt, E, 'Sites and Preservation of Prehistoric Basketry and Woven Fabrics', *CIBA Review*, 54, 1938-43, Basle, 1947.
Vogt, E, 'Woven Fabrics', *CIBA Review*, 54, 1955-66, Basle, 1947.
Vogt, E, 'Dyes and Dye Plants in Prehistory', *CIBA Review*, 54, 1967, Basle, 1947.
Vospicus, Vita Aureliani.

'W.N.', 'England's Efforts against Napoleon's Blockade', *CIBA Review*, 36, 1315, Basle, 1940.
Wagner, H, *Die Korperfarben*, 2nd ed, Stuttgart, 1939.
Walker, S, & Bierbrier M, *Ancient Faces*, London, 1997.
Wallert, A, 'Unusual pigments on a Greek marble basin', *Studies in Conservation*, 40, 3 (1995), 177-88, London, 1995.
Walton (Rogers), P, *Archaeology of York*, 17/3; 17/5; 17/11, c. 1987 (abbr 'AY').
Walton (Rogers), P, 'Textiles, Cordage and Raw Fibre from 16-22 Coppergate', *The Archaeology of York The Small Finds*, London, 1989.
Walton (Rogers), P, Wild J P, *Textiles in Northern Archaeology*, London, 1990.
Walton Rogers P and Taylor G, *Orientations*, April 1997, 1997.
Walton Rogers, P, *A Textile Lining in a Civil War Helmet*, unpubl, 1998.
Warren, P, 'A Textile Town — 4500 Years Ago', *Illustrated London News*, 252, February 17, 1968, 25-7, London, 1968.
Warren, P, *Myrtos: An Early Bronze Age Settlement in Crete*, Oxford, 1972.
Wedderburn, D, 'Wedderburn's Compt Book 1587-1630' and 'Shipping Lists of Dundee 1580-1618', *Publ Scot Hist Soc*, v XXVIII, May 1898, Edinburgh, 1898.
Weigle, P, *Ancient Dyes for Modern Weavers*, New York, 1974.
Weigle, P (ed.), 'Handbook on Natural Plant Dyeing', *Plants & Gardens*, Brooklyn NY; reprint of *Plants & Gardens*, v29, no2, 72, [1973] 1986.
Wells, H, *The Maddermarket Theatre*, Norwich, 1992.
Wescher, H, 'Dyestuffs and Chemicals' (Alum), *CIBA Review*, 62, 2287, Basle, 1947.
Wescher, H, 'Indian Cotton Prints in the Middle Ages', *CIBA Review*, 64, 2359-60, Basle, 1948.
Wescher, H, 'Development of the Fairs of Champagne', *CIBA Review*, 65, 2368-78, Basle, 1948.
Whitehead, R H, *Micmac Quillwork, Micmac Indian Techniques of Porcupine quill decoration, 1600-1950*, 1982.
Whiting, M C, & Sugiura, T, 'Additional Study of the Dyes'; Crowfoot E, 'Textiles', Lapp P W, Lapp N L, *Discoveries in the Wadi ed-Daliyeh*, *AASOR*, 41, 1974.
Whiting, M, 'Progress in the Analysis of Dyes of Old Oriental Carpets', *Hali*, Vol II, No 1, Spring 1979, 1979.
Wieczynski, J L (ed.), *The Modern Encyclopaedia of Russian and Soviet History*, Gulf Breeze Fla, 1981.
Wild J P, *Textile Manufacture in the Northern Roman Provinces*, Cambridge, 1970.
Wischnitzer M, *A History of Jewish Crafts and Guilds*, New York, 1965.
Wiskerke C, 'De geschiedenis van het meekrapbedrijf in Nederland', *Economisch-historisch Jaarboek*, XXV, 1952.

Wolff Dr, *Narrative of the Mission of Dr Wolff to Bukhara*, 1844.

Wood J, 'Colour in Mabinogion Tales', *Colour and Appearance in Folklore*, 16-21, London, 1991.

Woodcroft B, *Alphabetical Index of Patentees of Inventions, 1617-1852*, London, [1854] 1969.

Wouters J, *Studies in Conservation*, 30, London, 1985.

Wouters J, Maes L, Germer R, 'The Identification of Hematite as a Red Colorant on an Egyptian Textile from the Second Millennium BC', *Studies in Conservation*, 35, London, 1990.

Wouters J, 'Dye Analysis of Chinese and Indian Textiles', *DHA*, 12, 12-22, York, 1993.

Wulff, H E, *The Traditional Crafts of Persia*, Cambridge Mass, 1966.

Xenophon, *Cyropaedia* . . .

Yacovleff E, Herrera F L, 'El Mundo vegetal delos antiguos peruanos', *Revista del Museo Nacional*, 3, 241-322 (1934); 4, 29-102 (1935), 1934, 1935.

Yu Feian, tr Silbergeld J, McNair A, *Chinese Painting Colors* . . ., Seattle, 1988.

Yule H, Burnell A C, *Hobson-Jobson, The Anglo-Indian Dictionary*, London, [1886] 1996.

Index

Index